# Augustine's Problem

# Augustine's Problem

Impotence and Grace

Jeff Nicoll

Foreword by Kortright Davis

RESOURCE *Publications* · Eugene, Oregon

AUGUSTINE'S PROBLEM
Impotence and Grace

Copyright © 2016 Jeff Nicoll. All rights reserved. Except for brief quotations in critical publications or reviews, no part of this book may be reproduced in any manner without prior written permission from the publisher. Write: Permissions, Wipf and Stock Publishers, 199 W. 8th Ave., Suite 3, Eugene, OR 97401.

Resource Publications
An Imprint of Wipf and Stock Publishers
199 W. 8th Ave., Suite 3
Eugene, OR 97401

www.wipfandstock.com

PAPERBACK ISBN 13: 978-1-4982-2494-9
HARDCOVER ISBN 13: 978-1-4982-2496-3

Manufactured in the U.S.A.                                            05/12/2016

Unless stated otherwise, translations from the Bible are taken from the New Revised Standard Version. New Revised Standard Version Bible, copyright 1989, Division of Christian Education of the National Council of the Churches of Christ in the United States of America. Used by permission. All rights reserved.

To the memory of Jerome Ysroael Lettvin whom I once caught cribbing the form but not the matter of an argument from the *City of God*.

For, in certain moods, no man can weigh this world, without throwing in something, somehow like Original Sin, to strike the uneven balance.

—Herman Melville, "Hawthorne and his Mosses"

# Contents

*Foreword by Kortright Davis* | ix
*Preface* | xiii
*Acknowledgements* | xv

Introduction | 1

### 1 **The Two Augustines** | 11
Augustine in conflict
The Manichaean Augustine
Solving the problem

### 2 **True Confessions** | 29
On the road to the fig tree
The *Confessions* anew
Augustine on trial

### 3 **The Argument over Augustine** | 48
Augustine's modern critics
Augustine's modern defenders

### 4 **Augustine's Argument** | 75
The core of the conflict
The question of control
The Fall: deep or shallow.
Perfectibility and punishment
Augustine's view of Augustine's view

### 5 **Augustine and Pelagius** | 96
Pelagius the preacher
First phase of the conflict (411–18)
Second phase of the conflict (418–30)
Who were the Pelagians?

6 **Origen and Seneca** | 124
   Neoplatonism
   Origenism
   Origen's fall
   The Stoic alternative

7 **On Nature** | 142
   The nature of philosophers
   The Manichaean dilemma
   The big picture

8 **On the Will** | 161
   Augustine favors freedom
   Augustine retreats
   Obedience and guilt

9 **Toddlers in Hell** | 181
   The little ones
   The potter's clay
   Double, double toil and trouble

10 **On the Disobedient Member** | 203
   From fruit to phallus
   Bad sex
   Good sex

11 **Augustine's Problem** | 222
   Why did Augustine win?
   What about Jerome?
   What about Cassian?
   Who was Augustine?

*Bibliography* | 249

# Foreword

It has always been commonplace to hear people make the excuse that they are 'only human'. Whenever they do this, it is to be assumed that they are conscious of some deficit or imperfection in their life, or in their behavior, and that they are entitled to some form of accommodation, or forgiveness, or exemption, from what should otherwise be expected of them. What, in fact, they do, is to presume that there is a built-in answer to the question: "What does it mean to be human"? How do we wrap our minds around the broad contours and complexities of the human condition with all its frailties on the one hand, and its capacity to assume the commanding heights of (supra) natural endeavor? Of course, the issue is further complicated when we virtually ascribe a certain level of 'super-humanity' to persons and personalities who have been known to rise above the ordinary spheres of human endeavor and accomplishment, and who have risen to such heights of notoriety and superior valor that would mark them off as a "cut above the rest of us." This has always been common throughout human history. Ancient mythologies dealt with this phenomenon by attributing unusual origins and endowments to exceptional people – they may have terrestrial mothers, but they certainly must have had extra-terrestrial fathers. Because of their superior powers and accomplishments, they must certainly have been born under exceptional circumstances; and this would have given them the privilege of being considered almost, if not entirely, "super-human."

Was Jesus of Nazareth a super-human? If he was, then how could he be identified fully with the rest of us? The same question is posed if he was actually half-god and half-human, and perhaps to an even more problematic degree. Indeed, it was at the heart of the Cappadocian Fathers' theology about the historical Jesus, and the meaning of his saving worth, that "that which was not assumed could not be redeemed." There is also the oft-quoted assertion that the Jesus of history is not the historical Jesus, and the historical Jesus is not the Jesus of history. The obvious challenge for people of faith is to wring the juices of the real historical Jesus out of the swaddling cloths of the Christian Faith tradition, in which he has been so tightly wrapped for nearly two millennia. It is generally assumed that even though the historical Jesus lived an ordinary human life, there were significant aspects of his personhood, and pattern of existence, that would have distinguished him from his contemporaries. In spite of his tears and taunts, his anguish and his anger, his physical endowments, his social encounters, his contextual realities, and his cultural engagements, the one thing that the Faith tradition insists on is his "sinlessness." If the Jesus of history was "sinless," was the historical Jesus also "sinless"? The Letter to the Hebrews suggests that "he was tempted as we are, yet did not sin" (4:15). If all of this is inherent of the human condition, then what was it that seemed to exempt the historical Jesus from all that we experience as ordinary human beings? The debate will continue along such enigmatic and paradoxical lines; but this is not what Jeff Nicoll is concerned about in this volume *Augustine's Problem: Impotence and Grace*. He is concerned about "sinfulness" and one man's theory.

Just as we have been alluding to the problem of the "two Jesus," Nicoll begins his extensive study with looking at the problem of the "Two Augustines." It is more than likely that the Augustine of history is not the historical Augustine, and the historical Augustine is not the Augustine of history. In other words, behind all the noble literature and religious traditions that have adorned the memory and legacy of Augustine of Hippo, Nicoll contends that there is a major trait in his biography and actual personal existence that can account for some of the emphases on the human condition and moral proclivities for which Augustine has become well known. Nicoll argues that the anomalies that he finds in Augustine's life are rooted and grounded in Augustine's impotence rather than in any radical conversion to chastity. His suggestion is that "the anger of impotence would suffice to explain the strictures on sexuality and would easily be developed into a theory of the complete impotence of the will."

This is a study that is made even more significant for its scholarly value since the author is not a professional theologian as such. He has brought to bear on his many years of diligent and extensive research, a demonstrably passionate interest in search of a viable alternative approach to the origins of Augustine's pilgrimage of religious thought and theological positions. The history of Christian thought has been heavily overlaid by the approaches to the problem of human sin and the modes of divine salvation. The contributions of Augustine to the origins and morphology of sin have been heavily adumbrated by his dominant thought that the human will is unable to help itself unless aided by divine grace. Of course, this approach was reinforced by Augustine's conflicts with Pelagius and those who thought like him.

Nicoll takes us through a maze of historical, theological, scientific, psychological, and literary explorations that seek to consolidate Augustine's basic themes on human nature, and its many challenges in struggling through the moral universe, while dealing with the physical realities inherent in the human body.

In the process we would well to be reminded that Augustine, as one of the four Great Latin Doctors, was not alone in his struggles and challenges. The others, of course, were Ambrose, Jerome, and Gregory. For example, Ambrose was quite ambivalent about his religious discipline of fasting. He once admitted: "When in Rome I fast on Saturday, when in Milan I do not." Augustine, as we all know, held Ambrose in very high esteem; but, at the same time, he once admitted that "his (Ambrose's) celibacy appeared to me a painful burden." Jerome himself was accused of having an improper relationship with a widow named Paula. Several centuries later, even the great Thomas Aquinas was assaulted by his two brothers who wanted to do everything in their power to tempt him away from becoming a Dominican monk. It is said that they brought to him a prostitute to tempt him, but that he drove her away by wielding a fire iron. In short, the struggles with being fully human, with all its physical proclivities and moral challenges in dealing with the bodily endowments, have always accompanied people of faith who wrestle with the uniqueness of Christianity's claims to be an Incarnational Religion. Nicoll argues that Augustine's struggle was unique. Instead of struggling against temptation and complaining about female seductiveness, Augustine emphasizes the inconsistency of (male) desire, asserting that the lust's refusal to follow the will even when the will wants sex is the punishment for the disobedience in the garden. This unusual stress on impotence leads, Nicoll believes, to a radically negative assessment of human capability.

What does it really mean to claim that God became human in Jesus Christ? And what does it entail when Christians embrace the Hebrew claim that we are all created in the "image and likeness of God?" All these underlying issues present themselves as we travel along with Nicoll in his comprehensive study of Augustine and his major problem. In one definitive sentence towards the end of this work, Nicoll writes: "Only Augustine's impotence mandated the impotence of the will and everything that followed." Out this would emerge the plethora of issues for which Augustine and his theology have been closely associated – Sin, Sex, Sensuality, Disobedience, Origin Sin, Human Depravity, the Fall, Freedom of the Will, Baptism, Salvation, Damnation – just to name a few. The author skillfully provides for us a novel framework through which to re-visit these topics, while at the same time he triggers several fresh and contemporary vistas of enquiry that can, and must, engage the rational mind and stimulate the theological imagination. Ongoing debates about human sexuality, insightful reviews of context and contextuality, and fresh approaches to theological/psychological explorations regarding the morphology of evil and its generative tendencies, all suggest themselves as topics in urgent need of fresh investigation, and more robust responsible dialogue. If such intellectual activities begin to take shape in the scientific and theological spheres of scholarly discourse, then Jeff Nicoll and his ground-breaking work: *Augustine's Problem* will have provided an invaluable contribution to this very worthwhile endeavor.

Kortright Davis<br>
Washington DC<br>
January 2016

# Preface

> What, then, could tempt thee, in a critic age,
> Such blooming hopes to forfeit on a stage?
> Could it be worth thy wondrous waste of pains
> To publish to the world thy lack of brains?[1]

A BOOK WHOSE PREMISE consists of three words: Augustine was impotent, requires an apology. Several excuses are possible, the first being its novelty. This provokes two responses—it is obvious, or it is complete nonsense. Establishing its plausibility requires effort, especially considering the theological consequences. The origin of the thesis—there is something wrong with the received views of his biography, philosophy, and theology—requires demonstration. The sense that some element is missing is apparent in the incoherence of both his defenders and his detractors. Describing what is known can reveal the outlines of the parts that are missing..

The case of Richard III provides a less complicated example than the rewriting of the story of an immensely influential church father. The last Plantagenet king of England may have been responsible for the deaths of his nephews in the Tower of London in the summer of 1483. Shakespeare's play left a lasting impression, only slightly ameliorated by Richard's modern defenders. His successor, Henry VII, blackened his name at every opportunity but did not accuse him of the princes' murders until twenty years had passed. Something is wrong with the story. The lack of an accusation does not prove Richard's innocence, but it does mean something is missing; perhaps Richard's accomplice became an important Tudor ally. More fancifully, the princes might have survived Bosworth Field and died of the sweating sickness carried by Henry's army; no one would have believed Henry hadn't poisoned them. Without the discovery of some telling document, it may remain an unexplained anomaly; nevertheless, it *is* an anomaly.

---

1. Charles Churchill, *Rosciad*, 597–600.

In Augustine's case, his attitude to sex is one imperfectly fitting puzzle piece. He does not sound like a reformed reprobate. While he may have experienced tormenting desire, his words are strangely un-misogynistic; while being anti-sex, he is not anti-woman, more often directing his dissatisfaction toward the male. Without a clear prejudice against the female, the arguments of the critics who trace his theology to his sexual attitudes seem hollow. His defenders are equally unable to locate a source for his ideas.

A second anomaly is Augustine's insistence on the incapability of the will to choose the good without God's explicit grace. Even his defenders try to reduce the implications of his pessimism and despair. Adam and Eve initially have the ability never to sin, and they still fall. It would not have been necessary to assume anything more drastic for their descendants; if the first parents can sin in paradise, their children can sin in the world.

If there is a deeper, unconfessed issue underlying the twists and turns of his intellectual and personal life, then things become clearer. Impotence resolves the anomalies of his life, replacing the enthusiasm of the convert to chastity with the frustration of the impotent man. The anger of impotence explains his strictures on sexuality and the complete impotence of the will. Just as God arbitrarily chose to make him impotent while others were not, God could predestine all of humanity to salvation or damnation.

We need a discussion of his biography, his philosophical roots, and theological development to evaluate whether impotence fills the lacuna in our understanding of the origins of his doctrinal positions. Each needs a fresh assessment in the context of this reversal of the canonical view of his sexuality. Augustine's influence has been pervasive, and the arguments over his ideas have continued for centuries. Understanding Augustine requires understanding how he has been understood. The peregrinations are not just Shandian digressions but provide the complex web of ideas needed to understand how Augustine could have come to his positions.

The arguments between his attackers and defenders have a different tone when applied to a man unable to act on his desires, rather than a man who rejects those desires. A new explanation of Augustine cannot change how western Christianity interpreted, adapted and adopted his sexual theories. Nor can it affect Luther's and Calvin's application of his concept of grace—but origins still matter. Without an understanding of how his obsessions wove themselves together, the student of Augustine cannot pick apart the threads—either to focus criticism more sharply or to find the appropriate defense.

# Acknowledgements

Dr. Ronald E. Hopson and Dr. D. H. Kortright Davis of the Howard University School of Divinity provided guidance in areas where my expertise is lacking. Mr. Scott Simmons is thanked for many hours spent at the Café Central in Vienna talking about Augustine and Pelagius after attending Sunday services at the Augustinerkirche. I interrupted my colleague Dr. J. Dexter Fletcher with sidebar conversations on nature and grace too many times to count and I am grateful for his patience and interest. The staff at the Altstadt Hotel (off of Augustinplatz) are thanked for their toleration of my spread out manuscripts in the salon during afternoon tea. Finally, there is no way to sufficiently thank my wife, Dr. Alice Ogden Bellis for the many readings of drafts, corrections of infelicities, and help in striking out fascinating, but irrelevant, paragraphs.

# Introduction

AURELIUS AUGUSTINUS, ST. AUGUSTINE of Hippo, is indisputably one of the greatest figures of his age. He establishes the rapprochement between the church and the faltering Roman state, completes the integration of Platonism into Christianity, is the first psychologist of the will, and pioneers the autobiography. He contemplates the inwardness of personality and the character of memory and time. Equally, he helps seal western misogyny, creates the definitive theories of original sin and predestination, and places a spell of darkness over Christian understanding of mortal life. He is the proponent of love and the condemner of infants. He is the Doctor of Grace, but the Catholic Church ignores his most passionately held opinions. He is patient and churlish. He urges repentance and claims we are unable to repent. He is a beneficent, love-filled priest—attentive to his congregation and a loyal defender of the church. He also is a bitter and angry polemicist—declaring God only saves a few and those for no comprehensible reason.

His opponents point to the misogynistic denier of free will; his allies emphasize his images of divine love. The problem of Augustine is how to reconcile these contradictions and identify their source. Augustine does not make it easy. In his *Revisions*, written in the last years of his life, he corrects, explains, and expands on his works. He resists saying that his views ever changed, even when the simpler course would have been to say that they had. He is a theological and philosophical innovator who denies that he is saying anything new. Critics use the earlier works to attack the later ones while his defenders sometimes hold on to his consistency for consistency's sake.

The arguments have raged back and forth for centuries without resolution; neither the attackers nor the defenders of Augustine have been able to construct consistent theories of the sources of his ideas. He offers too many contradictions to classify him as a determinist or misogynist. Efforts to trace his doctrines to his heretical past or his relationship with his mother have been unsatisfactory. The purpose of this book is to offer a different hypothesis to link together his disparate parts. Rather than being a recovering profligate, incapable of giving up women until his miraculous conversion, he was a frustrated, sexually impotent man. The helplessness of the impotent man was enlarged into a general incapability of the human will. Many features of his controversial positions follow from this starting point.

The tension in Augustine's autobiography, the *Confessions*, is obvious. His conversion gives him the opportunity to withdraw from the world and his mother's expectations, but forced ordination involves him in the lives of his congregation. He comes to terms with his condition by assuming it is just one example of the impotence of the will. We can only choose between sins, and never can choose the good. Rather than being the rational beings of Greek philosophy, we are the prisoners of sexual desire. The impotent man can do nothing to alter his condition; correspondingly, the individual efforts of any person are futile. We are all justly damned. The hypothesis of impotence is strengthened by the mechanism Augustine adopts to demonstrate our damnation. He claims God punished the disobedience in Eden by making sexual desire uncontrollable. In contrast to the Greek consensus that reason can and ought to rule the body, concupiscence rules the mind. However, he does not simply condemn desire; he points to its unreliability. A man cannot will an erection, nor can he suppress one with a thought. Augustine repeatedly returns to this failure of the will; he describes the penis as the disobedient member that does not always respond when a man wants sex. Our damnation follows from the act of disobedience implicit in the erection required for our conception. Instead of being moral creatures who can choose between good and evil, we inescapably acquire sin and guilt simply by being conceived.

We can do nothing for ourselves. The only way out is an arbitrary pardon of the original sin of our existence; only God's grace, never earned or merited, can save us. God only gives mercy to a very limited number of predestined elect, but since we are all conceived through disorderly desire, the majority can be justly abandoned to their damnation. Augustine has to construct this theory in defiance not only of Greek philosophy but the consensus of the early church. More surprisingly, he has to deny God ever made a covenant with humanity. There is no partnership with the divine except for the elect, and they are not distinguishable from the damned.

Augustine's ideas are most easily seen in his polemical attacks against his opponents. In the last decades of his life, he takes on the preacher Pelagius and his allies. Pelagius represents the old Roman view of personal responsibility. His Christianity is dutiful rather than inspired; God commands us to be perfect, and we ought to be perfect. He objects strongly to the notions of original sin, predestination, the necessity of infant baptism, and the limitation of God's grace. When Augustine writes against the Pelagians, he reveals the details of his theology that readers might otherwise miss.

Augustine's dominance makes it hard to see how revolutionary he is. He radically alters the Hellenic basis of Christianity by postulating a damaged nature to accommodate original sin. To the Greeks, the nature of anything was its unalterable essence—it cannot be damaged. Augustine concedes that human nature, as God creates it, is good, but conception stamps us with sin and we are born marred. Augustine's adversaries find the concept of changing God's creation impossible philosophically and blasphemous theologically. Augustine is not very convincing in his redefinition of nature, and modern readers tend to skip the argument; we no longer believe in Platonic ideal chairs (chapter 6) and his contortions are painful to follow. He is more successful with his invention of an independent faculty of the will, separate from human nature. The Greeks recognize the opposition of the rational and irrational, Apollo and Dionysus, but the philosophers want reason to win and think irrationality is insanity. While correctly pointing to humanity's perverse choices, Augustine only discovers the will to make it impotent.

The philosophical innovations are difficult enough for his contemporaries to swallow, but his application of them to theology appalls them, contradicting their understanding of God's mercy and God's justice. One measure of Augustine's rhetorical genius is that critics and defenders alike become obsessed with the minutia of his elaborate arguments, debating Aristotelian nuances on nature or quibbling over questions of what makes a sin voluntary. The trees are fascinating, but they distract from the larger forest of Augustine's abandonment of the covenant.

Any re-evaluation of Augustine is difficult. Rebecca West says his thought "is the ring fence in which the modern mind is prisoner."[1] The discussion will inevitably be in Augustine's vocabulary. The Emperor Theodosius in 380 declares catholic (meaning Nicene) Christianity to be the only acceptable form, but each disputant claimed he was catholic. The tomb of Julian of Eclanum, Augustine's most stubborn opponent, defiantly reads, "the Catholic Bishop."[2] The final form of the Nicene Creed only emerges in 381 from chaotic Council of Constantinople, but it takes time to become standard. At the 393 conference at Hippo, Augustine does not preach on the Nicene Creed from 325 or its update of 381, but on the Old Roman

1. West, *Saint Augustine,* 161.
2. Brown, *Augustine of Hippo,* 385.

Creed used by Ambrose in Milan.[3] What seems orthodox and fixed today was more fluid in the fifth century.

Similarly, the term "Church" has too many resonances with the later Roman Catholic Church for casual use. In the fifth century, there is the church in Rome, in Jerusalem, in Constantinople, in Antioch, in Alexandria, in Carthage, and in Hippo. They all compete for primacy, occasionally giving a nod to Rome, but more as a tactic than a commitment. This period also marks the beginning of the separation of the church into eastern and western wings, but it would be premature to call them the Eastern Church and the Western Church with capital letters.

One must resist other anachronisms. Modern scholarship considers, for example, how the interpretation of the Eden story changes in the Hellenized Judaism of Paul's time. Barr concludes that the Hebrew canon never blames the evils of this world on Adam.[4] While this may represent a majority of Hebrew Bible scholars, it is not the framework of Augustine or the Pelagians. The combatants all agree Genesis tells the story of a Fall. They disagree about its depth and its significance. Returning Genesis to its Hebrew roots is of little value in assessing why Augustine takes his particular route.

Similarly, it is of no importance here that the scientific revolution undermines the historicity of the Fall. While the modern theologian must find other ways of accounting for evil and stating the meaning for Christians of the incarnation and resurrection, this is not a fifth-century problem. Redefining original sin for the modern era is irrelevant. Original sin here means Augustine's original sin, fueled by concupiscence and resting on the erratic nature of conception. The modern analysis of free will in a world apparently dominated by physics is interesting but does not provide much guidance in understanding Augustine.[5]

Finally, the modern reader has to struggle with the vocabulary used. Some of the concepts were established ideas of Greek philosophy, but others were still in development in the fourth and fifth centuries. For example, everyone believes all of God's creation is necessarily good. The word "necessary" has a particular philosophical meaning, perfected by the medieval scholastics. Necessary truths are true in all possible worlds God might have

---

3. BeDuhn, *Augustine's Manichaean Dilemma*, Vol. 2, 187.

4. Barr, "Biblical Faith and Natural Theology," 59.

5. For modern discussions of free will and determinism, see the two editions of *The Oxford Handbook of Free Will*, edited by Robert Kane. For attempts to bring Augustine's argument into a modern form see, for example, Rist, "Augustine on Free Will and Predestination," Rowe, "Augustine on Foreknowledge and Free Will," and Hopkins's replies to Rist and Rowe in his *Philosophical Criticism*.

created. God's *absolute* power has no limits other than logical necessity. God's *ordinate* power, on the other hand, reflects the world God chose to create, imbued with natural law. Normally, God operates in the world within his more limited ordinate power; miracles are the rare exception of an application of his absolute power. God has limits; not even God's absolute power can make 2 + 2 = 5.

A second distinction, important in the discussion of God's mercy and judgment, describes the mysteries of God's will. It seems that God wishes all persons to be saved: "This is right and is acceptable in the sight of God our Savior, who desires everyone to be saved and to come to the knowledge of the truth (1 Tim 2:3–4)." The question Augustine and the Pelagians battle over is why, in that case, some people are not saved. While God's *consequent* will cannot be thwarted, his *antecedent* will is occasionally not fulfilled. A just judge antecedently wills all men to live but consequently wills the murderer to be hanged, and the analogy applies to God: what he wills antecedently may not happen.[6] Augustine, using other terms, says God may wish all of us to be saved, and he could save us with his absolute power, but the arrangement of the world implies only a very few are saved within his ordinate power.

Following the philosophical discussion is ironically hindered by our better understanding of the Greeks. A modern undergraduate has better access to Plato than Augustine did. A fourth-century Latin-speaking student would have only the equivalent of the "Idiot's Guide to Plato." One of Augustine's intellectual phases was Neoplatonism, a nineteenth-century term applied to a late classical school of philosophy; it is primarily through the lens of Neoplatonism that Augustine draws on Plato. The relationship to Plato's *Republic* or the *Symposium* is weak, but there is a stronger connection to the *Timaeus*.[7] The reader has to deal with Greek philosophy in an unfamiliar form.

Part 1 consists of chapters 1, 2, and 3. Chapter 1 introduces the discussion of the two Augustines. Scholars disagree on whether it is fair to talk about two Augustines at all. If they support the theory of two Augustines, they differ on how to describe it. The alternatives include an early and late Augustine, a Catholic and a Protestant Augustine, and the defender and denier of free will. The tensions between the two Augustines are revealed in his idiosyncratic exegeses of scriptural texts, his varying attitudes to the freedom of the will and his uneven treatment of sexuality. One common

---

6. See discussion in Robertson "Augustinian Ecclesiology and Predestination," 407.

7. Pelikan, in *What has Athens to do with Jerusalem?*, traces how the cosmogony of Genesis and the *Timaeus* were woven together from Philo of Alexandria to Augustine and beyond.

theme is the influence of his long-lasting adherence to a dualistic variant of Christianity, Manicheism. His opponents and critics frequently accuse him of retaining elements of this heresy, connecting it to each part of his theology. This provides another taxonomy; the anti-Manichean Augustine and the still heretical Augustine. The hypothesis of impotence provides a different approach to combining the disparate Augustines into a single person. The internal tension of the impotent man is reflected in his theology and accounts for his contradictions.

Chapter 2 revisits Augustine's autobiography, the *Confessions*, in search of clues to reevaluate the received story. A critical reader of the *Confessions* will detect that Augustine is concealing something. Superficially, the *Confessions* describe a painful search for a philosophical and religious place of safety but it also may reveal an increasingly frantic effort to avoid the conventional life of a married Roman. The hypothesis of sexual impotence can help reconcile the internal oddities of this autobiography.

In chapter 3, Augustine's modern (from Erasmus onwards) enemies and allies battle over his influence on the western church and society. An understanding of the passions aroused by Augustine is vital. Augustine's denial of free will and supposed misogyny attract his critics; his defenders rally to mitigate his views. This exchange between Augustine's foes and allies creates the beginning of a portrait, or rather, two portraits, of the person he may have been.[8] The Enlightenment thinkers focus on Augustine's denial of free will while his views on women and sexuality attract more attention in recent times. Impotence provides an alternate view of both problems.

Having established some familiarity with Augustine and his controversial opinions, part 2 (chapters 4 and 5) returns to the fifth century to provide an orientation to Augustine's times. Chapter 4 outlines the field of battle between Augustine and his Pelagian critics. Augustine represents his fundamental sense of helplessness, first in relatively conventional language and then in more self-revelatory ways. The primary issues are human nature, the will, and the meaning of grace. Augustine believes the catastrophic Fall fatally crippled humanity. Our nature, derived from God is necessarily good, but our will, through sexual desire, damages it. The will is so weak that it can only choose between sins. We remain in this state unless God grants us grace, restoring the will's proper orientation. God is just, but we all deserve damnation and should be grateful for his random mercy. Original sin is transmitted by generation, not through the flesh, but through the will.

---

8. The battle over Augustine never ends. Oberman's survey. *The Harvest of Medieval Theology: Gabriel Biel and Late Medieval Nominalism*, and Adams's extensive two-volume study, *William Ockham*, provide informative introductions to the scholastic period with connections to the Pelagian struggle.

Disorderly desire recapitulates the disobedience of Adam and Eve in each conception. The Pelagians assert, on the contrary, that our punishment is the expulsion from paradise; our will and nature are unchanged. Our will, degraded by habit but fortified by teaching, can choose the good. We are responsible for our behavior, good and bad. Grace consists of the goodness of God's creation, the gift of rationality, and the example of the law and Christ. God is just and is an impartial judge of our deeds. Reproduction is part of God's good creation and is fundamentally good. Infant baptism becomes a nexus of the controversy. Augustine asserts babies are damned without it; the Pelagians declare God would not punish anyone without personal sin.

Fortified with an overview of the arguments, chapter 5 provides a blow-by-blow history of the Pelagian controversy. The issue is not the struggle between Augustine and the Pelagians, *per se*, but rather how Augustine fights. Since almost every argument over Augustine turns into an argument over Pelagius, understanding the history is important. Augustine is at his best and worst as a controversialist. A dispassionate discussion of the inner logic of his theological positions misjudges him, but the violence of his argument, even in a polemical age, is more and more revealing.

The dispute begins with a disagreement about the relative importance of human effort and divine grace. While Pelagius acknowledges the dependence on God's grace, he consistently maintains humanity has its role. The response to God must match the awesome offer of divine grace. We must choose to turn to God; God has too much respect for his creation to take this choice away from us. O'Donovan credits Augustine with the reply of western Christianity that God never waits for us but is always in action.[9] However, the scriptures repeatedly show God asking us to turn to him in repentance; a call waits for a response. Of course, God's initiative is always first in the trivial sense that God created the world, and he sends the prophets. However, Augustine's reply denies the central role of the return to God that runs through the scriptures.

Pelagius asserts each person has to *choose* to accept God's grace and we have the God-given power to do so. The scriptural injunctions to repent and return to God prove we have the responsibility to respond to the call. The flaw in Pelagius's view is that people continually disappoint our expectations; we never do as well as we should. In contrast, Augustine believes the burden of original sin is so great that humanity is incapable even of repentance without an individual grant of God's grace. The unaided will is unable to do anything but sin. History often supports Augustine's negative

---

9. O'Donovan, *Resurrection and Moral Order*, 102.

assessment, but it is impossible to reconcile with the covenant history of the Bible.

Augustine radically sexualizes the issue, submerging the original question of the possibility of righteousness. The dispute is lengthy with Pelagius playing the smallest part. Pelagian ally Caelestius provokes the fight and Julian holds on to the end. History ignores Pelagius's words, accepts Augustine's description of them, and makes his name an epithet. The treatment of Pelagius may have been unfair, but it was decisive in the development of western theology.[10] Alexander V. G. Allen comments that it does not matter what the Pelagians thought; Augustine and Jerome created an image of their opponents and their heresy that was useful to the church for centuries.[11]

With an understanding of the issues debated, part 3 (chapters 6, 7, and 8) goes deeper into fifth-century thought. Chapter 6 goes back to the end of the fourth century and the controversy over the third-century theologian, Origen. Trained as a Neoplatonist, Origen is the champion of the freedom of the will. He argues for the restoration of all souls to harmony with God (he understands 1 Tim 2:4 literally—God desires us all to be saved and will bring it about). His denigration of the material world and his belief in universal salvation make him unpopular in the late fourth century. When he falls from favor, long after his death, theologians and scholars scramble to make their positions consistent with the new orthodoxy. The fight over Origen frames the Pelagian dispute; the controversialists duck some issues but use others as weapons. An understanding of Origen is fundamental to the struggle. Chapter 6 concludes with some background on Roman Stoicism and its relationships to the implicit assumptions of Augustine and the Pelagians. Stoicism's dour confidence contradicts Augustine's view of our damaged nature and impotent will. With Origen unusable, Stoicism becomes the basis of the anti-Augustinian defense of human nature and free will.

Chapters 7 and 8 reexamine Augustine's convoluted theories of nature and the will. Human nature is dissected in chapter 7. The simplest route to Augustine's conclusions would have been to say the Fall damages our nature—but this is not available to him. By having the will damage nature though sexual desire, he finds a mechanism to carry his theoretical program. Our nature is good, but stained. It is not the Platonic ideal chair that God created but is now a scratched and dented chair. We are born deformed by original sin. His opponents don't follow his reasoning and claim Augustine is still a Manichaean dualist who condemns the flesh as evil. Augustine separates himself from his contemporaries by elevating the will to an

---

10. Pelikan, *The Christian Tradition*, Vol. 1, 313.

11. Allen, *Continuity of Christian Thought*, 154. The 1883 Bohlen Lectures.

independent and corruptible part of human psychology. The disorderly will produces the war between spirit and flesh, not dualism.

Chapter 8 describes his evolving position on free will. Having saved the initial goodness of human nature by denigrating the will, Augustine has to explain his defense of the will in his anti-Manichaean period. His early works support the strength of the will and the justice of God, who does not punish any sin unless it is truly voluntary. The later works express the utter failure of the will absent grace, a position more compatible with his feelings of helplessness. Since his fifth-century opponents identify the will with reason and the absolute capacity and responsibility to choose correctly, they cannot follow his evolving positions; they see his denial of human agency as an affront to God.

Augustine's doctrines of nature and the will lead to the questions of predestination and sexuality discussed in part 4 (chapters 9, 10 and 11). Chapter 9 discusses Augustine's use of the metaphor of the potter who can dedicate a vessel to an honorable or dishonorable purpose (Rom 9:20–23) to explain why God chooses us for damnation or grace before time. A universal original sin means damnation is always just; we should be grateful for the few who escape. The birth of defective infants demonstrates a prenatal sin, and the inability of children to repent shows the impotence of the adults. If children cannot ask, seek, and knock, because they are too young to understand, it would not be fair for the adults to achieve salvation by a route unavailable to infants. The brutality of his theology appalls many critics; the words chosen show the depth of his commitment to his system.

Chapter 10 focuses on the erectionalization of the entire argument. The erratic penis can disobey the will even when the will chooses sex. This disobedience provides a mechanism for the transmission of sin from parent to child and represents the catastrophe in the Garden of Eden. Augustine uses increasingly strange arguments about the possibilities of pre-serpent sex; he exposes a fantasy that reproduction under the command of the will would have employed a limp penis dispensing semen passively in analogy to urination.

Chapter 11 returns to Augustine's problem and forms the conclusion of the work. The first question is why the odd structure he creates for himself dominates the western church. Part of the answer is political. The adoption of Christianity by an increasingly fragile empire provides new opportunities for an ambitious church. Augustine exploits the empire's needs for the church and molds the church into a cooperative partner of the state.

The second question is whether there were different paths for the church to follow. Augustine's solution is compared with the alternatives presented by Jerome and John Cassian.[12] In different ways, they each show how the Pelagian challenge could have been met without the denial of free will, the odd sexuality, infant damnation, and the arbitrariness of grace. Augustine's victory over all these ideas is ensured by his better alignment with the historical necessities of the declining empire and his outstanding rhetorical skills. Finally, he is partly right about one crucial thing, the will. The classical consensus that reason rules human behavior, or should rule it, is inadequate. The will often makes perverse decisions that contradict what is good.

To the extent possible, the discussion will stay within Augustine's ring fence. The question remains whether the emphasis on the Pelagian controversy is appropriate. Some readers conclude that the oddities in Augustine's biography are sufficient evidence of impotence. However, Augustine's impotence shapes his answers to the hard theological problems he confronts. Exploring the battlefield reveals the positions Augustine clings to tenaciously, even when alternatives are more coherent. The issues are still challenging: freedom and determination; mercy and judgment; responsibility and punishment; evil and grace. There are no final answers to the dilemmas, but we still talk about them in Augustine's terms.[13]

The history of western Christianity depends on Augustine, the problems he faced, and the solutions he devised. Any reconsideration must try to prescind from that history, but Augustine's dogmatism forces readers to choose. As Gerald Bray writes, "In the end we must opt for Augustine or against him, and allow the rest of patristic thought on the matter to be seen in the light of that fundamental choice."[14]

---

12. Cassian is one of the founders of western monasticism. A follower of Origen, he was expelled from Egypt during the controversy over Origen and relocated to what is now southern France.

13. Wiggers, *Augustinism and Pelagianism*, 17.

14. Bray, "Original Sin in Patristic Thought," 47.

# 1

# The Two Augustines

IF MODERN READERS KNOW anything about Augustine's life, it is through his autobiographical prayer, the *Confessions*. He traces his journey from Manichean dualism to Nicene Christianity, and from degraded sex addict to virtuous priest. His sex and Manichean lives were roughly contemporaneous. He acquired a lover at seventeen and became a Manichean auditor, corresponding to the Christian catechumen, at about the same time. He loosened his connection with the Manicheans circa 384 and dismissed the lover in 385. After several zigs and zags, he has a powerful conversion experience in a Milanese garden and becomes a devout Christian. West is confident Augustine describes his life truthfully,[1] and R. L. Ottley speaks of his sincerity.[2]

If his autobiography is not confession, it may be denial and deception. As George Orwell wrote of Gandhi, "Saints should always be judged guilty until they are proved innocent."[3] His conversion may have been due less to his mother Monnica's[4] influence or his dangerous Manichaean past and more to his sexual dysfunction. The secret he cannot confess is that he is not the profligate he claims to be. The hypothesis defended here is that Augustinian impotence of the will is sexual impotence, plain and simple. It is not just a question of the bare biographical possibility, but if the hypothesis is correct, it recasts the foundations of his theology. Augustine bases much of

1. West, *Saint Augustine*, 15.
2. Ottley, *Studies*, 119.
3. Orwell, *All Art is Propaganda*, 353.
4. Monnica is the North African spelling; the secondary sources vary between Monnica and Monica.

theology on the waywardness of desire. Concupiscence produces an erection when it is not wanted and fails to do so when it is wanted. The dual nature of desire is reflected in the problem of two Augustines.

The division between the two Augustines depends on the classifier. The most common one is between his youth and maturity, with the dividing line being the work *To Simplician* composed shortly after his consecration as Bishop of Hippo in 396. The early Augustine, as portrayed in the touching search for peace in the *Confessions*, becomes the angry protagonist of his years of controversy. This thesis became dominant following Peter Brown's magisterial biography of 1967. He argues Augustine's conversion in Milan in 386 is to Neoplatonism rather than Christianity. His encounter with Paul in the 390s during the Manichaean controversies produces a revolution in his thought. While he longed for philosophical serenity, he is unable to shake off the body. His dream of independence lost, he has to accept he will never achieve the repose he desired.[5] In the first edition of his biography, Brown relies on John Burnaby's 1938 Hulsen Lectures. Burnaby believes the later books are the dyspeptic work of a tired old man and do not represent Augustine at his best.[6] The epilog of Brown's second edition allows more continuity between the younger and older Augustine. Brown accepts that the doctrines of grace, free will, and predestination are not just the reactions of a disappointed man but are nascent in the early work.[7]

J. B. Heard separates a sacramental theology from the Predestinarianism that Heard considers heretical.[8] N. P. Williams makes a similar separation into institutional and predestination elements.[9] The early twentieth-century polemicist Thomas Allin uses the terms Catholic and Protestant theologies. He complains that whenever critics attack the later Augustine, his defenders point to the earlier writings, even though he abandoned them later (and denied that the older works meant what they seemed to say).[10] The marathon Pelagian controversy (410–30) provides other milestones. Augustine crushes Pelagius and Caelestius in 418, but this just opens the way for the struggle against Julian, unfinished at Augustine's death.

Some scholars reject any division. There are those who think his later ideas are natural developments of his earlier ones, and those who think they

---

5. Brown, *Augustine of Hippo*, 139–50.
6. Burnaby, *Amor Dei*, 231.
7. Brown, *Augustine of Hippo*, 490.
8. Heard, *Alexandrian and Carthaginian Theologies*, 361. Heard's 1893 Hulsean lectures are filled with anti-Augustinian jibes.
9. N. P. Williams, *Ideas of the Fall*, 425.
10. Allin, *Augustinian Revolution*, 108–109.

represent a response to Pelagius. The scholars who reject even an indirect Pelagian influence point instead to an evolving vocabulary rather than any fundamental change. William Cunningham judges that Augustine's developed positions provoked the Pelagian opposition rather than the Pelagians compelling Augustine to exaggerate his views.[11]

Gerald Bonner feels Augustine is consistent from *Simplician* and the *Confessions* onward, and thus his ideas do *not* stem from anti-Pelagianism. However, Bonner acknowledges that the Pelagian period hardens Augustine.[12] Bonner goes too far for some defenders. Marianne Djuth criticizes his rejection of predestinationism and his preference for John Cassian. She says this constitutes an implicit acceptance of another taxonomy of two Augustines: the Augustine who defended free will when it was convenient in his anti-Manichaean period, and the anti-Pelagian denier of free will. Djuth argues for continuity in Augustine's treatment of the will.[13] Carol Harrison asserts Augustine was certain of the utter incapability of the will and the necessity of grace long before *Simplician*. Between 394 and 396, he experiments with the idea that the beginning of faith is within human grasp. However, he retracts these fragmentary thoughts in *Simplician*, returning, in Harrison's view, to his core beliefs.[14] Jason BeDuhn offers a compromise, stating that Augustine's formal *beliefs* are consistent with an evolving *understanding*. Words that begin as slogans become pillars of a system. His gradual education into the forms of his new faith partly masks any development.[15]

His rhetorical training also may conceal change; he may seem to contradict himself when he is only varying his words to fit the occasion. Augustine has no biblical training when he converts; his understanding and vocabulary is Neoplatonic. He needs to distance himself from his past, so the case he initially presents is anti-Manichaean; he chooses the texts and the approach to match the situation. The fight with the Manicheans is over dualism, materialism, and fatalism, so the emphasis is on the freedom of the will and the goodness of creation. Later, in his struggle against the Donatists, the central issues are the unity of the church and the validity of the sacraments. The subject having changed, the approach is different, and new texts are appropriate. The emphasis is on the description of the church as an encompassing organization, with a mixture of saints and sinners. With

---

11. Cunningham, *S. Austin*, 175–76. This is the published form of the 1885 Hulsean Lectures.
12. Bonner, "Augustine and Pelagianism," 28–29.
13. Djuth, "Hermeneutics of *De Libero Arbitrio*," 282.
14. Harrison, *Rethinking Augustine's Early Theology*, 151.
15. BeDuhn, *Augustine's Manichaean Dilemma*, Vol. 2, 14–15.

the advent of the Pelagians, the primacy of grace is threatened. The circumstances and texts again change, and any contradictions with the earlier struggles are irrelevant. Augustine is not a systematic theologian—rather he is a situational theologian. He draws on Manichaean, Donatist, Academic, and Neoplatonic thought as he requires. Even when condemning a position as wrong-headed or heretical, he is capable of packing elements of the enemy's thoughts into his new structures. While not denying the genuine struggle and change in Augustine, the contradictions may merely reflect the case at hand. The anti-Pelagian writings have the advantage of making Augustine angry, and angry debaters can make revealing mistakes.

The Donatist struggle was extremely important in Augustine's development as a fighting churchman. Although the issues were not primarily theological, the controversy partly overlapped the Pelagian era and provided Augustine with training and confidence. Augustine becomes a hero of the African church during the long campaign against the Donatists. That controversy began long before Augustine was born. During the Diocletian persecution (303–305), some North African clergy handed over the scriptures to the Roman authorities. The Donatists refused to acknowledge the baptisms and ordinations made by these *traditores* (those who hand over, the root of the word traitor). At the beginning of Augustine's priesthood, the schismatics probably outnumbered the catholics in Hippo. The matter was formally settled by a council in June 411 attended by two hundred eighty-six catholic bishops and two hundred eighty-four Donatist bishops. Pelagius was there, but he and Augustine didn't meet. The Donatists were defeated and their churches were seized, although remnants of the church remained up to the Arab conquest. The struggle taught Augustine how to mass support from the African clergy, a technique that he applied successfully against the Pelagians.

The controversy led him to an appreciation of the value of imperial support. Augustine argued, based on Luke 14:23, that heretics could be "compelled to come in" (*cogite intrare*). He recommended fear tactics to the proconsul Donatus (not the eponymous leader of the schismatics) to correct the heretics.[16] He took an even harder line later, saying he didn't favor more violence at the time because he lacked the experience of how much evil the Donatists would cause.[17] The issue of coercion is a substantial part of the Enlightenment reaction to Augustine; more than half of Pierre Bayle's massive *Philosophical Commentary* discusses Augustine's *cogite*.[18] One of

---

16. Aug., *Letter* 100.1.
17. Aug., *Revisions* 2.5.32.
18. *Letter* 185 to Count Boniface compares compulsion to the restraint of madmen

the factors contributing to Augustine's success as a controversialist is his ability and willingness to make theological disagreements an issue of state. The empire began to interfere with the church in Constantine's time at the Council of Nicaea in 325; it could no longer let religious argument disrupt the fragile stability of the besieged state.

Impotence provides an understanding of the two Augustines that resolves some of the difficulties of other explanations. If impotent, then his conversion initially makes him safe from conventional Roman family life. He can relax, bolster his anti-Manichean credentials, and lightly Christianize his Neoplatonism. After his forced ordination in 391 and consecration as bishop in 396, he has to deal with a sexually active congregation who are living the life he has abandoned. Contemplating his loss and isolation leads him to evolve his theory of grace; his impotence is just part of the wider human inability to do good. As Augustine changes, the differences reflect his gradual identification of every person's sin with his disability as well as the discovery of a Pauline vocabulary in which he could speak more clearly.

He has two theologies, raggedly held together. The first is an institutional theology of the church, its congregations, and its sacraments. As Christianity becomes the standard of the empire, the problem of running churches for all the new Christians is real. The ordinary Christian commits sins; they are not always major sins, but there is a continuous drone of insignificant transgressions.[19] The pastoral Augustine encourages the Christian to pray the Lord's Prayer daily (a theme he returns to frequently) for these sins and to give alms to the church. Praying, repentance, and seeking God's ear make sense. The steady streams of little sins and expiating funds stabilize life for the middling Christian, who is neither a notorious sinner nor a saint. Equally, consistent almsgiving provides reliable revenue to the bishop for building and maintaining churches, supporting the clergy, and caring for the ordinary poor.[20]

The second is a theology of nature, the will, and grace, in which morality and ethics play no part. Prayer, baptism, and repentance are meaningless; the church and sacraments are of doubtful relevance. The penitent sinner should pray and give alms but, aside from any temporary comfort it might bring, it has no bearing on her salvation. This theology focuses on our utter dependence on God and the real necessity of grace. All are justly damned; mercy is given arbitrarily to a very few. Salvation has nothing to do

---

for their own good.

19. Brown, "Crisis of Wealth," 20.
20. Brown, *The Ransom of the Soul*, 83–114.

with sins or virtues. God chooses his elect without regard to anything that human reason can comprehend.

Nothing resolves the tension between these theologies. Augustine switches between them smoothly, only rarely conscious of any conflict. While he manages the church of the *non valdes boni* (the not very good), he simultaneously considers them worthy of contempt. God is just, but he does not care if the justly damned greatly outnumber the saved.[21] The damage done by the Doctrine of Grace to the Doctrine of the Church is evidence of a hidden driver so powerful that their author cannot see what he has done. Augustine struggles to combine his doctrines with the responsibility of managing a congregation containing very few elect. Any strict adherence to an absolute predestination with a limited number saved makes it impossible to run a church.[22] Augustine, as will be shown, partly solves his problem by speaking soothing words of repentance, prayer, and almsgiving to his congregation, without telling them that human deeds and human merit are irrelevant.

The Pelagian ideas threaten both theologies. Pelagius was a layman, variously described as British, Welsh, or Scots, with a charismatic preaching style. When he arrives in Rome, he allies with the spiritually renewed rich centered in Rome and Italy. He emphasizes *authentic* Christianity, not *mediocre* Christianity and is interested in making saints. We all have free will and the capability of doing better; sinlessness is an achievable goal. Augustine, in his pastoral role, thinks Pelagius abandons the middling Christian. The possibility of sinlessness disrupts the need for the institutional church and may lead people to ignore their duty to pray and give alms. It is unlikely that Pelagius encouraged people to neglect any duty or to be proud of their virtue; he is particular hard on hypocrites.[23] More important to Augustine, perhaps, is the damage Pelagius does to Augustine's sense of despair. If we are fundamentally capable of good, then the bleakness of limited grace is dispelled. The practical Augustine may worry about church finances but the polemical Augustine clings to his guilt and impotence. Alms are inextricably connected to sin, but sin is more important.

---

21. Aug., *Letter* 190.12.

22. Harnack, *History of Dogma*, Vol. 5, 166.

23. Pelagius, *On Bad Teachers* 11.1. The authorship of *On Bad Teachers* is unclear. It states some of its positions more strongly than Pelagius's usual cautious style.

## AUGUSTINE IN CONFLICT

The sigh of relief in Augustine's early work may have been a conversion-related release from addiction. It is more likely under the current thesis that it was an escape from a revealing conventional marriage. The continuing obsession with sex reflects the failure of celibacy to provide any permanent solution. If a person conquers an addiction, the pain may go. However, if desire remains with no outlet, the frustration increases. Impotence does not trouble a man who has mastered his desire. Augustine's descriptions of his torments may well have been as intense and painful as he writes because no resolution is possible for the impotent man.

Augustine transforms his helplessness into a general theory of the will. He does not deny we make acts of will, but those choices are never for good, absent grace, and are only a selection among sins. He precludes *any* human initiative, even when the scriptural text or prior tradition requires it. Consider his exegesis of Zech 1:3; he begins with the Pelagian case:

> When the Lord says, "Turn to me and I shall turn to you" one of these actions seems to pertain to our will, that is our turning to him, but the other seems to pertain to his grace, that is, his also turning to us. Here the Pelagians can think that their view wins out by which they say that the grace of God is given in accord with our merits.[24]

He never addresses the text directly but presents other texts showing humanity begging God to turn them to him (Ps 80 and 85). He is obfuscating. All the texts refer to a call and response exchange. God calls for a response requiring *human* effort. The Psalms contain a *human* request for God's help with the turning. In Zechariah, God issues a call; in the Psalms, the first words are human, asking for help in responding to that call.

Augustine's inability to accept any notion of human initiative is telling. It is not just that he does not see the texts as describing a covenant; rather, he cannot imagine anything other than the total failure of human endeavor. Ignoring the biblical calls for the people to repent and turn to God requires a willful blindness. He expresses the conventional view in his sermons; his congregations would not have appreciated his full opinions. He preaches, "He invites us to turn back to him; he waits for us until we turn back to him;

---

24. Aug., *Grace and Free Choice* 5.10 (Teske, WSA, I/26, 77–78). The primary designation in terms of the book, chapter, letter or sermon number, and paragraph and subparagraph, if applicable, will be given first in footnotes. If a direct quotation is used, the translator and the page number in the translation used will be provided in parenthesis. All of the translations in the New City Press edition will be notated WSA, Works of Saint Augustine, along with the series number.

he pardons us if we turn back to him; he gives us the winner's crown if we don't turn away from him."[25] He urges repentance, "Do not be slow to turn to the Lord (Sir 5:8)."[26] Both sermons are after the *Simplician* revolution; the pastoral and polemical Augustines coexist, even if Augustine hides his predestinationism from his congregation.[27]

The text in Zechariah is an obstacle for many Augustinians. Luther analyzes it grammatically. He reasons that commands like "Turn to me" are in the imperative. This does not imply the indicative, just as a command to "Fly" does not give one the ability to do so. God's commands to turn, repent, love, are all empty speech designed to make us recognize our inability to obey. They are contrary-to-fact subjunctives: God would turn to us if we could turn to him, but we cannot.[28]

Augustine denies God has a universal will to save all people. He describes humanity in such dark terms that God has no reason to save it; there are no virtuous people. God is portrayed in darker terms; even if people are weak and sinful, a loving God might reach out to them. Augustine's God does not feel a genuine empathy for humanity. The biblical calls are empty gestures, and God cannot reward anyone's response to those calls. A few are given mercy, but merely as a proof that God can. Humanity is a *massa perditionis*, a lump of perdition, and God is an arbitrary judge. This radical change from scripture and the early church is incredibly shocking. Nothing in his autobiography suggests a motive and nothing in the theological climate of his times requires it. The abandonment of the idea of a covenant between God and his people—turn to me, and I will turn to you—needs a correspondingly radical explanation. A new picture is required.

An impotent Augustine differs fundamentally from the one presented in his autobiography. Both critics and defenders read the *Confessions* as an honest, if colored, description of sexual addiction. The discussion is entirely about the degree rather than the existence of his addiction. An impotent man has more to hide than a womanizer does. Many authors downplay his claims of *extreme* sexuality, but they generally believe him when he says he was a prisoner of his desire. Louis Sébastien, OSA, thinks he was ruled by desire;[29] Andrea Dworkin describes him as a champion among sinners.[30]

---

25. Aug., *Sermon* 29A.2 (Hill, WSA, III/2, 121).

26. Aug., *Sermon* 40.2. While most Protestants omit Sirach from their Bibles, Augustine considered the entirety of the Septuagint, which contains Sirach, to be divinely inspired.

27. Aug., *Gift of Perseverance* 22.57.

28. Luther, *The Enslaved Will*, 75–77.

29. Sébastien, *Life of Augustine*, 10.

30. Dworkin, *Intercourse*, 190.

Henry Chadwick believes he struggled between his desire for a philosophy dedicated to universal truths and his addictive desire for women.[31] Some doubts creep in. West warns that there were things in his life that Augustine cannot face, and the *Confessions* reflect that denial.[32]

Although he says he was incapable of controlling his desire, there is no child following his son Adeodatus (Given by God), born when Augustine was seventeen or eighteen. Augustine claims perfect fidelity to his lover but never gives her a name.[33] He calls her *unam* (one). He refers to a second lover as *aliam* (another). The secondary sources use concubine, mistress, companion, lover, partner, and common-law wife. Brown says the often-used term "concubine" is not technically correct (as well as having a pejorative sound). Concubinage was an established practice for Romans of a higher class than Augustine's rank. Augustine's marriage options were not restricted by law.[34] The coldness of his treatment attracts modern scorn but Lancel romantically defends him, saying he does not name her because it would recall her scent and sound.[35]

His account shows no real intention to marry, even under considerable pressure from his mother. The girl eventually chosen may have been as young as ten years old. Her age had the advantage of delaying marriage for two years—Roman law prohibited marriage for girls under twelve. If he wanted to get married quickly, if only to slake his lust,[36] Monnica could have found someone older. He claims he was impatient to have a sexual partner approved by Monnica, now that she had disposed of his lover.[37]

Augustine's biography provides negative evidence in the lack of the second child. Explanations include a perfect method of birth control, some infertility of his lover that prevented a second conception, or a failure on Augustine's part. The first possibility is intrinsically improbable, and the second would not address the absence of a child with his second lover. The third possibility is central to the current thesis. Paul laments, "but I see in my members another law at war with the law of my mind, making me captive to the law of sin that dwells in my members (Rom 7:23)." Augustine restricts the other law to the problem of erections. He complains we can direct the other parts of the body to do our will, but the members associated

---

31. Chadwick, *Augustine*, 24.
32. West, *Saint Augustine*, 17.
33. Aug., *Confessions* 4.2.2.
34. Brown, *Through the Eye of a Needle*, 150.
35. Lancel, *St. Augustine*, 27.
36. Aug., *Confessions* 6.12.22.
37. Aug., *Confessions* 6.15.25.

with conception defy us. We have to wait for them, rather than having them respond to our command. They are disobedient. First, they may not move when we wish it; and, second, they may move when we don't.[38] If Augustine was impotent, the lack of a second child is not surprising; the conception of Adeodatus may require explanation (chapter 2).

Missing in Augustine's rants about the disobedient member is the expected misogyny. There is no accusation of women and no complaint about their seductive ways. Felecia McDuffie distinguishes Augustine from other church fathers precisely because he does not attribute his desire to the seductiveness of women.[39] *Some* sexual tension is at his core. The first possibility is that he was a prisoner of desire as a young man, but his conversion freed him from his addiction. The focus on the disorderly desire, in particular on the inconveniently flaccid penis, makes this unlikely. A better explanation is impotence, whatever its source.[40] Augustine's lack of misogyny is astonishing. It is not surprising that a fifth-century monk writes from an androcentric perspective; he *is* condescending. It is perhaps even reasonable that, even after a claimed passionate youth and fourteen years with one lover, he remains ignorant of female sexuality; modern men, women might agree, often do no better. However, his theology is still surprising. He bases his entire theology on original sin, first contracted in Eden. Eve listens to the snake; Eve takes the apple; Eve persuades Adam to eat. The rebellion against God, if that is what it is, is Eve's choice. If, as Augustine theorizes, the punishment for that disobedience is unruly sexuality, then Eve should be portrayed (as she later is) as the ungovernable seductress. Nevertheless, when Augustine wants to identify the disobedience in the bedroom that replicates the disobedience in the garden, he emphasizes the male inconsistency, not the female enticements. His conversion liberated him, not from women but from male expectations.

His earliest post-conversion writing provides insight into the relief he felts after escaping from an official Roman marriage. Augustine thinks no woman, however virtuous, can be allowed to distract a scholar; there is no requirement for a sage to reproduce. He sniffs "anyone who has intercourse with a woman for this purpose only seems to me worthy of admiration rather than imitation. The danger of attempting it is greater than the happiness

---

38. Aug., *Marriage and Desire* 1.6.7.

39. McDuffie, "Augustine's Rhetoric of the Feminine," 103.

40. Is it possible that his unwanted erections were provoked by young men while the missing erections were in the presence of women? Burrus *et al.*, note, "The spectacularly anachronistic question of his sexual orientation has for the most part produced disappointingly uninteresting answers." *Seducing Augustine*, 29.

of achieving it."[41] This is an oddly detached statement from a man who has recently been torn from his lover, become engaged to a child, dumped her, and escaped from sexual addiction. The words are those of a virginal Oxford don, not a repentant Don Juan. The notion of the danger of reproduction is ludicrous, particularly in a doting father. He belongs with the Inklings, another C. S. Lewis (before *his* marriage). The reader cannot take his earliest writings at face value, especially when they reek of the high table. The detached don of the *Soliloquies* and the reformed rake of the *Confessions* are both literary poses. The writer of the *Soliloquies* sounds as if he never had a son, or even any sex, of any kind, ever.

His distaste for the mechanics of sex is prissy, not analytical. He doesn't deny sex in Eden would required some motion, but is aghast that it is now so shameful.[42] The shame is due to the erection's unreliability. He complains, "In the case of the sexual organs, however, lust has somehow taken such complete control of them that they are incapable of being moved if lust is absent, and they do not move at all unless it arises either on its own or in response to stimulation."[43] Foucault recognizes that Augustine is not simply saying the genitals are shameful. They are shameful because they move without the consent of the will, presenting the revolt against God.[44] Virginia Burrus points to the contrast between the predominant Roman fear of penetration and Augustine's innovation of making the erection itself the problem.[45]

Kate Cooper and Conrad Leyser disagree with Burrus and Foucault about the primacy of erection; they embrace impotence as a central theme of Augustine. They recognize that the unpredictability of the erection is Augustine's real point. The failure to achieve an erection represents humanity's full degradation.[46] Their analysis is very close to the perspective of the current hypothesis, but with a reversal of the direction. They correctly identify how important impotence is to Augustine, but see this primarily as his dismantling of classical Roman standards of masculinity and his criticism of the rabid asceticism of his times. These stress the achievement of control over desire and classify those who cannot control themselves as weak. Cooper and Leyser argue Augustine uses metaphors of impotence to illus-

41 Aug., *Soliloquies* 1.10.17 (Burleigh, 33).

42. Aug., *Marriage and Desire* 1.31.53.

43. Aug., *City of God* 14.19 (Babcock, WSA, I/7, 127).

44. Foucault, "Sexuality and Solitude," in *Religion and Culture*, edited by J. R. Carrette (Manchester: Manchester University Press, 1999) 182–87 at 186, in Cooper and Leyser, "The Gender of Grace," 548.

45. Burrus, *Sex Lives of the Saints*, 4.

46. Cooper and Leyser, "The Gender of Grace," 541.

trate the weakness of the will and the common status of all men (as usual, Augustine only considers women derivatively). If no man can control his penis, no man can exalt himself over another; we are all sinners. Even the monk hiding in the desert cannot control himself. In contrast, the current hypothesis is that his sexual impotence leads to his theological position. He does not start with a non-sexual understanding of our inconsistency in choosing the good over the bad and then use the inconsistency of the erection as a metaphor for this wavering. Instead, his helpless impotence is the foundation of his belief in our inability to do good. A similar question arises in the relationship between infant baptism and original sin. Augustine argues that original sin demands infant baptism; the tradition of the North African church of infant baptism proves original sin must exist. He wants us to believe his confidence in the custom leads him to original sin as an explanation. However, it is also possible his despair gives him a sense of universal damnation, and he uses baptism to justify it.

The centrality of the penis *is* an Augustinian innovation, contrasting both with the traditional Roman notions of measured restraint and with the rabid hostility to women of Tertullian and Jerome. Criticism of Augustine as a woman-hater is misplaced. Any neglect or suppression of the feminine is secondary, even if he weaves some standard misogyny into his work. He has no sustained interest in female sexuality—women are not his problem. It is not surprising his defenders can easily find pro-marriage ideas in Augustine and can contrast him positively with other more obviously misogynistic theologians. He cannot even bring himself to condemn Eve, a task any churchman should have found easy. Foucault captures part of his flavor in seeing the erection as a symbol of disobedience in Augustine's thought,[47] but he misses Augustine's interest in the inability to obtain one. It is not in passion that sexuality reflects and recapitulates the disobedience in the Garden; it is in penile unpredictability.

Personal impotence provides a new path into the mysteries of Augustine. The impotent man is never free from the knowledge of his impotence while the sex addict may achieve temporary relief from his obsession by acting on it. The impotence of the will is a good match with physical impotence—both are total failures. A weak will, like Adam's, could fit with a lack of restraint in sexual matters—sometimes we control ourselves, sometimes we don't. An impotent man may resent women, but he equally may be self-loathing. Augustine's particular form of misogyny makes more sense as a problem of failed masculinity, not seductive femininity. His biography, his books, and his last great struggle against the Pelagians provide the evidence.

---

47. Foucault, *The Use of Pleasure*, 138.

This controversy not only dominates his old age but also sets the framework for centuries of debate—any argument over Augustine includes a rehashing of the Pelagian controversy. His guard is down in the anti-Pelagian works, and the contradictions of his positions become clearer.

Even if we grant the hypothesis of impotence, it does not exhaust or classify the man—there is more in the *Confessions* than dissimulation and more in the *City of God* than bizarre sexual fantasies. A very different Augustine appears when he avoids his obsessions. He can speak about the love of God as the basis of the love of self and neighbor, or about the complex psychological phenomena of time and memory. The contrast between the two Augustines is telling; there is something primal about his reaction to the issues treated here—something painful and irrational.

## THE MANICHAEAN AUGUSTINE

Critics often trace the distasteful parts of Augustine to his Manichaean past. The Pelagians throw the accusation of Manichaeism at him at every turn, and he, in turn, valiantly attempts to separate his views from theirs and to turn the charge on his opponents. It is the faith of his youth and lingers, along with many other influences, throughout his life. It comes under attack politically; when Augustine distances himself from it, he becomes a fervid opponent. The ins-and-outs of its theology are important; Augustine retains the imagery even when he claims he has discarded its errors. To understand Augustine fully and to appreciate the attacks made on him by Julian of Eclanum, a detour into Manicheanism is necessary.

Manicheanism described itself as the true Christianity; the Manichees (or Manichaeans) claimed they avoided the primitive anthropomorphisms associated with naïve Christianity. Their embrace of reason and philosophy attracted the young Augustine. The social status of Manicheanism was uneasy, but the notions of orthodoxy were not yet rigid. They gained respect for their austere life, but the imperial authorities viewed them with suspicion. Manichaean bishops and congregations were scattered across the empire. The auditors (analogous to Christian catechumens) were not subject to the same ascetic discipline as the Elect but supported them as they wandered from place to place.

Like the earlier Gnostics,[48] the Manichees rejected the Hebrew Scriptures and referred to those who accepted them as semi-Christians. The

---

48. Gnosticism is a catchall term for a number of early divergences from the ill-defined orthodox path, all claiming a special revelation or knowledge, *gnosis*, was available to an elect. A dualistic approach to good and evil characterized most Gnostics,

third-century founder Mani described himself as an apostle of Christ but believed Christ was a purely spiritual being, unmixed with evil. He rejected the virgin birth; indeed, he dismissed the possibility of any birth of Jesus. The Manichees exploited the Pauline distinction between the spirit and the flesh. The spirit consisted of the particles of light—associated with the transcendent god, asceticism, and Christianity, The flesh was composed of matter associated with a lesser creator god, pagan practices, and Judaism.[49] Creation was the result of the battle between the forces of light and darkness. God permitted part of the divine substance to mix with the evil substance to ameliorate the effects of the invasion of Evil, creating the world we know. Every person, every material object, was a mixture of light and dark. Good and Evil are of roughly equal strength; we participate in the struggle by rejecting the dark elements within us, liberating the particles of light. Since these were dispersed throughout the material world, the Manichees were very fastidious about food and frequently fasted. They were vegetarian and imagined that the divine sparks were liberated in the stomachs of the Elect. They were strict pacifists and drank no wine. Augustine remarked that they recognized God in the grape, but not the cup;[50] he spoke derisively of the Elect as belching the divine.[51]

In the Manichaean framework, each person is in constant turmoil. Good and evil actions alternate in a chaotic sequence. In the unenlightened state, even the particles of light are fragmented; the seeker must combine the particles of light to achieve good consistently. Unenlightened people are helpless pawns, unable to control whether good or evil is temporarily in the ascendant. The Elect can discipline themselves; by focusing on uniting the good particles within them, they can reunite them with God. The Elect encouraged the auditors to approach this ascetic ideal and to avoid procreation of children. Each child represented a further imprisonment of particles of good in the matrix of evil matter, further delaying the eventual reunion of all of the particles of good.

BeDuhn believes Augustine did not understand Manichaean responsibility or even the differences between Manichaeism and Nicene Christianity

---

with a denigration of the Hebrew Bible as being pre-gnosis, or even the scripture of an evil god. Among the Gnostics were the second-century thinkers Valentinian and Marcion.

49. For the relationship of the spirit/flesh dichotomy to the development of Christian attitudes to the Septuagint and to the Jews, see Fredriksen, *Augustine and the Jews*. She shows how Augustine's rejection of his Manichaean past shapes his witness theory of the role of Judaism in a dominantly Christian empire.

50. Aug., *Against Faustus*, 20.13.

51. Aug., *Against Faustus*, 5.10.

at the time of his conversion.⁵² Augustine says he thought sins were due to an indwelling evil nature, and not due to choice; he was pleased to have his guilt removed so easily.⁵³ The Manichaeans only absolved people who lacked self-knowledge of the mixture of good and evil within them such as children and the unenlightened. This tolerance would not have applied to an auditor like Augustine. He should have been preparing himself for God's grace by self-discipline, confession, and study. Sin was foreign; it was a disease, not intrinsic to one's true nature. As the auditor improved his self-awareness, outbreaks of evil would be more quickly diagnosed and suppressed.⁵⁴ Augustine would have been considered responsible for dealing with these attacks by his Manichaean tutors.

God's grace is necessary to bind together the good particles into a coherent force; the auditor prepares for grace by proper control of desires. Unless a person comes under the influence of a member of the Elect to guide him, the forces within him will leave him in turmoil. Within this broad framework, the role of Christ is muted. Christ and his apostles (including Mani) act as wake-up calls—providing the incentive and instruction needed to begin the process of producing an integrated soul.⁵⁵

Manicheism included elaborate hierarchies of spiritual entities, a complex history of cosmic struggles and an altogether satisfying distinction between run-of-the-mill people and the Elect. The Manichaeans are easy to mock, but traditional angelology retains similar elements. The younger Augustine was intrigued with their system, but the older Augustine is easily able to shed the ridiculous parts of the cosmology when it proves convenient. Bonner identifies the initial attraction in the Manichaean explanation of the world's mixture of good and evil, along with its plan for humanity's eventual salvation. It offered a moral discipline and respect for all creation often missing in orthodox Christianity. The Manichees were willing to suffer torture and death for their beliefs, like martyrs of the early church. Bonner feels both theologians and historians have underrated Manicheanism.⁵⁶

The helplessness of the unenlightened person, the division into light and dark, and the sexual aversion would haunt Augustine's later years as echoes of his past. It may not be coincidental that the procreation-avoiding Manichees attracted an impotent Augustine. Accusing him of being a closet Manichee has always been appealing but it is insufficient. He does not sound

---

52. BeDuhn, *Augustine's Manichaean Dilemma*, Vol. 1, 86.
53. Aug., *Confessions* 5.10.18.
54. BeDuhn, *Augustine's Manichaean Dilemma*, Vol. 1, 87.
55. BeDuhn, "What Augustine learned," 39.
56. Bonner, *St. Augustine of Hippo*, 158.

like a Manichee—he sounds worse. The Manichean dualists believed in human effort; an auditor, properly instructed, could make progress in the virtues and with sufficient self-discipline, become one of the Elect. The impotence of the will cannot allow for that. The Manichaeans, as well as some Christians, advocated a boycott of the womb, but they are not responsible for Augustine's odd sexual hypotheses.

## SOLVING THE PROBLEM

Augustine's role is so dominant that it is difficult to see how radical his position is and to what degree he limits what had been a wide range of views. The second century Clement of Alexandria considers sexuality one of many desires to be moderated and controlled. Although Tertullian and Jerome produce an increased emphasis on the centrality of sex as *the* characteristic sin, everyone thinks controlling sexuality is possible. There would be no point in encouraging virginity, chaste marriages, and a celibate clergy, if it were not. Augustine changes all this; not only is it impossible to end desire, but it also does not matter if a person controls it. The emblem of disobedience is the inconsistent, even defiant, penis. While every man (and woman) might agree it has a will of its own, Augustine makes it the only will.

Sexual impotence is the key. His developed theology—predestination, original sin, the helpless will, irresistible grace, and infant baptism—can all be traced to that single source. Impotence drives his pessimism—if a man cannot control his penis, he cannot control anything. If the will cannot choose sex, then it cannot choose virtue. If we cannot choose good, then we can never earn God's favor, obey God's commandments, or seek God in repentance. Only God's grace can rescue us, and it will not be universal. Salvation will be individual, handed out stingily, one-by-one. No human action can affect God's decision to give or withhold grace. Just as there is no comprehensible reason for impotence, there can be no understanding of God's choice. Grace is arbitrary from any possible human perspective; no one can penetrate the mystery.

Individually each of the elements of his theory could have had nonsexual sources. A defective will follows from simple observation—people often behave perversely, contrary to what they know is right—or from the fact that it was Adam's weakness, too. When the Pelagians challenge him, the dark Augustine emerges. He relentlessly traces each idea to the penile rebellion. His critics do not make the linkage to sex; Augustine does that himself. He sexualizes the argument—not Pelagius, not Caelestius, not Julian, and not his later detractors.

The received story does not hold together. The sex fiend he describes is unlikely to have had only one child in a fourteen-year relationship or to have remained faithful so long. Ramirez cannot see how Augustine could be as profligate as he claims and maintain a stable life with his lover.[57] To reconcile this with Augustine's personal sense of his vast sinfulness, he concludes Augustine's confidence in his guilt convinces the reader. He emphasizes sexual addiction to provide a dramatic element—if you write a confession, you must confess something.[58]

The alternative proposed here is that his defenders are correct in believing his story of addiction improbable—not because he was not addicted, but because he was impotent. Ronald Hopson points out "the intensity of guilt is a good indicator of the sense in which the problem is internal, not a consequence of seduction. It is also an indirect measure of the extent of the sense of violation—an indirect measure of one's sense of abnormality."[59]

Erotic sex does not haunt Augustine's dreams; erratic sex does. He reserves erotic language for God; it is not bodily beauty or song, or perfume, "none of these do I love when I love my God."[60] His regret for his wasted youth is genuine: "Late have I loved you, Beauty so ancient and so new, late have I loved you."[61] Human love cannot compare. His loyalists point to these poetic expressions of the love of God with admiration, but this is not the totality of Augustine.

There is something missing in the structure of Augustine's thought. His central pillar is humanity's utter dependence on God. In the nineteenth century, Friedrich Schleiermacher defends a similar concept without invoking the penis. Augustine demands infant baptism; this liturgical requirement does not require disorderly desire. Vague notions of original sin are common in earlier church fathers; none of them speculates so elaborately about sex in paradise. Nothing requires his sexualization of these issues—and nothing requires his emphasis on the inability of men to control their erections. If he has to sexualize the Fall, the easiest thing would be to blame Eve and feminine wiles. If the wish to parallel Adam and Christ compels him to blame men, he could have woven a story around pride. While Jerome might have produced a sexualized theology (if he had been theologically inclined), only Augustine insists on an "erectionalized" theology.

---

57. Ramirez, "Demythologizing Augustine," 68.
58. Ibid., 81.
59. Ronald Hopson, Howard University School of Divinity, private communication.
60. Aug., *Confessions* 10.6.8 (Boulding, WSA, I/1 185).
61. Aug., *Confessions* 10.27.8 (Boulding, WSA, I/1, 203).

There *are* constraints on his thought. His Manichaean past makes the simple ascription of blame to a damaged human nature extremely unwise, and the Greek philosophical framework limits his language. Something sexual is implied, and the conventional explanations are all unsatisfactory (neither critics nor defenders are happy with them). His sense of complete and utter personal helplessness is evident in all his writings; impotence is the key.

We will explore his impotence by a rereading of Augustine, particularly his writings on the Pelagians and related works. These contain some of the strongest and strangest words on sex and sin. His position is distinct both from relatively mild demur from family life made by the Patriarch of Constantinople, John Chrysostom,[62] and from the virulent misogyny of Tertullian and Jerome. Augustine's attackers and defenders of the nineteenth and earlier centuries react strongly to him, better reflecting the passion and drive of the fifth-century protagonists than the more dispassionate twentieth and twenty-first-century commentators. The two Augustines are shown clearly, etched in acid.

The problem of Augustine is analogous to a famous psychological experiment: the subjects are told to watch a basketball game and count the number of times the ball is passed. They concentrate on the ball, and about half the subjects don't notice the man in a gorilla suit walking across the court.[63] Augustine is so caught up in his denial of his personal impotence that he does not, *cannot* notice, what Julian and his modern critics see. The example also applies to the students of Augustine. They focus on his contributions to theology, philosophy, and church governance. They do not see the impotent gorilla in the room.

---

62. Chrysostom is a near contemporary (347–407) of Augustine. See Harper, *From Shame to Sin*, 161–66, for a discussion of Chrysostom's role in the creation of a Christian revolution in the concept of marriage.

63. For one version of the invisible gorilla test, see www.youtube.com/watch?v=IGQmdoK_ZfY.

# 2

# True Confessions

ANY EXAMINATION OF AUGUSTINE begins with the *Confessions*. Even if it is less than perfectly honest, this autobiographical prayer establishes an image common to both his defenders and critics. George Orwell writes, "Autobiography is only to be trusted when it reveals something disgraceful."[1] Augustine wants us to believe in three things: his helpless inability to avoid sin, his sexual obsession, and his full-hearted conversion. This story may be secondary to his other purposes (whatever they were); the theology is there for a reason.[2] Others read the *Confessions* as an artful cover story, concealing the less convenient parts of his history, including his Manichaean past, his dubious sexuality, and the character of his conversion. Scholars don't agree on what he might have been concealing.

The *Confessions* portray Augustine as a reluctant bad-boy. He was born in 354 in a small North African town, Thagaste, to a minor official and his Christian wife. When he was sixteen, he took a year off from his studies while his father put together the cash to pay his school fees. Augustine ran with a rough crowd: "Afraid of being reviled, I grew viler and when I had no indecent acts that could put me on a level with these abandoned youths, I pretended to obscenities I had not committed, lest I be thought less courageous for being more innocent and be accounted cheaper for being more chaste."[3] The boys climbed over a garden wall and stole some fruit. Augustine makes the episode a metaphor for the pointlessness of sin. He

---

1. Orwell, *Benefit of Clergy*, in *All Art is Propaganda*, 210.
2. Chadwick, *The Early Church*, 219.
3. Aug., *Confessions* 2.3.7 (Boulding, WSA, I/1, 36).

chose to steal because his will was corrupt, and he was unable to resist. The pears were unimportant: "I had plenty of better ones, and I plucked them only for the sake of stealing, for once I picked I through them away. I feasted on the sin, nothing else, and that I relished and enjoyed."[4] Bonner believes Augustine's discussion of childhood sin, from the greed of infants to schoolboy pranks, reflects his life-long obsession with the nature of sin. The pear episode is insignificant in itself, but it exemplifies the emptiness of sin.[5]

He claims to have fully exposed his sexual obsessions. As a teenager, he attended church services just to pick up girls.[6] Most importantly, he confessed to his long love affair. Adeodatus was born at the beginning of the relationship. Augustine says he was reluctant to have more children and in fourteen years, there were none. The Manichaean Elect were celibate; auditors merely practiced birth control. Augustine practiced the rhythm method.[7] Ranke-Heinemann notes the fourth century had miscomputed the time of maximum fertility; dependence on the rhythm method would have led to many little Manichees.[8] He apparently also used *coitus interruptus,* and, perhaps, other forms of non-reproductive sex. The later Augustine insists any sexual relations not using the vagina are forbidden because they are associated with pleasure and not reproduction.[9]

Ramirez notes his contraceptive success exceeded that expected of mere auditors.[10] Several authors date the conception of Adeodatus before Augustine became an auditor and attribute the lack of another child to Manichaean influences. He joined the Manichees in Book 3, and he did not mention the lover until Book 4; however, it may be dangerous to conclude this was the order of events. More interestingly, Augustine might have chosen Manicheism because giving up sex is not a challenge for the impotent—avoidance of procreation provides a cloak of invisibility. The data do not suggest contraceptive discipline, but an absence of sex.

Augustine's supposedly purely sexual connection was long lasting. Adeodatus was born circa 372; Augustine and his lover were a loyal pair until 385. As his career as a rhetor in Milan developed, he put her aside as an impediment to a suitable marriage. Monnica was insistent, and a marriage

---

4. Aug., *Confessions* 2.6.12 (Boulding, WSA, I/1, 39).
5. Bonner, "Augustine's Doctrine of Man," 496.
6. Aug., *Confessions* 3.3.5.
7. Aug., *The Manichaean Way of Life* 18.65.
8. Ranke-Heinemann, *Eunuchs,* 83.
9. Aug., *Marriage and Desire* 2.20.35. Augustine quotes Rom 1:26, "For their women exchanged natural relations for those which are against nature," and interprets them as non-reproductive heterosexual relations.
10. Ramirez, "Demythologizing Augustine," 70.

was arranged.[11] His selected bride was a ten-year-old child, conveniently postponing the wedding for two years. His lover was sent back to Africa to enable the marriage; Augustine retained custody of Adeodatus. He says the loss shredded his heart. He wanted to take this opportunity to become chaste; his lover, after all, had vowed to do so, but his addiction immediately drove him to acquire another partner. The new lover was insufficient to heal him: "The wound inflicted on me by the earlier separation did not heal either. After the fever and the immediate acute pain had dulled, it putrefied, and the pain became a cold despair."[12]

The age of the prospective bride is uncertain. While the minimum age for marriage was twelve, fourteen might have been the median. The thought of a twelve-year-old bride appalls West, and she assumes the girl was twelve or thirteen at the time of the betrothal.[13] Brown surmises she was twelve and from a Catholic family close to Ambrose.[14] Serge Lancel also thinks she was twelve.[15] Other authors are content to call her ten.[16] Everyone seems to assume Augustine was marrying up. In contrast, West believes Monnica would have preferred him to remain a child. She sees the struggle as between his father Patricius's hope for grandchildren and Monnica's hope for his celibacy. In West's view, Monnica used religion as a tool to infantilize Augustine: "Very evidently Christianity need not mean emasculation, but the long struggles of Augustine and Monnica imply that in his case, it did."[17]

The engagement to a child was a risk; her age postponed the need to consummate a marriage, but marriages to upper-class Roman girls were for the production of children. Augustine had just two years to find a way out of his mother's plans. There is only a single mention of the second lover; how he terminated the connection is unknown. She may be a literary construction, permitting Augustine to contrast his long-time lover's declaration of future celibacy with his uncontrollable lusts. As the time for the wedding approached, the pressure on Augustine increased. He was wandering in a garden and sat under a fig tree in a state of despair. He heard the voice of a

---

11. Aug., *Confessions* 6.13.23.

12. Aug., *Confessions* 6.15.25 (Boulding, WSA, I/1, 113). His lover's vow of chastity was practical; a woman with only one lover, a *univira*, was still eligible for baptism.

13. West, *Saint Augustine*, 68.

14. Brown, *Body and Society*, 392.

15. Lancel, *St. Augustine*, 73.

16. Fredriksen, *Augustine and the Jews*, 132, Harper, *From Shame to Sin*, 166, and Cooper, "Augustine and Monnica," 17.

17. West, *Saint Augustine*, 26.

child uttering the famous words *tolle, lege* (take up and read) and discovered a way out of his problems.[18]

In 1950, Pierre Courcelle's *Recherches sur les "Confessions de sainte Augustin"* opens the door to reconsiderations. He suggests the fig tree was symbolic of the darkness of sin, and the child was a literary device indicating a divine answer to Augustine's turmoil.[19] Scholars now felt free to doubt every element of the *Confessions*: his choice of forms, his dramatic sense, and his reuse of older material. Burrus compares the *Confessions* to the *Golden Ass* of Apuleius, which also moves from carnality to divine revelation.[20] O'Donnell reanalyzes the urgency of Augustine's need to confess. He thinks it kinder to think the assertions do not represent an accurate account but rather are what Augustine needs to say to avoid facing what he wants to deny.[21] He concludes it would be naïve to assume the first great autobiography is also the first *honest* autobiography. Augustine wants to downplay his notorious Manichean past and to get back in the fame game, establishing himself on the map even from the awkward position of a provincial bishop. However, there may be other things to conceal.

Burrus *et al.* point out that it is the least lurid autobiography of a sex addict imaginable. Every time the reader expects a little salacious detail, even for the purpose of self-accusation, Augustine slips away. His reticence suggests the possibility "that he is faking the whole thing."[22] Augustine has the skill to suggest a sexual past he never reveals, leaving the reader to use his imagination.[23] If there is nothing to confess, Augustine might have been unwilling and unable to invent sex scenes in a prayer addressed to God.

West regrets the loss of the novelist she thinks Augustine could have been. She particularly admires the descriptions of the death of an unnamed boyhood friend and his long-time ally Alypius's addiction to blood sports; she finds his story-telling superior to Tolstoy's.[24] West reminds us Augustine was a capable writer, of fiction or non-fiction.

---

18. Aug., *Confessions* 8.12.29.
19. See Hadot, *Philosophy as a way of life*, 51.
20. Burrus, *Sex Lives of the Saints*, 80.
21. O'Donnell, *Augustine, a new biography*, 77. O'Donnell's biography is relentlessly revisionist, undercutting conventional treatments of Augustine's motives.
22. Burrus *et al.*, *Seducing Augustine*, 13.
23. Ibid., 15.
24. West, *Saint Augustine*, 16.

## ON THE ROAD TO THE FIG TREE

Augustine's conversion is central to his image, but the Milan conversion was his second—his first was to Manichaeism. He became an auditor when he was eighteen, distancing himself from his mother's simple Christian faith,[25] but retaining a devotion to the name of Jesus. The Bible disappointed Augustine stylistically, and he was unprepared to explore its deeper significance.[26] He joined the Manichees, whose materialism and glibness impressed him.[27] The Manichees had a well-developed criticism of the Hebrew Scriptures and could point to passages distasteful to a teenaged purist.[28] His natural arrogance was stimulated by his time with the Manichees. He found Aristotle's *Ten Categories* trivial.[29] His intellectualism motivated his first conversion from a vaguely Christian background to the elaborately metaphysical Manichaeism. He persuaded his friends Alypius and Honoratus and his long-time patron Romanianus to join as well and was active in the Manichaean community.

Augustine eagerly awaited the return to Carthage of the Manichaean bishop, Faustus. He hoped for insights into the hidden mysteries of the faith but was disappointed when he finally met him in 382. Faustus charmed Augustine with his piety and warmth but did not impress him with his brilliance. When Augustine confronted him with astronomical knowledge contradicting Manichaean cosmology, Faustus refused to engage on matters that did not bear on whether a person followed moral guidance or was learning to control his appetites. Nevertheless, they got along well—Augustine read recommended classical authors to him. Unfortunately, the empire was turning against toleration of anything other than the recently constructed Nicene Christianity; Faustus was at risk. There were anti-Manichean decrees issued in 381 and 382 slowly making their way to North Africa. Imperial decrees were not applied immediately and universally. In some cases, the decree was a description of imperial intent that had to be followed-up with specific instructions to specific governors. There were many ways to appeal and avoid them, but they represented a threat that could not be ignored.

Augustine fled to Rome in 383, escaping increased persecution of the Manichaeans, unruly students, and Monnica. He famously tricked her when

---

25. O'Donnell speculates in *Augustine, a new biography*, 212–13, she may have been a Donatist; Augustine exchanged letters with a Donatist relative, Severinus. See also Wills, *Augustine's Confessions*, 19.
26. Aug., *Confessions* 3.5.9.
27. Aug., *Confessions* 3.6.10.
28. Bonner, *St Augustine of Hippo*, 188.
29. Aug., *Confessions* 4.16.28.

she pursued him to the docks, slipping onto a boat without a word. In Rome, he was a member of the large Manichaean community and worked as a teacher in 383–84. Eventually, he distanced himself intellectually from the Manichaeans though he retained them as friends. He came under the influence of the skeptics of the New Academy. After his disappointment with Faustus, this was refreshing. He shared his new insights with his Manichaean hosts but did not break with them.[30] The New Academy was only a temporary stopping point before he adopted Neoplatonism. The Neoplatonists had a cosmogony as complex as Manichaeism but without the troubling astronomical implications.

The Roman students were unsatisfactory; they were better behaved than the Carthaginians but had a tendency to ignore tuition bills. He wanted to move again. With the assistance of his Manichaean friends, Augustine got the support of the pagan City Prefect, Symmachus. Symmachus provided a recommendation for a job opening in Milan as rhetor, a court-appointed teacher of rhetoric, possibly to irritate St. Ambrose by placing a Manichaean heretic in Milan.[31] Milan was one of the sites of the Western imperial court (along with Trier in the north) and was a more suitable location for an ambitious young man than Rome. It also had a smaller Manichaean community; the persecution had gotten hot enough that a lower profile was advisable.

The ever-diligent Monnica caught up with him in Milan.[32] She immediately began to work on getting rid of the lover, setting up an appropriate marriage, and making him a proper Christian. He did not immediately fall under Ambrose's spell. He occasionally went to listen to his sermons with Monnica, paying attention to his style; Ambrose was more sophisticated than Faustus but less charming.[33] He gradually replaced his Manichaean philosophy with Neoplatonism, the thinking man's religion.[34] Augustine, who had adopted Manichaeism because it attracted a better class of intellectual than his mother's faith, transferred his belief to an even tonier group. She rejoiced at the fact that, although he said he was not yet a Catholic, he no longer considered himself a Manichaean.[35]

Augustine characteristically chose a trendy mystical approach, rather than any scripturally based form of Christianity. The Bible still did not

30. Aug., *Confessions* 5.10.19.

31. Brown, *Augustine of Hippo*, 59–60.

32. Cooper, "Augustine and Monnica," 8, concludes Augustine chose to bring Monnica from Africa, possibly to help him with his political connections.

33. Aug., *Confessions* 5.13.23.

34. See discussion in Copleston, *History of Philosophy*, Vol. 1, Part 2, 216.

35. Aug., *Confessions* 6.1.1.

satisfy his philosophical needs. After Augustine's conversion in 386, Ambrose gave him a copy of Isaiah, which he did not understand. The vastly experienced Ambrose may have been suspicious of the sincerity of a dilettante, poseur, and flâneur with a dubious history. Ottley thinks Ambrose may have distrusted him as a stranger, an African, and a former heretic, who owed his job to the Roman city prefect, Symmachus, a pagan who had frequently collided with Ambrose.[36]

Augustine could make no sense of the prophetic God; only the transcendent Neoplatonic God resonated. His journey from abstract religion to the exegete of Romans is one of his more remarkable transformations. The Neoplatonism is strongest in his early post-conversion works while he was learning the actual content of the religion he had professed. The consensus is that even his mature works reflect a Neoplatonic framework in a Christian context. Harrison disagrees, asserting his conversion leaves only a few echoes. She maintains the incarnation, the creation of a good universe *ex nihilo* (out of nothing), the impotence of the will, and the necessity for grace distance Augustine from his Platonic roots and were part of his understanding from the early years.[37]

He had begun to make his way in a circle of like-minded amateurs.[38] Before his conversion, he and his friends had pondered retiring from the world to form a philosophical community; the ever-persuadable Romanianus was going to pay. They may have been motivated by a recent failed attempt of the Manichaean Elect in Rome to do so. They abandoned the fantasy when the wives of the married men objected.[39] It is not clear how interested Augustine was in consummating the marriage arranged by his mother. There is the echo of the high table and Victorian Oxford.

In 386, the pressure on Faustus in North Africa increased. He was tried and sentenced to death; his sentence was commuted to exile. Augustine was named as a Manichee in the trials, *in absentia*. It would have been dangerous to return to Africa as a Manichee in 386, and the threat might have pursued him to Italy. The politics were risky; the Manichees were the first targets of large-scale repression of theological deviation.[40] Closer to home, the Nicene champion Ambrose had won a staring contest with the

---

36. Ottley, *Studies*, 24. They clashed over funding the Vestal Virgins and the proper way of handling a famine.

37. Harrison, *Christian Truth and Fractured Humanity*, 84.

38. O'Donnell wonders whether his career was as successful as advertised. *Augustine, a new biography*, 52.

39. *Confessions* 6.14.24.

40. Brown, *Religion and Society*, 94.

Homoian[41] imperial court over the use of two basilicas in Milan in February 386. The outcome of the struggle between the Arian and Nicene sides was in doubt. Augustine does not show much awareness of these controversies in the *Confessions*.[42]

He does expose his inner turmoil. He approached Simplicianus, a priest who had been Ambrose's mentor at the time of Ambrose's baptism (and became his successor).[43] Discussing their shared philosophical ideas, the name of Marcus Victorinus (a famous rhetor and translator of the Neoplatonists Plotinus and Porphyry) arose. Victorinus's reading had led him to accept the truth of Christianity, but he would not immediately publically admit conversion. Upbraided by Simplicianus for his timidity, he eventually took the step of a public declaration to loud acclaim.[44] Victorinus's declaration may have been a significant nudge for Augustine, showing an accomplished scholar could accept the complete Christian package without embarrassment.

Augustine, Alypius, and a third African friend, Nebridius, continued their haphazard theological discussions. They were relatively ignorant of Christianity. Augustine was pleased to learn Christians did not believe in a corporeal or material God; Alypius was gratified to discover they did believe Christ had a human soul. On the crucial evening (Nebridius was away), they entertained another African, the Christian Pontitianus. Their visitor was delighted to see a copy of Paul's Letters lying on the table rather than some secular text. Pontitianus told them about St. Anthony of Egypt. Anthony had died in 356; he was famous for his piety and Athanasius had written his biography around 365.[45] Augustine and Alypius had never heard of the famous monk, nor were they aware of Ambrose's monastery in Milan. Previously, Augustine had associated ascetic withdrawal with the Manichaean Elect; a safe method of avoiding marriage was a miracle.

Pontitianus recounted the experiences of two colleagues at court; they had found a copy of Athanasius's *Life of Anthony* in yet another garden. They immediately decided to withdraw from the world while dumping their fiancés, who promptly and conveniently took the veil themselves. Augustine was overwhelmed. These men had been able to make the choice for God and

---

41. One of the many non-Nicene parties held that the Father and the Son were homoiousian, "of a similar substance," rather than identical, homoousian, "of the same substance," the Nicene formulation.

42. In *Confessions* 9.7.15, Augustine briefly mentioned that Monnica had been part of Ambrose's occupation of the basilica. He wasn't there.

43. Aug., *Confessions* 8.2.3.
44. Aug., *Confessions* 8.2.4.
45. Aug., *Confessions* 8.6.14.

against marriage while he was still paralyzed by indecision. He tore himself away from Alypius and paced deeper into the garden. Here he made the famous, and possibly theatrical, cry: "Make me chaste, but not yet." Summoned by the miraculous voice of the child, he returned to the copy of Paul that had provoked the evening's momentous conversations. Treating it as an oracular book, he opened it and read, "not in reveling and drunkenness, not in debauchery and licentiousness, not in quarreling and jealousy. Instead, put on the Lord Jesus Christ, and make no provision for the flesh, to gratify its desires (Rom 13:13–14)." He went to get Alypius, who found a symbolic verse of his own. The two friends announced their conversion, to Monnica's great joy.[46]

With the example of Pontitianus's friends, Augustine withdrew from his career and abandoned his fiancé. He does not describe the undoing of the marriage or the discarding of the second lover. He did not proceed immediately to the baptism Monnica had been encouraging. Instead, he took Alypius, Adeodatus, some of his friends (including a son of Romanianus),[47] and Monnica into a retreat at Cassiciacum (modern Cassago). They had a grand time writing Neoplatonic essays to each other. BeDuhn suggests the retreat to Cassiciacum may have been a political precaution. Augustine stayed away until a January 387 decree allowing Faustus and other Manicheans to return from exile.[48] Sorabji thinks the description of his retirement was partly literary. Augustine eventually informs his employers he is in poor health. Seneca suggested the same excuse.[49]

Augustine was profoundly joyful—he had resolved his religious turmoil and escaped marriage. Ambrose baptized Augustine, Alypius, and Adeodatus on Easter Eve in April 387. Easter was a traditional time for baptisms, but the timing may also reflect a cooling down of the anti-Manichaean frenzy that allowed him to appear in public. His joy was real; Monnica's primitive faith, Manichaeism, the New Academy, and Neoplatonism had all failed him. Similarly, his lover, the second lover, and the prospects of marriage to a twelve-year-old were all sexually unsatisfactory. Chastity and the church provided a refuge.

His conversion experience strengthened his intermittent desire to withdraw from the world but only now did he give up the concept of marriage. Monnica may not have been as eager for Augustine's complete

46. Aug., *Confessions* 8.12.30. It is not clear that Monnica rejoiced in his celibacy.

47. Having converted Romanianus to Manichaeism, Augustine had to reconvert him to Nicene Christianity.

48. BeDuhn, *Augustine's Manichaean Dilemma*, Vol. 1, 219–20.

49. Sorabji, *Emotion and Peace of Mind*, 401. Compare Seneca, *Letter* 68.3 (Gummere, 133).

withdrawal as he suggests. BeDuhn concludes he had been long seeking a Ciceronian retreat from the world, but the political situation had made that impossible in the Manichaean framework. When Pontitianus revealed the opportunity to retire safely, he leapt at it. The new life was not, as he understood it, radically different from the life of Faustus, and the path, once available, was easy to take.[50] The conversion did not require either the ending of the engagement or the abandonment of his career. Most Christians were married, and if Augustine and his child bride-to-be had so chosen, the marriage could have been celibate. Even his eventual ordination would not have been an insuperable barrier to marriage and children; Julian of Eclanum was a married bishop, the son and son-in-law of bishops. Augustine used the occasion of his conversion to flee into the newly respectable monastic retreat, truncating both his engagement and his secular career. Harrison accepts Augustine's statements that his hesitations were based on his inability to give up women and accept celibacy.[51] There doesn't seem to be a convincing reason for Augustine's stated conviction that celibacy was necessary for his conversion.

His subsequent biography shows he did not long escape from ambition; he was too natural a disputant for a peaceful withdrawal. He still sought honor, just in a different domain. BeDuhn's conclusion that Augustine wanted to escape domestic life—marriage—is consistent with impotence. Augustine needed to find a way to get out of the upcoming wedding without exposing himself. He could not use the Manichaean route because of the political dangers, his attempt to retire into a male commune in the countryside had failed, and the date of the marriage was looming closer and closer. He had every reason to jump.

It is hard to assess which motive was stronger: the fear of prosecution as a Manichaean or the fear of exposure as impotent. Either would have sufficed, and there may have been a genuine resolution of his religious doubts. Religious fervor for *Nicene* Christianity is unlikely to have been the proximate cause. Chadwick notes it took a long time for Augustine to separate his Christianity from his Neoplatonism.[52] The Nicene orthodoxy was not well established or even understood in the Latin-speaking regions of the empire as it was in the Greek empire. There is no clear indication Augustine had heard of the partial victory of Gregory of Nazianzus[53] at the Council of

50. BeDuhn, *Augustine's Manichaean Dilemma*, Vol. 1, 203.
51. Harrison, *Christian Truth and Fractured Humanity*, 90.
52. Chadwick, *The Early Church*, 218.
53. Gregory of Nazianzus and the brothers Gregory of Nyssa and Basil of Caesarea are collectively called the Cappadocian Fathers. They were the fourth century's vanguard of the evolving Trinitarianism.

Constantinople in 381. Augustine's ignorance of church politics makes his sudden adherence to Ambrose's side in the complex struggle between the church and empire surprising. It might indicate an astute assessment of the ultimate winner, a grasping at straws for any route out of the marriage, or the momentous revelation he described. It was by no means a safe bet: the church was both a subject of imperial favor and a political plaything of the emperors.[54]

He returned to Thagaste in 388 after his mother's death. There, he reproduced the Cassiciacum experience with Alypius and a few close unmarried friends, living off the proceeds of the sale of the family estate or continuing to depend on wealthy friends. Augustine might have happily stayed in this seclusion, but he visited Hippo to counsel an acquaintance about joining the Thagaste community in 391. The congregation seized him and demanded his ordination, a common risk in the fourth century. His knowledge of the scriptures was still so limited that he asked his bishop for time to develop the necessary familiarity. In a few years, he was consecrated as bishop of Hippo.

The rhetor displaying his brilliance at court became the bishop provoking Jerome over issues of translation,[55] debating the Manichaeans, demolishing the Donatists, and taking on the Pelagians. Augustine relished controversy throughout his entire career. In *Two Souls Against the Manicheans,* he traces his attraction to the Manichaeans to his love of winning debates. They armed him with arguments that defeated unlearned Christians; each victory massaged his ego and made his adherence to the heresy more stubborn. At the time, he had attributed his success to the correctness of the Manichean view. Later, he realized his triumphs owed a lot to his skills and the weakness of his opponents.[56] Bayle says if Augustine had not abandoned Manichaeism he might have used those skills to reform and strengthen it against orthodox Christianity.[57]

Different biographers point to his ambition or a need to cover his Manichean tracks as motivations lying behind the *Confessions.* The current hypothesis is that the *Confessions* hid his failed sexuality. His misogyny does

---

54. It is a mistake to think of the growth of orthodoxy as a series of conclusive victories. Arianism, condemned at Nicaea in 325, Manichaeism condemned in 380, and Nestorianism, condemned in 431, all survived into the seventh century (the last two reaching China) and traces may be found even later.

55. Augustine objected to new translations from the Hebrew, arguing that the Greek of the Septuagint was divinely inspired. *Letter* 28.2.2.

56. Aug., *Two Souls Against the Manichaeans* 9.11. Subsequently referred to as *Two Souls.*

57. Bayle, *Historical and Critical Dictionary,* 144.

not derive from a failure of the will to resist the body's hunger for sex, but from a failure of the body to respond to the will's desire for sex. Impotence adds a different flavor to his misogyny; he has the general condescension of his age, but he directs his rage at men. Sexual addiction is only a cover story.

## THE *CONFESSIONS* ANEW

If Augustine was impotent, the story in the *Confessions* reads differently. The lack of a second child points to sexual incapacity rather than a surprisingly effective Manichaean rhythm technique. The fact he remained faithful for many years reflects the desire to provide protective cover for the state of impotence, acting as a shield against Monnica's well-known nagging about marriage and grandchildren. The fact that he retained custody of Adeodatus suggests the hold he had over his lover was the child.

The question of Augustine and Monnica has created an entire industry; everything begins with Monnica.[58] She presses him toward conventionality, marriage, and career. His mother is made *the* central issue by many: "He is, after all, the man who virtually invented the closet."[59] Although his relationship with his mother provides sufficient resources for a thousand volumes, it is more interesting to consider what remained in that closet. The tensions with Monnica were real, but the constant coming and going from the closet may hide the real source of his conflict.

Augustine's description of his sex life is internally inconsistent. Men driven by desire do not remain faithful to lovers for fourteen years unless there is a non-sexual component. Augustine gives very little text to his lover; a few sentences acknowledge the beginning of the relationship, and a paragraph describes the tearful parting, but that is it. His pain at losing an unnamed male friend of his youth is deeper. Augustine mourns his sudden death for *six* of the sixteen chapters of Book 4; this is about the length of the discussion of the pear tree theft in Book 2. The disparity in the lengths devoted to the lover and the friend may indicate the latter relationship was more meaningful to Augustine.[60] He cannot control his grief; he marvels that other people still live when his friend is gone.[61] The loss shreds his soul.[62] His overwhelming pain does not keep him from using his friend for

---

58. Burrus, *Sex Lives of the Saints*, 77.

59. Burrus and Keller, "Confessing Monica," 119.

60. Aug., *Confessions* 4.4.9.

61. Aug., *Confessions* 4.6.11.

62. Aug., *Confessions* 4.7.12. See similar language in *Confessions* 6.15.25 about his loss of his lover.

pedagogic purposes. While his friend lay unconscious with fever, his family had him baptized. Augustine teased him over the baptism when he showed signs of recovery, but his friend, who had previously joined him in deriding such rituals, objected to the raillery. Augustine treats this in the *Confessions* as a portent, demonstrating not only the power of the sacrament but also his foolishness at mocking it. If he could use a friend's death so calculatingly, the sincerity of his briefer account of the relationship with his lover is problematic. When C. S. Lewis's wife dies, the pain is real;[63] in comparison, Augustine's heart, trailing blood at the loss of his lover,[64] is literary.

Presumably, Augustine was not impotent when Adeodatus was conceived. The loss of his friend may be a clue to the onset of his impotence; this would provide an explanation for the lack of a second child other than faultless birth control. The possibility arises that the nameless friend was Adeodatus's father. In this alternate history, Augustine wanted to raise the child as a memory of his friend and established the relationship with the mother to do so. The thesis that the pain in his life was impotence does not depend upon this idea, but it is tantalizing to imagine Augustine, the virgin. Another comparison with C. S. Lewis is apt. Lewis had made a pact with a fellow soldier, Paddy Moore. If either of them died in battle, the other would tend to the fallen comrade's family. Paddy was killed in 1918, and Lewis cared for his mother Jane Moore until she was hospitalized in the 1940s with dementia; she died in 1951. Biographers disagree about whether the relation was sexual. Lewis remained a bachelor until 1957. When he did marry, it may have initially been a favor to another friend. Joy Davidman needed to marry a British subject to remain in England. It is not impossible that Augustine adopted Adeodatus and married his mother as a tribute to his friend just as Lewis took care of Paddy's mother, then Joy Davidman and her sons.

Jostein Gaarder's novel *Vita Brevis* examines this period of Augustine's life from the perspective of his lover, whom Gaarder names Floria Amelia. Floria does not think much of Augustine's boasting; she says he was not much of a lover.[65] Floria has a point; his sex-talk is more like a high school locker-room conversation than the memoirs of an experienced roué. Floria mocks his declaration that he should have castrated himself before he had so many occasions to sin—not the Auriel she knew. The possibly less-fictional Augustine of the *Confessions* bemoaned the fate that left him prey to his desires. He blamed his parents for not having had him married as a

---

63. Lewis, *A Grief Observed*, 23–24.
64. Aug., *Confessions* 6.15.25.
65. Gaarder, *Vita Brevis*, 35.

young man, but he did have a sort of marriage with the real-life Floria from age seventeen to thirty-two. It is unclear how early marriage would have quenched the fires surrounding him, or why the stable life with his lover did not suffice. Nevertheless, he wished he had made himself a eunuch for the kingdom of heaven; untroubled by desire, he could have patiently awaited salvation.[66]

Floria's reaction to Augustine's post-coital whining is reminiscent of another renowned love affair. Peter Abelard was a twelfth-century theologian and logician in Paris, in frequent conflict with Bernard of Clairvaux. In his early thirties, he fell in love with the teenage Héloïse, the niece of Canon Fulbert. Their passion was reciprocal and uninhibited. The affair lasted only eighteen months but resulted in the birth of a son, named Astrolabe in honor of their common interest in astronomy. They debated ways to regularize their lives; marriage would end his academic career, and she was protective (she even used Jerome's *Against Jovinian* to oppose marriage (see chapter 10)). They eventually married in secret as a compromise, but this proved insufficient to assuage Fulbert's anger. Abelard was set upon and castrated. Héloïse retired to the convent of Argenteuil and Abelard retreated to the Abbey of St. Denis. He wrote the *Historia Calamitatum* (the *History of my Calamities*), describing his life up to the age of fifty. His autobiography provoked a series of letters demonstrating that Héloïse was one of the most remarkable women of any age. She declares, "The name of wife may seem more sacred or more binding, but sweeter for me will always be the word mistress (*amica*), or, if you will permit me, that of concubine or whore."[67] However irregular in its origins, there was nothing shameful in their passion. She prefers the title of whore (*meretrix*) over the title of Empress (*imperatrix*).[68] The flight to religion was his idea, not hers. She asks why he neglects her, never speaking to her when he makes a pastoral visit or even sending her a letter. Her memory was of a complete passion—no part of it regretted. She longed for him still.[69] Abelard insisted on his degradation; he forced his desire on her even during Holy Week.[70] Abelard cannot accept that Héloïse both loved him physically and emotionally, with a bond she had not severed when Abelard found himself severed from desire. Augustine's impotence may have answered his regret that he had not castrated himself in youth.

66. Aug., *Confessions* 2.2.3.
67. *Letters of Abelard and Héloïse*, 113.
68. Ibid., 114.
69. Ibid., 129.
70. Ibid., 147.

Augustine wants us to believe he could not be chaste like Adeodatus's mother. He suggests he would have been unfaithful in the new marriage as well, it being hard to imagine that a twelve-year-old would satisfy his uncontrollable lusts. However, his life looks more like avoidance of marriage than an ambivalence about chastity. The betrothal to a ten-year-old, his philosophy book club, and the fantasy of celibate retirement, are all attempts to avoid the marriage he cannot consummate. The unavoidability of the marriage triggers the final breakdown. Adeodatus's adolescence may have added to the threat by confronting the impotent father with a sexually active son. Augustine mentions his father noticing his adolescent state in the public baths;[71] this could have been a recasting of a day with Adeodatus. Augustine knew he would have to arrange a marriage for Adeodatus. The contrast between the young man's sexual initiation and his failure was painful.

Most scholars accept that his driving issue was inordinate, disordered desire—concupiscence. The word is unavoidable in Augustine; it has a nasty ring in English. The earlier Hebrew notion was the *yetser ha-ra'* (the inclination to evil): "for the inclination of the human heart is evil from youth (Gen 8:21)." The *yetser ha-ra'* is ambiguous; although the source of misplaced desire, it also provides the energy for action—a Jungian rather than Freudian libido—without it, nothing is done. It was a part of human nature, newly implemented in each soul, not inherited. Using the *yetser ha-ra'* correctly was part of being human; without it, Rabbi Samuel ben Nachman (third century) says, no one would marry or work.[72]

As it moves from language to language, the connotations change. The Greek term *epithumia* used to translate *yetser ha-ra'* is more negative, suggesting evil desire rather than an inclination to evil.[73] Paul was Gamaliel's student, and it is possible to hear echoes of the *yetser ha-ra'* in the epistles. *Epithumia* becomes even more negative in Latin, *concupiscentia*, as disordered desire. Although applicable to all desires, in Augustine's hands it came to mean primarily sexual lust. His work was the decisive step in the transformation.

---

71. Aug., *Confessions* 2.3.6.
72. Quoted by N. P. Williams, *Ideas of the Fall*, 67.
73. Wiley, *Original Sin*, 29–30.

## **AUGUSTINE ON TRIAL**

Augustine stands accused on two issues—misogyny and pessimism—connected by many critics to his Manichaean past. There are three grounds for attack:

1. The Manichaean ascetic ideal, particularly the avoidance of procreation, forms a foundation for an anti-sex, anti-female perspective.
2. The Manichaean distinction between good and evil matter is equivalent to that between spirit and flesh.
3. The Manichaean battle of good and evil within each of us is the same as original sin.

Augustine makes a great effort to distance himself from all of these positions, yet he does not wholly escape the Manichaean taint. Still, he was not an ordinary ascetic just as he is not an ordinary misogynist. His goal after his conversion was not the mortification of the flesh, but *deificari in otio* (to become godlike in leisurely retirement).

Augustine is not entirely innocent of these charges, but the usual indictments are not well drawn. The story changes if his pessimism and misogyny grow out of his impotence, and not his Manichaean past. If a man's sexual frustration is due to the inability to achieve an erection, self-anger is the result, rather than misogyny (although no one should underestimate the male's ability to blame the female).

Misogyny may take several forms. One attack is cosmological, blaming women for the fallen state of humanity. Tertullian chose this form:

> Do you not know that you are (each) an Eve? The judgment of God upon this sex lives on in this age; therefore, necessarily the guilt should live on also. You are the gateway of the devil; you are the one who unseals the curse of that tree, and you are the first one to turn your back on the divine law; you are the one who persuaded him whom the devil was not capable of corrupting; you easily destroyed the image of God, Adam. Because of what you deserve, that is, death, even the Son of God had to die.[74]

There is little of this vituperation in Augustine. He goes out of his way to exculpate Eve and blame Adam. His motive is not a pro-feminist one—but Eve lacks a disobedient penis.

---

74. Tertullian, *On the Apparel of Women*, 1. Accessed May 1, 2015, http://www.newadvent.org/fathers/0402.htm.

Augustine is guilty of a second form of misogyny, condescension. Eve's only purpose was procreation: "Had Adam needed a helpmate in the sense of a partner in really intelligent conversation and companionship, God would surely have provided another man."[75] His condescension is infuriating, but there are no accusations of seduction and corruption of the noble male. Augustine is a jerk, but he is not the only source of Christian misogyny.

A third type of misogyny is a fear of the irresistible sexuality of women. In Augustine's time, dramatic rejection of women was common. The smallest touch of a woman was considered sufficient to bring on overwhelming passions that might be immediately consummated, even if the occasion was a nun's care of an old bishop on his sickbed.[76] While Augustine avoided the company of unchaperoned women as Bishop of Hippo,[77] there is none of the anchorite's hysteria in his writings, even though this tone was common. Portraying women as dangerous seductresses would have facilitated his condemnation of sexuality, but he is not afraid of them; he despises the male more.

Finally, there is misogyny associated with sexual revulsion. The views of men and women about sex range from repugnance to indifference to enthusiasm. A person finding sex repulsive might express disgust about the physical, particularly sexual, attributes of the rejected partners. A woman might rail about the ugliness of the male genitals, male hairiness, or the violence of the male role in sexual intercourse. The erect and engorged penis would be the subject of opprobrium. A man revolted by sex would disparage women's bodies, recoiling from breasts and genitals, and be disgusted by menstruation and childbirth.

Augustine finds a good use of an evil in reproduction, but nothing negative about women's bodies or biology. Instead, when he attacks desire, either abstractly or concretely, the male body is the target. The disobedient member is the emblem of Adam's disobedience. Erections occur when a man does not want them, and they do not occur when a man wants them. The problem with the stronger resonance is clear—there are ads for Viagra, but no ads for chemical castration. Augustine divides his words roughly equally between the flaccid and the firm cases. He did not have an unreasonable resentment of women, but a reasonable resentment of his disobedient organ. Manichaeans avoid procreation because it prolongs the process of restoring good matter to its origin. For Augustine, procreation is the

---

75. Aug., *Literal Interpretation of Genesis* 9.9. As quoted by Chadwick, *Augustine*, 89.
76. Brown, *Body and Society*, 242.
77. Possidius, *Life of St. Augustine*, 36.

source and transmission mechanism for original sin using the disobedient member. In both systems, there is a disdain for sexuality but the logical foundations differ.

If Augustine is not guilty of a Manichaean rejection of sexuality, is he a dualist? The Manichaeans and Augustine both claim to provide definitive exegeses of Paul, which lend themselves to dualistic interpretations. In Manichaean cosmology, the particles of good and evil are in a constant struggle, with limited hope for the success of the good, but it is a winnable battle with discipline. When an auditor begins to make progress, God will provide assistance. The battle is winnable in the individual and, over time, it is winnable for all. The dualism is in the basic structure of the universe, but the universe can be made whole again by human effort.

Augustine believes in creation from nothing by a good God; therefore, he rejects the Manichaean interpretation of the war between spirit and flesh. The war must be on different terms because matter (flesh) is good. For Augustine, the war is a result of the disobedience in the garden. Without the first sins, the spirit would have ruled the flesh. When Adam and Eve sinned, they and all their descendants are punished with disorderly desire. The war between spirit and flesh is the war in the members, represented by the disobedient penis. There is no possibility of victory; the complete impotence of the will explains the inevitability of defeat.

Augustine thinks he has cleared himself of any taint of dualism. The world is good, there is no division, in principle, between spirit and flesh. The sin that is also the punishment of sin, concupiscence, provokes the war of the flesh against the spirit. If he absolved from dualism, is there Manicheanism in his concept of original sin? The similarity is closest in the case of ordinary people, unenlightened from the Manichean perspective, ungraced in Augustine's view. The Manichaeans assert the unenlightened are helpless victims of the conflict between good and evil. Their will is weak and only randomly produces good. However, it occasionally does do good; the ordinary failure of human effort is part of a grand metaphysical design and enlightenment is possible. In the Augustinian case, the ordinary human never performs any good act; it may appear to be good, but without grace, it is still a sin. This part of his doctrine makes Augustine's pessimism deeper. Original sin is darker than the Manichaean war. The helplessness of humanity is personal, not cosmological.

Augustine cannot abide the implication that he has remained a Manichaean. He cannot understand why Julian does not understand. The incapability of the will is apparent, and it is the only solution to the problem of mortal life. Does he not see the mystery of God's grace and the necessity for infant damnation? Julian cannot think the way Augustine does; he cannot comprehend how Augustine can be the strange and perverse person he seems to be. The differences between Augustine and the Manicheans are real, but they are too subtle for Julian. Although the charges against Augustine need re-evaluation in the context of his impotence, many modern readers will reach a mixed verdict: innocent of Manichaeism, guilty of profound pessimism, and an accessory to Western misogyny.

# 3

# The Argument over Augustine

THE DEBATE BETWEEN AUGUSTINE's critics and defenders is often frustratingly narrow. Discussions of his theories of grace fill thousands of pages without any mention of the radical sexualization; discussions of his philosophy ignore predestination. His critics fulminate about his errors without acknowledging the depth of his psychology. While feminist critics are not embarrassed to discuss his sexual attitudes, male scholars seem unwilling to examine the connections between performance and predestination. His critics despise him, and his allies are often defensive, trying to separate out the parts of Augustine they admire from those they disavow or explain away. The tone of the controversy since the Reformation has been as virulent as the original battle. Although sometimes lacking in detachment, the perspectives of the modern protagonists help to paint a picture, or two pictures, of the two Augustines. The argument begins and ends with sin.

Original sin links the two Augustines and is his most distinctive contribution to western theology.[1] What purpose does it serve in Augustine's theology? As a young man, he is a Manichaean. At first, he is an active proponent, converting his patrons and friends; later, he becomes more of a lapsed Manichee, though still willing to depend on old friends for advancement. Manichaeism offers a tidy solution to the problem of evil—the existence of suffering in God's good creation. For the Manichees and other dualists, there is no problem—the world is a battleground between two equally matched forces of good and evil. When he distances himself from them, he needs a new theodicy. Original sin provides an explanation as simple as dualism; if

---

1. O'Donnell, *Augustine, a new biography*, 296.

all are guilty, then any evil experienced in this life is only justice. Augustine feels a universal sin is the only solution that does not fall into Manichaeism.

Is an original sin necessary? The early church had only a vague notion of sin in Eden. In the second century, Irenaeus emphasizes human weakness. Adam and Eve are finite creatures, necessarily limited in their potential and childlike in their ignorance. God intended to bring them to gradual maturity, but in their innocent state, they are prey to Satan. Clement of Alexandria focuses on Adam's ignorance; Clement's student Origen, like the earlier Irenaeus, points to Adam's finite nature. Athanasius blames the clay God uses to form him. There is finitude, immaturity, inattention and materiality, not sin and guilt.[2]

If an original universal sin exists, what should it be? The obvious answer is pride—pride, stubbornness, and rebellion. Ambrose identifies its source as Adam's desire to be equal to God, or according to Ambrosiaster, to be God.[3] Satan falls as an act of pride; pride is the immediate cause of the Eden disobedience.[4] Augustine does not make pride the center of his argument since it is hard to see how it would apply to newborns. Augustine's choice for the descendants of Adam and Eve is not pride, but sex—more precisely, the unruliness of sexual desire. In this, he is in harmony with the ascetic temper of the times but breaks with the church fathers and philosophers, who consider sex as just one of the passions. This sexualization of the problem indicates an obsession his critics from Julian onwards cannot fathom.

How is this sin transmitted? It could have been in a defect in human nature—a genetic disorder. A flawed nature has two problems; first, it is easy to see how we could inherit a predilection to sin, but that is not sin. It is an original sinfulness, but not an original guilt. Second, it sounds Manichaean. Augustine's opponents will try to argue his transmitted sin is Manichaean dualistic nature—he will vehemently deny it.

Are our spiritual souls derived from our parents in the same way we inherit our fleshly bodies? If so, our souls would *be* Adam's soul, as our flesh is his flesh, and we would have his sin and his guilt. Augustine is uncomfortable with this idea. This notion of traducianism (the transmission of the soul from the parents) is too close to the Manichean notions of a mixture of good and evil particles in human nature for Augustine to endorse.

---

2. Bray, "Original Sin in Patristic thought," 39.

3. Ambrosiaster is the name given to the author of Commentaries preserved under the name of Ambrose, but referred to as Hilary by Augustine.

4. Aug., *Forgiveness of Sins* 1.17.27.

What are the consequences of original sin, transmitted sexually? He could have stopped at this point. All begin damned. Infant baptism would be necessary, and the sacraments would sustain its benefits. Earning salvation could have been daunting but doable. This is insufficiently dark for Augustine. Our will is unable to control the penis; *a fortiori*, he argues, it is unable to do anything but evil. We have free will but only the freedom to select our sins. Here his impotence takes its final step in the sexualization of the whole of the human condition. Along with this collapse of the will, it drives him ineluctably to the concept of unmerited and unmeritable grace, and predestination.

Christopher Kirwan questions whether original sin is a coherent concept. While it provides Augustine with a reason for universal damnation, he merely asserts it.[5] Kirwan claims that of Augustine's five favorite proof texts, three depend on mistranslations (Job 14:4–5, Rom 5:12, and Eph 2:3), one is directed to the sin of the mother and not the child (Ps 50/51:5), and the fifth has nothing to do with sin (John 3:5).[6] Kirwan will not even engage Augustine in an argument. To him, the very idea of original sin is absurd; no one should waste time in trying to make sense of it. His examination of the Augustinian *transmission* of original sin—if it existed—shows a similar impatience.[7]

The argument that Augustine's Old Latin translations were poor and, therefore, his interpretations are wrong is anachronistic. There was no consensus that Jerome's Vulgate should supersede the translations based on the Septuagint; in fact, the Old Latin translations were used well into the scholastic period. Some translation issues surfaced in the fifth century. Julian argued with Augustine over Rom 5:12, but Rist notes Augustine worked out his theories without regard to scripture and later attached specific texts to the argument. Thus, even if Rom 5:12 was misread, Rist maintains his theology would not change.[8] Scholarship has improved the texts since the fifth century and biblical scholars often use the New Revised Standard Version as a reference translation, but things that are clear to a modern reader were much murkier then. Pelagius probably spoke Greek and Julian may have had some ability in both Greek and Hebrew, but Augustine depends almost entirely on the Old Latin translations.

---

5. Kirwan, *Augustine*, 130–32.

6. Kirwan depends on N. P. Williams, *Ideas of the Fall*, 379. Job 14, Ps 50/51 and John 3:5 are discussed in chapter 4, Eph 2:3 in chapter 7, and Rom 5:12 in chapters 9 and 10.

7. Kirwan, *Augustine*, 150.

8. Rist, *Ancient Thought Baptized*, 20.

The poet Samuel Coleridge also thinks Augustine is talking rubbish. In a trivial sense, every sin is original; it has an origin in a voluntary act. Nothing that is not original in that sense is sin.[9] F. R. Tennant declares there has to be a deliberately violated moral law for anything to be a sin. In contrast to Augustine's view, the greed or jealousy of an infant is not sin, any more than the behavior of a cat with a mouse is evil. Sin requires moral agency. Only adults have complete agency; any imputation of sin to infants is nonsensical.[10] Tennant's opinion is Pelagian; we have a sinfulness derived from our culture, not an inherited guilt.[11] Tennant differs from Pelagius in emphasizing, as Augustine could not and Pelagius would not, that there *is* a fundamental weakness in our nature. While we are responsible for our decisions and shaped by our social environment (the Pelagian view), we are also limited by our organic and amoral nature.[12] N. P. Williams also interprets the inheritance from Adam as an original sinfulness (the *yetser ha-ra‘*), not an original guilt. It is a medical condition or natural state; the category of guilt does not apply. He does not find anything in Paul or Augustine that explains how a disease can have symptoms of guilt.[13]

Heard believes that without Augustine, theology would have been free to follow the Jewish Neoplatonist Philo of Alexandria and the Christian Neoplatonist Origen into allegorical interpretations of the Genesis story, eliminating the conflict of reason and faith. He proposes a maturation theory compatible with Darwin. The Genesis story represents the moment when God adds a new spirit of consciousness to the slowly evolving primates.[14]

Burnaby argues Augustine's anti-Manichean stance forced him to call every human evil either sin or punishment. Punishing the innocent undermines ethical intelligibility. Burnaby thinks that all of Augustine's efforts to provide a rational explanation of original sin fail. His attempted theodicy incorporating divine justice and universal damnation does not explain the problem of evil in the world and seems more like the devil's plan than God's.[15]

According to Reinhold Niebuhr, original sin is offensive both to Hellenic-influenced rationalists who consider reason to be the capstone of

---

9. Coleridge, *Aids to Reflection*, 204.

10. Tennant, *The Origin and Propagation of Original Sin*, xxv. 1901/02 Hulsean lectures.

11. Ibid., 72.

12. Ibid., 122.

13. N. P. Williams, *Ideas of the Fall*, 133–34.

14. Heard, *Alexandrian and Carthaginian Theologies*, 136.

15. Burnaby, *Amor Dei*, 191–92.

human faculties and to moralists who wish to improve human behavior and judge it fairly. Julian is both. Niebuhr notes Augustine's awkward position is that we are held responsible for actions we are fated to commit.[16] Critics and defenders alike must deal with the difficult problem of original sin as Augustine defines it.

## AUGUSTINE'S MODERN CRITICS

Distaste for Augustine has been common since the revival of his work by the Reformation. The ground is gone over again, with Erasmus as Julian and Luther as Augustine. Erasmus uses the same texts used by Pelagius in his *Letter to Demetrias* against Luther: "Before each person are life and death, and whichever one chooses will be given (Sir 15:17)," and "Choose life so that you and your descendants may live (Deut 30:19)." The impotence of the will makes the choice irrelevant.[17] John Donne complains that if the strings of the instrument of God's word are reprobation, limited salvation, an impotent will, and the inability to repent, then it is out of tune.[18]

As is often the case, the reception of Augustine's ideas tells us more about the critic than it does about Augustine. The seventeenth-century divine Jeremy Taylor captures the petulant tone of the debate; Augustine's original sin was a novel concept, "but when 'Pelagius had puddled the stream.' St. Austin was so angry that he stamped and disturbed it more."[19] The whole concept of original sin is nonsense, Taylor concludes, an argument about things that don't exist. Two centuries later, James B. Mozley takes Taylor to task but provides a defense resonating with Taylor's criticism. Taylor should not waste time ranting about the injustice and cruelty of original sin because the doctrine is intrinsically incomprehensible.[20] Tennant continues the discussion half a century on, describing Mozley's theory as an act of desperation.[21]

Edward Gibbon describes Augustine's scholarship as superficial, his Latin, bad, and his mind, argumentative. He concludes that for all of the

---

16. Niebuhr, *The Nature and Destiny of Man*, Vol. 1, 241.

17. Erasmus, *On Free Will*, 12. Erasmus liked Pelagius's *Commentary on Romans*, but attributed it to Jerome.

18. Donne, Sermon 133. Cited in Kirwan, *Augustine*, 143.

19. Taylor, *Whole Works*, Vol. 7, 566. English writers through the nineteenth century often used Austin instead of Augustine.

20. Mozley, *The Augustinian Doctrine of Predestination*, 363

21. Tennant, *Origin and Propagation of Original Sin*, 19.

praise given Augustine, his more difficult ideas are quietly ignored.[22] Augustine would have resented the criticism of his style; he thought himself a student of Cicero.[23] Joseph Priestley describes his doctrine as a disease of the western church.[24] John Adams also rejects original sin. He accepts responsibility for his own sins because they are his; broader theoretical speculations are of no interest.[25] The poet laureate Robert Southey declares Augustine influence to have been wide and deleterious.[26]

The nineteenth-century German historian G. F. Wiggers fumes that original sin eliminates accountability and destroys morality. The sexual transmission of sin is unphilosophical and not supported by the gospel or Paul. He feels Julian presented the anti-Augustinian case so well that attempting to expand on it is superfluous.[27] The Irish historian William Edward Hartpole Lecky calls Augustine the father of the Inquisition, who trained people to ignore their better instincts and adopt his terrifying ideas.[28] Allen is no fonder of Augustine, declaring he could find a way to make even the most drastic reversal of normal reasoning plausible.[29]

Adolph Harnack says Augustine redefined pessimism itself, replacing the optimistic core of Christianity with a darkened view. Augustine's influence made it impossible for anyone to think in other than Augustinian terms, but there is no scriptural support for predestination.[30] Heard is frustrated that Augustine escapes criticism by being one Augustine to the Catholics and Anglicans, who ignore predestination, and another to the Protestants, who dismiss his sacramentalism and dedication to the institutional church. He describes Calvinists and Catholics burying Augustine's bust in flowers, but from opposite sides.[31] Lecky remarks that each camp

---

22. Gibbon, Vol. 3, 431.

23. Chadwick writes, "His instinct for fine prose was irrepressible." *The Early Church*, 216.

24. Priestley, *A History of the Corruptions of Christianity*, 94. Scientists remember Priestley as the co-discoverer of oxygen, theologians recognize the Unitarian polemicist, and historians know the enemy of Edmund Burke.

25. Letter to Francis Adrian van der Kemp, February 23, 1815, quoted in Gaustad, *Faith of the Founders*, 77.

26. Southey, *The Book of the Church*, Vol. 1, 311.

27. Wiggers, *Augustinism and Pelagianism*, 373. Translated by Ralph Emerson but not Ralph *Waldo* Emerson.

28. Lecky, *Spirit of Rationalism*, Part 2, 21.

29. Allen, *Continuity of Christian Thought*, 4. An entire volume could be made up of vitriolic Victorian attacks on Augustine.

30. Harnack, *History of Dogma*, Vol. 5, 74–75.

31. Heard, *Alexandrian and Carthaginian Theology*, 195.

finds its doctrines in Augustine and uses him to berate the other.[32] Thomas Allin calls his ideas pathological and concludes, "Instead of a theology, he gives us an elaborate criminology."[33]

Paul Johnson calls Augustine the heretic, indeed the greatest of heretics.[34] John Ferguson declares Pelagius's views are in agreement with the basic tenets of Christianity, but this is not the case with Augustine.[35] Karl Rahner plaintively defends the Pelagians: "Was it all false, the case made by Pelagius and Julian of Eclanum against the apparently universally triumphant Augustine?"[36] Niebuhr, not a friend of Pelagius by any means, admits the earlier church fathers were essentially Pelagian.[37] It might be more accurate to say Pelagius was firmly in the traditions of the pre-Augustinian church.

The critics usually object to either Augustine's predestination or his misogyny. Part of the confusion about Augustine derives from this division; the incapacity of the will and his sexual obsessions are inseparable. Both his critics and defenders produce unbalanced arguments by overlooking the interrelationships. His insistence on the total failure of the will and the oddly un-misogynistic elements of his theology are traceable to his impotence.

## Will, predestination, and freedom

Augustine is the first theoretician of the will as an independent element of psychology. Alasdair MacIntyre even believes Augustine articulates Paul's own doctrine of the will better than Paul could himself.[38] In Greek philosophy the paramount faculty of the soul is the mind or reason; Aristotle famously defines the humans as *rational* animals. The issue is practical ethics, *choosing* one's actions; there are only errors, not sins. A person who fails to make the rational choice is ignorant or deranged. There is no theory of an independent will before Augustine. Separating the will from the essence of humanity would have seemed a philosophical impossibility to his contemporaries and predecessors.

32. Lecky, *Spirit of Rationalisation*, Part 2, 22.

33. Allin, *Augustinian Revolution*, 76. Allin felt Harnack was much too easy on Augustine.

34. Johnson, *A History of Christianity*, 122.

35. Ferguson, *Pelagius*, 182.

36. *Theologie der Gegenwart* (1977) 2, 76, as quoted by Ranke-Heinemann, *Eunuchs*, 77.

37. Niebuhr, *The Nature and Destiny of Man*, Vol. 1, 245.

38. MacIntyre, *Whose Justice?*, 157–58.

Augustine correctly points out the sheer bloody-mindedness of humanity; we can know what is right, why it is right, be in apparent self-command, and still do terrible things. The unreliable will, not reason, is in command. We do not know ourselves and cannot predict our behavior even one day.[39] His analysis is essential, but Augustine confines the will to the will to do evil, the *mala voluntas*.[40] For the mass of humanity, the will is incapable of good; there is no freedom but to sin. The inability not to sin (*non posse non peccare*) means nearly all are damned. Thomas J. J. Altizer describes him as the theorist of a free will that is a contradiction in terms. He argues Augustine's recognition of the impotence of the will was an essential part of his conversion.[41] If the will is incapable of pursuing truth, the only recourse is to throw oneself into the arms of faith and authority.

Paula Fredriksen contrasts Augustine unfavorably with Origen. Augustine interprets Paul as implying the just damnation of all but a very few. In contrast, Origen reasons that God's will to be all in all expressed in 1 Cor 15:28 includes the possible salvation of all rational beings—humans, angels, and demons. Augustine and Origin agree justice and mercy are divine attributes. However, Augustine's God applies one or the other, selectively and arbitrarily. God either is just (and damns, because all deserve damnation) or is merciful (bestowing an arbitrary and unmerited grace). Origen's God blends justice and mercy in every action and truly desires the salvation of every soul.[42]

Harvard political philosopher John Rawls attributes his loss of faith to doctrines depicting humans as puppets and God as a glory-seeking monster.[43] Rawls believes the darkness in Augustine's mind had enormous consequences for western philosophy.[44] Walter Kaufman rejects Augustine's argument that since all are worthy of damnation, the few who are spared should be grateful. Arbitrary treatment, even if it is arbitrary mercy, is the very definition of injustice.[45]

---

39. Aug., *Letter* 130.2.5.

40. The Latin word, *voluntas*, is multivalent. In a tautological sense anything that is done, we do. If we do it, it was by the will and *voluntas* is invoked. *Voluntas* can refer to what we desire, choose, or strive to achieve.

41. Altizer, "Ethics and Predestination," 232.

42. Fredriksen, *Original Sin*, 99–100.

43. Rawls, *A Brief Inquiry*, 264. Many critics refer to Augustine's reduction of humanity to puppets. Toynbee in his 1951–52 Gifford Lectures, also calls Augustine's God a monster. *Historian's Approach to Religion*, 182.

44. Rawls, *Political Philosophy*, 302.

45. Kaufman, *Without Guilt and Justice*, 59.

In Origen's view, to despair of the repentance of any created being concedes theology to Gnosticism. It would deny the use of God's gift of reason, relegating the creator to the status of an evil demiurge. Any text hinting of fate or predestination is, at most, a concept of God's foreknowledge; God sees what we will do (if left undisturbed) and calls us to repentance. Redemption is not a painless process granted to the few; there is a well-defined path to heaven, but we must climb.[46] Salvation is a gift, but it is also a prize requiring a human contribution.[47]

Elaine Pagels feels Augustine undermines political institutions by degrading humanity, leading to an increased dependence on the state. The early church stresses human moral autonomy, *autexousia*. God gives Adam overlordship of the world; this dignity requires a corresponding royal sense of duty and responsibility. In contrast, Augustine's humanity is incapable of managing itself, much less all of creation. At least before the Fall, Adam has the choice of obeying God directly, his descendants have only the option of obeying ecclesiastical and imperial authorities. Pagels concludes Augustine's theory of the Fall bound the church and empire together.[48] Her complaint echoes that made earlier by Lord Acton. If people are incapable of choosing the good, then they obviously cannot be trusted with freedom. If we are slaves to sin and cannot use our minds and wills to escape, we cannot and should not be free.[49] Pagels cannot quite believe Augustine won, overturning the consensus of the earlier theologians and concealing their contributions under his dominant views.[50]

If reason fails, the only alternative is to put oneself in the hands of the church. Augustine willingly does so: "In fact, I would not believe the gospel if the authority of the Catholic Church did not move me."[51] He is not solely responsible for the ossification of doctrine—the rise of the state-sponsored institutional church put a clumsy imperial hand on the intricacies of theology. He has a mixed history on coercion at best. When people stubbornly refuse to agree with him, he thinks the state should compel them.

---

46. Chadwick, *Early Christian Thought*, 119.
47. Meyendorff, *Byzantine Theology*, 139.
48. Pagels, *Adam, Eve, and the Serpent*, 125.
49. Acton, *Selected Writings*, 606–607.
50. Pagels, "Politics of Paradise," 68.
51. Aug., *Answer to the Letter of Mani known as the Foundation* 5.6 (Teske, WSA, I/19, 236).

## Sexuality

Criticism of Augustine for his influence on western sexual attitudes predominates in the twentieth and twenty-first centuries. The literature on Augustine's attitudes on sex, his lover, and his mother is beyond cataloging. Kirwan cannot understand him or his influence. His sexual obsessions are inexplicable to Kirwan, but the harder puzzle is the adoption of his doctrines by the church.[52] Kirwan and other critics miss the point. While Augustine's negative attitudes toward sex are absorbed by the church, the details are different. Augustine always blames the inconsistency and rebellion of male sexuality while the broader Christian culture is more consistently misogynistic, focusing on the supposed evilly seductive qualities of women almost completely ignored by Augustine.

Julie B. Miller concludes the entire sweep of Augustine's thought denies sexuality has any positive role. The idea that there could be a deep bond between marriage partners mediated by sex is foreign to him. He would have rejected as disgusting the thought that it could serve as a metaphor for the love of God.[53] It is not much of a defense to say he had a more generous view of marriage than Jerome or Tertullian. As chapter 10 will show, his rejection of any positive view of sex and intimacy in marriage is demonstrated clearly in his obsession with Julian's sex life. It is not surprising he had difficulty in thinking about sexuality in modern terms, but his discomfort has unique features. Uta Ranke-Heinemann describes Augustine as the man who placed a misogynistic asceticism at the center of Christianity. Like Miller, she blames him for neglecting love and equating sex with damnation; his theories are nightmarish.[54]

His discussion of the rape of Christian women by Alaric's Visigoths during the sack of Rome in 410 provides an example used both for and against him. The Roman pagans accuse the Christian God of abandoning the city. They sneer that the rape victims should have purged their dishonor by committing suicide as Lucretia had in pre-Republican times. In reply, Augustine argues their purity had not been affected; they had no need to commit suicide. He fatally qualifies his remarks by wondering whether *some* people might think the women had implicitly given consent by feeling the pleasure inevitably (!) associated with the act.[55] He does not say this is *his*

---

52. Kirwan, *Augustine*, 196.
53. Miller, "Augustine on Sexuality," 245.
54. Ranke-Heinemann, *Eunuchs*, 75–78.
55. Aug., *City of God* 1.16 and 1.19. The fourth century thought pregnancy required female pleasure, so if a raped woman became pregnant, she must have enjoyed it. In 2012, Senate candidate Todd Akin re-introduced the concept as "legitimate rape."

opinion, but he does say the shame felt by the women reflects either their guilt or their fear that *some* will assume they had pleasure and hence did consent. The raped women who did not consent directly or indirectly did not lose their purity and did not have the duty to commit suicide. If Lucretia had reasoned more carefully, she could have lived.[56] Melanie Webb suggests Augustine extends sympathy to the victims. She notes Augustine is the first philosopher to say rape is an occasion for consolation.[57] On the other hand, Kyle Harper thinks Augustine treats Lucretia badly, condemning her as either an adulterer or a murderer.[58]

Richard Sorabji feels reverence for Augustine has bundled poorer arguments with stronger ones. He prefers the Pelagian perspective that lust is a good thing that may be misused over Augustine's view that it is an evil thing that may be put to a good use. Like other British commentators, he would have preferred to see a local boy triumph, changing the western perspectives on sexuality and more.[59]

Augustine's theology is not without precedent. Paul writes, "it is well for a man not to touch a woman (1 Cor 7:1)." John describes the redeemed as those "who have not defiled themselves with women (Rev 14:4)." Tertullian says the only distinction between marriage and fornication are the laws regulating the former.[60] This harsh view of women is not universal among the church fathers, even if condescension is. Chrysostom prefers the calm life of a celibate monk, but he does not condemn marriage and business. They are, at best and at worst, a distraction from a life dedicated to prayer. If the monks and virgins represent the shock troops of Christianity, devout households of married couples still made up the rank-and-file congregants.[61] There is misogyny in Chrysostom; he believes in the natural headship of the husband and the need to curb female vanity, and he speculates that reproduction in Eden would have been somehow asexual, but accepts matrimony. He could contemplate conception very positively, "as if she were gold receiving the purest gold, the woman receives the man's seed with rich pleasure."[62] He is an advocate of the new Christian marriage, faithful and permanent. In this context, he encourages continence, chastity, and vir-

56. Aug., *City of God* 1.19.
57. Webb "Rape and Consolation," 58.
58. Harper, *From Shame to Sin*, 173.
59. Sorabji, *Emotion and Peace of Mind*, 417.
60. Tertullian *On Exhortation to Chastity* 9.
61. For a discussion of Chrysostom's view of women, see Ford, *Women and Men in the Early Church*.
62. Chrysostom, *Homily 12 on Colossians* 4:18 (Roth and Anderson, 76).

ginity. Nevertheless, his emphasis is on the care of the poor: "For without virginity, indeed, it is possible to see the Kingdom, but without almsgiving, this cannot be."[63] He scourges his congregation, "If he loves the poor, he is a human being; but if he is wholly involved in commerce, he is an oak tree."[64]

Augustine could not help dropping misogynistic bricks. In *On the Trinity*, he writes that man as God's image does not cover his head in church but the woman does because she is not quite the image of God. When she is considered as her husband's helpmate, they together are the image of God. A woman is not the image of God in her own right, unlike the man.[65] Augustine's early discourse on the Sermon on the Mount also emphasizes woman's secondary role. The good (male) Christian loves his wife as someone under his instruction but hates the sexual connection to her. He loves her as a human being [*homo*] but hates her as a wife [*uxor*].[66]

To many in the fifth century, women represent temporality and men, eternity. Kim Power argues that if the feminine is rejected, all of creation is devalued.[67] She discusses Augustine's innovations in his discussion of Wisdom and Knowledge (*Sapientia* and *Scientia*). Contrary to tradition and grammar in Hebrew, Latin, and Greek, he asserts *Sapientia* is male, leaving the lesser role of *Scientia* to the female.[68] Power describes the overwhelming fear, common to Roman men, of effeminacy and the loss of rationality to minds weakened by desire, causing them to suffer the loss of vital heat assumed central to masculinity and *Sapientia*. Giving in to mere *Scientia* would result in a catastrophic loss of the masculine self.[69] An impotent Augustine *has* lost his vital heat; he *is* emasculated.

Dealing with women sexually is degrading and dealing with them non-sexually is disappointing. For Augustine and his contemporaries, the headship and rationality of man and subservience and irrationality of woman are obvious. Augustine may even exceed Ambrose and Tertullian

---

63. Chrysostom, *Homily on Matthew* 47.5. Accessed June 1, 2015, http://www.newadvent.org/fathers/200147.htm.

64. Chrysostom, *Sixth Sermon on Lazarus and the Rich Man* (Roth, 107–108).

65. Aug., *On the Trinity* 12.7.10. See Matter, "De cura feminarum," 96, Ruether, "Augustine: Sexuality, Gender, and Women," 54, and Stark, "Augustine on Women: In God's Image but Less So," 215. Rist thinks the argument is mistaken, stressing that Augustine's words apply to woman in her role as helpmate; intrinsically, she is not disparaged. *Ancient Thought Baptized*, 115–18. Rist may have missed the point: if a woman is only valued if one prescinds from her femaleness, then she is devalued.

66. Aug., *Sermon on the Mount*, 1.15.41.

67. Power, *Veiled Desire*, 221–22.

68. Ibid., 140–43.

69. Ibid., 219.

along these lines, giving this subordination its lasting form. Nevertheless, his position goes beyond this condescension, arising much more from the inconsistent penis than the enticing vagina. The emphasis shifts from the persistent dangers of the female to the inconsistency of the male. He can display the usual male dismay at female enticements, but when Julian attacks his core beliefs, he relies on, or rather cannot rely on, his penis.

## AUGUSTINE'S MODERN DEFENDERS

The controversy swirling around Augustine has given him a bad press. John M. Rist dismisses some of Augustine's critics as uninformed and prejudiced opponents of Christianity in general.[70] Although he also criticizes Augustine, he calls the critics who do not engage him directly simplistic. Rist goes too far in suggesting that all criticism of Augustine represents post-Enlightenment ideas. Nevertheless, he provides a salutary warning; understanding the issues depends on understanding Augustine's times and the character of fifth-century debate. Augustine attempts to place his opponents on the horns of unresolvable dilemmas, sometimes at the cost of internal coherence. Rist thinks Augustine's ideas are worth studying, even when they are wrong-headed. He believes the Enlightenment warred against Christianity in the person of Augustine, unleashing unfounded criticisms.[71] Similarly, Paul Rigby attempts to counter those who feel Augustine reduces humanity to mere toys. He writes, "But how can one explain Augustine's ability to engage generation after generation for sixteen hundred years if the human puppet is at the heart of his anthropology?"[72] While this is special pleading, Rigby has put a difficult question; chapter 11 provides a partial answer.

Some defenders claim the Pelagians provoked Augustine into incautious positions. In his biography of Augustine, Brown suggests he was a worn-out campaigner, reflexively entering controversy once again.[73] Others suggest his strong positions energize the Pelagians, but his doctrines were formulated earlier.[74] Discarding selected parts of Augustine as polemical exaggerations is ultimately unconvincing because the source of his ideas—his impotence—is unrecognized. Leibniz rejects the automatic damnation of infants, virtuous pagans, and those ignorant of Christianity. He does not accept original sin as the sole basis of damnation. He is disinclined

---

70. Rist, *Ancient Thought Baptized*, 4.
71. Ibid., 292.
72. Rigby, "The Role of God's 'Inscrutable Judgments,'" 214.
73. Brown, *Augustine of Hippo*, 387.
74. Cunningham, *S. Austin*, 80.

to believe merit has no value, and God acts arbitrarily without sufficient reason. Putting aside some further difficult or disgusting ideas, he is willing to adopt Augustinianism![75]

The stigma of heresy is sufficient to make people uncomfortable with affirming Pelagius explicitly even if their position is essentially Pelagian. Leonard Hodgson initially takes the Augustinian position on the human need for grace. He declares truth is inaccessible to humanity without God's help. He then says all knowledge is a result of revelation. God the creator reveals himself through the totality of the universe, and God the redeemer is revealed through reflection on biblical events.[76] However, the former is the Pelagian position on the grace of creation and the latter is what Augustine calls "nothing but the law and teaching."[77]

However, it is more than the heretic's taint—a larger issue is involved. Southey speaks well of Pelagius, despite his status, calling him the greatest Welshman and the most reasonable of accused heretics.[78] The Augustinian revival led to the Enlightenment reaction with its insistence on reason. The reputations of the Pelagians improved as the philosophers scorned Augustine. The nineteenth-century belief in individuality and progress further supported the Pelagian surge. When Darwin upset literal interpretations of the Fall, the shallow Pelagian Fall (see chapter 4) is more amenable to reinterpretation. In this period of high European confidence, with the success of empire and the apparent banishment of internal conflict, it is not surprising Victorians rejected Augustinian pessimism and looked favorably on Pelagian optimism.

In the late nineteenth century and early twentieth century, the cracks begin to appear. Nietzsche proclaims the death of God. The Great War ends the belief in the myth of human goodness, moral progress and an unconditional freedom of the will. Reflecting on the horrors of that war, N. P. Williams feels evil requires an explanation going beyond the free choice of independent agents.[79] He rejects Augustinian original righteousness of Adam and an inherited original guilt but seeks a compromise, retaining

---

75. Leibniz, *Theodicy*, 300.

76. Hodgson *For Faith and Freedom*, Part 1, 80–90. 1955/57 Gifford Lectures.

77. Aug., *The Grace of Christ and Original Sin* 1.6.8 (Teske, WSA, I/23, 406). Mozley demurs from Augustine's use of this trope: "But with all deference to so great a name, I cannot think that this adverse explanation is altogether justified by the language of the Pelagians themselves." *The Augustinian Doctrine of Predestination*, 53.

78. Southey, *The Book of the Church*, Vol.1, 310–11.

79. N. P. Williams, *Ideas of the Fall*, 4.

a little more free will along with Augustine's penetrating analysis of our struggles with the darkness within us.[80]

Williams adapts a distinction of William James between the once-born or healthy-minded, and the twice-born or morbid-minded.[81] The once-born are the optimists who, at their core, cannot think ill of God or his creation. The glass is not only half full but also is continually filling. They cannot fathom the pessimistic twice-born who see the glass as half empty and rapidly draining. The morbid-minded think the healthy-minded are "blind and shallow," while healthy-minded think the twice-born are "unmanly and diseased."[82] The once-born are Pelagian, the twice-born, Augustinian. The once-born consider sin in the context of freedom and responsibility. They see God and the world as good—evil is a disease or weakness. As a disease, it is cured by faith; as weakness, it is corrected by instruction. The once-born focus on success, the twice-born, failure—but failure is often inescapable since evil is as much part of human existence as good. James concludes a satisfactory religion must develop the negative component as well as the positive.[83]

Williams observes that if Augustine's views were the only basis of doctrine there would be no future in Christianity.[84] As little as Williams likes unadulterated Augustinianism, he cannot endorse Pelagius, although he is strongly tempted to do so, proudly noting his British origin. An Englishman would think the Pelagians sound, representing sanity against fanaticism.[85] Nevertheless, he associates Pelagius with the unfettered will exposed as a dream by the Great War. Like James, Williams believes a useful religion must reflect the moral struggle humanity encounters, and judges Pelagian optimism inadequate.

Niebuhr, whose 1939 Gifford Lectures were occasionally interrupted by the German bombing of Edinburg, echoes Williams's ambivalence. He contrasts Augustinian and Lutheran Germany with the more Pelagian British. However, the expected praise is mixed; the Anglo-Saxons are sane and just in comparison, but also shallow and self-righteous.[86]

---

80. N. P. Williams, *Ideas of the Fall*, 382.

81. Ibid., 169–71. Rees thinks the distinction is overstressed. *Life and Letters*, Vol. 1, 84.

82. James, *Variety*, 152.

83. Ibid., 154.

84. N. P. Williams, *Ideas of the Fall*, 382–83.

85. Ibid., 354–55.

86. Niebuhr, *Nature and Destiny*, Vol. 1, 220.

Mozley looks for a balance between our consciousness of freedom and captivity. Pelagius supports our strength; Augustine stresses our weakness.[87] Burnaby also complains Pelagius does not pay sufficient attention to the depth of the moral struggle.[88] C. S. Lewis observes that we know what we ought to do, but don't do it; both facts must be accepted if we are to deal with the human condition.[89] Alan Jacobs similarly points to our consistent failure to come anywhere near the Pelagian standard.[90]

Augustine believes original sin has so devastated humanity as to remove the possibility of free choice of the good. The Pelagian alternative that we are creatures of bad habit is denigrated as explaining too little. However, in the *Letter to Demetrias* Pelagius describes our habitual sins as addictions accumulated over many generations.[91] Strangely, his critics often accuse Pelagius of ignoring the power of habit; it would be more accurate to say he emphasizes habit over innate weakness. William Bright thinks Pelagius did not sufficiently consider human limitations and neglected habit.[92] Tennant shares this view, thinking that Pelagian made an unnecessary error in neglecting habit, damaging his case against Augustine.[93] This criticism of Pelagius (representing a backhanded defense of Augustine) depends more on Augustine's anti-Pelagian works than Pelagius's own words.

What Augustine gets right is the fact of our perversity. We can tame lions but not ourselves.[94] Stortz says our hopes are Pelagian, but our experience is Augustinian. Pelagian optimism is re-assuring; we would rather be confidently working on our salvation than considering ourselves disabled with a fatal illness.[95] The Pelagian reply is that if we are recuperating from illness, we need to change our diet, get more exercise, and take charge of our medical condition.

A. H. Armstrong criticizes both Augustine and Pelagius for inadequate treatments of the external factors restricting a philosophically attractive free will. He rejects the Pelagian Christ because he is a primarily a teacher and exemplar, rather than a redeemer. Armstrong cannot be an Augustinian,

---

87. Mozley, *The Augustinian Doctrine of Predestination*, 61–62.
88. Burnaby, *Amor Dei*, 221.
89. Lewis, *Mere Christianity*, 8.
90. Jacobs, *Original Sin*, 114–15.
91. Pelagius, *Demetrias* 8.3. See chapter 5 for further discussion of the *Letter to Demetrias*.
92. Bright, *Anti-Pelagian Treatises*, viii.
93. Tennant, *The Origin and Propagation of Original Sin*, 14.
94. Aug., *Nature and Grace*, 40.47.
95. Stortz, "Pelagius Revisited," 140.

either, believing the ultimate responsibility is ours. We misuse our wills, but God has universally empowered humanity with the tools of salvation.[96] This is the core of Pelagianism. Even people who agree with the Pelagian system reject him.

Lancel believes Pelagius is too extreme. In his *Letter to Demetrias*, Pelagius affirms the ability of the will to make the best choice. While this appeals to Enlightenment and modern secular attitudes, Lancel thinks it is arrogant compared to the Jerome's acceptance of the inevitability of human failure. He thinks Pelagius replaced the cruelty of Augustine's grace with an unachievable morality.[97]

The twentieth-century controversy over natural versus revealed theology recapitulates the argument over Pelagian optimism.[98] In his 1937/38 Gifford Lectures, Karl Barth defends Reformation theology from natural religion, which he identifies with Pelagianism. Reform theology rejects any teaching that humanity possesses the ability to learn anything of value about God and the universe.[99] The Pelagians say God's grace lies in the creation of the world, the gift of reason to humanity, the law of Moses, and the example of Christ. Creation and reason are part of the common human heritage; they can grasp the essence of God's law. While the Pelagians lacked the further adumbrations of scholastic natural theology, their universalism places them on the side of natural theology. Augustine would be in an awkward position from Barth's perspective since he retained a sizable inheritance of Greek thought. He doesn't fit perfectly in the Reformation framework. Augustine is more precisely *sola gratia* (by grace alone), rather than *sola fides* (by faith alone) or *sola scriptura* (by scripture alone). Faith is a result of grace, and scripture is insufficient without grace.

Something is particularly disturbing about Pelagianism. Plato believes sin is the result of ignorance, and yet Plato is treated kindly. Stoic confidence is not dismissed as naïve. St. Francis's open-hearted optimism does not call down contempt. Whether Pelagius deserves this unequal treatment or not, he has a tainted legacy—an original cheerfulness—that still offends, and he makes a more convenient target than Plato, Seneca, and Francis. Pelagius does not acknowledge any darkness intrinsic to our nature, which leads, in anti-Pelagian minds, to arrogance and pride. Even critics who violently reject predestinationism will often side with Augustine on this heart of darkness. They are angry with Pelagius, with whom they almost entirely agree,

---

96. Armstrong, "St. Augustine and Christian Platonism," 22.
97. Lancel, *St. Augustine*, 342–343. Chapter 11 discusses Jerome's alternative.
98. Raven, *Natural Religion*, 212.
99. Barth, *Knowledge and Service of God*, 9.

for not anticipating the modern failures that have so clearly shown them the ineradicable poisons of our nature.[100]

## Will, predestination, and freedom

After the fervor of the Reformation fades, even Augustine's defenders feel the need to moderate his views on the will. R. L. Ottley thinks traces of Augustine's heretical past linger. The just damnation of the vast majority of humanity resembles the equality of evil and good in the Manichaean cosmology, a resemblance made stronger by his emphasis on sex.[101] Ottley does not want to address predestination or Augustine's theory of grace; he feels Augustine's unfortunate inconsistencies were introduced in his battle with the Pelagians.[102] Augustine's critics take him at his word on the impotence of the will and predestination; his defenders often glide over the difficulties. Bright offers several excuses, suggesting that we ignore predestination and other exaggerated positions.[103] Augustine's critics might counter that with such criteria, there will be little Augustine left. Harrison takes a stronger line and is willing to defend Augustine *in toto*. She chides scholars who discern a genuinely free will lurking in Augustine.[104] He tried to include free will but eventually had to concede the absolute centrality of grace.[105]

To be fair, Augustine struggles with the very challenging dilemma of free will and determinism. The early anti-Manichean work *On Free Will* is in the form of a dialog. Augustine's friend Evodius poses the question of how God can have foreknowledge of all things and yet we are responsible for our sins that must happen necessarily because of that knowledge.[106] Augustine's argument is verbal; we cannot say we will unwillingly or that we do not will (choose) our choices, or that a sin is not voluntary. What we do, we do, and the will mediates all actions. The distinctions he makes may or may not be coherent—Julian and the other Pelagians do not find them so. Niebuhr feels it is logically inconsistent to maintain our responsibility for the sins we cannot avoid committing.[107]

---

100. It is hubris to believe that only we have discovered the failure of rationality.
101. Ottley, *Studies*, 51–52.
102. Ibid., 81–82.
103. Bright, *Anti-Pelagian Treatises*, xiv.
104. Harrison, *Christian Truth and Fractured Humanity*, 111.
105. Harrison, *Rethinking Augustine's Early Theology*, 152.
106. Aug., *On Free Will* 3.2.4.
107. Niebuhr, *Nature and Destiny*, Vol. 1, 244.

Augustine insists God can justly punish sins *because* they are voluntary; we do will them. While the will is free, the will is not always good. The will can only become directed to good by God's grace, because "the will is prepared by the Lord (Prov 8:35 LXX)." Grace is required to redirect the will from evil to good. Once the will is good, God gives further aid. Augustine holds this formulation from *Simplician* on, and some defenders, while rejecting predestination, use this at least as a defense of his consistency. The Pelagians would have identified the grace that re-orients the will with creation, reason, law, and the example of Christ. Of course, Augustine eventually clarifies that the will is not just not always good; it is never good without grace. If God prepares the will, he only prepares the will of the predestined.

Augustine repeatedly uses Proverbs 8:35 to deny human initiative, but it is problematic. Augustine depends on Old Latin texts translated from the Greek Septuagint, which do read *voluntas praeparatur a deo* (the will is prepared by God). The Hebrew texts and modern translations differ from the Septuagint. The NRSV reads, "For whoever finds me finds life and obtains favor from the Lord." This is not just a modern choice; Jerome's Vulgate uses *hauriet salutem* (shall find favor). While the protagonists argue over the differences in the texts, Augustine prefers the hallowed Septuagint; he sees no need to return to the Hebrew and distrusts Jerome's ability to find something new.

For Augustine, it is pointless to ask God for the strength to obey the commandments. The will is incapable of repentance or asking, seeking, and knocking (Matt 7:7) without prior grace, which is withheld or given arbitrarily. Augustine's critics claim free will is a very different concept for the early and late Augustine. Bonner acknowledges a change in outlook; the initial optimism disappears in the anti-Pelagian period, and his mind becomes narrower. Nevertheless, Bonner thinks the changes are for the better. Losing his trust in humanity increased Augustine's understanding of our dependence on God.[108] Greek openness to the divine is not enough to bring us grace, and a confident estimate of human capability does not match the degraded human condition. Bonner calls predestination terrible and indefensible,[109] but he is glad Augustine won; believing humanity capable of achieving righteousness is far more dangerous.[110]

Mozley feels the *Pelagian* emphasis on the natural capabilities of the will undermines the basis of morality: a sense of sin. So rather than being the Puritanical ascetic he is often accused of being, Pelagius ends up

---

108. Bonner, *St. Augustine of Hippo*, 214.
109. Ibid., 392.
110. Ibid., 139.

diminishing both morals and virtue, reducing the human struggle to one of reason alone. Augustine is to be commended for crushing Pelagius,[111] even if his approach is excessive with dreadful consequences.[112] Mozley argues we must simultaneously accept God's grace and human free will as mysteries of the faith beyond the vagaries of an inadequate human understanding. Had the theologians understood their limitations, they could have avoided the long and futile fight over Augustine's ideas.[113]

The younger Rawls sought to reconcile Augustine and the Greeks. The classical consensus traced error to ignorance and assumed the mind could eliminate ignorance by instruction and reason. However, the Augustinian perspective is that the knowledge obtainable by reason alone is insufficient to address the realities of an evil world; we require divine instruction. Augustine asserts all knowledge requires divine illumination, even mathematics, but special grace is required to go beyond the truths of geometry. God, as our creator, is perfectly suited to be our teacher.[114]

MacIntyre assesses Augustine as having merged classical and biblical thought successfully, moving from Cicero to Paul. He believes Augustine solved a problem beyond Plato's reach. The Platonic view is that all may reach an understanding of justice and right action by reason if they make the effort; the point of the Socratic dialogs is to force the Athenians to think. Nevertheless, even if people do apply themselves to the understanding of justice, knowledge is insufficient to produce justice, a conclusion incomprehensible to Platonism.[115] The will, although ultimately in charge, has been misdirected for so long that it has lost the ability to right itself. Humanity chooses what it loves but cannot choose to love.[116] Although the will had been directed to good in Eden, Adam redirected the will from the love of God to his own selfish interests. Without a properly directed will, Adam could never recover the freedom he once had. MacIntyre asserts each person retains a commonality with Adam, hindering the will unless rescued by divine grace. He believes Augustine supported the view that while God's grace is necessary for the will's redirection, the will must assent to grace.

---

111. Mozley, *The Augustinian Doctrine of Predestination*, 106.

112. Ibid., 323.

113. Ibid., 326–27.

114. Rawls, *A Brief Inquiry*, 173–74. This is his undergraduate thesis, written before his loss of faith.

115. MacIntyre, *Whose Justice?*, 153–54.

116. Brown, *Augustine of Hippo*, 375.

He does so in the face of explicit Augustinian texts to the contrary and is indifferent to the question of how the contradictions might be resolved.[117]

MacIntyre does not address predestination or Augustine's sexual obsessions. He is more interested in the comparison between Aristotle's construction of society and Augustine's. Aristotle's city, the *polis*, is a narrow collection of citizens, excluding women, barbarians, and slaves. MacIntyre thinks Augustine's city is more embracing since no social category is excluded from the City of God. Sinners may not enter, and MacIntyre implies that is by their choice.[118] However, no one enters the City of God except by God's grace. God alone excludes or includes—his choice is arbitrary but is independent of gender, nationality, and slave status. Aristotle's city had a small but predictable citizenship; Augustine's city has even fewer members, who, as far as we can tell, are chosen randomly.

The differences between Augustine's defenders and critics mirror Catholic and Protestant attitudes towards him. The Catholic Church accepted his support for the institutional church, his defense of the sacraments, his insistence on the necessity of infant baptism, and his demonstration of original sin. It discreetly ignored predestination, absolute human incapability, the irresistibility of grace, and the limitation of grace. The Reformation revived all of the latter ideas while rejecting Augustine's sacramental past. Whatever their actual denominational affiliation, if any, his defenders argue as loyal Catholics while his critics respond as disaffected Protestants.

## Sexuality

Augustine's opponents are not simple-minded endorsers of sex, but it is easy to use its ambiguous character as a defense of Augustine. Julian is as unwilling as Augustine is for people to do it in the road, but it is not evil.[119] Augustine ridicules his unwillingness to call the emotion in question the concupiscence of the flesh, with all that phrase's negative connotations.[120] Julian's defense of marital sex is always awkward and is very modern. He sounds like a parent trying to give a balanced description of sex to an adolescent. Augustine's rhetorical certainties give him an advantage.

Hunter admits the difficulties of the concept of original sin. Nevertheless, he feels the negative assessments of Augustine depend too much on the later polemics and ignore the earlier works such as *On the Good of Marriage*

---

117. MacIntyre, *Whose Justice?*, 157.
118. Ibid., 163.
119. Brown, *Body and Society*, 412.
120. Aug., *Answer to Julian* 4.2.8.

and *On Holy Virginity*.¹²¹ These were part of a fourth-century battle over the relative value of virginity and marriage. The monk Jovinian initiated the controversy when he declared marriage is a suitable state for a Christian and moderated the praises of chastity. Jerome replied with a fervid defense of virginity; he summarizes Jovinian's theses as follows:

1. A virgin is no better as such than a wife in the sight of God.
2. A person baptized with the spirit as well as with water is not subject to the devil's dominion. Sin is avoidable and remediable by repentance.
3. Abstinence is no better than a thankful partaking of food.
4. There is but one grade of punishment and one of reward in heaven.¹²²

Jerome's *Against Jovinian* is more than a simple atack on marriage. Jerome believes in a hierarchy of virtue; there will be ranks in heaven (point 4) and virgins have to rank above wives (point 1). He is suspicious of any suggestion of the possibility of sinlessness (point 2) and is too much of an ascetic to trust moderation (point 3).

Augustine also prizes virginity above marriage. However, he thinks Jerome goes too far when he says marriage is bad. It is better to define marriage as a good thing, and virginity as a better thing. Augustine still objects to the equality of virgin and wife before God. He says Jovinian was popular in Rome because he elevated married women and "was even said to have dragged down into matrimony several nuns about whose purity no suspicion had preceded."¹²³ Augustine's defenders note the lack of Hieronymian invective, but are less sensitive to how "dragged down into matrimony" sounds.¹²⁴

---

121. Hunter, "Augustinian Pessimism," 156.

122. Jerome, *Against Jovinian* 3. Accessed June 1, 2015, www.newadvent.org/fathers/30091.htm. Kelly argues Jovinian was emphasizing the cleansing power of baptism, which made all Christians part of a single community. *Jerome*, 186.

123. Aug., *Revisions* 2.22(49).1 (Ramsey, WSA, I/2, 129). In the *Revisions* (*Retractationes*) Augustine reviews his works, correcting or excusing errors.

124. According to Augustine (*Marriage and Desire* 2.5.15) Jovinian had accused Ambrose of being a Manichean for maintaining Mary's perpetual virginity, *ante partum, in partu*, and *post partum*; Pelagius and Caelestius were committing the same error, throwing accusations of Manicheanism around. He repeats the accusation against Julian (*Two Letters* 1.2.4). Jerome had previously defended Mary's *post partum* virginity against the monk Helvidius. Helvidius argued that scripture supported the hypothesis that Mary had a normal marriage, bearing children, after the birth of Jesus. Helvidius thought Mary should be a paragon for married women as well as virgins. Jovinian support a true parturition, denying virginity *in partu*. For Helvidius and Jovinian, the emphasis on Mary's virginity slandered married women and diminished the humanity of Jesus; this was the basis of their accusation of Manicheanism. The Manicheans denied

Armstrong agrees Augustine's critics overlook his milder views, especially in comparison with Jerome. By locating sin in the will, he removes it from the body, distancing the argument not only from Manichaean dualism but also from the Greek emphasis on matter as dark and refractory.[125] Armstrong rightly identifies two crucial parts of Augustinian thought. Augustine does find a middle place between Manichaean materialism and Neoplatonic abstraction. Also, by separating sin from the body, he ends the identification of the female body as particularly earthy.

R. A. Markus asserts this is what is important to understand about Augustine; Augustine believes sexuality is intrinsic to humanity, at least as humanity is now. This is not a completely happy assessment, because, as Markus sees it, the central problem of humanity and the central problem of sex are the same.[126] This correctly identifies one Augustinian theme; sex, specifically the unreliability of the erection, is a symbol and basic exemplar of human disobedience. Our inability to control (male) sexuality is symptomatic of our inability to control any of our desires and actions. Transferring the problem from the earthy, seductive female to the male temporarily recasts the problem, even if the western church reverts to a more primitive misogyny. Augustine's novel approach can appear refreshing in comparison with simple-minded attacks on women. Matter makes the case that Augustine's problem with sexuality is not centered on women.[127] Chadwick thinks Augustine unjustly criticized; many of his remarks are positive reflections on women.[128] These defenses correctly distinguish Augustine from the standard misogynist, but sex is still the problem. Most men see sex through their desires; however, Augustine is relentlessly phallocentric. Women may be the object of male desire, but the core problem is penile unpredictability.

Other church fathers struggle with sex. Origen made the Garden story into an allegory of the loss of the spiritual state. God's granting of suits of skin marks the transition to the material world. This allows Origen to think of gender as a secondary state, not part of the original creation. Augustine leans toward Origen in his early work, but later he accepts the literal meaning of the pre-Fall words "be fruitful and multiply (Gen 1:28)," implying

---

that Jesus had been born after the flesh; Augustine admits that he had held a similar view during his Manichean period (*Confessions* 5.10.20). This history may have shaped Augustine's response to Jerome's *Against Jovinian*. While Augustine's own belief was not far from Jerome's, he needs to separate himself from the Manichean position. For a discussion, see Hunter, "Virginity of Mary," 47–71.

125. Armstrong, "St. Augustine and Christian Platonism," 10.
126. Markus, *End of Ancient Christianity*, 60.
127. Matter, "Christ, God, and Woman," 164–74.
128. Chadwick, *Augustine*, 89.

reproduction in paradise.[129] This is an advance on the opposing view that sex is an accommodation made *ratione peccati* (on account of sin). Nevertheless, Augustine's view of sex in paradise is his most bizarre excursion into speculative biology. As discussed in chapter 10, he assumes a flaccid penis, an intact hymen, and a urinary model of insemination.

While arguing Augustine makes too much fuss over his adolescent urges, Brown believes the expulsion of Augustine's lover caused him real pain.[130] He deflates the supposed intensity of Augustine's sexual obsessions by suggesting Augustine found living with lover and mother equally difficult; they are both Eves. He cites *Letter* 243 in which Augustine counsels a young man who is thinking of abandoning his life in a monastery to care for his widowed mother.[131] Augustine writes, "For this shadow of a son's love of his mother comes from the leaves of that tree with which our parents first clothed themselves in that damnable nakedness."[132] Augustine's basic argument is that Jesus requires us to abandon our families to follow him (Luke 14:26). However, suggesting that a son's feeling of obligation to his mother is analogous to the serpent's temptation is extreme, and he cannot avoid his obsession with genitals. It is certainly clear any affection for Monnica is swallowed up in Augustine's dedication to the force of original sin.

By downplaying Augustine's self-descriptions, his defenders distance him from the self-portrait of a fanatic—first wildly enthusiastic, and then, repulsed. He is treated as if he were just a stuffy and prudish Victorian. His emphasis on modesty and the shamefulness of sex is, from that perspective, nothing exceptional. Bonner argues Augustine expects his contemporaries to share his attitudes; sexuality is tainted and shameful.[133] Augustine is astonished when Julian resists. Bonner does not go far enough: Augustine expects his readers to agree that penile intransigence is the fundamental problem. The oddity in Augustine's argument does not lie in a denial of his sexual situation. He may or may not have confronted his sexuality. He does not blame women for inordinate desire or erectile failures. What he does not see is the extraordinary incongruity of using a peculiarity of reproductive physiology common to all male mammals as the foundation of theology and faith. He does not think all men are sexually impotent but takes his

---

129. Zevit, following Rashi, notes the grammatical form of the verb "knew" in Gen 4:1 implies Cain had been born in Eden before the serpent episode. *What Really Happened*, 185–90.

130. Brown, *Augustine of Hippo*, 79.

131. Ibid., 52.

132. Aug., *Letter* 243.10 (Teske, WSA, II/4, 169).

133. Bonner, *St. Augustine of Hippo*, 376–77.

feelings of helplessness as the key to understanding the entire human condition. Ignoring the utter strangeness of this is the gorilla in the room.

Mathijs Lamberigts appreciates that Julian is one of the very few of Augustine's contemporaries to state a positive view of desire. Still, he suggests Julian and modern critics over-sexualize Augustine's focus on concupiscence, which covers more than sex. Lamberigts accepts Augustine's description of his escape from addiction and notes Augustine displays negative attitudes about sex throughout his career; the Pelagians did not provoke them. Nevertheless, he uses Augustine's begrudging defense of marital sex as evidence of Julian's exaggerations. He unconvincingly argues that Augustine grants humans the ability to resist desire.[134]

Augustine's defenders usually stop short of endorsing the abandonment of Adeodatus's mother; some choose to blame Monica or the attitudes of the Milanese snobs.[135] J. J. Lias, the hard-working editor of Allin, is astonished by Augustine's callousness and appalled that Monica approved of the abandonment. Even given the lover's low status under Roman law and custom, Augustine's behavior is unacceptable. It should have disqualified him from sainthood; he certainly "would be scouted in English society at the present time [1911]."[136] The English clubbiness of this is delightful; Augustine's defenders in sexual matters seldom see anything more than this failure to act like a gentleman. More drastically, Ramirez assumes the lover was comfortable with dismissal as a fact of Roman life in the fourth century. She would not have "held this against him, any more than a slave-mistress of George Washington or Thomas Jefferson would have held that against them."[137] Ramirez overestimates their contentment in both cases.

Karl Jaspers describes Augustine as cold-hearted; he dislikes both the treatment of his lover and the mercenary character of his planned marriage. He accepts Augustine's greatness but thinks he falls short of the other greats.[138] Ramirez attempts a defense even in the case of the dismissal of the lover, asserting the remorse expressed in the *Confessions* absolves Augustine of any blame. Ramirez feels Jaspers has not appreciated what a mensch Augustine was and how much pain he felt when dumping her.[139]

---

134. Lamberigts, "Augustine's View of Sexuality," 176–97.
135. Brown, *Augustine of Hippo*, 52.
136. Allin, *Augustinian Revolution*, 173, editor's footnote.
137. Ramirez, "Demythologizing Augustine," 75.
138. Jaspers, *Foundations*, 224.
139. Ramirez, "Demythologizing Augustine," 73–74.

Elizabeth Clark shows a remarkable detachment, reserving judgment in the absence of a detailed account of the circumstances.[140] Cooper suggests it was a painful but understandable decision for an ambitious man.[141] She concludes that his sin was not the sex, but the callous discarding of the lover.[142] If he had thought so, then there was a simple way to purge that sin after his conversion. He could have sought her out and married her since he no longer had ambitions at court—but that is not what he chose to do.

While Augustine did not marry his lover, he does not share the virulent distaste for women of the married Tertullian. When young women dedicated to virginity wish to appear in church with their hair uncovered as a sign of their purity; Tertullian thinks they only want attention. He sneers, "There she is patted all over by the roving eyes of total strangers."[143] Tertullian is sure he was on solid ground—chastity does not make women any less seductive.

In comparison to this priapic urgency, Augustine is mild. His *lack* of conventional misogyny is in strong contrast to the female seductiveness feared by Tertullian.[144] Overall, Brown thinks Julian's attacks are unfair and deliberately distorted.[145] Julian *is* tendentious and occasionally silly, but the strangest Augustinian positions are his considered words, not Julian's. The most drastic expressions of predestination are in Augustine's letters to the puzzled monks of North Africa and Gaul, and the oddest sex appears in the *City of God*. Augustine caricatures himself.

Augustine's defenders feel he has been misunderstood, let down by his successors, or is the victim of anachronistic perspectives on sexuality. The most common theme is that Augustine is at least not Pelagius, overemphasizing free will and underestimating humanity's fallen nature. The loss of much of Pelagius's work means it is difficult to judge how much he differs from his contemporaries, all of whom encouraged the ascetic life to one degree or another. One source is Pelagius's *Libellus fidei* (declaration of faith), written as an attempt to overturn his condemnation by Innocent of Rome on January 27, 417. Pelagius places himself firmly in the Nicene tradition, anathematizing a broad range of heretics as well as making a statement

---

140. Clark, *Marriage and Sexuality*, 18, footnote.

141. Cooper, "Augustine and Monnica," 8.

142. Ibid., 17.

143. Tertullian, *On the Veiling of Virgins* 14 as given in Brown, *Body and Society*, 118.

144. Brown, *Body and Society*, 81. The problem of male desire is here identified as woman's fault.

145. Brown, *Through the Eye of a Needle*, 176. See also Brown, *Body and Society*, 396–427.

of his distinctive beliefs. Given his history of slippery answers, it may not represent the views that got him into trouble earlier. The *Libellus fidei* was preserved under the names of Augustine and Jerome. Peter Abelard, Peter Lombard, Bonaventure, Thomas Aquinas, William of Ockham, Duns Scotus, among others, quoted it favorably and considered it perfectly orthodox. At least in this late defense, Pelagius does not seem like an extreme ascetic. He does not demand perfection; if we fall after baptism, we can still be saved through reconciliation and repentance.[146]

Jacobs feels Augustine's universal depravity is not an assault on human dignity or an implicit criticism of God but is liberating. We are all in the same boat; we are all failures. Augustine gives "hope to the waverer, the backslider, the slacker, the putz, the schlemiel."[147] Jacobs may overestimate Augustine's sympathy for the schlemiel and, particularly, for the putz. While putz and schlemiel are common Yiddish words for jerk and loser, putz means a dirty penis.

In the case of the will, the critics and defenders could be notionally divided into loyal Catholic defenders and disaffected Protestant critics. In matters of sexuality, there is not much difference between the Catholic and Protestant traditions, so a denominational distinction is less relevant. The defenders and critics divide along lines of gender politics. The supporters are attempting to downplay Augustine's biography and the more drastic views while the opponents attribute the long history of Western sexual attitudes to his malign influence. The defenders sound overly detached and male-centric; the critics may exaggerate the extent of his influence on Western misogyny. They both miss the possibility of his impotence.

---

146. Pelagius, *Libellus fidei*, 18. Some manuscripts omit "reconciliation;" see Egmond, "Textual Tradition," 341.

147. Jacobs, *Original Sin*, 53–54.

# 4

# Augustine's Argument

TEASING OUT AUGUSTINE'S MOTIVATIONS is a challenge, not least because the fifth-century opponents use philosophical concepts distant from the modern reader. His conversion, evolution, and struggle take place in a context that forces the discussion into currently obscure channels. Augustine's enormous influence also hinders any re-examination. His opponents, ancient and modern, are compelled to speak on his terms. His precursors are lost in his shadow; when Luther and Calvin reform the church, they only go back to Augustine. This chapter provides an overview of the disputed issues that later chapters will re-examine in more depth, but the outline is hard to establish. Burnaby suggests that discerning a coherent Augustinian doctrine in the totality of the anti-Pelagian works is a hopeless task.[1]

The three primary texts are Rom 5:12–19, 7:14–25, and 9:13–26. The signature text is Rom 5:12. Augustine uses a faulty Latin text to establish the basis of original sin, inherited from Adam. In the second text, Paul describes the struggle of people who want not to sin but are overwhelmed by the sin that dwells within them. Augustine interprets Rom 7:23 ("the war in the members") as referring to sexual concupiscence and the disobedience of the male member. Finally, he uses Paul's discussion of God's supremacy and inscrutability in Romans 9 (God's preference of Jacob over Esau and the hardening of Pharaoh's heart) to define the doctrine of double predestination.

When trying to follow Augustine's path, one should not lose sight of the problem he is trying to solve—the fallen state of the world. The world is an unpleasant place with sin and suffering abounding; the mess calls for

---

1. Burnaby, *Amor Dei*, 191.

an explanation. Classical philosophy provides a framework but important differences, such as creation *ex nihilo*, have to be included. For personal reasons, the explanation needs to be separable from unfashionable alternatives, especially Manichean and Origenist ones. He finds his solution in sexual desire. When the word concupiscence is used by Augustine, it usually means the lust needed to arouse the body.[2] It is not John Coltrane's *A Love Supreme* he has in his ears, but *A Lust Supreme*.[3] Augustine made sex central so that sin is inevitable; it is an ever-present reminder of the Fall.[4] Since lust embodies the disobedience of the Garden, it can never be anything but evil, even if put to a good use.

## THE CORE OF THE CONFLICT

As difficult as it is to sort out Augustine's views, the Pelagian side is even harder to follow. The three allies have diverse and conflicting perspectives. Pelagius does not have a system. He accepts the Nicene Creed and denies his preaching is anything other than the ancient doctrine of the church; he only wishes to say people *can* and *ought to* do good. Caelestius is more of a natural controversialist and adds speculations of no real interest to Pelagius.[5] Julian provides the backbone to the controversy, but it is unlikely Pelagius could have followed his elaborate reasoning. The Pelagian-Caelestian-Julian system rests on a confident faith in God's justice and human freedom:

1. God is good and just. God's creation—all of it—is good.

2. The nature of a created thing cannot change. Human nature is unchanged.

3. It is *possible* to be sinless, and there may have been sinless people. There is no transmission of sin. We are born into a corrupted society and acquire bad habits—sins—by imitation.

4. God's grace consists of three parts:

    a. The grace of creation itself: we are God's creatures and created rational, with the unimpaired ability to choose to do good.

---

2. *City of God* 14.16.
3. Harmless, "A Love Supreme," compares Augustine to jazz standards.
4. Brown, *Body and Society*, 422.
5. Evans, *Pelagius*, 92, demurs from the common view that Pelagius was not much of a theologian. His theology depends, Evans believes, on three principles: orthodox Nicene Trinitarianism, the anthropology of man as a rational being in relationship to God, and strict anti-Manichaeism.

b. The grace of God's law: this guides our free will in choosing good.

c. The grace of Christ's example: this shows how to escape from the imitation of the corrupted society around us.

The Pelagians temporize and waffle on whether individual grace is necessary, an aid, or even exists. The grace of creation and reason give humanity sufficient power to do good. Targeted grace is welcome, but it is not required. There is a covenant between the human and divine; God calls, we turn to God, and God turns to us in return.

If the Pelagians celebrate free will and capability, Augustine's response is a story of grace and limitations:

1. God is just and good. God's creation is good, all of it. On this, all agree.

2. The nature of a created thing cannot change. Human nature is unchanged, at least if we consider nature technically. Again, there is agreement.

3. The sin of the Fall was so great that the *will* of Adam's descendants is corrupted; the will then corrupts the flesh. Concupiscence is a sin in itself and the punishment of the sin in the Garden, transmitting original sin to each generation.[6] The will is free only to choose evil. This is the crux of the disagreement.

4. Only God's grace can change the horrible situation of humanity.

    a. God's grace is unmerited and arbitrary. Human efforts are irrelevant.

    b. God's grace is from eternity. We are predestined to be either an honorable vessel (chosen for salvation) or a dishonorable vessel (abandoned to damnation).

    c. God's grace is effective. If a person appears to have God's grace but fails to persevere to the end of life, then he or she never had God's grace.

Neither synopsis includes the sacraments. Pelagius and Augustine both reduce their significance. If human will is sufficient to obey God's commandments, the sacraments can only have a strengthening and comforting role. If unmerited grace determines everything, it is hard to see even a tutorial role for the offices of the church. Rist comments that under Augustine's theory even one of the elect is "not more than an animated puppet."[7] Pelagius sees *adult* baptism as a watershed moment, marking a person's

---

6. Aug., *Unfinished Work Against Julian* 1.44.
7. Rist, "Augustine on Free Will and Predestination," 229.

commitment to righteousness, and Augustine makes *infant* baptism a cornerstone of original sin—but their support sits uneasily on their broader premises. Criticism of Pelagius recognizes this, but Augustine usually gets away with his destruction of the sacramental structure. Allen recognizes both problems. He acknowledges there is very little room in the Pelagian system for Augustine's institutional church; the educated human will is sufficient.[8] He then notes Augustine confines the benefits of baptism and the Lord's Supper to the elect; for the rest of the congregation the sacraments are pointless if temporarily comforting.[9]

The summaries don't contain Christologies.[10] Augustine pounds the Pelagians for spouting philosophical gibberish that has nothing to do with Christ.[11] If the grace of creation and the law is sufficient for righteousness, there is no need for the incarnation and crucifixion.[12] If there is no wound in human nature to heal, Christ's life was without purpose. If humanity needed an example to imitate, a prophet or righteous man would have sufficed. However, the situation is equally bad for Augustine. If the elect are predestined, there is not even the need for a new teacher.

The Pelagians never produce a coherent theological stance—they are not innovators and deny they are anything other than orthodox. They only strive to be *integri Christiani* (authentic Christians) rather than run-of-the-mill believers.[13] They may have felt superior to common Christians, as Augustine asserts, or simply thought the mediocre Christians were not even trying. As the scholastics would later say, the ordinary Christians did not *facere quod in se est,* they did not do what was in them to do, did not do their best. The search for genuine Christian discipleship permeates upper-class Roman society in the fifth century; Pelagius is just one representative.

If the Pelagians put too much faith in an all-powerful adult baptism, Augustine counters with a more magical infant baptism. The Pelagians may have been too optimistic Christians could easily discard their bad habits and choose the good. Augustine could have stressed that sinners require a church to nurture and sustain them through a long recovery; instead, he invokes the *massa perditionis*. When the Pelagians argue all should strive to be saints, Augustine does not show pity to the weak; he damns the children and all but the very few predestined honorable vessels. When Julian

---

8. Allen, *Continuity of Christian Thought*, 153.
9. Ibid., 163.
10. For a contrary view, compare Lamberigts, "Competing Christologies."
11. Aug., *Nature and Grace* 40.47.
12. Aug., *Sermon* 131.9.
13. Brown, *Religion and Society*, 192.

tries to maintain Roman restrained marital sexuality, Augustine denounces the disobedient penis. With a different opponent, the Pelagians might have been extremists, excoriating the rich, encouraging asceticism, and seeking a church of purified saints; against Augustine, they are the proponents of reason. They never can figure out how to respond to him because the argument is not with Augustine, it is with his impotence.

## THE QUESTION OF CONTROL

The underlying question is whether we are or can be in control of ourselves. The Pelagian answer is yes; the Augustinian answer is no. James P. Mackey captures the Pelagian attitude in his preface to Davies and O'Loughlin's *Celtic Spirituality*. God's creation is doubtless good, and newborns are especially good. There are demons to overcome with God's help, but everything is doable if we simply put enough effort into it. Mackey approves of this Pelagian optimism and rejects Augustinian despair.[14] All people are equipped to run the race of righteousness and all should; "I have fought the good fight, I have finished the race, I have kept the faith (2 Tim 4:7)." Even if we are not Olympic runners, we should at least jog. Pelagius's tone is typical of the times; Chrysostom also compares life to the arena. If an athlete wants to win the crown, he must not relax so "that after he has striven a short time here he may enjoy lasting honor hereafter."[15]

In Pelagius's understanding of Paul, running the race would be meaningless if we could not strive to finish it by obeying God's commandments. He is not saying anything new; he follows Chrysostom: "Let us not therefore suppose His injunctions impossible. Nay, for besides their expediency they are very easy if we are sober-minded."[16] This position, common to the ancient church, is both optimistic and rigorous. Pelagius allows some room for human frailty. In his *De Natura* (*On Nature*),[17] he emphasizes that success is contingent; he claims he is talking about what is possible, not how often it occurs.[18] Even with this slight caveat, possibly made under pressure, the basic Pelagian attitude is "yes, we can."

14. Davies and O'Loughlin, *Celtic Spirituality*, xvii.

15. Chrysostom, *Third Sermon on Lazarus and the Rich Man* (Roth, 68).

16. Chrysostom, *Homilies on Matthew* 18.2. Accessed August 1, 2015, http://www.newadvent.org/fathers/200118.htm.

17. The titles of all the competing books on human nature are quite confusing. To keep them clearly separate, Pelagius's work will be referred to as *De Natura*. Augustine's response is *Nature and Grace*.

18. Aug., *Nature and Grace* 7.8.

Heard is upset that the non-Augustinians place the responsibility on humanity for its life in this world and the next,[19] rather than throwing themselves on the mercy of God. Burnaby concludes the problem with the Pelagians is not an over-confidence in human nature but the Greek belief in the superiority of reason.[20] Augustine acknowledges the primacy of the rational mind, but that only magnifies the problem of self-satisfaction when we are boastful.[21] This view may be more humble than the Pelagian confidence, but the latter is consistent with the early church.

For Augustine, humanity is a complete mess, a *massa peccati*, a lump of sin, a *massa perditionis*, a lump of perdition.[22] We are quite definitely *not* in control. In parallel to Augustine's evolution on free will, his views appear to change. In the early *On the Sermon on the Mount*, Augustine declares that beatitudes are achievable in this life as they were by the apostles. He withdraws this notion of apostolic righteousness later. Whatever else the apostles achieved, they would still be afflicted with the movement of the flesh against the spirit. They were no more able to control the penis than we are.[23] The mature Augustine relentlessly argues we have only the freedom to choose between sins, and even our apparent good deeds are sins if they are outside of grace.

Augustine recognizes that the empire's church can no long hold itself to the high standards of the heroic age. The Pelagians feel they are still on the cutting edge of a missionary church, which needs its troops rallied to greater effort.[24] Augustine sees Pelagian encouragement as arrogance. God made us human, but if we can make ourselves just, we can make something better than God can.[25] He frequently cites 1 Cor 4:7, "What do you have that you did not receive? And if you received it, why do you boast as if it were not a gift?" He summons Cyprian to his aid; we have nothing to boast about. We pray because we are not saints and martyrs.[26]

Brown believes Augustine provides a defense of the middling Christian; the Augustinian church had mechanisms (praying and giving alms) for

19. Heard, *Alexandrian and Carthaginian Theologies*, 25.

20. Burnaby, *Amor Dei*, 59.

21. Aug., *Answer to Julian* 4.3.28.

22. Augustine gives Ambrosiaster's concept of the lump of humanity a darker connotation. Bonner, "Augustine and Pelagianism," 31–32.

23. Aug., *Revisions* 1.19(18).2. Augustine continues to ignore the problem of sin in women.

24. Brown, *Augustine of Hippo*, 371.

25. Aug., *Sermon* 169.13.

26. Aug., *Answer to Two Letters Against the Pelagians* 4.9.25. Subsequently referred to as *Two Letters*.

tolerating minor sins.²⁷ Markus agrees the sanctimonious Pelagians might have divided the church like the Donatists, who sought a church that was "spotless and without wrinkle (Eph 5:17)."²⁸ Brown and Markus endorse the sacerdotal Augustine but overlook double predestination. Within the doors of that welcoming church are only a very few selected for unmerited grace.

Augustine conflates the authentic Christians encouraged by Pelagius with the Donatist church of saints. He claims Pelagius advertises his followers as already perfect: "So how is the Church at this time free of stains and wrinkles when you are its stains and wrinkles?"²⁹ The church would not pray the Lord's Prayer if we were not all sinners; he asks if somehow God has canceled all his debts.³⁰ The Pelagians do not say they are perfect, just that they ought to be. Augustine's frequent use of the Lord's Prayer as a hammer is rhetorical overkill. The goal of perfection, even if immodest, does not imply that the Pelagians claim to be sinless or do not ask for forgiveness of their sins.

Neither protagonist admits any division of humanity into two classes: Pelagius declares there is a universal call to perfection, Augustine replies with the universal need for grace. In the end, Augustine distinguishes only the saved and the damned, separated only by inscrutable acts of God. The mediocre Christian and the ascetic monk are equally damned without grace.³¹

## THE FALL: DEEP OR SHALLOW.

The Fall provides an answer to the question of evil in a universe created *ex nihilo* by a benevolent and omnipotent God. Cardinal Newman faces up to the problem, writing "We seem to be faced with the dilemma of either denying the existence of God or accepting our radical estrangement from him. Some terrible disaster has separated humanity from God."³² The Augustinian Fall is a devastating step off a cliff. The collapse is so overwhelming and

27. Brown, *Augustine of Hippo*, 351.
28. Markus, *End of Ancient Christianity*, 53–55.
29. Aug., *Sermon* 181.3 (Hill, WSA, III/5, 326).
30. Aug., *Sermon* 181.6.
31. Markus, *End of Ancient Christianity*, 65.
32. Newman, *Apologia pro vita sua*, 217–18. Leibniz, who coined the word "theodicy," articulates a different approach. Since this is the best of all possible worlds, we must assume the evils present in it must somehow be the necessary consequence of the creation of a *possible* world. There is a "pre-established harmony" underlying the universe, which we must trust. For Leibniz's involvement with Augustine's work, see Backus, "Augustine and Leibniz."

the prospect so bleak that only a dramatic Rise including the incarnation, crucifixion, and resurrection, can overcome the Fall. This deep Fall/steep Rise emphasizes the uselessness of human endeavor without the grace of God provided through Christ. Augustine's Fall is deep, and the valley floor is flat. We are helpless; grace airlifts a few individuals from the valley, but the floor is still the floor—there is no notion of any progress.

Augustine and the church fathers are saddled with the Greek concept of nature; the nature of a thing is intrinsic to it and cannot change (chapter 7). The Fall has to fit into this overarching concept. One approach, popularized in the east by Athanasius and Gregory of Nyssa and in the west by Ambrose,[33] exalted the prior state of Adam, postulating a state of original righteousness. Adam had supernatural (beyond nature) abilities, both intellectual and moral, including the power to be sinless (*posse non peccare*). Humanity loses these powers after the Fall but retains its *essential* nature and its *natural* powers. Adam had these supernatural powers as a gift; they were not *naturally* his. Our natural powers are insufficient to prevent sin and misery. Loss of supernatural powers is not an entirely satisfying argument. It is hard to separate it from a corruption of human nature, which is philosophically impossible and too close to Manichaeism. Augustine selects the will as the source of corruption to avoid the condemnation of nature. For each person, the will sins in the form of paternal concupiscence and re-corrupts human nature—the spirit corrupts the flesh. His solution leaves humanity degraded and helpless unless the healing is provided "by the grace of God through Jesus Christ, our Lord (Rom 7:25)." His anti-Manichaean stance and his belief in original sin require the deep Fall: as N. P. Williams notes, original sin without a Fall is Manichaeism.[34]

In contrast, the Pelagians have a shallow Fall, so shallow that it was only a "failure to climb."[35] The Fall was not a plunge into a chasm but rather a relocation to a poorer neighborhood. People have to struggle harder for food and shelter than they would have in Eden. However, the basic choices offered to Adam and Eve are still available. Along with a shorter Fall, the Pelagians have a gentler Rise. The role of Jesus is less dramatic and is more in tune with the ethical teacher of the Enlightenment than the cosmic Christ. The history of humanity has been a gradual descent as bad examples accumulate. This process reaches its nadir, and, finally, Christ reverses the decline. The Pelagian exhortations address the perceived moral stagnation of Rome's Christians; Pelagius wants them to "run in such a way that you

---

33. N. P. Williams, *Ideas of the Fall*, 300–301.
34. N. P. Williams, *Ideas of the Fall*, 148.
35. Ibid., 455.

may win (1 Cor 9:24)." The Pelagians share this idea of accumulated habit with Ambrose, who contemplated the gradual degradation of human society, rather than focusing on the abrupt fall of Adam.[36]

Augustine believes Pelagius's shallow Fall is the root of his error. Pelagius sets goals he does not realize are unachievable without an individualized grace. He does not appreciate the depth of the wound done to humanity. According to Augustine, Pelagius describes the good of human nature as if it were independent of God, rather than being radically dependent on him. O'Donovan senses self-satisfaction, comparing Pelagius to the Pharisee, proud of his achievements and neglecting his dependence on God.[37] O'Donovan goes too far in comparing Pelagius to the Pharisee—Pelagius does not stress his achievement but the requirement to achieve more. Although the Pelagian Fall does not damage human nature, we still find it hard to be righteous. After all, Adam and Eve sinned—without changing our nature, we would also be able to sin.

The shallow Pelagian Fall is easier to recover from, and humanity can take active steps. Pelagius employs a theory of three ages. The time from Adam to Moses represents untutored nature (the descent into the valley). This is followed by the time of the law, from Moses to Christ (the valley floor). Finally, we now live in the age of grace, inaugurated by Christ (the ascent out of the valley). Even in the first age, people could respond to the law of nature, deducible by reflection, and live sinless lives. However, habits and ignorance makes the task harder. The law reduces the difficulty; it instructs us and establishes the standard we are to meet.[38] Even the law proved to be insufficient to overcome the habit of sin in the majority of humanity, necessitating the revelation and example of Christ.[39] Pelagian history is a smooth arc, falling from Adam to Moses, stabilized a little by the law, but redeemed and climbing with Christ.

Other theologies also have a rising valley floor. The eastern deification theologies define salvation in terms of gradually becoming more and more godlike by grace and the imitation of Christ. In deification or *theosis* theologies, the role of the cross is reduced; the assumption of humanity by the Logos is the central theme. Athanasius writes, "For He was made man that we might be made God."[40] Gregory of Nyssa explains how this

36. Brown, *Through the Eye of a Needle*, 132.
37. O'Donovan, *The Problem of Self-Love*, 100.
38. Evans, *Pelagius*, 99.
39. Ibid., 109.
40. Athanasius, *On the Incarnation of the Word* 54.3. Accessed June 1, 2015, http://www.newadvent.org/fathers/2802.htm.

is possible: "Then he mingled himself with our nature, in order that by this mingling with the Divine Being our nature might become divine."[41] This mystical notion has practical consequences in affirming the full humanity of Jesus; Gregory of Naziansuz writes, "For that which He has not assumed He has not healed; but that which is united to His Godhead is also saved."[42] The deification perspective differs from both the Pelagian and Augustinian ideas. The Pelagian Jesus is a paragon of righteousness to be imitated. The goal is not the majestic goal of *theosis* but the modest goal of obedience to God's commands. In strong contrast, the Augustinian human has no potential for divinity in this life. We are scum, only occasionally rescued without regard to our merit.

Just as the Pelagian Fall is milder than the Augustinian Fall, Pelagian grace is less dramatic than Augustinian grace. Julian explains the meaning of the grace of Christ:

1. We are made out of nothing, not from some Manichaean matter.

2. We have reason, which allows us to transcend the other animals.

3. With reason, we have learned we are created in the image of God and have been given the free will consistent with that dignity.

4. God continues to offer grace; for example, the law was given to help us.[43]

In the Pelagian perspective, grace consists foremost in God's creation; our essential nature is necessarily good. This is true of every creature's nature, but humanity also has the gift of reason. We can understand our responsibilities and order our lives. It is correct to say that grace comes first, but God gives this in the creation of the universe and throughout history from Eden, through the Exodus and the exhortations of the prophets, to the resurrection. God provides the ability to choose the good in our nature and repeatedly calls us to make our choice; we must respond. When people accept their responsibility freely, then God gives supplementary grace as an aid, not as a necessity. Augustine thinks this is dreadfully naïve:

> On such grounds he should at least admit that there is a terrible darkness in the human mind that knows how to tame a lion, but does not know how it ought to live. Or do free choice and

---

41. Gregory of Nyssa, *Catechetical Oration* 25 (University of Michigan reprint, 79–80).

42. Gregory of Nazianzus, *Letter* 101. Accessed June 1, 2015 www.newadvent.org/fathers/3103a.htm. Similar remarks are found in Irenaeus, Clement of Alexandria, and even Tertullian.

43. Aug., *Unfinished Work* 1.94.

the natural law suffice for one to know this as well? This is the wordy wisdom [*sapientia verbi*] that does away with the cross of Christ.[44]

Pelagius waffles on the character of grace, just as he does on infant baptism. In his *Libellus fidei*, he attempts to establish his orthodoxy and asserts "Free will we do so own, as to say we always stand in need of God's help."[45] He honestly thinks that is enough to get Augustine off his case, but Augustine just repeats his criticism that the Pelagians have reduced grace to instruction.[46] Pelagius adds, "But we say a man is always in a state that he may sin, or may not sin, so as to own ourselves always to be of a free will."[47] One can hear Augustine gnashing his teeth.

The Pelagian and Augustinian positions on the Fall are not the only ones available. Irenaeus even finds a positive outcome; the Fall is the first step in a process leading humanity to an even higher state than Adam and Eve had in their innocence.[48] Paradise was not enough. The Fall teaches that sin causes separation from God and leads to death; with that example in mind, we can actively cleave to God. Theophilus of Antioch declares the sin was not eating the fruit, but eating it prematurely. It would have happened eventually, but Adam was still, relatively speaking, an infant.[49] Justin Martyr takes no particular notice of a Fall; Adam and Eve provide the initial example, but everyone sins personally. The terms of the covenant are unchanged: "all men are deemed worthy of becoming gods, and of having power to become sons of the Highest."[50] Like Adam and Eve, all are subject to God's final judgment.

There was even another fall competing with the Fall described in Genesis 3. In Genesis 6:4, the sons of God lusted after the daughters of men to produce the giants of the earth, the nephilim, whose story was elaborated in late works like Enoch. Their tainted blood continued to plague humanity. Barr thinks the Genesis 6 fall was more significant than the Eden fall in the Hebrew scriptures.[51] Zevit agrees the fall in Genesis 2–3 had no influence

---

44. Aug., *Nature and Grace* 40.47 (Teske, WSA, I/23, 248).

45. Pelagius, *Libellus fidei* 25. To Augustine's irritation, Pelagius uses *auxilio* (help), not *gratia* (grace).

46. Aug., *Grace of Christ and Original Sin* 1.6.8.

47. Pelagius, *Libellus fidei* 25.

48. N. P. Williams, *Ideas of the Fall*, 195.

49. Theophilus of Antioch, *To Autolycus*, 2.25 (Dods, 104).

50. Justin Martyr, *Dialogue with Trypho* 124. Accessed June 1, 2015, www.newadvent.org/fathers/01288.htm.

51. Barr, *The Garden of Eden*, 74–94.

up to the destruction of the Temple in Jerusalem.[52] Williams detects traces of the *yetser ha-ra'* and the Genesis 6 fall in the gospels and epistles. Paul argues women should cover their hair, "because of the angels (1 Cor 11:10)." However, Williams notes there are many more gospel references to demons and evil spirits than to the *yetser ha-ra'* or the nephilim and no references, in his view, to an Augustinian Fall.[53]

Augustine sees *infant* baptism as confirming the depth of the Fall. Tatha Wiley notes *adult* baptism is implicit in the first-century *Didache* (*The Teachings of the Twelve Apostles*) since the participants fasted for two days before the ceremony.[54] Clement of Rome (first century) speaks in his *Letter to the Corinthians* of a universal need for redemption and a universal sinfulness without a detailed theology. The second-century *Shepherd of Hermas* states infants are free of sin but leans to the *yetser ha-ra'*, the inclination to sin. The *Epistle of Barnabas* agrees children are born without sin, but does have some discussion of the Fall. Adam has little to do with it, but Eve is tempted by the serpent and sins.[55] Justin Martyr is an early supporter of infant baptism, despite his rejection of a steep Fall. He places more emphasis on the influence of demons and is ignorant of any transmission of sin.[56] Baptism inoculates the infant against temptation. Irenaeus emphasizes the maturation of each individual on the path to deification rather than any anchoring of sin in Adam.[57] Tertullian opposes infant baptism: "let them become Christians when they have become able to know Christ."[58]

Origen believes there was an apostolic tradition of infant baptism, but the custom puzzles him since it is hard to attribute to newborns any offense in need of pardon. He accepts some contamination present in "the filth of birth" (*sordes*) that is cleansed in baptism. Even Mary goes to the temple to be purified and dedicate Jesus to holiness (Luke 2:22). He is uncertain *sordes* implies liability, guilt or sin (*reatus, culpa,* or *peccatum*). Whatever the defilement of *sordes* might mean, it is not original sin.[59] Baptism washes away

---

52. Zevit, *What Really Happened*, 19.
53. N. P. Williams, *Ideas of the Fall*, 108.
54. Wiley, *Original Sin*, 38–39.
55. Kelly, *Early Christian Doctrines*, 163.
56. Weaver, "From Paul to Augustine," 190. See also Kelly, *Early Christian Doctrines*, 167.
57. Wiley, *Original Sin*, 40–42.
58. Tertullian, *On Baptism* 18. Accessed June 1, 2015, http://www.newadvent.org/fathers/0321.htm.
59. Weaver, "From Paul to Augustine," 195.

an individual sin committed by each separate soul in the spiritual realm and not some universal inherited sin.[60]

Origen refers to two proof texts also used by Augustine. The first is Job 14:4–5; the Septuagint version reads, "Who shall be pure from defilement, not so much as one, even though his life on the earth be but a day." Other translations detach the defilement from the brevity of life; as given in NRSV, the verses read:

> 4 Who can bring a clean thing out of an unclean? No one can.
>
> 5 Since their days are determined, and the number of their months is known to you,
>
> and you have appointed the bounds that they cannot pass.

Marvin Pope's Anchor Bible translation marks verse 4 as a possible interpolation.[61] The text appears truncated; different approaches have been taken to fill in the missing words. The Targum adds "except God" to the end of verse 4. The Vulgate attempts, "Is it not you alone (*Nonne tu qui solus est*)?" These emendations have no implication of infant condemnation.[62] Clement has no patience for the idea that the text supports any sin or guilt; the responsibility lies with the supporters of an original sin to say how Adam's curse can fall on the innocent.[63] Athanasius thinks the word filth is a reference to the messiness of birth.[64]

The second text is Jesus's reply to Nicodemus: "Very truly, I tell you, no one can enter the kingdom of God without being born of water and Spirit (John 3:5)." Although Origen and Augustine think this is an endorsement of infant baptism, the gospel context is equally suited to an adult spiritual renewal and commitment.[65]

Cyprian is the African standard-bearer for infant baptism. It had been the tradition in some regions to baptize infants on the eighth day, paralleling the custom for Jewish circumcision. Cyprian thinks this is too long

---

60. Brown, *Body and Society*, 352.

61. Pope, *Job: A New Translation*, 104. Williams has the same opinion. *Ideas of the Fall*, 17, 224.

62. Pope, *Job: A New Translation*, 106–107.

63. Clement of Alexandria, *Stromateis*, 3.16.100.4–3.16.100.6. See also N. P. Williams, *Ideas of the Fall*, 207.

64. Beatrice, *Transmission of Sins*, 196.

65. Augustine makes no use in the anti-Pelagian works of the household baptism texts (Acts 10:24–48, 16:14–15, 16:26–34, and 18.8) in which believing individuals are baptized with all their households. The emphasis in these texts is on the act of belief. There is no explicit mention of the baptism of children, but neither is there a suggestion that the children were *not* baptized.

a delay, leaving the child vulnerable to the Adamic stain. The infant needs forgiveness even though she has no sins of her own, only Adam's.[66] Augustine agrees: An infant eight days old has no personal sins; why should it be condemned if it is not circumcised, unless it contracts a sin from its origin?[67]

The Cappadocians were too busy with Christological issues to spare much time for infant baptism. Gregory of Nazianzus describes it this way: "Here is the Seal of God our defender, *for innocent infants Only a Seal*, but for grown men a Seal and a Remedy Potent."[68] This is the two-level baptism for which Augustine pillories Pelagius. Gregory of Nyssa "declares that the new-made Christian ascending from the baptismal font is *as free from accusations and penalties as the new-born babe.*"[69] Theodoret of Cyrus (a student of Theodore of Mopsuestia[70]) accepts the tradition. However, since it cannot be for the remission of sins (infants have none), baptism has to have another signification, even for adults. It is the opening into a new life, the first step on the road to deification. The Pelagian baptism is well within the boundaries of the eastern church.

O'Donnell describes the road to infant baptism as rocky; it takes a while before Augustine figures out how to use it to tie his theories together.[71] It is the perfect argument; if we baptize infants, there is an original sin. If there is an original sin, it can only come from generation. From a liturgical choice, it becomes the decisive argument against the Pelagians. Calvin admits the idea develops slowly because there is nothing intuitive about the transmission of sin and guilt. He accuses the earlier theologians of cowardice in their silence.[72]

Augustine's insistence on the damnation of infants requires an explanation. It is partly the acceptance of the strong African tradition of infant baptism. More deeply, their damnation is central to his theodicy. If even newborns are damned, then the misfortunes of this life are well-deserved punishment and God is just. His other goal is to associate the source of sin with sex. If concupiscence is the fundamental sin, it must have victims. Bearing false witness damages your neighbor; theft means something is

---

66. Pelikan, *The Christian Tradition*, Vol. 1, 291.
67. Aug., *Answer to Julian* 3.18.35. See also *Letter* 166.8.23 and *Two Letters* 4.8.23.
68. Cited by N. P. Williams, *Ideas of the Fall*, 290. Emphasis in Williams.
69. Ibid., 279. Emphasis in Williams.
70. Theodore of Mopsuestia (350–428) and Chrysostom were students of the pagan philosopher Libanius. Theodore hosted Julian of Eclanum but later distanced himself from the controversy.
71. O'Donnell, *Augustine, a new biography*, 206.
72. Calvin, *Institutes of the Christian Religion* 1.2.1.5.

stolen; murder leaves a body. Pride is an intellectual sin with second order consequences—but sexual desire is very physical. Someone must suffer for it. Since Augustine believes sex provides those who can do it with overwhelming pleasure,[73] they cannot be the victims—it has to be the children. He sacrifices the souls of children for the disobedience of the penis.

Having established a theory providing every infant with an inescapable sin via conception, he could have left it there. Humanity would be born in bondage and would have to struggle to achieve freedom. Children would have an initial debt that, if the will were free, they could work off over time, but the will is not free and is incapable of freeing itself. We are born in sin and debt, "Indeed, I was born guilty, a sinner when my mother conceived me (Ps 50/51:5)." The wound is mortal; every infant is born in a state of damnation. Only a very few will escape from the torments of hell. No one can even attempt to escape through any act of their own; those who do escape are selected for salvation before birth. Augustine uses infant damnation to reinforce not only his late-life adoption of infant baptism but also his theories of strong predestination.

Augustine dwells on infant defects, deformities, and death. Their sufferings cannot be their personal fault. The Pelagians, Augustine asserts, must either accuse God of injustice or admit the infants somehow deserved their pain. Julian could have used Augustine's words in his *On Free Will* in which Augustine says the suffering of the children may do the parents good. The children will recover (and forget their pain) or die, and the parents may choose to live better lives as a result. If the parents don't reform themselves, they will be called to account at the last judgment. As for the children, he imagines God will have some reward. He speculates, "Who knows what good compensation God has reserved in the secrecy of his judgments for the children themselves who, though they have not had the chance of living righteously, at least have committed no sin and yet have suffered?"[74] The Pelagians preach against adult complacency; this leaves them unprepared when confronted with crying babies. Although a Celt, Pelagius is Roman in his focus on adult responsibility. It is hard to imagine Caesar, Seneca, or Cicero fussing over children.

Augustine's disaffected Protestant critics claim Augustine is the sole inventor of original sin, as we know it. His loyal Catholic defenders reply that Augustine expresses cogently and coherently the ancient doctrine of the church as expressed in Romans. Pier Franco Beatrice attempts a middle way in his 1980 book, *The Transmission of Sins: Augustine and the*

---

73. Aug., *Answer to Julian* 4.14.72.
74. Aug., *On Free Will* 3.23.68 (Burleigh, 211).

*Pre-Augustinian Sources.* He traces Augustine's view to Egyptian Jewish Christian Encratites of the late second century.[75] Beatrice's source is Clement of Alexandria's *Stromateis*. Book 3 discusses several attitudes to sexuality, devoting a large portion of the book to Julius Cassian.[76] Julius was no friend to sex; just because the penis fits neatly into the vagina, we should not conclude sex was part of the divine plan.[77] Beatrice suggests the gap between Julius and Augustine is small. Whether there is a direct line between these heretics and Augustine is more speculative. Augustine himself lists the Encratites in his *Heresies*,[78] but the classification of a belief as a heresy does not preclude it from having an influence.

Augustine's position is drastic, but it is a logical consequence of his notion of the Fall. He stringently denies that any amount of good works would provide the virtuous pagan with any claim on God's forgiveness outside the church. God has predestined such a person to damnation, and because all are damned, his damnation will be just. Baptism washes away sins and is a requirement for salvation; an infant rushed to baptism who dies too early was not predestined to receive this benefit and is justly damned. In the one case, a long list of meritorious deeds has no influence with God; in the other, he is compelled to wash away sins by a ceremony.

## PERFECTIBILITY AND PUNISHMENT

Augustine's Fall and Rise are sharply defined events. Quoting Chrysostom, he says the world was saved by Christ's sacrifice just as it was damned by Adam's disobedience.[79] For Augustine, salvation is only by grace because sin has been transmitted by generation, rendering us incapable of doing good. We are abruptly damned by conception; we are abruptly saved by grace. In contrast, the Pelagians focus on imitation; we earn salvation by imitating Christ; we sin by imitating Adam. Things happen slowly; we gradually remove gradually remove the rust of ignorance and become obedient to God's will. The covenant has simple rules. Julian says sin "is contracted by imitation, committed by the will, blamed by reason, revealed by the law,

---

75. De Simone disagrees with Beatrice's thesis, arguing Augustine is no innovator and no Encratite. "Sources of Saint Augustine's Doctrine of Original Sin," 205–27.

76. Not *John* Cassian.

77. Clement of Alexandria, *Stromateis* 3.91.

78. Aug., *Heresies* 25.

79. Aug., *Answer to Julian* 1.6.27.

and punished with justice."[80] Given these differences, it is not surprising they disagree on righteousness.

Pelagius believed the Fall damages neither human nature nor human will. The bedraggled world is the accumulation of individual bad choices. The process restarts with the Flood, with Moses, and, finally, with Christ. We are now on the long road back to the Father. The journey is challenging, but we have the capability to choose the good and a positive duty to do so. With capability come responsibility, judgment, and punishment. Pelagius defends himself at Diospolis by insisting the wicked will burn with eternal fire.[81] Such a harsh punishment can only be just if people have the ability not to sin. Each person, inside or outside the church, has a chance for salvation, but the penalty for failure is severe. Pelagius condemns Origen's speculation that Satan and the fallen angels can eventually join the saints.[82] In his certainty of punishment, Pelagius is closer to Jonathan Edwards than to an Enlightenment liberal. He admonishes, "Let us make haste then, while there is still time, and strive with all our might to overcome all our sinful habits and steep ourselves in works of righteousness and holiness."[83] Only then can we avoid the torment of the damned. Pelagius speaks in the language of many preachers, ancient and modern. Chrysostom adjures his congregation: "we have not ceased from reminding you of the terrible court, the inexorable judgments, that unquenchable fire, and the undying worm."[84] Bonner thinks Pelagian hellfire is less a theological position and more a style of energetic preaching.[85]

Mozley is ambivalent about Pelagian confidence in human ability; it is logically true and avoided determinism, but it fails to maintain the proper distance between humanity and God.[86] Mozley over-emphasizes Pelagius's perfectionism and neglects the discussion of the difficulties of overcoming accumulated habits in the *Letter to Demetrias*. Augustine feels the possibility of righteousness is a pipe dream. Pelagian optimism ignores the reality of human weakness. When Pelagians refer to Matt 11:30 ("For my yoke is easy, and my burden is light"), Augustine explains the yoke is only light if God's grace lightens it. He invokes the Lord's Prayer again; if we were sinless, we

---

80. Aug., *Unfinished Work* 2.74 (Teske, WSA, I/25, 195–96).
81. Aug., *Deeds of Pelagius*, 3.9.
82. Aug., *Deeds of Pelagius* 3.10.
83. Pelagius, *On Bad Teachers* 25 (Rees, 252).
84. Chrysostom, *Seventh Sermon, on Lazarus and the Rich Man* (Roth 125).
85. Bonner, *St. Augustine of Hippo*, 355.
86. Mozley, *The Augustinian Doctrine of Predestination*, 57–58.

would not need to pray.[87] The accusation is misplaced; the Pelagians stress the need for all of the customary practices of the church, including prayer.

Augustine initially makes a statistical argument. It is possible to make a single choice for the good, but living righteously would be like flipping a coin repeatedly and getting heads every time. Later, he states people cannot even repent without a prior divine intervention. Any suggestion of an initiative is an error. Julian is mistaken if he thinks asking, seeking and knocking (Matt 7:7) merit God's response; if so, then grace would be given as a reward.[88] Augustine insists people cannot ask, seek or knock unless God wills them to do so. He returns to infant baptism; if the Pelagians argue the adult can choose the good, they cannot impose such an obligation on infants. God is even-handed: if children cannot repent, ask, seek or knock, then neither can adults.[89] Since God arbitrarily predestines some children to deformity, it is not surprising adults are also arbitrarily given justice or mercy.

The ecclesiastical Augustine contradicts the polemicist; he explains the role of the rich is to give alms:

> He has practically slammed the door in the face of the rich. "What will happen, what will happen? The door's shut." Knock, and it will be opened to you. "How?" say the rich," How shall we knock?" How else but with your hands? What does this mean, "with your hands"? Knock with your good works.[90]

By this date (403), Augustine firmly believes in the impotence of the will and the uselessness of merit. However, he has a congregation to comfort and a roof to repair. Persuading people, especially the rich, to contribute is the priority. The practical challenge of managing a church overrules his central conviction that most of his congregation is damned. He suggests that giving alms will get their prayers heard and persuade God to change their lives.[91] He preaches the need for prayer even in the midst of the Pelagian crisis; we should beg for God's help.[92] Augustine's defenders can often find solace in his sermons.

The grace-based Augustine withdraws fund-raising and prayer from relevance: only the predestined can repent. He beats against 1 Tim 2:4, "who

---

87. Aug., *Answer to Julian* 3.1.2. See also *Letter* 215.3 and *Answer to Julian* 4.3.29.
88. Aug., *Answer to Julian* 4.8.41.
89. Aug., *Answer to Julian* 4.8.42.
90. Aug., *Sermon* 114B.9 (Hill, WSA, II/11, 107–108). Dolbeau 5.
91. Aug., *Sermon* 39.6.
92. Aug., *Sermon* 348A.2.

desires everyone to be saved [KJV: Who will have all men to be saved] and to come to the knowledge of the truth." Augustine claims "all" refers to all the elect.[93] God will save all those whom he wills to save. Since these are a tiny fraction of humanity, "all" means "a few." If God wills all to be saved, "all" means the predestined are drawn from all of humanity.[94] The elect include all types: black, white, slave, free, tinker, tailor, soldier, sailor, sinner, saint.

Augustine has the deepest historical (in contrast to cosmic) Fall imagined.[95] After the Fall, people are utterly incapable of changing their condition and begin life with a burden of sin so great as to ensure their damnation. Adam's disobedience precipitates the Fall, and all humanity inherits the consequences. Augustine then sexualizes the argument in ways that become more and more bizarre. Jerome is a passionate opponent of Pelagian ideas he sees as Origenist, but his *Dialog Against the Pelagians* focuses on the necessity for humility, rather than odd sexual fantasies (see chapter 11).

Because human nature cannot be the source of sin, Augustine needs a sin of the will. While pride is the cause of the Fall in Eden,[96] it does not guarantee a universal damnation for humanity outside of Eden. He depends more and more on making this universal sin *original*, in the sense of stemming from our origin, staining even the newborn child. For that purpose, pride will not do. The universal sin must begin at, indeed, before, conception. Augustine cannot make sex itself a sin. God enjoined Adam and Eve to be fruitful and multiply. There would have been reproduction in Eden, and it would have had to be good, not evil because it was part of God's good creation. It would have differed greatly from that observed in the fallen world—it would be rational and free from passion. His views are very strange; only encountering them in full does them justice (chapter 10). In summary, impregnation would follow the model of urination, with a flaccid penis under the control of the mind.

The universal sin separating us from Eden is not located in the material flesh, but in a defect of the spiritual will. Conception now reflects disorderly desire and recapitulates Adam and Eve's disobedience. Erectile dysfunction

---

93. Aug., *Answer to Julian* 4.8.44, *Rebuke and Grace* 14.44.

94. Aug., *Rebuke and Grace* 14.44. See also *Predestination of the Saints* 8.14, *Letter* 149 written to Paulinus of Nola, *Letter* 217 to Vitalis, among many other texts.

95. Cosmic falls explain the evil in the context of the divide between the material and spiritual worlds. Historical falls emphasize the events in the Garden. *Paradise Lost* contains two falls, the battle in heaven, which has the high drama, and the more boring encounter with the serpent.

96. Toews analyzes the first sin as mistrust; the serpent persuaded Eve that God had misled her. She sins by questioning God's judgment. *Story of Original Sin*, 5.

is primary. The rebellious member satisfies his need for a universal sin. Conception somehow transfers the sin of disobedience to the child, stamping the child with the punishment of that sin—an impotent will, incapable of even seeking God's help. After adolescence, the child will be the plaything of disobedient and disorderly desire—if male, inheriting the contrary member. Altizer identifies the orgasm as the point of the transmission of sin; lust is at its peak and the will is absent.[97] The mechanism is specified, but Julian cannot see how it amounts to a transfer of guilt.

## AUGUSTINE'S VIEW OF AUGUSTINE'S VIEW

Augustine always has the last word, so it is appropriate to let him define the issues. In *Letter* 217 to his correspondent Vitalis, he lists the twelve crucial doctrines:

1. The unborn and newly born have only the sin of Adam, not a personal sin or a sin committed in a previous existence.
2. Grace is not given for merits.
3. Grace is given to enable specific actions, such as belief. There is no general grace available to all. The "will is prepared by the Lord."
4. Grace is not given to all. It does not depend on actions or intentions.
5. God's mercy is a gratuitous gift.
6. It is not unjust that grace and mercy are not given to all.
7. We are judged by our actual deeds and not by potential deeds of a longer life.
8. This applies to the young; their judgment is based on their short lives and original sin.
9. It does not matter whether believers might have sinned in a longer life.
10. We freely choose to believe. This has to be carefully understood because the "will is prepared by the Lord."
11. We should pray that unbelievers should be converted.
12. We should give thanks when an unbeliever believes.[98]

---

97. Altizer, "Ethics and Predestination in Augustine and Levinas," 238.
98. Aug., *Letter* 217.5.16. Augustine suspects in late letter (426–428) that Vitalis has Pelagian leanings.

Augustine derives some of these from the Pelagian controversy but others from the interactions with the monks who are disturbed by his theories of free will and grace. In particular, numbers 11 and 12 refer to customs of the church Augustine is loath to reject. He hears that Vitalis believes the beginning of faith, the *initium fidei*, is a human capability, but Augustine wants him to accept that it a gift of God.[99] This human contribution has to be denied because it contradicts the capriciousness of God's grace. If the church prays for the conversion of the infidel, the *initium fidei* cannot come from human effort. Otherwise, we would not need to pray for the pagan. This idea sits uncomfortably on a foundation of arbitrary grace.

Augustine gives a different summary in the *Gift of Perseverance*; his list of doctrines is boiled down to three, the first two of which he claims support from Cyprian.[100] First, grace is not a reward for our merits because all our merits are gifts of God. Second, no one can be sinless; and third, we are born already subject to Adam's sin, remediating by baptism. He uses the Lord's Prayer to make his points; in this analysis, each clause re-enforces his conviction that persistence in the faith is one of the gifts of God.[101] For example, "May your name be holy" means we are asking God to give us the gift of perseverance in those virtues; perseverance and the virtues themselves are gifts and not as the Pelagians say, the result of human effort.[102] In both the letter and the *Gift of Perseverance*, Augustine's central point is that all the positive actions of humanity are God's gifts. There is no merit, and the negative aspects of life are fully deserved. The balance between them is part of God's inscrutable, but just, will.

99. Aug., *Letter* 217.6.29.

100. See Komline, "Grace, Free Will, and the Lord's Prayer," for a discussion of Augustine and Cyprian.

101. Aug., *Gift of Perseverance* 2.4–5.9. See also *Two Letters* 4.9.25–4.9.26. The *Gift of Perseverance* is a response to queries from discontented monks of Provence, written in 429–30.

102. Aug., *Gift of Perseverance* 2.4.

# 5

# Augustine and Pelagius

THE VERY ORTHODOX CATHOLIC writer Hilaire Belloc captures the essence of the argument in his wonderfully titled "Song of the Pelagian Heresy for the Strengthening of Men's Backs and the very Robust Outthrusting of Doubtful Doctrine and the Uncertain Intellectual." Belloc accurately says Pelagius claimed we were responsible for our own salvations rather than dependent on the church and that Pelagius laughed, or, more accurately, fumed, at original sin.[1] The saga includes condemnations (*in absentia*), recantations (of dubious sincerity), vindications (temporary), papal support (unreliable), and banishment (final). Some supporters, like Caelestius, got him deeper into trouble, and others, like Julian, provided depth after he had retired from the fight. Some friends were worse than enemies; Nestorius, who was soon to be tagged with his own eponymous heresy,[2] hosted Pelagian refugees. Pelagianism might have vanished from history if Augustine hadn't made the struggle the locus of his definitive views on sex, sin, freedom, and grace.

Augustine may have inflated the number and influence of the Pelagians.[3] Bonner characterizes them as inadvertently achieving immortality by angering the well-organized African bishops.[4] Pelagianism as a threat may have been the product of Augustine's imagination as he shaped the

---

1. Belloc, *Four Men*, 117.

2. Nestorius (386–450) was the target of the 431 Council of Ephesus, partly for rejecting the title *theotokos* (mother of god) for Mary.

3. Bonner, "Pelagianism Reconsidered," 237.

4. Bonner, "Augustine and Pelagianism," 27.

unique African perspective.[5] The Africans were adamant that the whole church should adopt their version of the faith.[6] Although the first hint of the controversy dates to 405, it didn't heat up until Alaric began to drive people out of Italy in 409. The exodus from Rome diluted the cohort of the Pelagian patrons. Caelestius was initially condemned in 411. Pelagius was alternately vindicated (415) and condemned (416). After several reversals of fortune, they were finally condemned in 418. Caelestius made futile overtures in hopes of rehabilitation, but Pelagius disappeared. The slogging match with Julian then began and continued beyond Augustine's death in 430. The swirl of letters and books does not do much to endear the protagonists to modern readers. Augustine is sarcastic and testy; Caelestius, hairsplitting; Pelagius, slippery; and Julian, arrogant. Brown believes an opportunity for a productive debate was lost.[7] Emerson welcomes this gladiatorial match because it keeps the reader awake.[8]

It is unclear why Pelagius became the center of the dispute—he was not an innovator. His views on wealth and the corruption of society were Ambrose's. His hell-fire tone was Chrysostom's. His optimism was that of Plato and the Alexandrians. His opinions on infant baptism were those of the Cappadocians. Finally, his advice to the rich renouncing the world was almost indistinguishable from Jerome's. He was an accidental heretic.

## PELAGIUS THE PREACHER

The primary sources for Pelagius include Jerome and Augustine, neither of whom ever gave a sucker an even break, making it difficult to establish just what sort of person he was. Abuse was poured on him by the most skilled polemicists of the age. Like Augustine, he seems to have contrasting characteristics. He was the scourge of the wealthy and the friend of rich patrons. He was a leader of a spiritual elite and a defender of the moral capabilities of the whole of humanity. He is hard to see under the mountain of abuse provided by his enemies.

He was most likely a layman, not a priest, or a monk. Jerome described him as an overfed Celt. He was comfortable as a counselor in Rome, but out of his depth as a controversialist. He was an ordinary man, "no one

---

5. Brown, *Augustine of Hippo*, 346.
6. Bonner, "Augustine and Pelagianism," 28.
7. Brown, *Augustine of Hippo*, 389.
8. Emerson's introduction to his translation of Wiggers, *Augustinism and Pelagianism*, 9–10.

special."[9] His following included the super-rich in Rome, Campania, and Sicily.[10] He deferentially tended to the needs of the *pars melior generis humani* (the better part of humanity), the stern patricians of Roman society. His popularity with the wealthy Victorians who shared the Roman sense of their own nobility and responsibility makes perfect sense.[11] His popularity among the rich might seem surprising, given the criticisms of the uncaring wealthy attributed to him, but there was a growing movement of renunciation among Rome's oldest families. Melania the Elder[12] and the priest (and future pope) Sixtus were among Pelagius's fans, along with, in decreasing order of respectability, Paulinus of Nola,[13] Theodore of Mopsuestia, and Nestorius.

Pelagius called the whole church to imitate the example of the martyrs of the past. The fifth-century heroes were visible in the authentic Christians under his instruction.[14] Pelagius was comfortable with the old Roman families, but he wanted them to be standard-bearers for Christianity as they had been for Rome. Pelagius thought anything less than an authentic Christianity was an insult to humanity and God.[15] He was not a fanatic appealing to desert monks; he spoke to conservative Romans whose religious beliefs are calm and orderly. His target audience was a *prudens*, the prudent man.[16]

He arrived in Rome sometime between 380 and 399. He had a sharp eye for hypocrites and the failings of his times. People were condemning lawful marriage and indulging in unnecessary fasting while they showed hatred to their brothers. They feign humility but inwardly are filled with pride.[17] Christians neglected Christ's teaching, and everyone pursued his own advantage to the disadvantage of his neighbor. He condemned those who considered themselves to be holy and disdained others as unworthy.[18] Often accused of naïve optimism, Pelagius understood weakness and was

---

9. Mathewes, "Career of the Pelagian Controversy," 203.

10. Brown, *Religion and Society*, 185.

11. Ibid., 188.

12. Melania the Elder (325–410) was a leader of the pro-Origenist faction.

13. Paulinus (354–431) is a representative of the rich Roman renunciators. He is a central figure in that community; he maintains epistolary contact with Augustine and Jerome and hosts the Pelagians amicably. He was a cousin of Melania the Elder. Brown, *Religion and Society*, 211.

14. Stortz, "Pelagius Revisited," 139.

15. Kelly, *Early Christian Doctrines*, 357.

16. Brown, *Religion and Society*, 189.

17. Pelagius, *On Bad Teachers* 11.1. The authorship of *On Bad Teachers* is unclear. It states some of its positions more strongly than Pelagius's usual cautious style.

18. Pelagius, *On Bad Teachers* 11.2.

very cognizant of sin—but he insisted people could do better. He focused on the individual; our failings are our fault.[19] The difference between Pelagius and Augustine was not their assessment of humanity's present but its future. Augustine emphasized the status of humans as irretrievably damned—Pelagius, their correctable immorality.

Pelagius was confident we could carry out God's commandments, even given our frequent abject failure to succeed and our whining about it. He insisted, "We cry out against the face of God and say, 'It is hard, it is difficult; we cannot do it, we are but men; we are encompassed with frail flesh.'"[20] He was concerned with behavior, not dogma. J. N. D. Kelly accepts the charge of Pelagius's insensitivity to human weakness. Nevertheless, he feels Pelagius's work reflects the glory of God and humanity's exceptional status in creation.[21]

In 405, Pelagius heard Augustine's prayer *da quod iubes et iube quod vis* (give what you command and then command whatever you will).[22] It may have been recited by Paulinus of Nola[23] or by the African bishop Evodius, an ally of Augustine in the conflict to come.[24] In this prayer, Augustine declared his submission to God's will. God can command anything (*iube quod vis*), but humanity is powerless to obey unless given specific aid to perform the command (*da quod iubes*). Some might hear this as a statement of humility, but Pelagius understood it as a terrible anthropology: we were playthings of the divine, with no responsibility for our lives.[25] He did not hear it as "give me strength" but "make me do it." If sins were not voluntary but were part of our nature or inevitable, then striving, repentance, and baptism would be meaningless. Since Pelagius attempted to persuade comfortable Christians to act like Christians, this was intolerable. While some of his

---

19. Ferguson, *Pelagius*, 165.

20. Pelagius, *Demetrias* 16.2 (Rees, Vol. 2, 53).

21. Kelly, *Early Christian Doctrines*, 360. On the other hand, Caelestius "made it his policy to stress the irritating tenets which the more conciliatory Pelagius himself tried to soften down." Ibid., 361.

22. Aug., *Confessions* 10.29.40.

23. Brown, *Religion and Society*, 212, suggests Pelagius and Julian had studied Augustine's anti-Manichaean works in Paulinus's library. TeSelle, "Prehistory of the Pelagian Controversy," 80, adds Pelagius may have seen *Simplician*. Bonner, "Rufinus of Syria and African Pelagianism," 45, suggests Rufinus the Syrian had seen it.

24. Lancel, *St. Augustine*, 362.

25. Rist believes this interpretation is mistaken. Pelagius "failed to understand Augustine's point about the need for God's prior action to promote love in human beings." *Ancient Thought Baptized*, 158. Pelagius might have responded that while God's prior action *is* necessary, it had been given universally in the goodness of creation, the teaching of the law, and the example of Christ.

audience might respond to a call for renunciation, he only wanted to give the remainder a swift kick. All Christians were under obligation to obey the commandments of a just and righteous God, leaving a few super-athletes like Paulinus to choose the higher road.[26]

Augustine claimed Pelagius was reviving the narrow-church Donatist ecclesiology he had defeated in 411. The common accusation of favoring a narrow church may be misplaced; declaring all people have the duty to improve is not the same as saying they are all saints. Lamberigts rejects the accusation of narrowness. Pelagius spoke of a holy church but, Lamberigts argues, it was not a static church of satisfied saints, but a dynamic church of determined strivers.[27] For Augustine, there can be no church of saints because we have the duty to pray the Lord's Prayer.[28]

Pelagius and Augustine did not immediately cross paths. This was partly geography; Pelagius was a man of Rome and the Roman establishment. The Donatist struggle that obsessed Augustine would have seemed provincial to him. In turn, Augustine may have heard only vaguely positive things about Pelagius. Augustine hated sea travel and depended on his friend Alypius, by then Bishop of Thagaste, to transport his books to Italy. This isolated him from the cosmopolitan elites throughout the empire. He was loosely connected to Rufinus of Aquileia's group through Paulinus of Nola but was not part of the cozy Rome of the Romans that welcomed Pelagius; Alypius was much better at schmoozing.

The Germans abruptly ended the separation of the protagonists. Pelagius and Caelestius went initially to Sicily where they had or made friends. Some works, such as *On Riches,* may have been written there,[29] as well as Pelagius's treatise *De Natura* and Caelestius's *Definitions*.[30] They continued to North Africa, passing through Hippo without meeting Augustine before arriving at Carthage. Augustine says he noticed Pelagius during the anti-

---

26. Evans, *Pelagius*, 62.

27. Lamberigts, "Competing Christologies," 165.

28. Gaumer, "The Development of the Concept of Grace," 164–65.

29. The relationship between Pelagius and his allies is ridiculously muddled. He probably travelled with Caelestius to Carthage, but they may never have been together again. Pelagius and Julian had a common friend in Paulinus of Nola, but Julian's attacks on Augustine do not depend on Pelagius or Caelestius directly. There may have been no Pelagian movement. Some of the strongest Pelagian writing may not be his work, including *On Riches, On Bad Teachers,* and *On Christian Life*. The *Letter to Demetrias* is claimed directly by Pelagius in his letter introducing his *Libellus fidei*. That, and *De Natura*, may provide the most reliable insights.

30. There is uncertainty about the authorship of the *Definitions*. See Dodaro, "The Carthaginian Debate over Sinlessness," 195, for a discussion. The views on sinlessness are close to those condemned at Carthage in 411.

Donatist Council in the spring of 411 but did not have the opportunity to speak with him. Rees wonders whether Augustine, stuck in the backwater of North Africa, would have ever heard of Pelagius without the intervention of Alaric.[31] Pelagius went on to Palestine, leaving Caelestius in Carthage. Harnack speculates Pelagius left Africa because he realized remaining would stir up conflict he wished to avoid.[32] Many other rich and powerful exiles descended on Africa, including Melania the Younger (granddaughter of Melania the Elder) and her husband, Pinianus. They initially stayed with Alypius in Thagaste, where they constructed two monasteries.[33] Augustine became entangled in a controversy over an attempt to ordain Pinianus forcibly (see below) and did not endear himself to Melania.

Although Pelagius had completed his commentary on Romans, Augustine was unsure of his position, in many senses. He wasn't sure whether Pelagius had the support of Paulinus of Nola and other notables and he wasn't sure what he was saying. His reputation for piety made Augustine hesitate to attack him directly, and he sought out accurate accounts of exactly what Pelagius and Caelestius were doing. He replies to an earlier letter from Pelagius in deferential terms, "To Pelagius, my beloved lord and brother for whom I long very much."[34] The goodwill didn't last.

## FIRST PHASE OF THE CONFLICT (411–18)

The first period covers the outbreak of hostilities after the anti-Donatist conference in Carthage through the acquittal of Pelagius at Diospolis in Palestine and the final condemnation by Rome in 418. The delays characteristic of fifth-century correspondence frequently left Augustine in the dark. He claims in the *Revisions* that any deference to Pelagius was courtesy employed to wean him from his errors.

Caelestius's desire for ordination in Carthage precipitated the strife. Paulinus of Milan,[35] who wanted the job for himself, brought charges against Caelestius. A synod led by Aurelius of Carthage condemned Caelestius's

---

31. Rees, *Life and Letters*, Vol. 1, 1.

32. Harnack, *History of Dogma*, Vol. 5, 175. Dunphy, "A Lost Year," 463–64, provides an alternate chronology suggesting Pelagius left after the condemnation.

33. Pinianus, Melania, and her mother Albina, may have travelled to Africa in the company of Pelagius. Dunn, "The Poverty of Melania the Younger and Pinianus," 101, cites the dissertation of M. R. Green, *Pope Innocent I: The Church of Rome in the early Fifth Century*, Oxford 1973, 83, to this effect.

34. Aug., *Letter* 146 (Teske, WSA, II/2, 316).

35. Keech theorizes that Augustine, under pressure from Rufinus's *Liber de Fide*, encouraged Paulinus in his attack. *Anti-Pelagian Christology*, 139.

views in late 411. They were all to have resonance in the controversies to come. There are lists of six or eight views depending on the source. Here, Rackett's organization of the list of eight into two primary themes and six subheadings is followed.

The first major thesis focuses on the events in Eden. Caelestius believes Adam was created mortal; he would have died whether he sinned or not. Consequently, Caelestius argues:

1. Adam's sin affected only himself and not the entire human race.
2. Newborn infants are in the same state as Adam was before his transgression.
3. The entire human race neither dies through the death or sin of Adam nor rises through the resurrection of Christ.
4. Infants, even though they are unbaptized, have eternal life.

The Fall did not have the cataclysmic effect demanded by the Africans. Adam was mortal, as we are, and we are as Adam was. There is no original sin—Adam's sin was Adam's, not ours. Without original sin, unbaptized and sinless infants are not damned. The third point is more complicated since it downplays the role of Christ and the resurrection. Caelestius's point, shared to some degree with all the Pelagians, is that our salvation depends on ourselves and not merely the result of Adam's sin or Christ's incarnation, life, death, and resurrection. His second thesis continues this line: people can be without sin and (easily) observe the commands of God. Since we can obey the commandments, Caelestius concludes:

1. There were people without sin before the coming of Christ.
2. The law leads to the Kingdom of Heaven, as well as the gospel.[36]

Caelestius insists on human dignity and responsibility. God would not have given us impossible commandments. God works incessantly to make us listen to him. He sent the law, the prophets, and Christ to make it easier. God called Abraham righteous (Gen 15:6), a status the Pelagians equated with sinlessness. Caelestius was a strong anti-Manichaean and defended the value of the Hebrew Bible against dualistic denigration of the law.

Augustine was not in Carthage for the condemnation of Caelestius; he was dealing with the aftermath of the Donatist crisis. However, the controversy prompted Marcellinus, Augustine's ally against the Donatists, to seek advice about infant baptism. He received his reply in Augustine's *The Punishment and Forgiveness of Sins and the Baptism of Little Ones* (subsequently

---

36. Rackett, "What is the matter with Pelagianism?" 227

referred to as the *Forgiveness of Sins*). Marcellinus, was disturbed by Augustine's suggestion of the possibility of sinlessness, and returned the first two books (written in 411) to him.[37] Augustine then added in 412 a clarifying third book in the form of a long letter. He suggested that new reports of Pelagian ideas about infant baptism prompted the writing of the third book.[38]

The common element uniting the Pelagians and their allies was the denial of original sin. This was the particular domain of Caelestius and the mysterious Rufinus the Syrian.[39] Caelestius linked original sin to infant baptism. Since there was no original sin, baptism was *beneficial* to infants, not *required*. Infant baptism was not for the remission of sins but was a form of sanctification and initiation. He tried to identify a destiny for infants dying before baptism and postulated a kingdom of heaven as distinguished from eternal life.

Augustine overheard people denying the need for infant baptism at the Donatist conference. The speakers were not under his authority, so he let it slide. It seemed like a minor episode, but he says he had to intervene when the idea spread and was enthusiastically discussed.[40] Augustine pointed to the liturgy; if infants are not damned for original sin, why do their parents bring them to the font to be healed by Christ?[41] The accusation of preaching two baptisms was partly justified, but it also applied to the very orthodox Cappadocians.

He did not mention names in the first two books of his *Forgiveness of Sins*—some have speculated he may have been responding to Rufinus the Syrian's *Liber de Fide*, rather than Pelagius.[42] He mentions Pelagius in the third book with the greatest respect: "I read certain writings of Pelagius, a holy man, as I hear, and a Christian of considerable religious development."[43] He may have hesitated to take on Pelagius's Roman allies.

37. Aug., *Letter* 139.3. Augustine claims he has forgotten why the books were returned. Dunphy thinks Marcellinus was unhappy with them. "A Lost Year," 405.

38. The confrontation between Paulinus of Milan and Caelestius is usually dated to the autumn of 411, followed by the request from Marcellinus to Augustine, and the rapid writing of *Forgiveness of Sins* before the end of the year. Dunphy believes the standard chronology has internal weaknesses and proposes that the trial of Caelestius was *before* the Donatist conference, possibly prompting Marcellinus's letter. "A Lost Year," 463–65

39. TeSelle, "Prehistory of the Pelagian Controversy," 86. The confusion about Rufinus the Syrian's identity is discussed below in a later footnote.

40. Aug., *Forgiveness of Sins* 3.6.12.

41. Aug., *Forgiveness of Sins* 1.18.23.

42. Bonner, "Rufinus of Syria and African Pelagianism," 36. See discussion of Rufinus in chapter 6.

43. Aug., *Forgiveness of Sins* 3.1.1 (Teske, WSA, I/23, 121). It is possible Augustine

He claimed he omitted the names because he hoped for the correction of the new heretics. He used respectful language for Pelagius because he was being praised by many.[44] He reiterated this self-defense in a 416 sermon; he had refrained from naming them to give them time to repent their errors.[45]

Caelestius denied the transmission of sin from Adam to his descendants, citing the support of "the holy priest Rufinus, who resided at Rome with the holy Pammachius."[46] By naming Pammachius and the apparently well-known Rufinus,[47] Caelestius may have been pointing to his noble birth and the nobility of his friends and allies. When pressed by Paulinus of Milan to name others, Caelestius replied, "Isn't one priest enough for you?"[48] The dispute was off to an edifying start. Caelestius would not abandon his positions, and the synod excommunicated him. He continued to Ephesus, where he finally became presbyter, the locals ignoring the African condemnation.

From 411 to 415, Pelagian cells flourished in Sicily, Rome, and Palestine. Letters began to arrive in Hippo with descriptions of Pelagian teachings. Augustine entered the fray with sermons against Caelestius. He wrote *The Spirit and the Letter* in 412 or 413, also dedicated to Marcellinus. While *Forgiveness of Sins* suggested sinlessness was possible if one had a sufficiently strong desire to be sinless, *The Spirit and the Letter* clarifies that only

---

had already seen Pelagius's *De Natura*. If so, he may have been writing against Pelagius, and not Rufinus the Syrian or Caelestius. See Dodaro, "The Carthaginian Debate over Sinlessness," for a discussion of the possible sources of the doctrine of sinlessness at Carthage. Dunphy, "A Lost Year," 448, speculates that Marcellinus may even been counted among the *amici Pelagaii* (the friends of Pelagius). In this reading, Marcellinus was concerned that the views of his friends were in question.

44. Aug., *Revisions* 2.33.60.

45. Aug., *Sermon* 348A.5.

46. Bonner, *St. Augustine of Hippo*, 321. Pammachius was a member of the highest nobility and Jerome's friend, but chided him for his over-reaction to Jovinian. He was married to the second daughter, Paulina, of Paula, Jerome's financially wobbly patron. He hosted a number of travelling theologians, including the Rufinus sent by Jerome to Rome. Pammachius apparently suppressed Jerome's conciliatory letter to Rufinus of Aquileia. See TeSelle, "Prehistory of the Pelagian Controversy," 63.

47. The identity of the holy priest Rufinus has generated an industry. There are four Rufini: (1) Turranius Rufinus of Aquileia, the translator of Origen; (2), Rufinus, a priest, sent by Jerome to Rome to patch up his quarrel with Rufinus of Aquileia; (3), Rufinus "the Syrian," so named by Marius; and, (4), Caelestius's "holy priest." Some Rufini may be the same person. Rees, *Life and Letters*, Vol. 1, 9, supports the identification of Rufinus the Syrian with Caelestius's holy priest, but was that the same person as the Rufinus sent by Jerome? Dunphy speculates in *Rufinus the Syrian: Myth and Reality* that Rufinus the Syrian may have been Rufinus of Aquileia, arguing that Marius Mercator had given Rufinus a Syrian origin to strike at Theodor of Mopsuestia.

48. Bonner, *St. Augustine of Hippo*, 321.

grace can produce such a desire.⁴⁹ Augustine received a copy of Caelestius's *Definitions* after Caelestius departure from Africa. He wrote the *Perfection of Human Righteousness* to refute Caelestius arguments on the possibility of sinlessness. The date is uncertain, with scholars varying in their estimates from 412 to 418.⁵⁰ The delay is a reminder of how the difficulty of obtaining reliable manuscripts governed the timing of responses. The emphasis on Caelestius in the early years is reflected in the nomenclature. Augustine calls his opponents the Celestines⁵¹ and Jerome names it the "Caelestian heresy."⁵²

In the meantime, Pelagius's aristocratic connections led to further controversy. Demetrias was the fourteen-year-old daughter of Anicia Juliana, and granddaughter of Sexus Petronius Probus and his widow, Anicia Faltonia Proba. Proba, head of the Anicii, had elevated Ambrose to a provincial governorship before his baptism and was the grandfather of two emperors. Demetrias was dedicated to a life of virginity in 413; Bishop Aurelius conducted the ceremony among the exiles in Carthage. The Anicii asked both Pelagius and Jerome (but not Augustine)⁵³ to write letters of advice. Ironically, the letter of Pelagius was preserved under Jerome's name, as was his *Commentary on Romans*.⁵⁴ They would both have been appalled. Jerome used his letter to take a swipe at Origenism, saying that it is "defiling the purity of the faith and gradually creeping on like an inherited disease till it assails a large number."⁵⁵

In the first edition of his biography, Brown describes Pelagius's message as harsh⁵⁶ but later assesses it as balanced.⁵⁷ Pelagius began his *Letter to Demetrias* with a fundamental defense of human nature. We measure the goodness of human nature by the goodness of its creator. If God made all of nature and called it good, then humanity, made in his image, is the pinnacle

---

49. Aug., *The Spirit and the Letter* 34.60.

50. See discussion in Squires, "Augustine's Changing Thought on Sinlessness," 455, footnote.

51. Aug., *Heresies* 87.1.

52. Jerome, *Letter* 143.1, accessed August 1, 2015, http://www.newadvent.org/fathers/1102202.htm.

53. Augustine may have encouraged Demetrias's decision to abandon her forthcoming marriage; see *Letter* 30.

54. See A. Bonner, "Manuscript Transmission of Pelagius's *Ad Demetriadum*," for the history of the text.

55 Jerome, *Letter* 130.16. Accessed June 1, 2015, http://www.newadvent.org/fathers/3001130.htm.

56. Brown, *Augustine of Hippo*, 342.

57. Brown, *Through the Eye of a Needle*, 304.

of creation.[58] Demetrias's task was to live up to this good start; the rational mind God gave her must always be in the process of choosing between good and evil. There is no final achievement of perfect virtue; in fact, our good deeds would not be meritorious if we were not always free to sin.[59]

Pelagius used Rom 9:20 ("Why have you made me like this?") to decry those who complain about not being immune to temptation. The pagans showed virtue lay within our natural power; surely, Christians could exceed this standard.[60] Sin had accumulated from the time of Adam to the time of Christ. Even after the expulsion from Eden, while human nature was new, we could live well. When human nature became "tainted with the rust of ignorance, the Lord applied the file of the law to it, and so, thoroughly polished by its frequent admonishments, it was enabled to recover its former brilliance."[61] The law and the imitation of Christ allow humans to scour off the rust sin and habit had deposited. The task was doable, but not trivial. We have been trained to ignore God and have to undo that training.[62] This training in evil goes beyond our lifetimes as the detritus of human society accumulates. Pelagius deferred to Demetrias's noble ancestry, declaring she had transferred the *noblesse oblige* of the civic life to the spiritual. He further distinguished the universal obligation for righteousness from the limited call to chastity. Having accepted a restriction, she had made herself liable for punishment if she faltered.[63]

Her family gave her material wealth but could not give her righteousness. She is now responsible for her virtue. The resources for virtue were her own: "They are things which cannot be within you unless they come from you."[64] He reminded her not to neglect good works and to pay attention to both weighty and easy commandments.[65] God created us and knows our strength. God understands how well we can follow his commands; he does not command the impossible or condemn anyone who could not avoid a

---

58. Pelagius, *Demetrias* 2.2.

59. Pelagius, *Demetrias* 3.1.

60. Pelagius, *Demetrias* 3.3. This interpretation is radically different from Augustine's, who interprets it as a statement of God's power to choose whether to save or damn.

61. Pelagius, *Demetrias* 8.2 (Rees, Vol. 2, 44). Seneca writes similarly, "But your dull, sluggish fellow, who is hampered by his evil habits, must have his soul-rust incessantly rubbed off." *Letter* 95.26 (Gummere, 257).

62. Pelagius, *Demetrias* 8.3.

63. Pelagius, *Demetrias* 10.1.

64. Pelagius, *Demetrias* 11.1 (Rees, Vol. 2, 48)

65. Pelagius, *Demetrias* 15.

transgression.⁶⁶ Augustine did not see the *Letter to Demetrias* for at least four years, but, when he did see it, it infuriated him.

Things drifted along quietly for several years. Hilary, a layman, wrote to Augustine in 414 or 415 from Syracuse. He was concerned about a local Pelagian cell. They supported the possibility of sinlessness and the ability to keep God's commandments. They did not think unbaptized infants were damned and encouraged the rich to give away their wealth. Finally, they were firm on the injunction never to swear.⁶⁷ Unnamed speakers were claiming the church can and ought to be without wrinkle or spot (Eph 5:27). Augustine replied that sinlessness might be an acceptable concept, but he denied a person could *easily* keep God's commandments. He referred to the need for grace and assistance exemplified by the recital of the Lord's Prayer. He used Rom 5:12 to justify the necessity of infant baptism. He mentioned Caelestius's inconsistency in accepting it liturgically, but Augustine did not name Pelagius. He included a defense of the rich by noting Abraham did not sell his flocks.⁶⁸

Things warmed up when Paul Orosius, who had fled from the Vandals in Spain, arrived in Hippo, asking questions about the errors of Origen. He left with the new purpose of opposing the Pelagians, arriving in Jerusalem in 415. He brought an Augustinian library including *Forgiveness of Sins* and *The Spirit and the Letter*, several of Augustine's letters and a file of documents citing Caelestius's condemnation at Carthage. He may even have been carrying an early version of Augustine's *On Nature and Grace*, written in response to Pelagius's *De Natura*.⁶⁹ Bonner thinks Orosius was a born troublemaker.⁷⁰

His temper and purpose endeared him to Jerome. Orosius denounced Pelagius to Bishop John of Jerusalem, who arranged a public confrontation. Pelagius appeared before a largely friendly synod on July 28, 415. Jerome despised John, not least because of the argument over Origen (see chapter 6), and did not come to the synod, probably realizing his presence would make

---

66. Pelagius, *Demetrias* 16.3.

67. Aug., *Letter* 156.

68. Aug., *Letter* 157. Augustine clarifies that the church is not now spotless but is being prepared to be so. *Revisions* 2.18.45.

69. Augustine says in the *Deeds of Pelagius* 23.47 that he wrote *On Nature and Grace* in response to material sent to him from former Pelagians Timasius and James. He says he was not certain Pelagius was the author and refrained from naming him as a kindness, but this may be face-saving. The final form of *Nature and Grace* was included in a letter to Jerome in 416.

70. Bonner, *St. Augustine of Hippo*, 332.

things worse.[71] When Orosius confronted Pelagius with Augustine's questions, Pelagius declared, "Who is Augustine to me?"[72] John of Jerusalem may have resented Orosius's efforts to exert Augustine's authority in John's domain and added, "I am Augustine here."[73] With his usual tactlessness, Orosius challenged John: "If you are going to assume the role of Augustine, then follow the sentiments of Augustine!"[74] The issue at Jerusalem was the possibility of sinlessness, not the infant baptism that had tripped up Caelestius in Carthage. According to Orosius, Pelagius admitted teaching people could be without sin and easily keep the commandments.[75] John supported him by pointing to Abraham, Zacharias, and Elizabeth. Pelagius affirmed the need for God's grace and escaped censure. However, he had a very different view of grace than Orosius and Augustine.

Orosius complained about the interpreters (he spoke only Latin) and demanded a Latin judge. John was content to bind all to a temporary reconciliation until a ruling by Innocent of Rome because the antagonists were Latin speakers. With all the terms murky, Pelagius escaped. Subsequently, John became more hostile to Orosius and accused him of claiming a person could not be sinless even with God's help. The exoneration of Pelagius stood temporarily unchallenged.

Pelagius was not safe. A second synod of fourteen bishops met in Diospolis (modern Lydda) in December 415. His new accusers were Heros and Lazarus, two bishops expelled from Gaul as supporters of the usurper Constantine III. They did not attend the synod, and Pelagius was able to take advantage of their absence. Pelagius again escaped by techniques that later infuriated Augustine. Pelagius avoided some issues, dumped Caelestius overboard,[76] gave over-careful answers, and quoted one of Augustine's friendly letters. Brown remarks on how blithely Pelagius proceeded, confident in his rectitude, but casually discarding his ally.[77]

Pelagius explained his statement from *De Natura* that no one could be sinless without the law as meaning knowledge of the law helps us not to

---

71. Harnack characterizes Jerome's anti-Pelagian writing as a "model of irrational polemics." *History of Dogma*, Vol. 5, 178. While the argument *about* Pelagius is between Augustine and Julian, Jerome has the argument *with* Pelagius.

72. Hanson, *Defense against the Pelagians*, 119. Orosius's self-pitying account of the Jerusalem synod is the primary source.

73. Ibid.

74. Ibid.

75. Ibid.

76. *Deeds of Pelagius* 11.24.

77. Brown, *Augustine of Hippo*, 358.

sin.⁷⁸ Pelagius admitted to saying our will governs our actions, but God aids us when we choose the good. He defended as scriptural the punishment of the unrepentant (this offended Augustine because it denied God the power to save an unrepentant sinner). He qualified his statement that evil does not enter the mind of a Christian to mean we should endeavor to avoid such thoughts.⁷⁹ He defended himself on the charge of teaching the possibility of sinlessness by again quibbling that its possibility did not imply anyone had achieved it. He claimed other statements were Caelestius's views, and he did not have to respond to them, but if they desired, he would join in the anathema. In some cases, the weaseling is obvious. He rejected the Caelestian statement that "Adam's sin injured only himself and not the human race."⁸⁰ However, he did not affirm an original sin or an injury to human nature, but only described the expulsion from Eden as a misfortune. He admitted he had said the church was without spot or wrinkle, but only in the sense that it was made so by baptism and Christ wished it to remain so.⁸¹

The synod decided the revised positions were canonical. Pelagius declared the remaining notions were speculations or open questions, not subject to doctrinal discipline, which he was willing to anathematize as foolish, but not heretical. The synod concluded he was orthodox.⁸² After the exoneration, a mob trashed Jerome and Paula's establishments in Bethlehem. Augustine blamed Pelagian supporters, but he may also have suspected John of Jerusalem.⁸³ Pelagius felt vindicated and circulated letters boasting of the result. He may have moderated his views in a revised *De Natura* and a defense of free will, *De Libero Arbitrio* (On Free Will or Choice), written in the post-Diospolis glow. He endorsed infant baptism but only for sanctification. On infants who die unbaptized, he remained agnostic: "I know where they do not go; I do not know where they do go."⁸⁴ At birth, a person is morally a *ta-*

78. Rees provides a list of Pelagius's answers at Diospolis. *Life and Letters*, Vol. 1, 135–39.

79. This may reflect the evolving notion among the ascetics under the influence of Evagrius Ponticus that evil thoughts were equivalent to their corresponding actions.

80. Rees, *Life and Letters*, Vol. 1, 136.

81. Ibid., 137.

82. Aug., *Deeds of Pelagius* 20.44. For the mismanagement of the case at Diospolis, see Burnett "Dysfunction at Diospolis," 155–59. Burnett concludes it is likely Pelagius was able to speak Greek while his opponents were confined to Latin.

83. Lössl in "Who attacked the Monasteries" concludes Pelagius was guiltless and hypothesizes that the attacks were part of the Origenist controversy or a general rejection of the Latin speakers in Palestine.

84. Ferguson, *Pelagius*, 96. One codex of the 419 Code of the Canons of the African Church includes a reference to John 14:2 "in my Father's house are many dwelling places [KJV: mansions]," which may have been used by some Pelagians as a solution to

*bula rasa*, on which free will writes. He clarified what he meant by grace (he avoided the term *gratia*, preferring to speak of God's aid, *adiutorium*[85]). By our nature, we are *able* to do good (*posse*). This is part of the basic design of human nature, common to all. The *choice* to do good or evil (*velle*) and the actual *action* (*esse*) are human responsibilities.[86] Ferguson argues Pelagius was clumsily stating grace is humanity's unique gift, but it is not a source of boasting. God's grace has given us the gift of choice, and we should be grateful.[87] Pelagius added, uncertainly, that God will supply sustaining grace to the earnest striver, and had provided guidance in his law and the example of Christ, limiting grace to this co-operating role. He admitted Adam's sin had injured the entire human race, but only by example, not transmission. Children were not in the same state as Adam, but only because they were children and lacked the faculty of reason.

Augustine knew the result of Diospolis but lacked a copy of the official proceedings. He gave a sermon based on a pamphlet of Pelagius (which did not directly address Diospolis) brought to Hippo by a congregant.[88] He listed the familiar Pelagian errors. If a man could make himself just, he would be greater than God, improving on creation.[89] The Pelagian emphasis on free will undermined the need for prayer, specifically the requirement to repeat the Lord's Prayer daily. Augustine undermined his position in the advice preached to his congregation: "We too have got to do something. We've got to be keen, we've got to try hard, and to give thanks insofar as we have been successful, to pray insofar as we have not."[90]

Pelagius's respite and Augustine's frustration soon ended. Orosius arrived in Africa with the hot news from Jerusalem sometime between spring and autumn of 416. He was carrying Jerome's *Dialog Against the Pelagians*, a cover letter, and the relics of St. Stephen. Infuriated by the news, Augustine and Aurelius made good use of their anti-Donatist experience and convened large meetings of bishops at Milevis and Carthage to condemn Pelagius and Caelestius. The Africans sent *Letters* 175 and 176 to Innocent seeking his support. Continuing the epistolary barrage, Augustine, Alypius, Aurelius, Evodius and Possidius (Augustine's first biographer) followed up with the

---

the unbaptized. Augustine dismissed the idea since the "mansions" were in his "Father's house," and it would not be appropriate for any unbaptized person to call God Father. *Nature and Origin of the Soul* 2.10.14.

85. As does Augustine in his *Propositions from Romans*. See chapter 6.
86. Aug., *Grace of Christ and Original Sin* 1.3.4.
87. Ferguson, *Pelagius*, 96.
88. Aug., *Sermon* 348A.7. Dolbeau 30.
89. Aug., *Sermon* 348A.8.
90. Aug., *Sermon* 348A.14 (Hill, WSA, III/11, 318).

much longer *Letter* 177. They usefully included copies of Pelagius's *De Natura* and Augustine's response, *Nature and Grace*, with the relevant passages highlighted to guide Innocent's reading.[91] The letters accused Pelagius of giving slippery answers and asked for the condemnation of the idea of human sinlessness no matter what Pelagius said in exculpation. Innocent was pleased to have Peter's Chair elevated to a position of primacy; the Africans worried about Pelagius's friends in Rome—they needed to be persuasive.

Brown thinks this letter campaign was an attempt to frighten and intimidate Innocent, implying Pelagianism would undercut the episcopacy, undermine the exclusive role of the church, and impede the imposition of a uniform orthodoxy.[92] Frightened or flattered, Innocent aligned himself with the Africans in three letters dated January 27, 417. With the usual delays, they did not reach Africa until spring. It was the first official pronouncement linking Pelagius and Caelestius. The earlier synods had attacked them separately or had been more of a grand jury investigation than a trial. Innocent's condemnation was replete with caveats, leaving the Africans unsatisfied. Pelagius sent the *Libellus fidei* defending himself to Innocent, but Innocent died on March 12, 417 before he could read it. The new Bishop of Rome, Zosimus, had to review the material, causing further delay.

Sometime after Innocent's death, Augustine and Alypius wrote to Paulinus of Nola. Their uncertainty about Paulinus's sympathies is apparent. Paulinus had loved Pelagius, "but we do not know how you are at present disposed toward him. For we too not only have loved him but still love him."[93] The Africans had heard people at Nola were saying Pelagius had gone too far in appeasing his critics.[94] The letter reviewed all of Augustine's positions, even those which had not figured directly at Diospolis. It discussed the mercy of God shown to Jacob and the justice of God's hatred of Esau, the inability of humanity even to begin to believe (see chapter 8), and the question of vessels of honor and dishonor (see chapter 9). The caution of Augustine and Alypius was warranted; Paulinus permitted the exiled

---

91. Aug., *Letter* 177. They noted that Pelagius may have denied he said the things included in *De Natura* (they do not insist he is the author) but demanded in *Letter* 177.7 that he anathemize them.

92. Brown, *Augustine of Hippo*, 359. Augustine sent many letters. *Letter* 179 went to John of Jerusalem and *Letter* 4* to Cyril of Alexandria. Toczko "Rome as the Basis of Argument" points to a rhetorical device used by Augustine in all these letters. The recipient is warned that the heretics have infested his city and are spreading deceit and lies. Toczko cautions that these scare-mongering tactics do not prove that there were Pelagian cells of any size anywhere. Innocent, in his reply to Augustine (*Letter* 186) condemns Pelagius and *De Natura*, but cannot put his finger on any actual heretics.

93. Aug., *Letter* 186.1.1 (Teske, WSA, II/3, 209).

94. Aug., *Letter* 186.8.29.

Pelagians to receive communion in his church up to his death in 431. Augustine's victory was not complete, even if people kept their heads down.[95]

By the winter of 417, Augustine had finally gotten the official Diospolis transcripts from Cyril of Alexandria. With renewed anger, he wrote *The Deeds of Pelagius*, addressed to Aurelius of Carthage, possibly originally intended for forwarding to Innocent—but it had not been needed to get Innocent's condemnation in January 417. Augustine and Alypius obtained Pelagius's *Letter to Demetrias* in 417 or 418 and sent a late response to Demetrias's parents. The bishops warned them that Pelagius's letter could cause great harm; attributing Demetrias's anticipated virtue to her inner resources was disastrous.[96] They complained about the deliberate ambiguity of Pelagius's words; they might be interpreted in many ways, some consistent with the African concept of grace and some depending only on human nature.[97]

In a sermon preached in Carthage at the shrine of St. Cyprian on September 23, 417, Augustine declared *causa finita est* (the case is closed), but Pelagius had not recanted.[98] Worse, two days earlier, on September 21, 417, Caelestius and Pelagius received pardons from Zosimus.[99] A chastened Caelestius had joined Pelagius in an appeal to Rome, forwarding letters of praise from Praylius, the successor of John of Jerusalem. Zosimus examined the backtracking Caelestius face-to-face and declared him orthodox; a synod said the prodigals were in full communion with Rome. Zosimus dismissed the complaints of the Africans as frivolous—none of the anti-Pelagians had come to Rome. Zosimus gushes, "How deeply each one of us was moved! Hardly anyone present could refrain from tears at the thought that persons of such genuine worth could have been slandered."[100] Zosimus had Pelagius's *Libellus fidei*; it included his last stand on the will:

> We confess free will in such a way that we say we always have need of God's help; and that they err as much who say with the Manichaeans that man cannot avoid sin, as they err who say with Jovinian that man cannot sin [after baptism]; for each removes freedom of the will. But we say that man always is able both to sin and not to sin, so that we confess that we always have free will.[101]

---

95. Trout, *Paulinus of Nola*, 235.
96. Aug., *Letter* 188.5.
97. Aug., *Letter* 188.11.
98. Aug., *Sermon* 131.10.
99. Lancel, *St. Augustine*, 328.
100. Brown, *Augustine of Hippo*, 361.
101. Pelagius, *Libellus fidei* 25.

AUGUSTINE AND PELAGIUS    113

The Africans were horrified by the backsliding of Zosimus. Their respect for the Bishop of Rome did not extend to accepting his opinions.[102] They would still call the Pelagians heretics until they admitted grace was more than an aid but was, instead, the *only* source of righteousness. Zosimus vacillated; in a letter dated March 21, 418, he asserted his displeasure that the Africans had ignored his decisions, but hinted the matter had not been finished after all. The African bishops proposed another council to meet in May 418, but imperial politics intervened.

On April 30, 418, Emperor Honorius, possibly provoked by a riot in Rome attributed to Pelagian supporters, issued a rescript from the imperial court in Ravenna exiling both Caelestius and Pelagius from Rome.[103] It accuses them of elitism, defying convention just for the sake of being different.[104] From the emperor's point of view, they were trouble makers; the theology was not the problem. On May 1, 418, the Council of Carthage, with several hundred bishops attending, condemned the Pelagian views in nine canons; in particular, the possibility of sinlessness without grace is strongly condemned. The canons were renewed a year later in the 419 Code of the Canons of the African Church.[105] Under increasing African pressure, Zosimus finally condemned Pelagius in his letter, *Tractoria*, in the summer of 418. Pelagius and Caelestius wrote letters to their allies but to no avail. Augustine continued fighting, writing to Sixtus, a former friend of Pelagius and future pope, in *Letters* 191 and 194, to ensure that the last remnants of the Pelagians were being stamped out. A decree sent to North Africa by the emperors Honorius and Theodosius in June 419 confirmed the expulsion.

The Roman exiles Melania the Younger, her mother Albina and husband Pinianus spoke with Pelagius in Jerusalem, perhaps hoping for a reconciliation. In probable ignorance of *Tractoria*, they wrote Augustine to report their conversation. They quoted Pelagius on grace: "I declare anathema anyone who thinks or says that the grace of God by which Christ came into this world to save sinners is not necessary, not only at every hour and

---

102. Bonner, "Pelagianism Reconsidered," 239.

103. Brown describes it as the "most depressing edict in the later Roman Empire." *Augustine of Hippo*, 363. Pelagius was probably not in Rome, but remained in Palestine.

104. Brown, *Religion and Society*, 189.

105. The 418 Canons can be found at http://www.monergism.com/thethreshold/sdg/Canons of the Council of Carthage to Investigate Pelagianism.pdf. Text translated by The Right Rev. Charles Joseph Hefele, DD & Henry Nutcombe Oxenham, MA. Edited by Rev. Daniel R. Jennings, MA. The 419 Code is available at http://www.newadvent.org/fathers/3816.htm. Translated by Henry Percival. From *Nicene and Post-Nicene Fathers, Second Series*, Vol. 14. Edited by Philip Schaff and Henry Wace. Buffalo, NY: Christian Literature, 1900. Revised and edited for New Advent by Kevin Knight.

at every moment but also for every act of ours."[106] Augustine responded in his book-length letter, *The Grace of Christ and Original Sin*. He fumed that Pelagius's statement was meaningless, given his limited notion of grace. Augustine dismissed the acceptance of God's help in Pelagius's *Libellus fidei*; Pelagius does not mean the awesome power of grace, but the aid provided by the law and teaching to a fundamentally capable human nature.[107] Chadwick believes Pelagius was incapable of denying that there had to be at least one element of salvation that was human responsibility.[108]

This long letter to the exiles (if it is correctly dated[109]) occupied a rare pause in the anti-Pelagian struggle. Augustine received a congratulatory letter from Jerome describing him as the second founder of the faith.[110] In Augustine's mind, the victory was won, and he could, unrestrained by the polemical and political situation, say what he meant. Augustine may have thought the matter settled; it was only the end of the first and shorter phase.

## SECOND PHASE OF THE CONFLICT (418–30)

Eighteen Italian bishops led by Julian of Eclanum refused to accept *Tractoria* and resurrected the Pelagian cause; doing this in defiance of Jerome, Augustine, and Rome took considerable courage.[111] The rebellious bishops proclaimed the Five Praises: praise of creation, praise of marriage, praise of God's law, praise of free will, and praise of the merits of the saints. Augustine said the five praises were traps laid by the Pelagians to persuade people to three evils. First, if grace is given for our merits then grace is not grace. Second, the denial of infant baptism leads to their damnation by neglect. Finally, the belief in the sinlessness of the saints denies the need to pray the Lord's Prayer daily.[112] The second phase had begun.

Julian was well connected. He was born around 386 in Apulia to Bishop Memorius and his noble wife, Juliana. Innocent sent his father-in-law, Aemelius of Beneventum, to Constantinople in support of John Chrysostom.[113] Memorius had written Augustine in 408 for a copy of his Cassicia-

---

106. Aug., *Grace of Christ and Original Sin* 1.2.2 (Teske, WSA, I/23, 403).

107. Aug., *Grace of Christ and Original Sin* 1.33.36.

108. Chadwick, *The Early Church*, 230.

109. Rees believes *The Grace of Christ and Original Sin* was begun in the autumn of 417, probably before Pelagius sent the *Libellus fidei* to Innocent. *Life and Letters*, 141.

110. Jerome, *Letter* 141. *Letter* 195 in the list of Augustine's letters.

111. Bright, *Anti-Pelagian Treatises*, xliv.

112. Aug., *Two Letters* 4.7.19.

113. Lamberigts, "Competing Christologies," 161.

cum period *On Music* for Julian to study as a young deacon in his father's church. Paulinus of Nola wrote a poem celebrating his marriage, projecting him as a father of a long line of bishops. He declared Julian and his bride had recovered the simplicity of Eden. Julian sold his lands to relieve a famine caused by the depredations of the Goths. He became Bishop of Eclanum in Campania between 412 and 416; it was a short episcopate. His position that people could be chaste was consistent with the ancient traditions of the church, but he was surprisingly modern in his claim that sexual desire did not have to be renounced at all.[114]

Julian wrote two letters appealing to Zosimus, who deposed him instead. After Zosimus's death in December 418, (popes died rather than face the Pelagian mess), Julian wrote to his successor Boniface without result. His Italian friends wrote to another Augustine, the Bishop of Aquileia, calling for a general council. Julian wrote to Rufus, Bishop of Thessalonica, looking for eastern support. He petitioned Count Valerius for an imperial review and accused Augustine of denigrating marriage, a sensitive issue for a high Roman official. Alypius had once sent Valerius a gift of eighty horses; Julian, as befitted his rank, assumed an appeal was his right and sent no stallions. Augustine was no advocate of separation of church and state when he could gain an advantage. He declared it unthinkable that the authorities would give Julian a hearing (they did not). The coercion applied to other heretics was more appropriate. He threatened Julian with the same treatment as was meted out to the Donatist mobs.[115]

Augustine wrote the first book of *Marriage and Desire* in 418 or 419, taking care to praise Valerius and his chaste marriage. Julian countered with *To Turbantius*.[116] Valerius sent some mangled excerpts to Augustine, who then wrote the second book of *Marriage and Desire* in 420. Julian had written that Augustine's party, like Jerome, condemned marriage and the God-blessed process of reproduction. Augustine clarified his view; while sexual desire was always an evil, marriage made a good use of that evil. He later received copies of Julian's letters to Boniface and Rufus via Alypius and wrote another rebuttal, *An Answer to the Two Letters of the Pelagians* (subsequently referred to as *Two Letters*). Julian was exiled from Italy in 419; he visited Theodore of Mopsuestia in Cilicia, remaining there until Theodore's death in 428. He moved to Constantinople, visiting the soon-to-be infamous Nestorius with other deposed bishops.

---

114. Brown, *Body and Society*, 412.

115. Aug., *Unfinished Work* 1.10.

116. Turbantius was an ally when this was written but eventually packed it in and was reconciled with the Roman church under Celestine; see Lancel, *St. Augustine*, 417.

Augustine received a full copy of *To Turbantius* in 421 and prepared a systematic response. Julian had objected to misquotations of his work in *Marriage and Desire*, and Augustine needed to be more careful. The *Answer to Julian* appeared in 421; Alypius carried it to Italy (Alypius traveled as far as Jerusalem for Augustine). Julian's last entry in the argument was *To Florus*, written sometime between 423 and 426 in response to the second book of *Marriage and Desire*. Alypius brought *To Florus* to Augustine in 427, triggering Augustine's final effort, the *Unfinished Work Against Julian* (subsequently referred to as the *Unfinished Work*).

Augustine was tired of the dispute. He hectored Julian, saying he should realize he is saying nothing and just shut up.[117] The *Unfinished Work* was found on Augustine's desk at his death as the Vandals besieged Hippo. He only completed his reply to six of the eight books of *To Florus*; all trace of the last two books is lost. The *Unfinished Work* does not add much new theologically but is revealing of the inner Augustine. Jesse Couenhoven describes it as lengthy, maligned, and often ignored.[118]

In the 420s, Augustine also contended with the reactions of bystanders. The monks at Hadrumetum in North Africa wondered if monastic discipline was pointless if all persons were predestined to salvation or perdition. Augustine replied with *On Grace and Free Choice* in 426, and *Rebuke and Grace* in 427, affirming his position on the necessity of grace. He later received letters from Prosper of Aquitaine and Prosper's friend, Hilary, reporting that monks in Gaul were disputing Augustine's theory of grace. John Cassian, Vincent of Lérins, and Faustus of Riez were the core of the opposition. They were later inaccurately called the semi-Pelagians. They declared that the will freely makes a beginning (choosing to believe) that is completed by grace. The monks thought Augustine had left them helpless, a view with which Bonner concurs.[119] Harrison disagrees with the robotic characterization of grace. Grace is irresistible for the elect not because it compels the will, but it summons forth a response from the depths of the true nature of the chosen ones. Harrison correctly captures Augustine's tone and reasoning but misses the force of the objection. The nature of a person in a state of grace is not disputed. Augustine's God only grants this to a few. The chosen elect and the abandoned damned are still unable to affect their fate.[120]

---

117. Aug., *Unfinished Work* 2.126.
118. Couenhoven, "St. Augustine's Doctrine of Original Sin," 359.
119. Bonner, "Augustine and Pelagianism," 30.
120. Harrison, "Delectatio Victrix," 300,

As a sidebar, it is one of the ironies of disputes over doctrine that slogans of the losers are adopted. Vincent is the author of the great criterion of orthodoxy: *quod ubique, quod semper, quod ab omnibus* (that which was everywhere, always, by all believed), which was originally used against Augustine. Heard agrees with Vincent that Augustine fails this test and Pelagius, supported by eastern tradition, passes.[121]

Augustine answered the monks with the *Predestination of the Saints*, and the *Gift of Perseverance* written in 429 or 430. The tone was condescending as befitted a bishop addressing lowly monks, and the sexualization was reduced in comparison to the anti-Julian works. Some of his more antagonistic attitudes directed towards Julian may reflect the equality of their ranks as bishops and his resentment at Julian's attempts to condescend to him, the conqueror of the Donatists. His statements on the will, grace, and predestination are more uncompromising in these works than in the meandering *Unfinished Work*.

Cassian asked, "how can whatever is true in each case and admits of no exceptions be considered other than attributable by nature to the very stuff of humanity after the fall of the first man?"[122] Sexuality is common to all and must be a part of our nature. Even if the management of it is complicated, we should conclude God intends human sexuality as it is now to be for our well-being. Sexual desire, moderated in marriage and controlled by the monk, was part of God's good created nature. Cassian was not as comfortable with marriage as Julian was; he aligned himself with the athletes of the desert. Desire is a thermometer—a monk might measure his success at withdrawal from the world by the number of his wet dreams. Cassian initially suggested six erotic dreams annually[123] but later he was more optimistic, expecting only three.[124] Whether he had more experience or was talking to older, gaunter, ascetics is not clear. The control of sexual desires was just a metric of progress: pride, hunger, anger, and greed were as important or more.[125] Of course, near-starvation would help reduce nocturnal emissions without any actual spiritual growth.

Pelagius was expelled from the churches under Jerome's influence and disappeared; he may have died as early as 418, or he may have lived in seclusion, regretting he had ever opened his mouth. Caelestius petitioned

---

121. Heard, *Alexandrian and Carthaginian Theologies*, 122.

122. Cassian, *Conferences* 4.7.1 (Ramsey, 159).

123. Cassian, *Institutes* 6.20.

124. Cassian, *Conferences* 2.13.1.

125. Diogenes wrote, "If only I could free myself from hunger as easily as from desire." Davenport, 173.

Caelestine, Zosimus's successor, for a hearing in 424, but was refused, and joined Julian in Constantinople. Pelagius had already irritated Jerome by allying himself with John of Jerusalem. Associating with Theodore of Mopsuestia and Nestorius attracted the attention of Cyril of Alexandria, reducing further the potential refuges of the Pelagians.

Nestorius endeavored to help his guests, writing to Rome to clarify their status. In a letter dated August 10, 430, Celestine confirmed their expulsion; a small council at Ephesus the same year added its condemnation. Julian continued his opposition even after Augustine's death on August 28, 430. Things came to a formal end at the Third Ecumenical Council at Ephesus the next year. Ephesus denounced Nestorius, but it also took the time to condemn the Pelagians. Julian attempted to preserve flexibility about the notion of original sin; he applied to Sixtus in 439 but to no avail. He died, possibly in Sicily among Pelagian friends, somewhere between 443 and 445. His tomb inscription defiantly read, "Here lies Julian, the Catholic bishop."[126]

An invitation to attend the Council of Ephesus arrived shortly after Augustine's death; it would have been a capstone to his career to dominate at one of the grand councils. Allen hypothesizes that the condemnations at Ephesus were a *quid pro quo*. The Latins agreed to condemn Nestorius (for things they didn't understand) and the Greeks agreed to condemn Pelagius (for things they didn't care about).[127] Harnack notes few Greeks disapproved of the Pelagians and the Latins condemned without considering the consequences.[128] This joint condemnation may not have been arbitrary. Nestorius was an adherent of the Antiochian school, which strove to preserve the humanity of Jesus as opposed to the Alexandrian School, which carefully guarded his divinity. If, as Pelagius reasons, the incarnation provided the perfect example to imitate, then Jesus's ability to avoid temptation could not mean he was not subject to temptation. To be a sinless exemplar, Jesus had to overcome temptations, not be immune from them. From the Alexandrian perspective, there was a danger in this emphasis on Jesus's humanity. Bishop Charles Gore's epigram goes, "The Nestorian Christ is the fitting savior of the Pelagian man."[129] Julian might respond that "the Apollinarian Christ is a suitable savior for the Augustinian man." Apollinaris's enthusiasm for the divinity of Christ led to his condemnation at the 381 Council of Constantinople for denigrating the humanity of Christ. Apollinaris was

---

126. Brown, *Augustine of Hippo*, 385.
127. Allen, *Continuity of Christian Thought*, 154.
128. Harnack, *History of Dogma*, Vol. 5, 188
129. Gore, "Our Lord's Human example," *Church Quarterly Review* 16 (1883) 98.

held to assert that the *Logos* had replaced the human rational soul (mind or *nous*) in Christ. Julian (see chapter 10) argues that Augustine reduces Christ's humanity to a cipher and varies his attack by suggesting Augustine had combined the errors of Mani and Apollinaris.[130]

## WHO WERE THE PELAGIANS?

The opprobrium makes it hard to form a balanced view. Julian attempted a metaphor drawn from Roman society. When a boy becomes a man, he is *emancipated* and is now responsible for his actions. Julian argued this is what becoming sons of God means. Augustine replied that Roman emancipation meant the son was no longer part of the household of the father; did Julian mean to imply we are no longer in God's house?[131] Julian never had a chance. The Pelagians were not systematic thinkers, much less systematic theologians: Pelagius was a preacher, Caelestius, a lawyer, and Julian, a bishop.

Pelagius was a spiritual advisor to Roman aristocrats; Bonner suggests they were mostly women.[132] The pairing of spiritual advisers and female supporters has persisted into the modern era. Jerome's fans were mostly women during his stay in Rome; in Bethlehem, he depended on his patron Paula and her daughter. His friend and rival Rufinus of Aquileia was funded by Melania the Elder. Pelagius's single idea was Christian authenticity. We are commanded to be perfect, we ought to be perfect, and, more controversially, we can be perfect. It may be easy to imagine wealthy women listening to these exhortations. However, Pelagius was also friendly with male aristocrats like Paulinus of Nola.

His *Commentary on Romans* was derivative; he rejected any hint of determinism without providing a complete framework—he was no Origen. He is accused of being a rabid ascetic, and he did use hellfire rhetoric at times, but he is not a desert monk like Anthony. He could not have held his patrician admirers otherwise. Bonner still considers him too ascetic; if he had been successful, the church would have been transformed into a monastery.[133] This is not tenable, given his audience. In the *Libellus fidei* 21, Pelagius condemns not only those who say God's commandments are im-

---

130. Aug., *Unfinished Work* 4.47.

131. Aug., *Unfinished Work* 1.178. Lamberigts suggests Julian's statement should be translated as emancipated *by* God rather than emancipated *from* God. "Competing Christologies," 163.

132. Bonner, "Pelagianism and Augustine," 39.

133. Ibid.

possible but also those who suggest that righteousness can only be achieved *ab omnibus in commune*, by all in a community. This may be a rejection of the idea that only the monks in desert retreats were capable of resisting temptation.

Pelagius wanted Christian virtues added to the Roman ones, without denigrating the proper Roman way. He spoke to and for the *prudens*. Brown admits his earlier assessment of Pelagian exclusivity may have confused Pelagius with his more radical supporters.[134] One of those associates might write "take away the rich, and you will find no poor,"[135] but Pelagius would have been too cautious to offend his patrons.

Augustine represented Pelagius as saying people could be without sin, not only in principle (which Augustine conceded) but also in practice. Pelagius certainly thought such perfection should be the defining goal, but he described it as a continuing challenge. Progress will become easier as we discard evil habits.[136] Augustine repeatedly accused him of denying the need to pray the Lord's Prayer, but he enjoined Demetrias to set aside special hours to pray privately in a closed room as directed in the gospel.[137] Life is measured not by our accomplishments but the distance to the goal. Patience is required: "as long as we strive towards the objective ahead of us, we do not slip back, but when we begin to stand still, we take the downward path, and it is our lot not to advance but already to go backwards."[138]

Augustine acknowledged Pelagius correctly analyzed the instances of sin recorded in scripture. They did not intend to make us accept our fate as sinners, but to teach us humility, encourage repentance, and give us hope of salvation.[139] This is the pastoral Augustine. The polemical Augustine would later clarify the pointlessness of repentance.

Chadwick describes Caelestius as "too elegant."[140] He was adept at logic chopping and arrogant, with Rufinus the Syrian's aggressive tone. He was principled enough to refuse to back down in Carthage in 411 in the face of excommunication and left town to try elsewhere. This contrasts with Pelagius, who was slippery and quite willing to dump Caelestius and his

---

134. Brown "Crisis of Wealth," 18, footnote 41.
135. Pelagius, *On Riches* 12.1 (Rees, Vol. 2, 194).
136. Pelagius, *Demetrias* 17.3.
137. Pelagius, *Demetrias* 23.1. See Matthew 6:6.
138. Pelagius, *Demetrias* 27.3 (Rees, Vol. 2, 67).
139. Aug., *Nature and Grace* 35.40.
140. Chadwick, *The Early Church*, 227.

ideas at Diospolis in 415. Bonner likes him, and regrets so little of his work is available.[141] He was combative, pushy, irritating—in a word, a lawyer.

Without *Tractoria*, Julian was destined to be a prince of the church. Bonner assesses Julian as able but unlovable. He had the best brain of the trio but with less range than Pelagius.[142] Burnaby finds him more interesting than the others, calling him fourteen centuries ahead of his time.[143] He had the arrogance of his rank, but he does not match Augustine or Jerome as a polemicist. He latched onto Augustine's Manichaean vulnerability and pounded relentlessly on that single note. Beyond that, he was a gentleman, and he could not accept Augustine's God—Julian would not have invited him to dinner. Lancel describes him as a "spoilt child of southern Italy,"[144] looking down on the descendants of Punic Hannibal. Augustine taunted Julian's pretensions, saying birth cannot overcome the Carthaginians when argument fails.[145] Augustine might have been the senior bishop, but he was redbrick while Julian was Oxbridge. He was a snob, deriding Augustine for appealing to popular religion rather than reason. However, he could also appeal to the masses when he said no one would say God is unjust.[146]

Although Julian is primarily known for his battle with Augustine, he might have made a mark without it. He wrote an exegesis of Hosea, Joel, and Amos eschewing fanciful allegorical interpretations and sought the plain meaning of the text, following the historical approach of Theodor of Mopsuestia. He avoided the Septuagint, which had added a layer of obscurity over already difficult texts and favored the use of Jerome's fresh translation from the Hebrew and the direct use of the Hebrew texts.[147] This directness goes far to explain Julian's reaction to Augustine's theology. The same approach informed his incomplete but stubbornly held views on grace. Lamberigts attempts to give Julian's theories an assessment independent of his criticism of Augustine. He takes Julian's position on the role of Christ to be that of improving humanity, created fundamentally good, by adoption.[148] A similar path was described by Cassian, who traces our status from slave to

---

141. Bonner, "Pelagianism and Augustine," 38.
142. Ibid., 41.
143. Burnaby, *Amor Dei*, 59.
144. Lancel, *St. Augustine*, 415.
145. Aug., *Unfinished Work* 6.18.
146. See Rebillard "*Dogma Populare*," for the ways Augustine and Julian appeal to popular rhetoric.
147. Lössl, "A Shift in Patristic Exegesis," 166–70.
148. Lamberigts, "Julian Aeclanum on Grace," 342–43.

hireling to child as we progress from the fear of God to the love of God.[149] God was merciful, only denying forgiveness to those who truly rebelled against him and refused reconciliation. God continually offered his help for those who turned to him in partnership.[150] Julian had a balanced perspective, even if he did not consistently answer the hard questions such as infant death and deformity, extensively used by Augustine.

What united the Pelagians was their Romanness, even if Pelagius was Roman by adoption. They mingled with the great, the rich, and the saintly. They expected a Roman attitude to life and religion organized around duty—obligations to the city and God. Augustine was never part of this world. When he met Anicia Faltonia Proba, Melania the Younger, her husband Pinianus, and Albina, her mother, he was deferential, but he did not manage them well. Melania and Pinianus were making plans to divest themselves of their vast wealth while staying as guests of Alypius in Thagaste. On a visit to Hippo, Augustine's congregation demanded the ordination of Pinianus to keep the money local. In *Letter* 126, Augustine claims he opposed the ordination but admits to talking to Pinianus about accepting the situation. The congregation made Pinianus promise not to leave town; he retreated to Thagaste instead. Augustine nagged him to keep his oath, but Pinianus said he had spoken under coercion. Melania, used to the prerogatives of the wealthy, put her foot down, preventing Augustine from witnessing a pledge to keep the oath.[151] Augustine wrote apologetic letters to her mother (who had accused Alypius and Augustine of greed) and others as the escapees eventually made their way to Jerusalem perhaps as late as 417.[152] They retained enough cash to give substantial alms and live in some comfort. He tried playing catch-up with his *Letter* 188 advising Anicia Juliana not to pay attention to Pelagius's *Letter to Demetrias*. She haughtily replied that it was not the place for obscure bishops to suggest that her family could be associated with heresy.[153] His tentative approach to Paulinus of Nola is another example of his discomfort around the rich. Augustine never escaped from being provincial, at least in Roman eyes. O'Donnell even suggests one of Augustine's motives in the Pelagian debate was competition for

---

149. Cassian, *Conferences* 11.7.6.

150. Lamberigts, "Julian Aeclanum on Grace," 348.

151. Dunn wonders how much of their wealth Melania and Pinianus had given up if they retained enough to be a target in Thagaste. "The Poverty of Melania the Younger and Pinianus," 93.

152. Lancel, *St. Augustine*, 313.

153. Brown, "Crisis of Wealth," 9.

the patronage of the rich. Pelagius was comfortable with the wealthy, and Augustine was an outsider.[154]

Brown describes Pelagius and Augustine as "religious geniuses."[155] Pelagius might be better described as the accidental advocate of the ancient position of the church on freedom and autonomy. His views were appropriate when Christians were an isolated minority, but awkward for a dominant majority religion in a Christian empire. Increasing Pelagius's status as an opponent has the effect of justifying the extremes to which Augustine goes. Kyle Harper compares the fight to the one between Trotsky and Stalin in the 1920s. Trotsky held to the Leninist ideals, but Stalin was the better strategist.[156] It is true the Pelagians were attempting to maintain a high moral standard, and Augustine was the more skilled politician, but the comparison needs some adjustment. Pelagius was smug, but neither Caelestius and Julian could match the founder of the Red Army in intellectual arrogance. Other comparisons work better; Julian considered Augustine a rural boob much as Trotsky ill-advisably sneered at Stalin. Trotsky was ruthless, a superb orator, and an efficient warrior—none of the Pelagians had these traits. A better comparison would be between the hapless Mensheviks (like Martov and Dan) and Stalin. The Mensheviks clung to an outmoded theoretical model and trusted in the truth of their ideas. Stalin easily swept them away. Like the Pelagians, the Mensheviks have remained sentimental favorites.

---

154. O'Donnell, *Augustine: A New Biography*, 254.
155. Brown, *Augustine of Hippo*, 370.
156. Harper, *From Shame to Sin*, 180.

# 6

# Origen and Seneca

THE PRIMARY FOCUS OF this chapter is on the wreckage left behind by the downfall of Origen. Almost everyone was an Origenist in 380 but by 400, all avoided even the slightest contamination of his more dangerous ideas. It is impossible to understand the positions of the antagonists without reviewing the rabid passions aroused 150 years after his death. Origen was considered a paragon of piety and scholarship; his imaginative interpretations of scripture were very influential. The controversy explodes in 375 and, after a period of chaos and recrimination, Pope Anastasius condemns Origen. Almost everyone, theologian or aristocrat, takes sides. Augustine, isolated in North Africa, takes some time to catch up while John Chrysostom is deposed as a part of the chaos. Origen represents the deepest Christianization of Neoplatonism and can be understood in those terms. Augustine switches from Manicheanism to Neoplatonism before his conversion and then comes under the influence of Origen. Traces of both Neoplatonism and Origenism stay with him to his death. The chapter begins with a brief review of Neoplatonism, followed by a discussion of Origen's contributions, and the history of his posthumous fall.

Origen falls but rebounds. Many critics of Augustine are fans of Origen and he certainly is the most admired church father never honored with sainthood. The contrast with the reception given to Augustine is striking. Erasmus remarks, "one page of Origen teaches me more of Christian philosophy than ten of Augustine."[1] Bigg calls him more logical than Augustine[2]

---

1. Quoted in Bigg, *Christian Platonists*, 329.
2. Ibid., 279

and declares every great member of the church loves Origin, at least a little.[3] Coleridge says he was misunderstood.[4] N. P. Williams cries, "Away with Augustine and back to Origen!"[5] Raven thinks a church that made Cyril a saint and condemned Origen had lost track of the word of God.[6]

In addition to his role as the epitome of the eastern approach, Origen serves as the primary defender of the free will from the theological perspective. When he falls, no one can turn to him to support the will. However, the practical and very Roman philosophy of Stoicism provides a comfortable backup position for the anti-Augustinians. While Stoicism lacks the grandeur of Origenism, it is confident virtue can be achieved by the strength of the will. The final section of this chapter will explore how Augustine deals with the Stoic ideas assumed by opponents like Julian.

## NEOPLATONISM

The Neoplatonists share with Plato the belief in an abstract world of true being beyond the physical world perceived by the senses. The sourcebook, the third-century *Enneads* of Plotinus, is not easy to follow; it consists of notes arranged by his student Porphyry. Plotinus begins with the One, who (which) is wholly transcendent and incomprehensible. The One is Being Itself or even beyond Being. Predicating existence of the One would set a limit, and the One is limitless, beyond essence, being, and life. The One is self-contained and has no awareness of anything, even of itself. Although the One is the source of everything, it is not a conscious creator. Emanations of diminishing status flow out of the One in a volcanic superabundance. The first of these is the *Nous* (Mind, Thought). The *Nous* is aware of the One and of itself. The One is not intelligible by any entity other than the *Nous*. The *Nous* is intelligible to humanity, and can reach both up and down.

The term "intelligible" has a technical meaning. Rational souls have several distinct faculties, including the intellect. Something intelligible is accessible to the intellect, comprehensible, understandable by reason. This is in contrast to "sensible," which means something available to the senses. Just as unhelpful as the Latinate "sensible" is the original Greek "aesthetic." The distinction between the noetic and the aesthetic remained of great interest to philosophers for millennia. The Cappadocians use it in the exegesis of the two creation stories in Genesis. The Genesis 1 story corresponds to

---

3. Ibid., 288.
4. Coleridge, *Notes on English Divines*, Vol. 1, 313.
5. Williams, *Ideas of the Fall*, 507.
6. Raven, *Natural Religion*, Vol. 2, 100.

the creation of an invisible, noetic, intelligible cosmos; and Genesis 2 story represents the visible, sensible, aesthetic cosmos.[7]

Within the *Nous* are all of the Platonic ideas (the ideal chair, the good, the beautiful and the true, etc. See chapter 7). *Nous* is identified with the demiurge from Plato's *Timaeus* (the ideas and the demiurge are distinct in classical Platonism). The Soul (or World Soul) proceeds from *Nous*. Soul looks both upwards to *Nous* and downwards to the natural world. These two roles divide Soul into the upper Soul and the lower Soul. The lower Soul is the soul of the material world. Human souls are generated in their turn and finally matter at the lowest level of being. Gnosticism identified the demiurge as the evil god of the Hebrew Bible. In Neoplatonism, the demiurge is necessary because the One is too transcendent to notice creation. Matter is good because it derives from the One as the final emanation, but it also represents non-being and is a source of evil. Christians mapped the Neoplatonic triple of the One, *Nous*, and the World Soul, to the Father, Son (Logos), and Holy Spirit. The soul falls down the hierarchy of being into the material world. To return, it must shake itself free from material distractions, remember its true self, and rise. This ascent is easy to appropriate for mystical Christianity.

The Manichaeans believe all material objects are mixtures of evil matter and good matter. There is an analogous, but more abstract, dualism in Neoplatonism. True being is intelligible. Sensible objects are mixtures of being and non-being. Evil is a privation of good; or it could be described as non-being (or better, privation-of-being). This abstraction permits Augustine to discard his youthful materialism and opens the way to understanding the universe in non-material or spiritual terms. There were nuances within the Neoplatonic position that allowed the Christian philosophers some room. Matter was more strictly non-being for Plotinus than for Porphyry, who acknowledges some minimal degree of being, at least a potentiality, for matter. Augustine leans toward this slightly more Aristotelian point of view, partly so that matter, as created by God ex nihilo, has some measure of good.

## ORIGENISM

Origen retains most of Neoplatonism but with twists. God the Father is an active creator, not a passive eruption. However, the material world is not the first world created. The universe begins as purely spiritual; each rational intellect is initially united with the divine but, by inattention to God, falls

---

7. Pelikan, *What has Athens to do with Jerusalem/* 98–100.

away to varying degrees. Satan falls the furthest and angels the least. Only one intellect is faithful, the Logos. God utilizes the Logos to create the material world as a part of redemption. Souls descend into bodies as part of the divine disciplinary process—pedagogy, not punishment. Our mortal existence is a time-out—a pause for reflection in the soul's eternal life. *Theosis*, or deification, returns the soul to the divine. Origen casts the Eden story in the spiritual realm, referring to the fall of pure spirits into material bodies. When God provides Adam and Eve with garments of skin, Origen takes that to signal their acquisition of material bodies; only then did gender come into being.

There is no problem in explaining why all are prone to sin—we would not be human if we had not already sinned—or why circumstances differ. We fall, not as descendants of Adam, bearing his sin, but individually, because of our own. Origen's belief in absolute freedom tempers his belief in universal salvation—each of us retains the ability to turn away from God. Gregory of Nazianzus and Gregory of Nyssa state a general restoration (*apocatastasis*) is, at least, an open question, so "God may be all in all (1 Cor 15:28)." The *apocatastasis* represents the return of the soul from the sensible (material) world to the intelligible (spiritual) world. It is the culmination of the history of each soul.

The incarnation forms the dividing line between the fall of human souls and the springing back. The infinite and eternal Logos voluntarily follows the same path to the material and sensible world that humanity has involuntarily taken. This amazing event ends humanity's fall and initiates its return. By his life, Christ offers the lessons on how to work for the return, and his death and resurrection are the first fruits of the *apocatastasis*. Perfection is possible because we are made in God's image, but we have to acquire the likeness by striving to imitate God.[8] The Origenist view survives in many forms; Emil Brunner writes, "The incarnation of the word of God is at once the insertion into time of the eternal God."[9]

Representing the early church consensus, Origen defends free will against Gnostic fatalism in his *On First Principles*; a free will is needed to enable the return to God. We are not stones moved about by external agents or fate. He embraces the Platonic axiom that error derives from ignorance and not a corrupt or corrupted nature. Education can alter us to the degree that profligates become better than the always chaste and savage men become so gentle that they improve on others who seem mild.[10] This is our task; "what

---

8. Origen, *On First Principles* 3.6.1.
9. Brunner, *Christianity and Civilisation*, Vol. 1, 49.
10. Origen, *On First Principles* 3.1.5.

does the Lord require of you but to do justice, and to love kindness, and to walk humbly with your God (Mic 6:8)?"[11] Pamphilus writes that anyone disagreeing with Origin is a plague bearer, undermining confidence in divine justice.[12] This remains the view of the eastern church. Sin is individual and to ascribe sin to our nature (as Augustine's original sin seems to do) is heretical.[13]

The Gnostic heretics find support in Romans, but Origen fights back: "And, from one handful of words from this letter they attempt to subvert the meaning of the whole of scripture, which teaches that God has given man freedom of the will."[14] He vows he will not permit any interpretation compromising freedom of the will, defending human nature against the Gnostic denigration of creation and free will against Gnostic determinism. Origen uses Rom 6:12–14:

> [When Paul says] "Do not let sin exercise dominion in your mortal body, to make you obey its desires" he is showing the matter lies within our power, that sin should not exercise dominion in us. For unless it were in our power that sin should not exercise dominion in us, he would not have given the command at all.[15]

When Origen falls, the freedom of the will loses its strongest supporter.

## ORIGEN'S FALL

In Neoplatonism, the World Soul's fragmentation into individual souls within the material world is a necessary consequence of the flow away from the One. In Origen, the descent of the pre-existent soul into the physical world is willful but individual. Its transformation and return to God involves shedding the husk of the body; the resurrected soul would be spiritual, neither male nor female. This lack of respect for resurrected flesh proves to be irritating to a society emphasizing the body in a negative sense. The mortification of the body and the elevation of the virgin require a fleshly paradise, cleansed of desire but still physical. A dissatisfaction with Origen's abstractions grows.

---

11. Origen, *On First Principles* 3.1.6.
12. Pamphilus, *Apology for Origen* 33.
13. Meyendorff, *Byzantine Theology*, 143.
14. Origen, *Commentary on Romans,* preface 1 (Scheck, 53).
15. Origen, *Commentary on Romans* 6.1.4 (Scheck, 2).

For Origen, the Son is co-eternal with the Father ("begotten before all worlds"), but distinct, being the Father's communication with the created world and the means by which creation is accomplished. The Holy Spirit is distinct from both the Father and Son, being the head of the created order. This perspective becomes unacceptable after the Councils of Nicaea in 325 and Constantinople in 381, representing an impermissible subordinationism.[16] Although the Cappadocians begin as strong Origenists, they move away. Gregory of Nyssa's changing view of the *apocatastasis* illustrates the process. Initially, he follows the standard Origenist model. Salvation is a long process and Christ, although his incarnation is crucial, is primarily a bystander and example. Later, Gregory emphasizes the incarnation implies the *apocatastasis* will be the establishment of a balance between the intelligible and sensible worlds, reconciled in Christ, rather than a return to a purely spiritual world.[17] These intellectual distinctions were not enough to doom Origen; rough politics brings him down.

Epiphanius, Bishop of Salamis, initiates the attack in 375. He objects to Origen's allegorical interpretations of scriptures and his intellectual approach to matters of dogma. Epiphanius supports the anthropomorphists, who favor the use of literal depictions of the divine in contrast to Origen's spiritual approach. Epiphanus sends his emissary Artarbius to Jerusalem in 393, and what might have been an abstract argument rapidly becomes political. Artarbius demands that everyone disavow Origen. Jerome, "that prince of theological trimmers,"[18] caves, but Rufinus of Aquileia dismisses the ultimatum, beginning the division between the two old friends. Before the disaster, Jerome described Origen as second only to Paul[19] and an "immortal genius."[20] He abandons him abjectly: "We were once zealous in our praise of Origen; let us be equally zealous in condemning him now that he is condemned by the whole world."[21] Epiphanius visits Jerusalem himself in 394, meeting opposition from John of Jerusalem. Epiphanius's interference in John's domain (including ordaining Jerome's brother uncanonically) incenses John, and he excommunicates Jerome. Theophilus, Patriarch of Alexandria, eventually brokers a settlement in 397, but it does not last.

---

16. The eastern church preserves "a Biblical and Orthodox subordinationism, maintaining the personal identity of the Father as the ultimate origin of all divine being and action." Meyendorff, *Byzantine Theology*, 183.

17. Mosshammer, "Historical Time and Apokatastasis," 82.

18. Heard, *Alexandrian and Carthaginian Theologies*, 162.

19. Bigg, *Christian Platonists*, 273.

20. Jerome, *On Illustrious Men* (Halton, 78).

21. Jerome's reply to Rufinus of Aquileia's *Defense* (Butterworth, xlvi).

Rufinus inadvertently makes things worse. Relocating to Rome in 398 with Melania the Elder, he translates Origen's *On First Principles* as a defense of Origen's teaching. He claims any doubtful passages are corruptions and edits them, replacing dubious texts with extracts from other works. Jerome responds with a more literal translation after his assistance is sought by Pammachius. This translation has the effect of spreading Origen's controversial speculations to a naïve Latin audience. Jerome's Roman anti-Origenist allies keep up the pressure there, and the relationship with Rufinus deteriorates further in an exchange of letters. A rapidly assembled synod at Rome condemns Origen in 400. The decree is not definitive, and Rufinus continues to fight.

Jerome had depended on Origen's scholarship and his exegesis. His praise of Origen causes him considerable embarrassment. For example, in his *Commentary on Galatians*, written in 386, he follows Origen meticulously. He explains "The one who is righteous will live by faith (Gal 3:11)" means "that before having faith and the intention to live by it, one must already be righteous and must by the purity of his life have climbed certain steps that lead to faith."[22] His commitment to human endeavor continues, "It is therefore possible for someone to be righteous without yet living by faith in Christ."[23] Even after his abandonment of Origen, Jerome tries to balance his continuing admiration for Origen's scholarship while condemning his theology. After the fall of Origen, Paulinus of Nola asks Jerome about the difficult problem of why God hardens Pharaoh's heart. In his reply, Jerome endorses Origen's treatment in *On First Principles* and simultaneously recommends his translation of the book to guard against Origen's heresies.[24] This measured attitude proves impossible to maintain.

Origen's fall is the pretext for the destruction of John Chrysostom. Among the Origenists are the four Tall Brothers, who reject literal depictions of God. The previously pro-Origenist Theophilus expels the brothers and John Cassian (see chapter 11) from Egypt in 399. The Tall Brothers flee to Chrysostom in Constantinople. Chrysostom summons Theophilus to Constantinople in 403 to answer charges, but Theophilus conspires with Chrysostom's local enemies to bring him down. His criticisms of wealth and emphasis on the care of the poor irritated the rich; he even suggested that private property was a consequence of the Fall.[25] As soon as Theophilus destroys Chrysostom, he reconciles with the Tall Brothers and starts using

---

22. Jerome, *Commentary on Galatians* 2.3.11–12 (Cain, 137).
23. Ibid.
24. Jerome, *Letter* 85.3.
25. Chadwick, *The Early Church*, 181.

Origen again. Theophilus's nephew, Cyril, continues the battle of Alexandria against Antioch and Constantinople, leading the charge against Nestorius at the Council of Ephesus in 431. Kelly provides a readable account of the incredibly complicated eastern politics from the perspectives of Rufinus and Jerome.[26] The dispute spreads from the Near East to every part of the empire; Chrysostom dies in exile in 407.

Melania the Elder and Rufinus are firmly in the pro-Origen, pro-Chrysostom camp. Chrysostom's allies lodge with Melania the Younger when rallying Italian support. Brown believes the Rufinus-Origen-Chrysostom cluster frames the Pelagian controversy, even if the Pelagians also distanced themselves from Origen.[27] Origen's cosmology is so rich that when he falls there are ample elements to offend everyone. Many theologians hold Origenist and anti-Origenist positions simultaneously. Everyone picks at least one idea to oppose.

Shortly after the condemnation in 400, the *Liber de Fide* (book or declaration of faith) of one Rufinus the Syrian starts to circulate in the empire.[28] He rejects the pre-existence of souls and a birth taint. He attacks *all* forms of traducianism (the transmission of the soul from the parents) leading to the damnation of infants. He suggests Adam's flesh was created mortal, but might have earned immortality. He is certain there are eternal torments, against Origen's pedagogical punishments. His style is sufficiently inflammatory that the frequently expressed idea he is Jerome's emissary is plausible. Marius Mercator accuses him of being the true source of the Pelagian heresy in Rome, which he further traces to Theodor of Mopsuestia.[29]

Although Jerome discussed the *apocatastasis* without qualms earlier, he rejects it in the 390s, possibly because it implies an equality of heavenly ranks when God becomes all in all.[30] The prospect of the Virgin Mary rubbing shoulders with a prostitute horrifies him.[31] He objects to the descent of souls, the return to a spiritual existence (denying a physical resurrection), and the possible repentance of Satan. He is sure God creates new souls daily and condemns traducianism as well as the descent of pre-existing souls. As a

---

26. Kelly, *Jerome*, 195–209, 227–58.

27. Brown, *Religion and Society*, 215–21. Chrysostom's homilies were translated by Annianus of Celeda, who points to John's exile as a parallel to the Pelagian case.

28. While the consensus is that Rufinus the Syrian is the author of the *Liber de Fide*, some argue Caelestius is the author. See Dodaro "The Carthaginian Debate."

29. Bonner, "Rufinus of Syria and African Pelagianism," 35. Bark argues Mercator used the supposed Mopsuestian connection as a weapon against Julian. "The Doctrinal Interests of Marius Mercator" 211–16.

30. Clark, *Origenist Controversy*, 99.

31. Ibid., 128.

part of the denial of Origen's remedial processes, he rejects *apatheia*, the notion that a person can transcend the emotions entirely. His diatribe in *Letter 133* (see chapter 11) equates Pelagian sinlessness, *impecantia*, with *apatheia*. Jerome exaggerates; *impecantia* is not the same as *apatheia*. Pelagius permits thoughts of sin, as long as a person does not act on them. On the other hand, *apatheia* has as its goal the elimination of even the thought.[32] In contrast to *apatheia*, Jerome emphasizes the cycle of sin and repentance as expressed in the scriptures. He stresses the continuing process of salvation in his anti-Pelagian works—rejecting simple-minded perfectionism, but not adopting the finality of infant damnation or predestination.

Pelagius's position is awkward after 411; he is staying in Jerusalem under the sponsorship of Origenist Bishop John of Jerusalem, but lurking in Bethlehem is John's enemy, Jerome.[33] Pelagius demonstrates his slippery political character frequently during his Palestinian stay. He uses the charge of Origenism against his accusers at Diospolis in 415, arguing for the eternal punishment of the unrepentant, and is happy to dump Caelestius when challenged. After his condemnation by Innocent of Rome in 417, he takes careful anti-Manichaean and anti-Origenist positions in the *Libellus fidei*. Pelagius shares with Rufinus and Jerome an objection to any form of traducianism. He prefers the fresh creation of the soul and rejects Origin. God creates each soul, but not from his substance (as in a Neoplatonic interpretation). The souls did not sin in a prior state nor did they dwell in heaven before being placed in bodies.[34] He again takes an anti-Organist position on the resurrection, affirming his belief in bodily resurrection and immortal life in that form.[35] Nevertheless, Pelagius's position on free will is Origenist. His *Commentary on Romans* never acknowledges his dependence on his predecessor's commentary, but it often reads like a clumsy paraphrase. Although he affirms eternal punishment, his uncertainty about the fate of unbaptized babies and his suggestion of the possible salvation of the virtuous pagan is fundamentally Origenist.

Augustine has several Origenist problems. His *Forgiveness of Sins* allows for the possibility of sinlessness.[36] His early writings lean toward

---

32. Kelly, *Jerome*, 315, fn. 35.

33. Some scholars (Evans, *Pelagius*, 31–37, Kelly, *Jerome*, 187, Rees, *Life*, 4–6), identify Pelagius with a monk who criticizes Jerome's *Against Jovinian*, possibly explaining Jerome's animus.

34. *Libellus fidei* 20.

35. *Libellus fidei* 15. For a discussion of the relationship of the *Libellus fidei* to the anti-Origenist movement, see Egmond "Pelagius and the Origenist Controversy," 634–39.

36. Aug., *Forgiveness of Sins* 2.6.7.

the pre-existence of souls. The common base of Neoplatonism creates similarities even when there is not a direct link. Augustine's early concept of humanity as the image of God is Origenist. Augustine says the Fall turned humanity away from God, thereby destroying God's image (and leaving us damned).[37] The difference between this and Origen's position is slight. It describes the Fall as causing the turning away of the soul from God—Origen would say the Fall is the result of turning away.

Augustine and Aurelius of Carthage frequently write to Jerome in the 390s asking for more translations of Origen's exegetical texts. However, they may not have seen Origen's *First Principles* until Rufinus's translation becomes available circa 399. Augustine wrote to Jerome in *Letter 40* seeking clarification on Origen's errors. In maintaining original sin, even in a very different form, Augustine runs the risk of an accusation of Origenist tendencies. Elizabeth Clark argues it achieves the same effect as Origen's fall of the pre-existent souls. In both theories, newborns have guilt.[38] However, in Origen's picture, the guilt is earned; in Augustine's theory, it is the stain of the father's concupiscence.

Augustine's early work supports the *apocatastasis*: "But the goodness of God does not permit the situation to go so far, and it orders all the things that are falling away in such fashion that they may be where they can be most appropriately until by their well-ordered movements they return to that from which they fell away."[39] This is precisely Origen's bungee cord anthropology; souls fall away from God by different distances, but they all bounce back. Satan is on the longest cord, but God will reel him in, eventually. Augustine has to have a new explanation for this image of the soul's return to God when Origen is condemned. He retains the falling metaphor but only the predestined return; the rest stall at the bottom, at an appropriate location for their specific punishment.[40] The souls that return to God are the souls that return to God—the souls that don't return to God, don't return to God. This is the same tautological claptrap used to explain that when God *wills all men to be saved*, it does not mean God wills all men to be saved, but God wills to be saved all the people God wills to be saved. In more

---

37. Bonner, "Augustine's Doctrine of Man," 505. Bonner notes that this abstract doctrine sits uneasily on the base of original sin with its materialist basis in generation, but Augustine seems to have no trouble maintaining both ideas.

38. Clark, *Origenist Controversy*, 6.

39. Aug., *The Manichean Way of Life* 7.9 (Teske, WSA, I/19, 72). Bammel concludes the early Augustine had adopted the entire Origenist theodicy. "Augustine, Origen and the Exegesis of St. Paul," 348.

40. Aug., *Revisions* 1.7(6).6.

human terms, "when I said forsaking all others, I meant I would forsake all those I chose to forsake."

Augustine's Neoplatonic roots appear in early work. The soul, "if it serves God with the mind and a good will, it will undoubtedly be restored, and will return from the mutable many to the immutable One."[41] He later explains such a restoration will be part of the resurrection of the dead and not something achievable in life.[42] In *Nature and Grace*, he distances himself further from deification in an uncharacteristically tentative way. As creatures, he is not convinced we can become truly equal to God; it is up to the proponents of such an idea to explain its possibility.[43]

Augustine moves dramatically away from any notion of *apocatastasis* in Book 21 of the *City of God*, affirming the eternal punishment of the damned including the devil and his angels. Origen and others who try to ameliorate eternal punishment might as well say the blessed life of the saved is not eternal either. Some people are saved, and some are burned to demonstrate both mercy and judgment (*City of God* 21.12). The vast majority is justly damned because punishment is due to all; a tiny number are given mercy to preserve a formal, if not numerical, balance. In chapter 13, Augustine rejects a general purgatorial punishment. God reserves his mercy to the predestined few (chapter 16). Nothing can reverse the predestination to damnation. He goes through the list of possibilities: He dismisses Origen's hopes in chapters 17 and 21. Chapters 18 and 24 dispose of the intercession of the saints. Participation in the sacraments is eliminated in chapters 19 and 26. Correct catholic baptism is down-graded in chapters 20 and 25. Even belief (chapters 21 and 25), and the giving of alms (chapters 22 and 27) are unable to spare someone from eternal torment. The intensity of the punishment may vary. The flames may have different temperatures, or the tormented may have different levels of pain tolerance (chapter 16). In response to the spineless defenders of God's mercy who cite Ps 77:9, "Has God forgotten to be gracious? Has he in anger shut up his compassion?" he asserts God remembers his mercy to his chosen vessels (chapter 24).

After this impressive display of hellfire preaching on the *eternity* of punishment, Augustine demurs from Pelagian *certainty* of punishment, considering it to be the flip side of Origenist universalism—one must allow for arbitrary grace.[44] Mercy will be shown to some sinners after some ill-

---

41. Aug., *On True Religion* 12.24 (Burleigh, 236).

42. Aug., *Revisions* 1.12(13).4.

43. Aug., *Nature and Grace* 33.37.

44. See also *Letter* 4* to Cyril of Alexandria; Augustine argues that denying random mercy would make a mockery of the Lord's Prayer.

specified pains (chapter 24) and it is possible there could have been some purgatorial preparation between death and resurrection (chapter 26) for a few. If there are no sinners elevated by unmerited grace, then it could appear grace is earned.

The piecemeal abandonment of Origen leaves all sides with incomplete systems. He provided an integrated solution to four issues dividing the fifth-century protagonists. Pre-existence solves the question of the origin of the soul. The differing degrees of fall determine the disparate lots for different individuals. There is absolute moral autonomy guaranteeing free will, and the *apocatastasis* vindicates God's justice. Augustine's solution is different. Original sin explains the state of the world. Augustine reverses the meaning of the will; he saves God's justice by asserting all are damned. He can find no theory of the soul that works for him and Julian complains endlessly about his mangling of the will and divine justice. The Pelagians opt for the separate creation of the soul, moral autonomy, and a fierce loyalty to God's justice. However, they have no explanation for the varying human situations—particularly the state of newborns.

Dominic Keech thinks Augustine inflates Caelestius and Pelagius to the status of heretics to protect himself from accusations of Origenism.[45] Keech may overestimate Augustine's direct dependence on Origen. His Neoplatonic past is sufficient to create a need to distance himself from Origen just as he distances himself from his Manichaean past. Nevertheless, the downfall of a giant like Origen makes all the survivors very sensitive and confuses the arguments as each participant claims to be free of any Origenist taint.

## THE STOIC ALTERNATIVE

Origen's fall does not eliminate the use of Stoic philosophy to defend the will. Stoicism pervades Roman attitudes to the problems of life. Julian assumes every sensible person will take the stoic attitude—we can control our behavior and emotions, deal with life, and bear our pains. With this Roman perspective, Julian considers Augustine a whiner or a pervert—finding evil where it need not be found—while Augustine thinks Julian is naïve. Augustine's elevation of the will to an independent faculty is one of the sources of the confusion. Julian and his Stoic mentors think of reason as determining our actions. Reason is the defining element of human *nature*. After all,

---

45 Keech, *Anti-Pelagian Christology*, 240. Compare Dunphy, "A Lost Year," 416–417, who argues Augustine is ignorant of Rufinus's *Liber de Fide* except in fragments, weakening Keech's argument.

Aristotle defines humans as *rational* animals.[46] By separating the will from our essential nature, Augustine escapes from the trap of changing our nature or attributing evil to God's creation.

Julian, Pelagius, and Caelestius are part of the Roman establishment. They share values with Symmachus and Petronius Proba: restraint, dignity, and duty. Stoicism enters Christianity through the standard education of the wealthy. Its simplicity and asceticism are a natural fit to Christianity, distinguishing it from pagan excesses. The early theologians asses the Platonists as sound on metaphysics, but the Stoics are better on ethics. Julian's use of Stoicism is often implicit since he does not think of Stoicism as an approach—it is the only way to reason correctly. A Roman gives alms out of duty to conform to the second great commandment. She does not do it for the expiation of her sins, as Augustine insists; it is just the right thing to do. The sage pursues the same goals of emotional control as the Origenist, without the sense of ecstatic ascent.

The Greeks attempt to control the emotions and, ideally, eradicate them. Aristotle emphasizes moderation of the emotions or passions, *metriopatheia*, the middle way or golden mean. Going further, the Cynics want to be free of them, *apatheia*. The Stoics, more modestly, aim to overcome them. Seneca chooses the Latin word, *impatientia*, to indicate the triumphing over suffering, not a lack of feeling.[47] These general attitudes are common to all the schools; the Stoic Seneca, a contemporary of Paul, often borrowed from Epicurus. The Stoic plan for achieving *impatientia* is rooted in their theory of the genesis of emotions. First, there is an "appearance," a bodily shock to the system. The shock might be a blow, a loud noise, or any other disturbance. The reaction could be raised blood pressure, pallor, goose bumps, or a shiver. These are not emotions; Seneca calls such an appearance a "first movement" (*primus motus*). First movements are distinct from emotions. First movements are not voluntary—they just happen, "and we cannot forbid these feelings any more than we can summon them."[48] First movements become emotions following two *judgments*; judgments are voluntary in the sense that we choose to make them, but they are actions of the intellect rather than of an independent will. The first judgment determines whether the appearance is *good* or *bad*—is it a love tap or an assault? The second judgment is to *assent* to a particular *action*. The emotions can be controlled either by modifying the first judgment or the second. The sage may judge

---

46. See Harper, *From Shame to Sin*, 117–22, for more discussion of the Christian and Stoic formulations of the freedom of the will.

47. Seneca, *Letters from a Stoic*, 9.3 (Gummere, 21).

48. Seneca, *Letters from a Stoic*, 11.6 (Gummere, 25).

a situation bad, but choose not to respond in a reactive way, or, better, the Stoic can learn to suspend the judgment of good and bad. If virtue is the only true good, and vice the only true evil, then the sage should develop an indifference to the events of the world. He prefers health but is indifferent to sickness; he loves his child and bears up under her death. The first-century Stoic philosopher and slave, Epictetus, calmly warns his master that the beating he is receiving will break his leg, and then just as calmly reports it has. Whatever one has to bear, one bears, and forbears from complaint.[49]

Of equal importance is the insistence that the first movements are involuntary—they might not ever go away. Since they are involuntary, the sage need not be ashamed of them—just not give in to them by judging appearances as good or bad, or by taking an action rashly. Crucially, erections are first movements. They are no more shameful than jumping when the door slams, or a growling stomach. Julian holds this perspective and Augustine, rather strongly, does not.

For Stoics, foolish reactions to the first movements come from desire and not the will; with a trained will, the wise man rises above desire.[50] Augustine's defense of human nature implies the Stoic distinction between desire and will is unsustainable. Everything is the will for both the wise and the foolish, and their emotions are the same. Emotions are part of God's good creation; anything negative comes from the will. The moral value of an emotion depends on the orientation of the will; if the will is properly directed, the emotions will be laudable.[51] The wise experience emotion with a will oriented to the soul's salvation, and the foolish with a will not so ordered. Even a wise man should feel grief and sorrow at his knowledge of his sinfulness and humanity's fallen state and joy at the thought of salvation.

Augustine rejects *apatheia* and *impatientia* because they imply the trainability of the will. In the process, he defends emotion—when directed toward salvation.[52] He admits we may be overcome by emotions and involuntarily yield to them. All of these uncontrolled emotions are part of this life and will disappear in the next; during this life, we should feel them, as long as they are correctly directed.[53] Seneca would demur that the sage can feel carefully constrained emotions (he gushes over the loving attention he is getting from a younger wife), but would never be dominated by them.

---

49. Seneca, "On Providence," in *The Stoic Philosophy of Seneca*, 30.
50. Aug., *City of God* 14.8.
51. Aug., *City of God* 14.6.
52. Aug., *City of God* 14.9.
53. Aug., *City of God* 14.9.

The description of first movements changes with Christianity. Origen re-casts first movements as pre-passions to describe otherwise unsuitable reactions in the saints, like Abraham's grief for Sarah, or Christ's waverings at Gethsemane. The pre-passions evolve into temptations. Evil thoughts might be provoked by demons, but they remain for Origen involuntary and are not sin. Manuals for desert solitaries even provide exercises to combat one particularly troubling demon (gluttony) by briefly entertaining another (avarice). Lust is seldom at the top of the list: anger and pride are more difficult to conquer. The monk begins with vows of fasting and celibacy; then he has to work on the hard stuff.[54]

The terminology begins to suggest the pre-passions are the initial stages of emotions, which differs significantly from the Stoic idea. As the beginnings of emotions, the first movements are themselves blamable if the emotions associated with them are culpable. The first movements are becoming the occasions of sin. Hunger pangs become tantamount to gluttony. In the fourth century, the monk Evagrius Ponticus puts Origen's bad thoughts into a list of eight temptations: gluttony, fornication, avarice, anger, depression, distress, vainglory, and pride. As the monks have little opportunity for actual sins, even thoughts of these things are dangerous, but they are not quite evil. The first three temptations are desires for things God created: the plants and animals we eat; the bodies of women; silver and gold. They cannot themselves be evil. The desire for them may be immoderate, and overindulgence could be sinful, but thoughts of them cannot be evil.[55] John Cassian uses the categories in the development of western monasticism, and, in the sixth century, Gregory the Great rearranges them into the seven deadly sins.

*Apatheia* comes under attack when Origen is condemned. Origen's Neoplatonic ascent begins with Aristotelian *metriopatheia* before rising to *apatheia*. The possibility of *apatheia* becomes unacceptable at the end of the fourth century. If we can control or eradicate emotions, there is no necessity for grace. By stages, Sorabji believes, Augustine comes to think of first movements as the beginnings of emotions, and equivalent to their consequences. If so, then an erection is not an innocent first movement but a shameful movement, identical to lustful action and independent of the will.

Sorabji observes that lust is central to Augustine's thought; lust is the problem because it is disobedient to our wills. This emphasis rings false to Sorabji, who believes Augustine fails to realize the source of his rejection of

---

54. Meyendorff, *Byzantine Theology*, 68.
55. Clark, *Origenist Controversy*, 77.

lust.[56] Whether Augustine recognized his deeper reasons for his objections or not, the argument he puts forward is less than clear and convincing. This opens Augustine to the Julian attack. Julian notes that while erections may arise involuntarily, it still takes a willful action to have sex. Sorabji believes Julian is the first to separate clearly the command of the will (choosing our desires) from the consent of the will (acting on our desires). The erection no more ineluctably leads to intercourse than a rumbling stomach leads to eating. Sorabji believes Augustine never found a response to Julian's criticism, even if he won the political fight. Sorabji misses the point about impotence. Impotence is not a first movement to be given or denied assent; it is the absence of movement.

Augustine is aware of the role of consent but characteristically uses this to heap further blame on desire. Even if the erection is not acted on, it is still an erection; chastity is not sinlessness if one feels desire.[57] For Julian a desire resisted cannot be a sin, but for Augustine any sexual desire is pollution, its inescapability being a reminder of original sin. Julian does not deny the fact of our desires, but he considers them parts of our good nature. When Augustine obsesses about one of them, Julian concludes Augustine accuses God of creating a flawed nature. Williams credits Julian with being the first Christian writer to understand that the appetites are morally neutral and laments the opportunity lost for the development of western philosophy.[58]

Even in an ascetic age, Augustine's focus on lust is novel. The Stoics, Origen, Clement of Alexandria, and the Egyptian monks consider the full range of human weakness. The desert ascetics worry about gluttony, avarice, and anger while urban Stoics emphasize the temptations of power and pride. An emphasis on one emotion over another is unnatural—all emotions ought to be controlled. Some desires do have a priority. Seneca writes that if a person can look at sex as just a means for reproduction and not a source of pleasure, then other desires for food and drink could be tamed.[59] Nevertheless, sex is not the only thing to be controlled; other temptations exist, in other hierarchies. Seneca declares that if the sage suppresses avarice, then ambition poses no problem. Seneca is no prude; a Roman who served Tiberius, Caligula, Claudius, and Nero would make an unlikely monk.

Augustine distinguishes between sexual desire and all other emotions, not by their sinfulness but their reliability. He points out that we can speak

56. Sorabji, *Emotion and Peace of Mind*, 12, 409
57. Aug., *Marriage and Desire* 1.27.30.
58. N. P. Williams, *Ideas of the Fall*, 343.
59. Seneca, "Consolation of Helvia," 13 (Hadas, 126).

angry words or hit someone even when we are not angry. This is not the case with the sexual organs, which cannot be controlled.[60] They have an independent will and have become an alien intrusion.[61]

Augustine claims that while anger and hunger can be feigned, and the usual actions performed (striking or eating), sex is different; a man cannot fake an erection. Sorabji thinks there is a logical confusion in Augustine's analysis. Just because the will sometimes cannot produce an erection, it does not mean that an erection (however obtained) is not subject to the will in action.[62] Sorabji concludes Augustine has misunderstood first movements. With a proper understanding, he would realize the first thoughts of lust, anger, and gluttony are all first movements, They are not sinful if the will does not assent to them. There is no difference between one sort of first movement or another; the consent of the will is equally required for anger and lust.[63] Augustine's misunderstanding is confined to sexual desire—although he may confuse first movements with emotions, only lust bypasses the will. Arguing that Augustine should have seen the parallel to hunger or thirst misses the point that the objection is not to lust in general but the failure of his particular genitals to respond to it.

Augustine does not understand Julian's attempt to distinguish command and consent; if the genitals submit to the will in the act of consent, why do they not respond to the will?[64] Julian believes neither hunger pangs nor erections are shameful even though neither is under the command of the will. Acting on hunger by eating, or utilizing the erection for sex does require the consent of the will, and may be shameful or not depending on circumstances. Julian does not understand why Augustine does not see it. Augustine cannot see it because the involuntary erection is not the issue—it is the sought-after, but absent, erection. Something that doesn't exist cannot be subject to the will's consent. Since it is obvious that acting on an erection does require the will's consent even if the will did not summon the erection, the case Augustine chooses is the failure to get an erection. We cannot summon erections with a thought, but neither can we will to be hungry or thirsty. We can eat when we are not hungry, punch someone when we are not angry and have sex when we have no overwhelming desire.

Augustine abandons the Stoic position that first movements are not sins because he cannot hope even to get that movement, much less resist it

---

60. Aug., *City of God* 14.19.
61. Loughlin, *Alien Sex*, 208.
62. Sorabji, *Emotion and Peace of Mind*, 380–81.
63. Ibid., 405.
64. Aug., *Answer to Julian* 5.5.20.

before it turns into sin. His anti-Stoical stance places him in an uncomfortable position. He adopts an ascetic life. His celibacy is part of his conversion; he desires more than anything to retire to a community of like-minded individuals separated from the world living a life of simplicity. Even with imperfect monks, he is successful at running a monastic community. All of these actions require a confidence in self-control that his theoretical position denies.

The ascetic movement relies on the Stoic principle that the mind could make rational, controlled, judgments, and thereby moderate, subdue, or eliminate the emotions. Even if the flight to the desert reduced the level of distraction, there would be no point to the seclusion if the monks could not control their emotions. Pelagius appeals to the extremely comfortable Roman elite, so his injunctions to perfection are, like everything else Roman, moderate. His sermons simply assume a person can do good, and not evil; Christians can behave like Christians. Augustine also lectures his congregation about repentance and runs an ascetic community, but has difficulty reconciling these practical actions with his theology of grace.

The fundamental question remains of whether or not people can choose the good and have moral responsibility. The Pelagians argue for capability and responsibility; the possibility of a sinless life exists (even if it is extraordinarily difficult), just as the Stoics assert that *apatheia* and *impatientia* are achievable. However, *impecantia* is a little easier since it allows for successfully resisted temptations, rather than true passionlessness. Augustine dabbled with sinlessness in *Forgiveness of Sins* and had to be circumspect, particularly after Jerome's diatribes. Nevertheless, the temptations of Stoic vocabulary are always there. He encourages his congregation on the path to sinlessness; they should direct their wills, so there is no lust to combat,[65] which is the desert form of the Stoic quest. In *Marriage and Desire*, Augustine sticks to the same theme. It would be best to have no desires (Exod 20:17) but at least we should not allow ourselves to pursue them (Sir 18:30).[66] The former is *apatheia*, the latter, *impecantia*.

---

65. Aug., *Sermon* 151.3.
66. Aug., *Marriage and Desire*, 1.22.24.

# 7

# On Nature

THE DISPUTE ABOUT HUMAN nature revolves around the question of the state of humanity, before and after the Fall. Is human nature good or evil? If good, is it healthy or injured? If injured, how is it injured and what are the consequences? This chapter will look more deeply at Augustine's theory of nature, asking why it has to have the structure he chooses, and how it supports his overall stance. Modern readers seldom have patience with this part of the argument. We no longer feel constrained by Aristotelian categories and the debates over free will and sexuality are of more interest. Nevertheless, for the fifth-century opponents, the character of human nature is central to every controversy.

Given his general pessimism about our injured nature, Augustine's convoluted defense of it can come as a surprise. He has to follow a narrow path. First, he needs consistency with the Neoplatonic philosophical consensus shared by the church. Plato identifies the nature of anything with its intrinsic characteristics, its essence. By definition, the nature of anything is unchangeable: an altered human nature would not be human. Second, he has to ensure no one can accuse him of Manichean dualism. The Manichaean description of humans as a mixture of two material entities, good and evil, provides a convenient description of the conflict in action and intent in human beings but is inconsistent with the goodness of creation. The problem is complex; dualism creeps into any theological discussion giving weight to Satan or original sin. He has to avoid accusations of continued heresy. Third, he wants a solution supporting his overall stance and consistent with creation *ex nihilo* by a good and beneficent God.

His final answer is that human nature is unchanged but is damaged anew in each person by a disordered will. This is expressed by the uncontrollability of sexual desire involved in our conception. Our fundamentally good nature is injured, but the injury comes from outside nature. No matter what else he adds—he must maintain this goodness.

## THE NATURE OF PHILOSOPHERS

Conforming Christian concepts to Greek philosophy remains acutely important to theologians from the church fathers through the Reformation. This obsession is hard for some readers to understand since Greek elements so thoroughly penetrate Christian thought that they are barely discernible as Greek. Augustine's need to treat human nature in this philosophical context is not the only instance of stretching Jerusalem on the Procrustean bed of Athens. The torturing of the two great commandments: to love God and to love one's neighbor (Matt 22:37–39) gives a simpler example. A straightforward reading is that Jesus divides the law into the obligations to God and the obligations to other people. Precisely how we love God and who is our neighbor and what are the duties implied have occupied millennia. Adam Smith points to excessive self-regard as the basic problem; rather than setting the goal of loving our neighbor, we should love ourselves no more than our neighbor can love us.[1]

Ethical speculations are not of first importance if the goal is a Platonized text. There are three loves mentioned: love of God, love of neighbor and love of self. The philosopher begins with the love of self. Eudaimonism, the theory that the goal of life is happiness, is a common idea in classical philosophy. It seems simple enough, but people can be, and usually are, wrong about what makes them happy (or so the philosopher says) and the philosophers themselves disagree. If a person says wealth or power made him happy, he is mistaken. No matter what he thinks, the true goal is something else Plato is glad to tell him. Real happiness includes all the cardinal virtues: prudence, justice, temperance, and courage. A tyrant cannot be happy. The philosopher must cultivate all the virtues. In Aristotelian terms, a person is only truly happy while seeking the highest good, the *summum bonum*. Aristotle defines this as maximizing one's individual talents, seeking excellence, or *arête*, as a citizen of the city.

Plato identifies happiness not with the full range of virtues, or even a single summary virtue like Aristotle's *arête*, but with a mystical ascent. The goal is union with the ideal forms of the Good, the Beautiful, and the

---

1. Smith, *Theory of Moral Sentiments*, Section 1.1.5.

True. As the seeker climbs, he or she would realize all virtues are all fundamentally the same. For a Christianizing Platonist or Platonizing Christian, the road to happiness is also an ascent but the goal is now the Triune God, not an abstract One. Happiness is the goal of self-love, and true happiness is union with God. Any self-love that is not the love of God is an error or misunderstanding; it is essentially self-hate. Augustine agrees all wish to be happy, but true happiness requires a dedication to the highest good, which is God.[2]

The identification of love of self with the love of God makes it hard to squeeze in loving our neighbor. It might seem to a naïve thinker that self-love is on the bottom of a hierarchy. The second great commandment lifts a person up to the love of the neighbor, and the first great commandment is the final goal of the love of God. If the mountaintop and the starting place are the same, there is no room for the middle—loving one's neighbor is meaningless. Augustine says the love of neighbor is a second-hand love of God; our primary duty to our neighbor is to encourage her to achieve her own mystical union with God. Just as self-love is salutary if it means loving God more than yourself, then love for neighbor means bringing her to God.[3] There is only one commandment, to love God.

Altruism makes no sense if every virtuous action is true self-love, that is, the love of God. There is no notion of demonstrating the love of God with the love of the neighbor—only the ascent to God matters. This is a limitation of love, as self-interested as the miserliness of Ebenezer Scrooge. Each of the classical virtues is part of the ascent to God. Temperance is not moderation; it is the desire to achieve perfect continence. Courage is the acceptance of all ills for God's sake. Justice is an understanding of humanity's place in the order of creation, accepting responsibility for the management of the world under God's sovereignty. Finally, prudence is the ability to determine which choices lead more directly to God.[4]

The focus on self-love in Neoplatonic form is an outlandish exegesis. Cramming Greek thought into the gospel text takes priority over understanding Jesus's injunctions in their original context; something is lost in the insistence on a Hellenized view of love. O'Donovan believes the tension between the two commandments is overcome in the universality of God's presence in all creation,[5] but the solution is not entirely satisfactory. The

---

2. Aug., *The Catholic Way of Life* 6.10.
3. Aug., *The Catholic Way of Life* 26.49.
4. O'Donovan, *Resurrection and Moral Order*, 223.
5. Ibid., 226.

Love of Neighbor disappears into the Love of God, rather than maintaining a separate status as one of the great commandments.

Rist is more sympathetic to Augustine's argument from love. Since the love of God is the foundation of all human activity if the will (*voluntas*) is correctly directed, every human action must be interpreted in the context of that love. While we can value lesser goods, we must always understand them in the context of the greatest good.[6] He does not deny the ethical consequence of preferring our neighbor's suffering to damaging our own souls but suggests these oddities make sense in the larger context of Augustine's celebration of love. Nevertheless, Rist concludes Augustine places too much emphasis on the first great commandment at the expense of the second.[7]

Burnaby has a stronger aversion to the consequences of Augustine's analysis. He feels Augustine perverts Luke 6:37–38 into "give and you shall be forgiven." The love of the neighbor becomes merely a means to salvation. If alms are recommended to obtain forgiveness of sins, it suggests we might buy our way to heaven and manipulate God.[8] Burnaby concludes that both ethics and religion are sacrificed to selfishness.[9]

The discussion of "nature" is drenched in even more jargon. In classical philosophy, the nature of anything refers to its *essence*, an abstraction from the characteristics of individual objects. Plato uses the term *eidos* (idea). For Plato, the world of material objects is secondary and inferior to the world of ideas, available only to the mind. Each object in the material world is what it is because it is an imperfect copy of the corresponding ideal object in the world of ideas. Each chair is a chair to the extent that it participates in or resembles the ideal chair; the idea of a chair represents what is common to all chairs and what is superior to each of them. We understand what a chair is because we have an imperfect and incomplete (confused) understanding of the ideal chair. The world of ideas is the *real* world; the sensible world of actual objects is effectively an illusion.

In the *Republic*, Socrates propounds the Allegory of the Cave. He asks his interlocutor Glaucon to imagine prisoners chained from birth in a cave and only allowed to look outward to the cave wall. Behind them is a fire, providing a dim and inconsistent light. They can only see shadows cast upon the wall by the activity behind them. Believing the world of shadows is all of reality, they judge someone by her ability to predict and describe the patterns of shadow. If a prisoner somehow turns to the light, she will

---

6. Rist, *Ancient Thought Baptized*, 159–69.
7. Ibid., 239.
8. Burnaby, *Amor Dei*, 134.
9. Ibid., 255.

initially be unable to comprehend either the fire or the things illuminated by it; gradually she understands. When she leaves the cave and sees the sun, she realizes the sun's light is the source of all things and achieve true clarity. In Plato's view, the sensible world is only the shadow of the intelligible world. The world of ideas is unchanging and permanent while the sensible world is transient and unstable.

In the *Symposium*, Socrates tells the story of Diotima's Ladder—the model of all Platonic ascents. He builds on his audience's familiarity with the physical beauty of an individual, exemplified by the charismatic Alcibiades. He contrasts the appreciation of a particular person's beauty and higher forms, generalizing from one body to all bodies, and then, gradually, to the abstract idea. Climbing higher and higher, the philosopher eventually arrives at the idea of Beauty itself. This is the world of the Good, the Beautiful, and the True that captures the romantic undergraduate; the prosaic prefer Aristotle. Some of Plato's contemporaries find his idealism ridiculous: "I've seen Plato's cups and table, but not his cupness and tableness."[10]

Aristotle rejects the actual existence of the realm of ideas as an unnecessary duplication of reality but retains the notion that there are realities beyond the senses. Instead of the term idea, Aristotle uses the term *morphe* (form). The *form* of something *informs* passive and undifferentiated matter (*hyle*) to make it what it is. There is no ideal chair in an ideal world, but rather there is an underlying design (the form of the chair) of every extant chair making it a chair and not a table. A particular person or thing is a compound of matter and possibly many different forms, creating an *ousia*, or in Latin, *substantia*, substance, or *essentia*, essence. The substance of any thing persists through all change; we grow old, we are injured, but our substance, our nature, our essence, does not change. Although Aristotle's *ousia* is always a combination of form and matter, its unchanging character makes it the functional equivalent of Plato's matter-free *eidos* for some purposes. The concepts are often used interchangeably in Hellenistic thought and are confusing both to the modern reader and the church fathers; there would not have been so many arguments over the terminology if they were clear. Cicero coined Latin term *essentia* as a translation for *ousia*. The different meanings given *ousia* by different schools of thought are confusing enough, and the Latin terms *essentia* and *substantia* do not provide any relief; the reader must do what she can.[11] Confusing in themselves, the terms and the Greek term for matter, *hyle*, are also not good matches for the Hebrew *ruach*, spirit, and *nephesh*, living thing, soul. The Septuagint translates these

---

10. Diogenes of Sinope in Davenport, *7 Greeks*, 183.
11. Hadot, *Philosophy as a way of life*, 75–76.

as *pneuma* and *psyche*. Paul generally uses *sark* for the flesh and *pneuma* for the spirit. A more complicated example is represented by "May the God of peace himself sanctify you entirely; and may your spirit (*pneuma*) and soul (*psyche*) and body (*soma*) be kept sound and blameless at the coming of our Lord Jesus Christ (1 Thess 5:23)."

The mature Augustine retains an underlying Platonic metaphysical framework. The independent realm of ideas is located in the mind of God (specifically in the Logos, the Son), guaranteeing their immutable and eternal character. The picture is of a spare room in the back of God's head, storing ideal chairs, tables, and other furniture, under ideal sheets. A special grace of God provides an intellectual illumination, a divine flashlight allowing a glimpse of true reality. Where Diotima's Ladder speaks of a process of elevating one's gaze from material instantiations to the ideal, Augustine denies we can discover Beauty in the beautiful by ourselves. Only God can provide the final understanding.

The nature (idea, form, substance) of anything is unchangeable. If you change the nature of any species of thing (as Aristotle would put it), it is not the same species. If one alters the nature of a chair, it becomes a stool, a pile of wood, or nothing. We can damage an instantiation of a chair, but the nature of a chair is untouched. The Greeks separated matter from the forms or ideas, so matter does influence actual things. A chair is a chair, but there are strong chairs and weak chairs. The dualist Manicheans point to the evil particles in matter to show how chairs and people can vary. However, the growing belief in creation *ex nihilo* eliminates any solution incorporating a lesser matter. Even the mud formed into Adam is created from nothing and cannot be the source of evil. Human nature is particularly good because Adam is made in God's image. This is difficult enough for a Jewish Platonizer, but the Christians have a further problem. Nicene orthodoxy requires Christ be truly human and truly God. Human nature has to be worthy of the incarnation. Christ is *homoousios* (of the same substance) with man concerning his humanity just as he is *homoousios* with the Father concerning his divinity.[12]

Augustine tries to solve his problem by distinguishing between essential and accidental properties. A chair is a chair whether made of wood, plastic, or steel; the material is not an *essential* feature of a chair but is rather an *accident*. Human nature, as a divinely created *form* or *substance*, is good; original sin is an *accident* adhering in it. His opponents might have agreed that by *voluntarily* sinning, we mar our natures in this way, but it is

---

12. This is the formula of Apollinaris (died 390). A prime example of the adoption of a part of a heretic's ideas.

impossible to be *involuntarily* stained by birth: accidents adhere in our nature over time. Augustine argues accidents are inheritable, giving ill health as an example.[13] He imagines characteristics are transferred in a Lamarckian fashion; the tyrant Dionysius placed a handsome portrait in his wife's sight during sex to improve the appearance of their child. Accidents do not pass from substance to substance directly but by a process of infection. The black skin of an Ethiopian child is not the literal blackness of the parents but is a cloak their bodies impose.[14] In this way, the sin of the father, as represented by the disorderliness of desire, passes by osmosis to the child.

Julian does not accept a transmission of guilt through generation; he cannot see how the will could affect the semen in this way. Augustine's response is infant baptism; if there is no guilt, why do we baptize?[15] Whether or not Julian understands how, the defect *is* passed. The disorderly will injures nature, which acquires an *accidental* defect. The philosophers err when they condemn the flesh—it has an evil; it is not itself evil.[16] Augustine insists concupiscence transmits the *accident* of original sin to God's good *substance*; Julian does not understand how this could happen. According to Aristotle, a migration of accidents is impossible.[17]

However, Aristotle allows for a combination of substances in a single concrete being. For example, the soul is the fundamental form of a living being, plant, or animal. Aristotle postulates a three-fold division of souls of living beings. The nutritive soul is common to plants and animals, enabling them to satisfy their basic needs for growth and reproduction. Animals add the sensitive, or animal, soul, allowing them to interact more fully with the sensible world. Finally, humans also include the rational soul. If sin were a substance, it could combine with other substances in the make-up of humanity. However, in that case, sin would be one of God's good creations, which is preposterous, and the argument fails. The Pelagians conclude there can be no transmission of sin. Pelagius argues that sin is an action, neither a substance nor an accident. He asks, "Is it a substance, or it is a word completely lacking substance, which expresses not some thing, not any existence, not some body, but an act of wrong doing? I believe it is the latter."[18]

---

13. Aug., *Marriage and Desire* 1.34.57.

14. Aug., *Answer to Julian* 5.14.51.

15. Aug., *Answer to Julian* 6.9.24.

16. Aug., *Unfinished Work* 3.189.

17. Beatrice, *The Transmission of Sins*, 32, says Marius Mercator cites this argument of Julian's.

18. Pelagius, *De Natura*, quoted by Augustine in *Nature and Grace* 19.21 (Teske, WSA, I/23, 234).

Sin is what we do, not what we are. This escape from the arid metaphysics of the Greeks contributes to Pelagius's modern popularity.

Part of the tension arises from different notions of the origin of the soul. How exactly does the soul fit into the dichotomies of spirit and flesh? Is the soul partly material or purely immaterial? Greek ideas again form the background. Plato discusses a tripartite division of the soul in the beautiful dialog *Phaedrus*. The soul is likened to a chariot driven by two horses. The driver is the mind, intellect or reason—the part of the soul that yearns to climb Diotima's Ladder. The first horse symbolizes the positive emotions of seeking honor and excellence but also including righteous indignation, courage, and other masculine virtues. The second horse symbolizes the soul's irrational appetites. Only by controlling both horses can the driver achieve the soul's ascent. All the emotions are important parts of the soul; reason tames them but does not discard them. Aristotle has his three-part human soul. Neither of these pictures is a good match for the less theoretically developed notions of soul in the Hebrew or Greek Bibles. Nor is the popular notion of souls surviving after death to be visited by Odysseus or Aeneas easy to conform to the theoretical constructs. Nevertheless, the theologians tried.

The Greek tradition strongly favors the pre-existence of the soul. The soul descends from the spiritual realm into the body. Socrates reasons in the *Meno* that all acquired knowledge in life is the memory of the accumulated knowledge of the pre-existent soul. The soul is attracted to the material world and descends into it, forgetting what it knew. The young Augustine accepts this, as did many of his contemporaries. He writes in *On the Magnitude of the Soul*, "It seems to me that the soul has brought with itself all the arts, and that what is called learning is not else than remembering and recalling." In the *Revisions*, he claims he meant the intellect has contact with immutable things and hence can grasp them by the intellect alone and not the senses.[19] In Manichaeism, the good soul is *sent* from the spiritual realm to contend with evil. For Origen, the fact that human souls *fall* from the spiritual realm into the material realm explains the differing birth outcomes.

Contrasting with this classical idea are two Christian alternatives: traducianism and separate creation. Traducianism is the biological notion that all human souls are present in Adam (as usual women get short shrift) in his semen. It has the advantage of explaining how Adam's guilt is passed to his descendants, but it reeks of Manichaean flawed nature. Separate creation hypothesizes that God creates each soul individually at conception, quickening, or birth. This makes it impossible to inherit original sin unless

---

19. Aug., *Revisions* 1.8(7).2.

it is a produced by birth—the bloodiness of birth being a symbol of the acquisition of a taint. Jerome and the Pelagians are resolute creationists—Julian persists in calling Augustine a traducianist (he can make no sense of original sin otherwise), but Augustine repeatedly denies it.

Augustine never establishes a single clear view—but the logic of avoiding Manichaeism and the need to keep human nature good before the action of the will eliminates any public acknowledgment of traducianism. In *Answer to Julian*, he compares a single traducianism (flesh only) with a double (soul and flesh). He refuses to state a preference. Both spirit and flesh may have been inherited from Adam in their current weakened state, or one corrupts the other.[20] He cannot sustain the idea that the flesh corrupts the spirit since nature, as God's creation, is fundamentally good, so he chooses the other alternative, the spirit corrupts the flesh. This may not seem any more acceptable, but Augustine treats the will as an independent faculty separate from the essential nature in a Platonic sense. The defect in the will is a series of sins passed down through each conception. Julian claims Augustine implies double traducianism since to be human is to have both body and soul. Augustine answers that we speak of Christ being taken down from the cross, not just his body, and asserts he has solved the problem by this synecdoche.[21]

His early post-conversion works use the Neoplatonic metaphor of a descent of a pre-existent soul; he also shows some interest in separate creation. Neither is compatible with original sin because a pre-existent soul could not share Adam's sin or parental taint and a newly created soul would be coming fresh from God's hands. His need to defend original sin means he has to abandon pre-existence and separate creation, but he cannot simply adopt traducianism. In *Letter* 166, written in 415, Augustine criticizes Jerome for his advocacy of fresh creation. If souls are freshly created, how can God justly damn them?[22] In this letter, Augustine summarizes some of the views he had previously analyzed in *On Free Will*. The possibilities are: (1), the soul is derived from Adam's soul; (2), the soul is newly made; (3) the soul pre-exists its material incarnation and is sent to bodies by divine decree; or (4), it glides spontaneously into them. By the time of *Letter* 166, all of these solutions are unsatisfactory because of their relationship to original sin or traducianism. In 416, he repeats his criticism of separate creation to the Roman nobleman, Oceanus, explaining Jerome's error in similar terms. He is

---

20. Aug., *Answer to Julian* 5.4.7.
21. Aug., *Unfinished Work* 2.178.
22. Aug., *Letter* 166.4.10.

unwilling to provide an answer to the question of the origin of the soul. Any clear statement on the soul would be problematic for original sin.[23]

He writes in 420 to Optatus, Bishop of Milevis, to discuss the origin of the soul and the origin of sin. He is still not certain of the mechanism but the fact that the soul of the infant bears Adam's sin is certain.[24] His solution is a mystical analogy. The flesh is propagated through the parents, but God is still the ultimate source. Analogously, the soul is also propagated from the parents while leaving God as the author of all things.[25] *The Nature and Origin of the Soul* is a response to the otherwise obscure Vincent Victor, who supports fresh creation and dislikes the letter to Optatus. Augustine reiterates his earlier points, dismissing Vincent's arguments. However, he does not quite endorse traducianism; he suggests Vincent join him in uncertainty. Otherwise, Vincent runs the risk of falling into the recently discredited Pelagianism.[26]

If the fundamental nature of the flesh is good, and the soul is pre-existent or new, there is no mechanism for the transmission of sin. In his *Revisions*, Augustine repents of his early language in *Against the Academics* favoring the pre-existence of the soul but he retains doubt about the other alternatives. He oscillates and admits he simply does not know.[27] He wonders whether the soul is propagated in the same way as the flesh or, if not, whether it is weighed down by the flesh. If the soul is not propagated, but renewed by God, then God's complicity in guilt might be implied.[28] Eventually, he gives up; the problem is too hard for our limited minds.[29] Keech describes Augustine's failure to explain a non-material transmission of guilt as diplomatic,[30] but no choice available to him is both coherent and safe. He is peeved that Julian keeps bringing up obscure points about the origin of the soul.[31] Julian correctly identifies a weakness of Augustine's theory—there is no completely convincing way to combine a non-traducian theory of the origin of the soul and original sin.

---

23. Aug., *Letter* 180.1.2.
24. Aug., *Letter* 202A.2.6.
25. Aug., *Letter* 202A.5.11.
26. Aug., *The Nature and Origin of the Soul* 1.13.16. Kirwan argues Augustine should have embraced traducianism since it alone could support the notion of an inherited guilt. *Augustine*, 142.
27. Aug., *Revisions* 1.1.3.
28. Aug., *Forgiveness of Sins* 2.36.59.
29. Aug., *Forgiveness of Sins* 3.10.18.
30. Keech, *Anti-Pelagian Christology*, 17.
31. Aug., *Unfinished Work* 2.178.

## THE MANICHAEAN DILEMMA

Augustine and Julian share a common commitment to Greek philosophical roots. However, Augustine has to make a special defense of nature against the Manichaeans with whom he is too easily associated for comfort. His past is frequently used against him—Julian claims that no matter how he squirms, Augustine is still a Manichaean, denigrating the flesh. He has to be consistent with the philosophers—and not be a Manichaean.

In cosmic myth terms, the Manichaeans are mid-way between the Gnostics and the Catholics. For the Gnostics, the evil demiurge is the creator. The demiurge is the lord of this world, the anthropomorphic God of the Hebrew Bible. For the Manicheans, the world comes into being as part of the conflict between good and evil—it is their battleground. Any form of dualism has an easy job in explaining the troubles of human life—it is just part of the cosmic struggle. For the orthodox Christians, creation is unquestionably good, the *ex nihilo* creation of the one God.[32] Introducing weakness and evil in this context is a difficult challenge. The earlier fathers depend on our finitude, immaturity, inattention, and materiality to explain the Fall and our continuing sinfulness. The greater emphasis on the perfection of God's work combined with Greek idealism makes it more difficult to comprehend the human condition in the fifth century.

While Augustine sometimes suggests a flawed nature, he typically modifies his remarks to clarify that although the flesh may be corrupted, it is not corrupting. In *Marriage and Desire,* he puts the ultimate blame on the devil. He writes, "This wound inflicted upon the human race by the devil compels everyone who is born through it to be subject to the devil, as if the devil has the right to pick the fruit from his own tree."[33] He says this is not Manichaeism because the devil is not the source of human nature, but only the source of its defect. Our divinely-created nature is not condemned in itself but for its ruinous defect. He more often describes the wound as self-inflicted rather than by the devil. Even in Eden, the serpent persuades but Adam and Eve choose. Because of their choices, the good of marriage no longer can be produced without the evil of desire. The ability of desire to arouse what the will cannot summon shows it is the most fundamental sin and particularly shameful.[34] We are under the power of the devil because

---

32. Aug., *Answer to Faustus* 21.5.
33. Aug., *Marriage and Desire* 1.23.26 (Teske, WSA, I/24, 45).
34. Aug., *Marriage and Desire* 1.24.27.

we are conceived by concupiscence, which cannot achieve the good of birth without shameful desire.[35]

Augustine's dualism emerges when he makes humanity subject to the devil because it gives the devil the same role in corrupting humanity as the evil matter of Manichaeism or the demiurge of the Gnostics. Augustine thinks the criticism is not apt; the devil does not create any part of human nature, but he injures it by introducing an *accidental* defect, not an *essential* flaw. He is unconvincing on how the devil's temptation of Eve results in concupiscence, but he is clear about the consequences. The soul cannot be made pure in the presence of lust if we ever act on our desires sinfully.[36] While procreation is a good use of an evil, sex for pleasure is an unmitigated evil. Julian thinks the language is inescapably Manichean whether Augustine focuses on Satan or concupiscence; either Augustine is elevating evil to a par with good, or he is describing an evil matter. Julian lists Augustine's condemnation of marriage and sexual desire, and the separation of Christ from his humanity as examples of Augustine's heresies. Julian acquits Augustine of Apollinarianism but insists on his Manichaeism.[37]

The Pelagians relentlessly accuse Augustine of retaining his old Manichaean dualism. The despairing view of humanity caught in the Manichean struggle is replaced by its total depravity caused by original sin and sexual desire, the emblem of primal disobedience. The transmission of sin through intercourse is close to the Manichean view of the entrapment of the good, as Julian will unceasingly maintain.[38] When the Bishop of Eclanum listens to the Bishop of Hippo, he hears a Manichaean. Augustine's story of a nature so damaged that it is unable to choose anything but sin sounds suspiciously like Manichaean nature caught between opposing forces. Julian constantly defends the legitimacy of all human emotions, including sexual desire, when they are moderated. Augustine's sexual revulsion reeks of heresy to Julian, who thinks God's creation must be good in its entirety, including sex.

The problem Augustine faces is nearly insurmountable; anything he says about an inevitable sin can be criticized as Manichaean. In several places, he describes the result of the Fall as a damaged nature. It is Adam and Eve's fault: "So terrible was the sin of these two that, due to their sin, human nature was changed for the worse and was also transmitted to their

---

35. Aug., *Marriage and Desire* 2.5.15.
36. Aug., *Answer to Julian* 5.7.26.
37. Aug., *Unfinished Work* 4.50.3.
38. Lancel, *St. Augustine*, 419, believes Julian's Manichaean attack is purely tactical. Lancel doesn't ask which of *Augustine's* positions are merely tactical, although he notes, "throughout his last twelve years, Augustine was a prisoner of his anti-Pelagian polemic." Ibid., 434.

posterity under the bondage of sin and the necessity of death."[39] He uses the same vocabulary right up to the end of his life; he writes in his *Revision* for *On True Religion* that humanity could have been immortal if sin had not damaged human nature.[40] He occasionally backtracks in case this sounds too Manichean. He denies ever accusing the substance or nature of the flesh.[41] What sounds like self-contradiction is an attempt to appeal to Platonic abstractions and Aristotelean distinctions. God created the *form* of Adam (his *substance*, his *nature*). It could not be evil because Adam is (as Eve is not quite) the image of God. If it is not defective as created, it is not defective now at the level of its form, its nature. If humanity's nature is injured, it must be freshly injured in each person, acquiring an *accident*. Augustine has to locate the source of the ever-renewed injury without blaming nature itself, or its biblical equivalent, the flesh. Nature must remain innocent of fault until it is injured, and yet it *has* to be injured.

Julian claims Augustine is not a Catholic because Catholics believe sin is an act of will, but Augustine and the Manichaeans derive it from an evil nature.[42] In Greek thought, the mind is higher than the body; our bodies cannot force us to sin. Reason is the highest part of human nature, the rational soul. It distinguishes us from animals and has to be able to dominate the animal and nuitritive souls. Julian hears Augustine as a Manichaean because Julian believes human nature and the will are both undamaged. If Adam and Eve could have remained sinless, then so can their descendants, who have the added benefit of the law and the example of Christ. For Augustine, disordered desire is a defect of the will that corrupts the flesh and injures human nature.

Julian cannot follow Augustine's innovation in separating human will from human nature, and even Augustine is sometimes muddled. In the early *On Genesis against the Manichaeans* Augustine's says sins harm only one's own nature and not anyone else's nature. He later retracts this, explaining, "Infants, who after all possess human nature, contract original sin, because human nature sinned in the first human beings, and that it is on this account that no sins but their own have harmed human nature."[43] To the extent that this is coherent, it is traducianism and seminal guilt, which he usually avoids.

---

39. Aug., *City of God* 14.1 (Babcock, WSA, I/7, 99). See also, for example, *Marriage and Desire* 1.32.37 and *Answer to Julian* 3.26.60.
40. Aug., *Revisions* 1.13(12).8.
41. Aug., *Answer to Julian* 6.23.74.
42. *Unfinished Work* 1.24.
43. Aug., *Revisions* 1.10(9).3 (Ramsey, WSA, I/2, 54).

Julian attempts to force Augustine into the Manichean mold by saying Augustine must assign blame either to the creator or to procreation itself. He asks who sins—God, the parents, or the newborn. He declares Augustine has not identified sin in anyone. God directly creates Adam and Eve; the form of their descendants comes from God, whether inherited or freshly created. There is no room for sin. Augustine has no answer in Julian's terms. He retreats behind Paul; eventually Julian will have to admit he has no way around what Augustine thinks is Paul's clear doctrine.[44] Augustine retreats to these bald assertions of authority frequently; Paul, Cyprian, and Ambrose are his favorite choices.

Augustine cannot permit himself to be associated with a defective or even mixed human nature; he insists nature is good, but the will is defective. Before the Fall, Adam and Eve have the ability to obey or not obey, but their descendants lose the ability. The untutored Manichaean will is incapable of *reliably* controlling human actions but *occasionally* does good. The Augustinian will is less capable; not only is it unable to choose the good consistently but also can never choose the good. Even if people other than the elect appear to be doing good, without the correct faith their will is not properly oriented, and their good deeds are sins.[45]

Augustine pays the price of being more pessimistic than the Manichaeans because he wants a universally impotent will. Adam's pride leads to his disobedience but for his descendants the source is in the disorder of desire. The desire of the parents mysteriously transmits the sin to the children, whose conception stains their flesh. Although he desperately wants this argument to be about the disordered will, the erectionalized account he gives makes it hard for Julian to hear anything other than an assertion of a fault in human nature. Augustine never escapes this trap.

Bonner compares the Pelagian emphasis on teaching and the law to the Manichaean program of gradual control of the self. Both assume that with education or enlightenment, we have the ability to follow the correct path.[46] This general program is also the program of the Stoics, the Platonists, and the monks in the desert—all believe enlightenment can and will lead to control of the flesh.

---

44. Aug., *Unfinished Work* 2.29.

45. Aug., *Answer to Julian* 4.3.25.

46. Bonner, *St. Augustine*, 174. If depending on illumination is a fault, it is shared by Augustine.

## THE BIG PICTURE

The third thread to pull on is Augustine's overall theological objective. Without the double burden of Greek philosophy and a Manichean past, it would be easy to say the Garden sin *does* damage human nature. In modern terms, the Fall introduces a genetic flaw, passed down like mitochondrial DNA from generation to generation.[47] There are scriptural texts supporting the hypothesis, but the idea does not satisfy Augustine. A flawed body reflects only the damage and not the guilt. Being lame is a weakness, but it is not a sin. If we actively injure our own good natures, the will's perversity requires an explanation. Augustine finds its source in the dominance of sexual desire exemplified by the uncontrollability of the erection. His carefully constructed view of human nature is the foundation of the impotence of the will, absent explicit grace.

If nature itself has become defective, then the Pelagians argue that human weaknesses would be part of our nature. If they are natural, they are not sin. A stone falling to the earth is responding to its nature; it is not a moral failing. Caelestius defends the possibility of human sinlessness in his *Definitions*, arguing the unnatural can be avoided. Augustine replies that he agrees sin is not natural, but human nature has a defect.[48]

Augustine turns to Paul; "All of us once lived among them in the passions of our flesh, following the desires of flesh and senses, and we were by nature children of wrath, like everyone else (Eph 2:3)." Our will is of useless unless grace heals it. We are children of wrath because our conception is mediated by sexual desire.[49] This text is one of Augustine's favorites, but critics dispute its meaning. N. P. Williams treats the issue contemptuously. If the text is understood properly, there is no support for original sin; nature does not have the Greek technical meaning here, and the children of wrath are just the people with whom God is angry.[50]

Augustine initially describes Pelagius as being on his side in the defense of nature. He comments on Pelagius's *De Natura*: "I found in it a man aflame with ardent zeal against those people who ought to lay the blame for their sins on the human will, but try to excuse themselves by laying the blame on human nature."[51] However, Augustine means that Pelagius is anti-Manichean; when he goes beyond that to defend free will, Augustine thinks

---

47. If the fault were in our mitochondria, it would be our mothers' and not our fathers' fault; a result that Jerome might have preferred, but not Augustine.

48. Aug., *The Perfection of Human Righteousness* 2.3.

49. Aug., *Forgiveness of Sins* 2.10.14–2.10.15.

50. N. P. Williams, *Ideas of the Fall*, 113.

51. Aug., *Nature and Grace* 1.1 (Teske, WSA, I/23, 225).

he has gone too far. They agree the will is to blame but their concepts of nature and the will are wildly different. The Pelagian defense of human nature is broader than Augustine's, just as their shallow Fall is less consequential. They feel there is no change in human nature or capabilities to explain. All of us, including Adam, have a will that can sin or not sin. The Pelagians believe praise and blame derive from what we do, not from anything we are at birth. We are begotten without virtue or vice and are born similarly; until we make willful choices, we are what God created.[52] The will creates sin, but the *individual* must sin; it is insufficient for the father to have sinned with his concupiscence.

Augustine wants us to be born with sin and guilt, but he has a vocabulary problem. Much of his language implies human nature has been damaged, a conclusion he wants to avoid. He needs to shift the blame. He quotes Vergil on the corporeal origin of sins but responds that the corruption of the body is not the cause but the result of sin; it is the soul that opens the flesh to corruption.[53] Our created flesh is good but it is immediately corrupted by the will at conception. Corruption belongs to the will. His further difficulty is that the corrupt will belongs to the parents, in particular, the father. Nevertheless, it corrupts the child.

This corruption has to be located carefully in the sequence of events in the Garden. He is adamant Adam and Eve did not feel sexual desire before the Fall. They would have been happy, healthy, and placid. The same serenity would have been the inheritance of their descendants. Humanity would have calmly increased in number until the missing ranks of the fallen angels were filled with the predestined elect.[54]

There has to be a sin inserted to corrupt the flesh, yet the sin cannot be the *result* of a defect in nature, it has to be the *cause* of that defect. Since Augustine makes the whole of human destiny hang on the first sin, he has to explain how eating fruit can be so portentous. The sin cannot be in the fruit because the fruit is part of God's creation. He concludes Adam's disobedience is significant because the prohibition would have been trivially easy to obey.[55] Like Augustine's theft of the pears in his neighbor's garden, the insignificance of the sin symbolizes a deeper disruption in the will.

A disobedience of the will proceeds the physical act of disobedience in the garden. Pride leads the first couple to exalt their independence over

52. Aug., *Unfinished Work* 2.6.6.

53. Aug., *City of God* 14.3.

54. See, for example, *City of God* 14.10 and *Revisions* 1.13(12).8. Augustine thinks number of replacement souls is nearly met; analyzing Ecclesiastes 3:5, he concludes the time for embracing is over. *Two Letters* 1.13.

55. Aug., *City of God* 14.12.

their obedience to God. The willful thought of disobedience is more important than eating the fruit. Sounding like Origen, Augustine postulates that if Adam and Eve had stayed focused on the unchanging God, and not turned away, Eve would have ignored the serpent and Adam would not have followed her suggestions.[56]

God forms human nature, and it is not naturally defective. For Adam and Eve, the act of pride is the moment the defect enters their nature. A modified approach is needed for their descendants since we cannot depend on the snake tempting each of us individually. Augustine argues the punishment of the disobedience in the garden has to be disobedience. Before the Fall, Adam can do anything he wants because his will is properly oriented; there are things he could not have done, but a correctly directed will never chooses such things. After the Fall, this changes. Adam did not do what he could have done, and we now cannot do what we want to do. With a misdirected will, we always choose inappropriately. The disobedience that is the punishment of disobedience is the inability to control sexual desire; we have lost control of our minds, our desires, and our bodies.[57]

Augustine's sexualization of the Fall provides a universal way for sin to re-enter our nature. The primal disobedience is replicated in every generation by generation itself. A voluntary sin is a sin that is only sin; concupiscence is the sin that keeps on sinning. It is the source, via conception, of the rebellion preventing humanity from doing as it wills.

Original sin is not technically a voluntary sin—it is created and transmitted by sexual desire, the sin that is also the punishment of sin. Kirwan does not believe this makes any sense; Augustine is making a category error, a sin cannot be the punishment of sin.[58] Augustine needs this error, however. It allows him to explain away his early free will expressions. Concupiscence is the involuntary sin that is the punishment of sin. All other sins are voluntary. Augustine uses similar words in many places: "there I wanted that sin to be understood which is not also the punishment of sin."[59]

It is a difficult concept for Julian; he pours out his complaint in *To Florus*. Saying sin is natural would make the devil humanity's creator and God unjust. It would destroy free choice and reason, which protect the church from error. Augustine's original sin forces us into sin all our lives; it even contaminates the saints. Augustine makes God's creation, human nature, corrupt and incapable of obedience, rendering God a tyrant. Finally,

---

56. Aug., *City of God* 14.13.
57. Aug., *City of God* 14.15.
58. Kirwan, *Augustine*, 135.
59. Aug., *Revisions* 1.16(15).2 (Ramsey, WSA, I/2, 76).

Augustine's appeal to the genitals is impious and itself shameful.[60] After adding some further insults, Julian states his position positively. God is just and fair; he would not command what is impossible, the scriptures cannot be interpreted to falsify his justice, and he is always just. He creates humanity in a state of innocence, without sin, and they are capable of maintaining virtue.[61] Julian says Augustine supports the Manichean doctrine of an evil intrinsic to nature; either Augustine is making the devil the creator of humanity (like other dualists) or he is attributing sin to God. Augustine replies the flesh is good, but it is now injured. It begins perfect, but it acquires a defect through an act of the will.[62]

For Augustine, the fundamental error of Pelagius is his over-confidant estimate of human nature. Pelagian nature is intact; discipline can scrape off the rust of ignorance and habit and reach for higher goals. O'Donovan incautiously describes Augustine as saying Pelagius underestimates how much the Fall damages human nature.[63] Julian repeatedly accuses Augustine of this, in contradiction to God's goodness and logic. Our nature is God's creation and is necessarily good. Augustine rejects the accusation utterly, at least when he is careful. The Manicheans believe the soul is a mixture of good and evil. The Neoplatonic view has a similar duality; the soul is a mixture of being and non-being. Neither approach works for Augustine; he must affirm that human nature is good. The problem has to be elsewhere. He locates the failure in the will, which corrupts the flesh. He separates the will from the Aristotelean description of nature so it can act independently. Julian cannot fit this novelty into the Greek philosophical framework. The chain of desire links the damage to the Fall. Adam and Eve fall, but their descendants keep digging the hole deeper.

When nature is used in its technical sense, both sides agree it is the same in and out of Eden. For Augustine, our good nature is subsequently corrupted by conception. For the Pelagians, we are unchanged and face the same choices and circumstances as Adam. Augustine believes concupiscence has so corrupted our good nature that it requires an act of grace to choose any good. The Pelagian belief in a rusted, but polishable, nature, make it a human responsibility to clean up our acts. One of Augustine's favorite proof texts is 1 Cor 4:7, "What do you have that you did not receive?

60. Aug., *Unfinished Work* 3.67–3.74. Julian's cry is pained: "You ask me why I would not consent to the idea that there is a sin that is part of human nature. I answer it is improbable. It is untrue. It is unjust and impious. It makes it seem as if the devil were the maker of men." Translation by Brown, *Augustine of Hippo*, 390.
61. Aug., *Unfinished Work* 3.82.
62. Aug., *Unfinished Work* 3.141.
63. O'Donovan, *The Problem of Self-love*, 99.

And if you received it, why do you boast as if it were not a gift?" For Augustine, this means any human action depends on individual acts of grace; anyone who believed otherwise is making himself equal to or superior to God. The Pelagians interpret it differently; we *have* received grace: creation, the gift of reason, the granting of the law, and the example of Christ.

Charles E. Raven's defense of natural religion provides a modern analog of the divide between Augustine and Pelagius. By the time of the Enlightenment, nature refers to the whole of creation, rather than to the essence of humanity; it is the nature of Rousseau and Wordsworth. Raven celebrates nature and hopes to derive theological insight from it, recognizing in nature an evolutionary principle, mediated by the Holy Spirit, which forms his theodicy. He notes Karl Barth considers any natural religion as at least heretical and possibly self-contradictory. If Augustine is correct about human nature, no recourse to reason and reflection is possible; belief to the contrary is a denial of the need for grace.[64] Raven comments ironically that Europeans think the British are all Pelagians because Pelagius was Welsh, and the British refuse to become Barthians.[65]

---

64. Raven, *Natural Religion*, Vol. 1, 1.
65. Ibid., 213.

# 8

# On the Will

WHETHER OR NOT AUGUSTINE successfully defends his theory of damaged nature, he has a similar challenge with respect to the capabilities of the will and the possibility of human righteousness. If people are free to choose, then they bear responsibility for their actions. If they do not have the ability to choose, then it is difficult to hold them responsible. The early church leans in the direction of freedom and responsibility. Theophilus of Antioch writes, "For God has given us a law and holy commandments; and every one who keeps these can be saved, and, obtaining the resurrection, can inherit incorruption."[1]

Augustine begins with an anti-Manichean defense of the will's capabilities that is fully consistent with Origen and the early church; he then moves through several stages to the impotence of the will. He later asserts he has always been consistent in his meaning; the will is helpless without grace. Nevertheless, his critics use his earlier words against him. The following sections present the early and late forms of his statements on the will; the reader can decide whether Julian is right to charge him with contradiction.

## AUGUSTINE FAVORS FREEDOM

Different schools of thought mean different things by the will and by free will. Platonic will is inevitably oriented to the good—it is not the will if it is not. The question of its freedom does not arise; if the will is not free, it is not the will. A person fails to use his will correctly only if subordinate goods are

---

1. Theophilus of Antioch, *To Autolycus,* 2.27 (Dods, 105).

confused with the true good. Only ignorance or insanity limits the will—there are no other excuses. The moral conflict is in some ways trivial in Greek philosophy; it is all education and discipline. Both the Hebrew and Greek scriptures have deeper concerns. If we make incorrect choices out of ignorance, we discover we cannot easily retrace our steps, even when we understand our mistakes. The Pelagians attribute this to habit, Augustine to original sin.

In Romans, Paul describes a person as divided into contraries. The substance of one central dispute over Romans is the explanation of this inner conflict. For Pelagius, the creation, the history of God's dealings with humanity, the law, and Christ are sufficient to re-energize the will, remove the rust of ignorance, and dislodge the acquired habits. The Manichaeans think waves of grace in the form of instructors such as Jesus and Mani will awaken the conflicted soul and lead to its unification. Augustine's final answer is that only unmerited grace can do the job—the notion of a will is a fiction. While this is his final view, it is not where he appears to start.

The early writings provide an outline of a near-perfect Pelagian position; indeed, Brown describes Augustine as "on paper, more Pelagian than Pelagius."[2] In his debate with the Manichaean Fortunatus, Augustine declares the will has to have full power. Otherwise, there is no justice in punishment, no merit in good deeds, no relevance for penace, and no forgiveness of sins.[3] Sin does not derive from evil matter but by our free choices.[4] He completes the Pelagian theory by emphasizing the power of habit. Initially, we can choose our actions freely. Later, we find habit is so strong we cannot undo our original voluntary choice.[5] Augustine substitutes habit for Manichean evil matter.[6] He nearly says habits are unbreakable, but ends up supporting free will. He considers Mt 12:33, "Either make the tree good, and its fruit good; or make the tree bad, and its fruit bad; for the tree is known by its fruit." He concludes we must decide to make the tree good or bad.[7]

In the first book of *On Free Will*, he adopts the standard Greek position that the mind controls the body; the higher dominates the lower.[8] Plato argues that a person who has not established the superiority of the mind has not adopted virtue as the guiding principle of the soul—the chari-

---

2. Brown, *Augustine of Hippo*, 141.
3. Aug., *Debate with Fortunatus* 2.20.
4. Aug., *Debate with Fortunatus* 2.21.
5. Aug., *Debate with Fortunatus* 2.22.
6. BeDuhn, *Augustine's Manichaean Dilemma*, Vol. 2, 345.
7. Aug., *Debate with Fortunatus* 2.22.
8. Aug., *On Free Will* 1.10.20.

oteer has dropped the reins. Nevertheless, a person *can* and *must* establish the mind's control and pick up the reins. We have a duty to place spiritual things above material and the capability to do so; this leads to our deepest happiness.[9] A person's freely chosen actions shape her life and are rewarded or punished accordingly with happiness or unhappiness.[10] God gives us free will so punishment will be just.[11] Adam's descendants can make a better use of their will than Adam did. If a person turns to God, God does not stand in the way but extends help.[12] A sinner must take responsibility for his actions. Our natures do not force us to sin; we choose to sin.[13] If an irresistible force compels us[14] or if an uncontrollable fever overtakes us,[15] there is no sin.

Augustine evaluates the role of free will within different theories of the soul's origin: traducianism, fresh creation, and pre-existence. In all cases of interest, the will is free. He dismisses the traducianist concept of a single soul, inherited like the flesh since that would too easily provide a common ownership of sin and a limitation of grace. The idea is inherently contradictory: a single soul cannot both be given and denied grace.

If the soul is freshly created for each person, then it will have sufficient natural goodness to regain Adam's state. He says that "before there has been any merit gained by any good work," God gives us the power to determine the proper way to live and the knowledge that we must strive for the good.[16] If the soul shirks its responsibility, it can justly be punished for failing to strive.

If the soul exists prior to its combination with the body, then it ought to seek salvation by its own efforts to restore its previous state. It must learn what it has forgotten, persevering, and seeking God's aid.[17] In both cases, the soul has the obligation to strive to do good and banish ignorance. If we begin in darkness, we can seek the light and ascend to true happiness.[18] If a person neglects study and piety, he deserves the state of ignorance. God

9. Aug., *Two Souls* 13.20. The Manichees speak of two minds, two wills, or two natures, competing for control, but never two souls. Bonner points out that whether the Manichees believe in two souls or not, Augustine may honestly think they do. "Augustine's Doctrine of Man," 497.

10. Aug., *On Free Will* 1.10.30.

11. Aug., *On Free Will* 2.1.3.

12. Aug., *On Free Will* 3.20.55.

13. Aug., *On Free Will* 3.15.46.

14. Aug., *On Free Will* 3.18.50.

15. Aug., *On True Religion* 14.27.

16. Aug., *On Free Will* 3.20.56. (Burleigh, 204).

17. Aug., *On Free Will* 3.20.57.

18. Aug., *On Free Will* 3.22.64.

has given him sufficient power and provides additional aid along the road to enlightenment.[19]

Many scholars detect a shift between the first two books of *On Free Will* and the third book, written perhaps as late as 396. Babcock argues justice requires free will and human agency, both of which are well represented in the first two books. By the third book, however, human agency becomes problematic.[20] Augustine begins in Book 3 with something resembling Pelagian habit. He argues, "It is not to be wondered at that man, through ignorance, has not the freedom of will to choose to do what he ought . . . in the face of carnal custom, which, in a sense, has grown as strong, almost, as nature, because of the power of mortal succession."[21] This is consistent with the support for free will in the earlier books. However, Augustine immediately undercuts it by confining it to Eden; full free will applies only to Adam before the Fall.

Harrison, on the other hand, maintains all of *On Free Will* is consistent with the primacy of grace; any indications to the contrary are misunderstandings. Harrison sees a hint of the need for unmerited grace in the phrase "before there has been any merit gained," which Augustine applied in the case of a freshly created soul.[22] The surface words only represent, she believes, Augustine's continuing self-defense against the Manichaeans, as he states in the *Revisions*. The deep meaning is always grace; the will is always prepared by the Lord.[23] He denies the Pelagians can refer to his earlier work for their arguments. He admits he said the will makes both good and bad choices, but the will is misdirected without unmerited grace. The ungraced will makes bad choices; the graced will makes good ones.[24]

Augustine does not present an argument. He acknowledges the will is the mechanism by which humanity sins or is righteous, but this is the vacuous meaning of *voluntas*. By definition, all acts are voluntary because they are done by that faculty of the soul. He simply asserts the will does not have the capacity to do good without grace. He claims his opposition to Pelagian ideas pre-dates Pelagius's arrival on the scene.[25] He does have to make some excuses; the early anti-Manichean *Answer to Adimantus* clearly states we have the duty and capability to change the direction of the

---

19. Aug., *On Free Will* 3.22.65.
20. Babcock, "Sin, Penalty and Responsibility," 225–226.
21. Aug., *On Free Will* 3.18.52 (Burleigh, 201–202).
22. Harrison, *Rethinking Augustine's Early Theology*, 198–237.
23. Aug., *Revisions* 1.9(8).2.
24. Aug., *Revisions* 1.9(8).4.
25. Aug., *Revisions* 1.9(8).6.

will.[26] He amends himself; we have the power to change our will but only if we have been given the gift of the power to do so. He cites those whom "he gave power to become children of God (John 1:12)" in support of this argument.[27]

Djuth is a firm defender of the consistency of Book 3 of *On Free Will*. She objects to the notion that ancient or modern critics have a better understanding of Augustine's works than he expresses in the *Revisions*. Augustine's path, she maintains, correctly steers between the Manichaean and Pelagian extremes. There is only one Augustine, who maintains a consistent theory of the will, evolving along with his growth.[28] Nevertheless, it is hard to avoid the conclusion that his early work places the responsibility for sin on the sinner. The difficulty this later puts him in is comical. Having argued the will is only free to sin, he has trouble explaining efforts to control and discipline behavior, whether in the congregation or the monastery. In *Rebuke and Grace*, he twists himself into knots to approve the rebuking of a lazy monk, even though the rebuke cannot move the monk to repentance or change his predestined state. In the *Gift of Perseverance*, he suggests manipulating the congregation into obedience.[29]

In the middle 390s, Augustine drifts toward the great renunciation of the freedom of the will in *Simplician*. In his *Propositions from Romans* he discusses the stages of grace in Origenist terms. First is the grace (*gratia*) freely offered to all in the call (*vocatio*), and the divine aid (*adiutorium*) given to those who freely respond to the call of grace. Harrison thinks this defense of the will is not heartfelt; it contradicted his deep beliefs that had only been confirmed by life as a priest and bishop.[30] Already by 394, she detects his retreat from the merit of faith beneath his attempts to maintain it, but he does still hold on. He addresses Rom 3:20, "for through the law comes knowledge of sin," and sounds like Origen. Augustine writes, "Such statements must be read, with great care, so that the Apostle seems neither to condemn the Law nor to take away man's free will."[31]

Fredriksen traces Augustine's retention of the human role in the beginning of faith in this period to the influence of the Donatist Tyconius. Tyconius's *Book of Rules* provides methods of interpretation integrating the Septuagint translations of the scriptures and Paul. Augustine's study

26. Aug., *Answer to Adimantus* 26.1.
27. Aug., *Revisions* 1.22(21).4.
28. Djuth, "Hermeneutics of *De Libero Arbitrio*," 289.
29. Aug., *Gift of Perseverance* 22.57.
30. Harrison, *Rethinking Augustine's Early Theology*, 142.
31. Aug., *Propositions from Romans* 13–18.1 (Landes, 5).

of Tyconius helps him break free of the Manichaean prejudice against the Hebrew Bible and is formative in the development of his attitude towards Jews.[32]

Augustine introduces four states of man: before the law (*ante legem*), under the law (*sub lege*), under grace (*sub gratia*), and in peace (*in pace*). In the first stage, we pursue desire. Under the law, we are pulled by desire but resist. Under grace, we neither pursue desire nor are pulled by it. Finally, in peace there is no desire remaining. Moving from being under the law is the beginning of faith, and is initiated by human petitioning. The sinner should seek the aid of Christ. When we pray for assistance, grace is granted; our prior sins are forgiven and help is given.[33] This is semi-Pelagian; we confess our weakness, ask for grace, and the request is answered. He has a Pelagian answer to Rom 7:15, "I do not understand my own actions. For I do not do what I want, but I do the very thing I hate." This is not a denial of free will because it represents Paul or another person under the law, not under grace. Augustine maintains we freely choose to believe and receive grace in the form of aid in return, which helps us not to sin.[34]

The distinction between being *sub gratia* and *sub lege* is common to many commentators, but it is also a source of confusion. Origen understood Romans 7 as applying either to a recent convert who is still establishing control over his body or to Paul before the road to Damascus.[35] Cassian, in his *Twenty-Third Conference*, suggests Paul speaks of himself but the sins into which the holy fall are those of distraction (similar to Origen's primal sin of falling away from God) rather than of action (theft, murder, adultery, etc.). For Cassian, a state of sinlessness is achievable, prescinding from such losses of concentration. Augustine later abandons this view, saying he had subsequently concluded the words apply to Paul, even under grace, not only under the law.[36] Paul never escapes the war in the members, particularly the sin that is the punishment of sin, sexual desire. Dodaro argues Augustine's change of perspective reflects his growing pessimism about the depth of human corruption, and the impossibility of even Paul to transcend the emblem of sin, sexual desire.[37]

Augustine's early solution to the problem of Jacob and Esau is that God foreknows but does not predestine. God hates Esau because he foreknows

---

32. Fredriksen *Augustine and the Jews*, 157–69.
33. Aug., *Propositions from Romans* 13–18.7.
34. Aug., *Propositions from Romans*, 44.1–44.3.
35. Origen, *Commentary on Romans* 6.9.4.
36. Aug., *Revisions* 1.23(22).1
37. Dodaro, "Ego miser homo," 142–44.

that Esau will freely sin. He loves Jacob because he knows who will make the free choice to believe, earning the merit of faith. Augustine accepts both God's aid and the grace-earning merits of faith: "Belief is our work, but good deeds are his who gives the Holy Spirit to believers."[38] God will add compassion and good works to the believer. Pharaoh deserved the hardness of his heart because of his prior lack of faith; faith initiates grace, lack of faith, penalty. He interprets Rom 9:16, "So it depends not on human will or exertion, but on God who shows mercy," in a way that maintains freedom. If we freely believe, God is merciful; if we refuse to believe, punishment will follow.[39] This is later modified; grace must be independent of even foreseen merits or faults.[40]

God provides the call and adds his mercy, but the *initium fidei* is human. God spares those who repent their sins and allows punishment to fall on those who spurn his call. The evil befalling a believer is explained as discipline and instruction.[41] Augustine allows for the free acceptance or rejection of God's call and declares that the worst of heretics may repent and return to the fold of the church.[42] This generosity is extended even to baptized Christians who profane the Holy Spirit if they repent.[43]

Harrison concedes that if the answering of God's call in the *initium fidei* is a human capability then God's subsequent grace might be a merited reward.[44] Nevertheless, she says this delicate mechanism of the *initium fidei* is an ultimately futile effort to stay within the conventional doctrines of human capability.[45] The traditional reading has been that he begins as Pelagian, moving to a semi-Pelagian position in the mid-390s. She believes these are only wobbles and waverings from his true faith. In her view, Augustine never abandons his conviction that the unaided human will is incapable of good.

It is also possible to see the early 390s as a continuation of the anti-Manichaean effort. He barely holds off Fortunatus in a two-day debate in the summer of 392, not long after his ordination.[46] As a result, he feels

---

38. Aug., *Propositions from Romans* 60.12 (Landes, 33).

39. Aug., *Propositions from Romans* 62.1.

40. Aug., *Revisions* 1.23(22).1–1.23(22).4. Calvin admits the notion of foreseen merits as a basis of grace was the belief of Origen, Ambrose, and Jerome. *Institutes of the Christian Religion* 2.3.22.8.

41. Aug., *Unfinished Commentary on Romans* 9.10.

42. Aug., *Unfinished Commentary on Romans* 15.16.

43. Aug., *Unfinished Commentary on Romans* 16.1–16.8.

44. Harrison, *Rethinking Augustine's Early Theology*, 137.

45. Ibid., 141.

46. So argue Fredriksen, *Augustine and the Jews*, 142–48, and BeDuhn, *Augustine's*

the need to defend Nicene Christianity by restoring the Hebrew Scriptures (in their Septuagint form) to canonical status and by rescuing Paul from the extensive Manichaean exegesis. His solution is narrowly drawn to meet those objectives. The law is saved, and Romans 7 brought into analytical coherence by conceding much of the Manichaean perspective in a modified presentation. Humanity is, in general, a plaything of its desires, but this is indecisiveness, not a civil war between two material natures. The law is not the product of the evil god, but a necessary stage in human development. The law does not cause sin but makes us aware of transgression, preparing the way to an acknowledgment of sinfulness, a prerequisite for confessing need and the beginning of faith. By using the language of habit, and allowing the *initium fidei* to remain within human power, Augustine remains in touch with the precedents established by Origen, Ambrose, and the overall Nicene church. Human responsibility is (barely) saved by the answer or refusal of the call; God's justice is similarly (barely) recognized in the offering of a refusable call.

Augustine's junior status is a final element of his tentativeness in the 390s. Sometime in 394 or 394 his boss, the bishop Valerius, decided to have him consecrated as a coadjutor bishop, an even more uncanonical idea than his use of Augustine as a preacher in his church. The Primate of Numidia, Megalius, rose in opposition to Augustine, partly on the grounds of his Manichaean past. Exactly how the matter was resolved is unclear, but eventually, probably after a declaration of faith to an episcopal council, Megalius consecrated Augustine in 396. BeDuhn speculates that the central books of the *Confessions*, in which Augustine describes his Manichaean period, represent a reworking of his defense.[47] His consecration gives him independence. He becomes convinced that God's omnipotence and sovereign freedom makes it impossible to imagine anyone refusing God's call. We cannot prepare ourselves for a call and cannot refuse it if it comes. Whether it is God's omnipotence or his own impotence that drives him, after his consecration he shows his hand.

## AUGUSTINE RETREATS

When Augustine shifts his apparent position, he leaves behind sufficient evidence to allow scholars to choose what they want.[48] Nevertheless, Au-

---

*Manichaean Dilemma*, Vol. 2, 122–63. Lancel, on the other hand, thinks Augustine won easily. *St. Augustine*, 154–55.

47. BeDuhn, *Augustine's Manichaean Dilemma*, Vol. 2, 239–73.
48. See, for example, the discussion in Taylor, *The Whole Works*, Vol. 7. 566–67.

gustine moves away from his original position decisively in his responses provided to his old mentor Simplician shortly after his consecration in 396. In his response to Simplician's first question, he initially recapitulates his position of 394. We do not have the capacity in ourselves to be righteous, but we can turn to God, who will provide the necessary strength.[49]

He lays the groundwork for a more negative view in his answer to the second question. He earlier used God's foreknowledge to explain the distinction between Jacob and Esau, but the difficulty is how to distinguish between foreknowledge of faith and foreknowledge of works. Foreknowledge of works sounds too much like merit, but how is the foreknowledge of faith different?[50] Thinking it through, he begins with a semi-Pelagian position that we can exercise the will even without a call. If our will is meaningless, he asks rhetorically, what would the injunction "Do you not know that in a race the runners all compete, but only one receives the prize? Run in such a way that you may win it (1 Cor 9:24)" mean?[51]

Doubt enters with Rom 9:16, "So it depends not on human will or exertion, but on God who shows mercy." He then invokes a different letter: "work out your own salvation with fear and trembling; for it is God who is at work in you, enabling you both to will and to work for his good pleasure (Phil 2:12–13)." He emphasizes the second part (God's work within us) over the first (the need to work out our own salvation). Even the presence of a good will is a result of God's work. Our will is not sufficient for us to live righteously unless we receive God's aid. Augustine temporarily allows we have some role; we must accept God's grace and mercy. This sounds symmetrical, but even assent requires God's prior call.[52] Later, Augustine makes clear the call is only for the predestined; there is no general call, open to all. Only the elect can run the race, and keep the faith: "I, in fact, strove on behalf of the free choice of human will, but God's grace conquered."[53] Fredriksen declares that even if Augustine's abandonment of freedom astonishes modern readers, this transformation presents us with the Augustine of history.[54] He shakes off the optimistic superstructure of his philosophical training and can be himself, defiantly helpless.

---

49. Aug., *Simplician* 1.1.14. The first numeral refers to the book, the second to the question, and the third to the section of the answer.
50. Aug., *Simplician* 1.2.5.
51. Aug., *Simplician* 1.2.10.
52. Aug., *Simplician* 1.2.12.
53. Aug., *Revisions* 2(1).28.1 (Ramsey, WSA, I/2, 110).
54. Fredriksen, *Augustine and the Jews*, 183.

In Teske's analysis, before *Simplician* Augustine separates human and divine authority. Reason can bring you to the knowledge of God—revelation and faith provide the final steps. After *Simplician*, even the assent to faith has to be the result of a predestined grace and is beyond human capability. It is no longer true that beginning to believe is within our power.[55] Babcock concludes Augustine deliberately discards human freedom and divine justice to preserve the arbitrariness of grace and the uselessness of human endeavor.[56]

He certainly stresses our hopelessness throughout the Julian period; we cannot freely choose to believe because the will cannot will the good if grace has not freed it.[57] He reinforces our bondage to Satan; in our current state, the will can only sin.[58] He explains away in the *Revisions* his defense of the will in *On True Religion*, in which he stated that a sin must be voluntary to be a sin.[59] He makes the tautological point that even sins committed in ignorance or under compulsion are voluntary. The person does them, and you can do nothing without the will. He continues incoherently, "And what is called original sin in infants, when they still do not have use of the choice of their will, is not absurdly called voluntary as well, because it was contracted from the first bad will of man and in some way became hereditary."[60] An involuntary sinful action is voluntary because it is an action; the original sin of infants *is* voluntary because Adam's sin *was* voluntary.

In the *Revisions*, Augustine cancels the potency of human nature described in the anti-Manichean *Two Souls*. In the earlier work, he says we can love spiritual things by nature. More carefully, he says this is only the case when grace has healed nature. We may say human nature is capable of choosing spiritual things over bodily things because *some* particular, predestined, saved human natures can.[61] In his *De Ordine* (*On Order*) he says we should strive to do our best so that God will hear us. He corrects himself because his words might imply God does not hear sinners, but he does not explain how hearing or not hearing our prayers is relevant.[62]

Julian sees Augustine's contention that free choice is lost in Adam's sin as Manichaean; he interprets Augustine as saying we are forced into sin by

---

55. Teske, "Saint Augustine as Philosopher," 14–15.
56. Babcock, "Augustine's Interpretations of Romans," 67.
57. Aug., *Two Letters* 1.3.6.
58. Aug., *Two Letters* 2.5.9.
59. Aug., *On True Religion* 14.27.
60. Aug., *Revisions* 1.13(12).5 (Ramsey, WSA, I/2, 60).
61. Aug., *Revisions* 1.15(14).8, correcting *Two Souls* 13.20.
62. Aug., *Revisions* 1.3.3.

our flesh.[63] Augustine retorts that Julian is another Jovinian, making good Catholics look bad by smearing them as Manichaeans. Pelagians show their arrogance when they trust in free will and not God.[64] Augustine proclaims, "Why so hostile to the grace of Christ? Why so trusting in yourselves?"[65] Augustine claims he does not deny free will, but insists the character of free will changes after the Fall. Humanity goes from the freedom to have no sin to the choice between sins.[66] Free choice is not lost, but it is deformed.

There can be no such thing as repentance as an act of human will. Even the prayers of the church have this displaced meaning. We do not pray to have sinners repent, but to have their will redirected. This suggests prayers can cause God to revise the predestined status of the sinner; all of Augustine's similar injunctions to prayer have the same inconsistent character. Julian points to Paul: "Do you not realize that God's kindness is meant to lead you to repentance (Rom 2:4)?" Augustine replies God only draws to repentance the predestined elect, who were chosen before the creation of the world.[67] The chosen are the chosen; the drawn are drawn. The church's prayers are reminders to God to do what he already decided to do.

God alone prepares a person for repentance. There is no role for human endeavor, teaching, or correction. In *Two Letters*, he again interprets a text in a novel way. Prov 16:1 reads, "The plans of the mind belong to mortals [KJV: The preparations of the heart] but the answer of the tongue is from the Lord." Augustine treats this as a denial of human initiative because while we may prepare our hearts and minds, God prepares us first.[68] The Pelagians cite Isa 1:19–20, "If you are willing and obedient, you shall eat the good of the land; but if you refuse and rebel, you shall be devoured by the sword." Augustine rejects the covenant offered; the Pelagian interpretation that human choice merits God's gift contradicts the meaning of grace; grace is not a free gift if it is a repayment for human action.[69] Again, he declares, "the will is prepared by the Lord."

Every human action is a result of a prior divine intervention. Augustine requires orthodox belief as a prerequisite for salvation, but even faith is meaningless because we cannot seek or study it. Even to pray requires a separate grace; the Pelagians err if they believe prayer makes us worth of

63. Aug., *Two Letters* 1.2.4.
64. Aug., *Two Letters* 1.2.5.
65. Aug., *Sermon* 131.9 (Hill, WSA, III/4, 321).
66. Aug., *Two Letters* 1.2.5.
67. Aug., *Answer to Julian* 5.4.14.
68. Aug., *Two Letters* 2.9.19.
69. Aug., *Two Letters* 4.6.12.

grace.[70] By contrast, Julian says we are to blame if we do not ask for what God is willing to offer, seek what he will show, and knock on the open door. Augustine responds, "but those infants refute this idea of yours by their very silence."[71] If we can fault adults for not asking, seeking, and knocking, we cannot fault infants for not doing so. If babies can't knock, no one can. Only those predestined to ask have their petition answered. He repeats his assertion that "[God] desires everyone to be saved (1 Tim 2:4)" means all of the elect; they "come to the knowledge of truth" because Gods wills them to do so. All of us are created by God's will and he wills which of us are saved. We are like infants who cannot will; God wills for his elect, preparing the will and providing help. Julian asks why God does not transform the will to allow all to seek him. Augustine repeats that God arranges for some infants not to be baptized; it is all a mystery beyond our understanding.[72]

Determinism and materialism have long histories, but while satisfying the requirements of a dormitory argument, it is hard to construct a church on them. If there is no freedom, there is no blame and no way to build a society. Augustine confronts the practicalities of his position in his odd little book *Rebuke and Grace*. The monks at Hadrumetum question the logic of rebuking a sinner under the theory of predestination. Augustine understands the abbot needs to enforce discipline, but he cannot find any plausible explanation why the abbot should do so. The notion that the rebuke is only punishment is not an acceptable idea. A typical admonition is an attempt to induce the wayward monk to repent and improve his behavior. Since the will is impotent without explicit grace, the rebuke cannot aid the sinner to repent; repentance does not lie in the sinner's hands, but in God's. God can give the sinner repentance as a grace with or without the rebuke, and the human rebuke has no effect on God. The rebuke might alter the monk's behavior, but that is not true repentance unless God gives the gift of repentance. Different behavior does not change anything of importance, even if it makes the lives of the other monks easier.

The sinner is responsible for his sins, but even that ultimately doesn't matter. We are born damned, and our actions have no effect on that state—only grace does. Grace that is not freely given is not grace (*gratia vero nisi gratis est, gratia non est*). Augustine is reduced to saying the abbot's rebuke reminds God to do whatever he already predestined. The abbot should both rebuke and pray for the errant monk's repentance. If the sinner is predestined to grace, God will make the rebuke work for his good. If the sinner

---

70. Aug., *Two Letters* 4.11.30.
71. Aug., *Answer to Julian* 4.8.42 (Teske, WSA, I/24, 405).
72. Aug., *Answer to Julian* 4.8.45.

is damned, the rebuke is wasted but the abbot cannot know. If the rebuked monk is one of the elect, then God grants him mercy. However, if he is not one of the elect, God imposes his judgment.[73] It is hard to imagine this argument brought peace to the monastery. Augustine frequently repeats the notion that God gives mercy to one, but judgment to another. The same applies to all of God's gifts. If someone is freed from desire, that is mercy. If he is not set free, that is judgment.[74] Mercy and judgment always hang on God's arbitrary choice.

Near the end of Augustine's life, monks in Provence under the guidance of John Cassian provide more trouble for Augustine. They object to his statement that grace is required for every good thing; no thought, no deed, no act of love is possible without it.[75] His responses to their objections in the *Predestination of the Saints* and the *Gift of Perseverance* strengthen the argument of *Simplician,* two decades after the original work. He claims he is only defending more carefully his consistent position that God does not give grace in response to merits and shows mercy only to his elect. Augustine frequently cites Rom 9:16 in support; it doesn't matter how we strive unless we are given mercy.[76] Cassian maintains, in contrast, that at least the *initium fidei* reflects human initiative, completed by grace. Augustine does not yield an inch, noting even Pelagius abandons the assumption of human achievement without grace at Diospolis.[77] Augustine is being as slippery as Pelagius in this case. At Diospolis, Pelagius says we require grace, but his grace is a very different grace. None of us can do without the grace of creation because we are creatures. None of us can do without the grace of reason because we are more than animals. However, Augustine has no interest in explaining the nuances of the Pelagian position to the recalcitrant monks.

Augustine uses his *Revisions* to clarify his earlier murky commentaries on Romans.[78] He carefully explains that no gift, including belief, comes as payment for merits. As for his earlier remark that belief is our work,[79] "I certainly would not have said this if I already knew that faith also belongs among the gifts of God."[80] He redirects them to *Simplician* to see that he

---

73. Aug., *Rebuke and Grace* 9.25.
74. Aug., *Letter* 2*.10.
75. Aug., *Rebuke and Grace* 2.3.
76. See, for example, *Predestination of the Saints* 3.7 and *Predestination of the Saints* 14.27.
77. Aug., *Predestination of the Saints* 2.3.
78. Referring to *Propositions from Romans,* 60.12.
79. Aug., *Propositions from Romans* 60.12.
80. Aug., *Predestination of the Saints* 3.7 (Teske, WSA, I/26, 153).

conclusively says grace is unmerited. He has already demonstrated that the beginning of faith and its end are both in God's hands.[81] His change of position is only apparent—the Pelagian over-emphasis on human capability requires a balancing response.

## OBEDIENCE AND GUILT

Can we obey God's commandments? If cannot obey, are we guilty? Augustine gives different answers in his early and later works. In the *Catholic Way of Life,* Augustine stated the love of God is a purifying fire burning away our vices,[82] implying an achievable virtue. He withdraws this in the *Revisions*; the Pelagians use this against him, but he claims he has always said perfection is unachievable in this life. Otherwise, Christians would not be directed to repeat the Lord's Prayer, asking for forgiveness.[83] It is impossible to be sinless, but constant prayer mitigates sinfulness. In *On Genesis Against the Manichees*, Augustine says people could both turn to God and obey his commands. Obedience is possible if we ask for and receive God's help. Nevertheless, people are only capable of repentance and obedience if God has chosen them and prepared their will.[84] The early answers support obedience, but the later works insist that obedience depends on predestined grace.

Even after the beginning of the Pelagian dispute, Augustine occasionally appears to give some credit to human capability. The first two books of *Forgiveness of Sins* are interpretable as admitting the possibility of sinlessness. This apparently disturbed Augustine's ally, Count Marcellinus. In the third book (written as a corrective) Augustine acknowledges its bare possibility, but only Jesus realized it; all of us fall short.[85] He dodges some of the questions about the human role in salvation in the *Spirit and the Letter* also written for Marcellinus. He admits his early work says the power to accept or reject God's call is within our will, but God is the source of our will, and no independent human capability is implied.[86] Augustine qualifies his words to specify that sinlessness is possible "if, with God's help, the

---

81. Aug., *Gift of Perseverance* 21.55.
82. Aug., *The Catholic Way of Life* 30.64.
83. Aug., *Revisions* 1.7(6).5.
84. Aug., *Revisions* 1.10(9).2.
85. Aug., *Forgiveness of Sins* 3.15.22.
86. Aug., *The Spirit and the Letter* 34.60. Keech, *Anti-Pelagian Christology*, 65, thinks *The Spirit and the Letter* was a response to Jerome's *Letter* 133.

will was not lacking."[87] The crucial addition is "with God's help." This argument changes from the unlikeliness of a sinless life to the certainty that it could not even be attempted without divine assistance to heal, redirect, and strengthen our injured will.

Augustine battles Caelestius in the *Perfection of Human Righteousness*. Caelestius, in his *Definitions*, suggests that sin, being voluntary, can be avoided. If sin is part of our nature, then it is not sin. If it is not a part of our nature, then it can be separated from it. If it is separable from human nature, then it can be avoided and, if it can be avoided, a person can be free of sin by a consistent exercise of the will. Augustine answers we can only avoid sin if our nature is healed by grace and the spirit is no longer at war with the flesh. Absent that grace, the question of avoidability is irrelevant.[88] For Caelestius, the call to righteousness is real; we can and must strive for it. If we ought to be without sin, which is obvious, then we can.

Augustine responds that knowing we ought to do something does not mean we can. A person with a limp cannot simply stop limping, but a doctor can heal her.[89] It is *unnatural* (contrary to nature) to have a physical imperfection. A person *ought* to walk straight; this does not mean she *can* walk straight without a physician. The divine physician is God's grace made available through Christ; the patient has no role, she neither merits nor cooperates with grace. Originally, this model of Christ as physician included the thought that the patient seeks out a physician; Augustine cancels that option later. God's physician does not make house calls or accept appointments.[90]

Caelestius persists with dogged pedantry. If we are commanded to avoid sin, it must be possible.[91] Augustine returns to his medical metaphor. Limping humanity is commanded to walk straight to demonstrate it cannot do it without seeking the appropriate medical treatment, the healing grace of God through Jesus Christ.[92] He may seem to be implying the sinner can pursue grace. However, Augustine denies we can turn to God unless he

---

87. Aug., *The Spirit and the Letter* 35.62 (Teske, WSA, I/23, 193).

88. Aug., *The Perfection of Human Righteousness* 2.3.

89. Aug., *Perfection of Human Righteousness* 3.5–3.6. See also *Perfection of Human Righteousness*, 2.4 for a similar exchange.

90. Harmless points out that in the anti-Pelagian works Christ is transformed from physician to pediatrician. "Christ the Pediatrician," 17. Augustine argues Julian was denying infants their only physician.

91. Aug., *Perfection of Human Righteousness* 3.6. Niebuhr notes the resemblance of this argument to the Kantian "I ought, therefore I can." *The Nature and Destiny of Man*, Vol. 1, 247.

92. Aug., *Perfection of Human Righteousness* 3.6.

redirects our will. Augustine blames Adam for our helpless state.[93] Adam's willful disobedience set up conditions leading the will always to fail; the propagation of the species requires the paternal desire that is always at war with the spirit.[94]

Augustine eventually throws up his hands and lists all of the scriptural references quoted by Caelestius urging people to perfection. The list includes Deut 18:13 and 23:17, Matt 5:48, 1 Cor 15:34, 2 Cor 13:11, Col 1:21–22 and 1:28, Phil 2:14–15, Eph 1:3–4 and 5:27, 1 Pet 1:13–16, Ps 15:1–2, Ps 119:1, ending with Prov 22:11. Augustine replies these are not commandments but (unobtainable) goals. Those who are running toward perfection are called spotless because of the character of their goal, not because they are righteous. The middling Christians pray and give alms; walking on the road to salvation is made pure by humble acknowledgment of the need to ask for forgiveness in the Lord's Prayer.[95] A steady stream of prayer and alms guarantees there will be no sins to forgive at the resurrection. Running or walking is only completed in paradise.

Augustine further tightens up his position, denying there is any real possibility of obedience and casually dismissing much of the Bible as mere rhetoric. Caelestius cites the covenant text of Isa 1:19–20 in which God contrasts obedience and the good life, on the one hand, with disobedience and death, on the other. Augustine sneers, "He acts as if the whole law were not full of such conditions or as if such precepts were given to the proud for any reason than that 'the law was given for the sake of transgression until the offspring should come to whom the promise pertains.'"[96] Striving to run along the road to perfection is ultimately pointless; the many scriptural injunctions only demonstrate our impotence. Our failures along the way humble us and make us realize we are hopeless without grace. Augustine does not explain why humility would matter; grace that is not freely given is not grace. A humbled sinner cannot compel God to change his mind and grant grace—humility, like any human effort, cannot affect salvation.

Augustine concludes *Perfection of Human Righteousness* with a summary of all his arguments. They seem conclusive to him, but he appends a strange coda; he says we should not challenge those who don't agree with him, at least not some of them. Augustine is either suddenly uncertain about himself, or afraid of some challenge. Teske suggests in his introduction to

---

93. Aug., *Perfection of Human Righteousness* 6.13.

94. Alexander connects Augustine's rebellious member to Plato's charioteer; the punishment of the Fall is precisely the loss of control of sexuality. "Sex and Philosophy in Augustine," 205.

95. Aug., *Perfection of Human Righteousness* 9.20.

96. Aug., *Perfection of Human Righteousness* 19.42 (Teske, WSA, I/23, 313).

his translation that Augustine was worried about the authority of the deceased Ambrose.[97] If *Perfection of Human Righteousness* dates from 416 or later, another possibility arises. Squires points out that Augustine received Jerome's *Dialog Against the Pelagians* and an ambiguous letter enclosed with it[98] when Orosius returned from Jerusalem. Jerome says in the letter that he hasn't had the time to comment properly on the two books Augustine had sent him (probably *Forgiveness of Sins* and *The Spirit and the Letter*). The letter praises Augustine's ingenuity (a possibly loaded word), but it may represent a subtle threat from Jerome that Augustine is departing from tradition. Jerome suggests it would not be appropriate for the two of them to be seen in disagreement.[99] In 416, Augustine has not yet achieved his untouchable status; he writes tentatively to Paulinus of Nola and waffles about sinlessness.[100]

Julian picks up Caelestius's cause. If we cannot pursue perfection, are we excused our failure? Julian points out that Augustine argues in his *Two Souls Against the Manichaeans* that sin is precisely the avoidable choice to do something forbidden. Sin is a result of a voluntary action; if you do not will the sin, it is not sin. *A fortiori,* infants, who all agreed lacked the will, cannot be guilty of sin. Augustine responds that children are still guilty through the sin of the concupiscence of their conception. He defends himself by saying the early works focus only on conventionally voluntary sins. The sin and guilt of the newborn is the sin that is the punishment of the sin of sexual desire of the child's father.[101]

Desire dominates the will, and the will can do nothing: "For it is free to the extent that it has been freed and to that extent it is called will. Otherwise will must properly be called utter desire."[102] What we commonly call the will is too weak to deserve the name. Its weakness is not the weakness of Adam and Eve but is the derived punishment of their sin. Original sin is not a sin anyone voluntarily commits. It is a sin imputed to all as a punishment, firstly, for the disobedience in the Garden, and, secondly, for its recapitulation at conception. All are conceived as an act of concupiscence; or, in the case of perfunctory sex, it still involves the emblem of disobedience, the erection.

---

97. Teske, WSA, I/23, 288.
98. *Letter* 172 in the list of Augustine's letters, *Letter* 134 in Jerome's works.
99. Squires, "Augustine's Changing Thought on Sinlessness," 458–461.
100. Aug., *Deeds of Pelagius* 30.55.
101. Aug., *Unfinished Work* 1.44.
102. Aug., *Revisions* 1.15(14).4 (Ramsey, WSA, I/2, 71).

Pelagius makes an argument from God's grace. We have the prior grace of God's creation and the gift of reason. An understanding of natural law can be the result of reflection. People can avoid sin, even without instruction by the church or knowledge of Christ. All people have the capability of being righteous and God will judge all accordingly. Augustine replies that, if we could be righteous based on natural law and reflection, even without the knowledge of Christ, then the Fall would not require the redemption of Christ and Christ died in vain. Since Christ cannot have died in vain, human nature cannot suffice: only faith in Christ's redeeming blood can save us.[103] Although Augustine continually refers to Christ's incarnation, crucifixion, and resurrection, he does not clarify how these have any value in the context of an absolute and arbitrary election.

The Pelagians insist on imitation over generation. People have the capability of not sinning and of sinning; we can either imitate Christ or imitate Adam. The ability not to sin comes from God, the source of human nature.[104] Just as Christ is the exemplar of a perfect life, Adam is the model of the life *not* to lead. Sin does not arise from generation, a flawed nature, or a defective will. There is no need to explain sin. God's direct creation, Adam, sinned under the best of all possible conditions—living in paradise with God as a neighbor. In fact, Julian declares infants are *less* culpable than Adam and Eve because infants are incapable of receiving commands.[105]

Augustine explains Julian's position carefully. Julian believes we can achieve any degree of virtue with God's assistance and denies there is any intrinsic evil tendency in human nature. As we are created good, we remain fundamentally good. Our basic goodness ought to make us ashamed of our sins and, therefore, repent and increase our efforts.[106] Augustine thinks that even being ashamed of one's failings is impossible without predestined grace. The advantage of his position is its absolute character: it explains everything. If we are all redeemed in Christ, we must all be damned in Adam. Since Paul traces things to Adam, it must be propagation. If sin passes by imitation, then we are not be blamed for another's sins but only for our own actions, and nothing is "through one man (Rom 5:12)."[107] Paul's comparison between Christ and Adam *must* mean we are condemned for Adam's sin. Augustine concludes that *must* mean damnation through generation and concupiscence.

---

103. Aug., *Nature and Grace* 2.2.
104. Aug., *Nature and Grace* 44.52.
105. Aug., *Answer to Julian* 1.5.19.
106. Aug., *Answer to Julian* 3.26.64.
107. Aug., *Answer to Julian* 1.7.22.

Julian does not find Augustine's arguments against imitation convincing; we choose whom to imitate.[108] Imitation is praiseworthy when we imitate good examples and blameworthy when we imitate evil ones. Augustine says if Paul had been talking about imitation, the parallel would have been between Adam (the initiator of sin) and Abel (an example of righteousness). Augustine is sure Paul is clear—Adam is the author of sin and Christ the author of righteousness.[109] Again, if Paul intended to imply immitation, he might have pointed to the first sinner, Eve. However, Paul insists sin came into the world through one man; Eve cannot be "one man." Therefore, he insists, transmission is not by imitation but by generation.[110] Generation always means in Augustine the erectionalization of disobedience. Women have only a passive role in reproduction, which is resolutely seminal.

Augustine never reconciles his internal contradiction. There is no sin if we are forced to sin. Without the grace of Christ, we can only sin. Sin is unavoidable, so there is no sin. Julian cannot see whatever it is Augustine sees. Julian acknowledges John 15:5 ("because apart from me you can do nothing") on the necessity of Christ, but we are *not* without Christ; we have his example. We do not lack the Logos; we have reason.

There are several ways of understanding Augustine's journey from his early defense of free will to the total collapse of the will. The first is to accept his statements that the evolution is more apparent than real. He always has believed in the primacy of grace. Becoming more confident of its necessity, he follows its logic to the denial in *Simplician* that people can even choose to believe. Any variation in tone only reflects the opponents of the day: Manicheans, Donatists, or Pelagians.

A second interpretation allows for a change in perspective brought about by disappointment in life. Embracing Christianity and celibacy does not give him personal peace. Distracted either by his congregation or by a continuing sexual desire, he becomes discouraged. Experience crushes any initial optimism about human capability. Unable to secure a complete triumph over his opponents or create a church of saints, he finally concludes humanity is irretrievable without direct divine intervention.

The hypothesis of impotence blends these interpretations together. For a man, impotence is the ultimate denial of the will. The frustration of desire renders useless even the most basic (male) endeavor. The young Augustine hopes that putting aside the conventions of Roman life will allow him to focus on philosophical investigations, using his will where it could still be

---

108. Aug., *Unfinished Work* 2.52.
109. Aug., *Unfinished Work* 2.54.
110. Aug., *Unfinished Work* 2.56.

effective. Without inner peace, sexual impotence continues to plague his thoughts. The common thread is not the primacy of grace, but the arbitrariness of impotence, which becomes the arbitrariness of God's mercy. If this is at the back of his mind, then managing a congregation and confronting his adversaries only reinforces his feeling of despair.

# 9

# Toddlers in Hell

PREDESTINATION IS ONE OF the hardest Augustinian doctrines to swallow, from the damnation of unbaptized newborns to the condemnation of virtuous pagans. The cruelty and arbitrariness revolt Julian of Eclanum. He cannot accept Augustine's arbitrary and unjust God. With a shallow Fall, the Pelagians argue it would be unjust to condemn someone to hell who conforms to God's law by the natural use of reason merely because she has not heard of Christ. Moreover, whatever their fate might be, unbaptized infants cannot deserve damnation. Augustine says Julian's God might be pleasing to Julian, but he is not the God of Paul and the church.[1] Augustine stands on Rom 5:12, Rom 7:23, and Rom 9:20–23. His deep Fall entails the impotence of the will and an unmerited grace. Damnation is never a question of any human notion of justice. All are justly damned by the concupiscence instrumental in their conception; God makes the occasional exception, whimsically.

Augustine's defenders struggle with predestination and especially the damnation of infants, flailing about with a range of explanations. West claims Augustine's attraction to damnation derives from childish petulance. She compares him to a favorite child who rejoices at the thought of less fortunate children.[2] James Wetzel tries to defuse predestination by focusing on Augustine's understanding of conversion for those predestined to convert. Predestination is the prior action of God's love. No one desires God's love unless God selects him or her for love. Only the predestined want

---

1. See, for example, *Unfinished Work* 1.50–51. *Unfinished Work* 1.129.
2. West, *Saint Augustine*, 108.

salvation; the damned just don't give a damn. Augustine's critics accuse him of limiting God's love, but this is not the case if only a few people want God's love.³ Susannah Ticciati interprets Augustine as placing God's presence in every human act, as a necessary relationship between creator and creature. What looks like God's participation in evil and an arbitrary salvation, must be re-analyzed in eternity.⁴ These explanations would have no made sense to Pelagius, Julian, or Cassian.

## THE LITTLE ONES

Augustine finds his decisive argument in infant baptism. His success astonishes O'Donnell. He believes infant baptism is so important to Augustine that he constructs his theory of original sin to support it. Nevertheless, Augustine's argument for infant baptism "has the quality of a mathematical equation that requires you to fail to notice that it divides by zero on two or three occasions in order to get its results."⁵ The reverse may be the case; Augustine wants a universal damnation and needs an argument for it. If it is universal, it applies to infants. If infants are damned, they must be baptized. Then he uses the argument in the opposite order. The church supports infant baptism. Thus, children must have guilt. Their sin necessarily stems from their origin, which is conception. Conception requires an erection, which requires concupiscence. The disobedient penis represents the disobedience in Eden. The evil of desire overwhelms the good of reproduction.⁶

In his anti-Donatist period, Augustine held a relatively flexible view. For example, martyrdom supersedes the requirement of baptism. Similarly, faith and repentance can suffice; belief saves the thief on the cross.⁷ He abandons this more open view with the insistence on timely infant baptism and has to find other explanations of the thief's salvation. He wonders if the water issuing from Jesus's side baptized the thief,⁸ or perhaps he was baptized in prison or earlier.⁹ Eventually, he admits he doesn't know but says we should assume he was baptized somehow.¹⁰

3. Wetzel, "Snares of Truth," 132.
4. Ticciati, "Augustine and Grace Ex Nihilo," 419.
5. O'Donnell, *Augustine, a new biography*, 206.
6. Aug., *Marriage and Desire* 1.5.15.
7. Aug., *On Baptism, Against the Donatists* 22.30. Accessed May 1, 2015, www.newadvent.org/fathers/14084.htm.
8. Aug., *The Nature and Origin of the Soul* 1.9.1.
9. Aug., *The Nature and Origin of the Soul* 1.9.12.
10. Aug., *Revisions* 2.55(82).3

Augustine's use of children catches the Pelagians off guard. Pelagius is an opponent of cheap grace and lectures adults on their obligations. It does not occur to him to consider the problem posed by infants; of dying children, he writes, "I know where they do not go; I do not know where they do go."[11] Augustine does not accept this casual dismissal of the question. He finds the Pelagian neglect of infant baptism appalling; repeatedly returning to the liturgical emphasis on early baptism is also a powerful rhetorical approach. When Julian accuses Augustine of Manicheanism, Augustine points to crying babies.

The first two books of the *Forgiveness of Sins* did not address the question of the sins of infants; Augustine remedies this in the third book. Augustine claims he was surprised to discover that Pelagius, in his commentary on Rom 5:12, denied the little ones are born with sin. Augustine excuses his earlier neglect of the subject because he did not believe anyone would deny their guilt.[12] He clarifies his position; children are good by nature, but their generation from the evil of concupiscence damages them irrevocably. Parents carry babies to the font; this proves they need healing.[13] Augustine counters the Pelagian denial of original sin with custom; the parents offering their children must "either admit that sin is being cured in their babies or stop presenting them to the doctor."[14] He begs Julian to accept original sin and let the little ones be saved.[15]

In *On the Grace of Christ and Original Sin*, Augustine cites Pelagius's *Libellus fidei*. In his final defense, Pelagius accepts a single liturgy for the baptism of children and adults but still denies the infants have any sin to be forgiven.[16] Augustine points out that Caelestius admitted openly in his examination by Zosimus what Pelagius is hiding. Accepting infant baptism is for the forgiveness of sins does not imply acceptance of a sin passed through generation if you still maintain infants are guiltless. Sin, Caelestius asserts, cannot be born with a person, it must be something the individual commits.[17] Augustine thinks the fallacy in the Caelestian argument should be obvious, even to a Bishop of Rome. If the infants are guiltless, what sins

---

11. Ferguson, *Pelagius*, 96.
12. Aug., *Forgiveness of Sins* 3.1.1.
13. Aug., *Forgiveness of Sins* 3.4.8.
14. Aug., *Sermon* 176.2 (Hill, WSA, III/5, 273).
15. Aug., *Two Letters* 1.27.47.
16. Aug., *Grace of Christ and Original Sin* 1.32.35. See also *Unfinished Work* 1.53–54.
17. Aug., *Grace of Christ and Original Sin* 2.6.6.

are they being forgiven for in the baptismal liturgy? He attributes the mild reaction of Zosimus to inappropriate pity.[18]

Although Pelagius agrees with the Cappadocians (see chapter 4) on baptism, he does not have the skill or the reputation of Gregory of Nazianzus. Gregory makes the distinction between infant and adult baptism (a seal for infants and both a seal and a remedy for adults). The Pelagians accept baptism for infants as a traditional adoption into the Christian community. It differs from the adult sacrament, even if the liturgical form is identical. For adults, it marks a formal commitment and a radical discontinuity between manners of living; for children, it is sanctification.[19] Julian agrees baptism is a requirement for all, including infants (although he tempers that with a belief in God's justice for virtuous pagans), but it has an effect proportionate to the need of the recipient.[20] Baptism does not snatch babies from the devil, but dedicates the children to God.[21] It changes adult sinners from evil to good, but children from good to better.[22] Although the Pelagians are uncomfortable with challenging infant baptism, infant damnation is intolerable. Julian cannot see how any acceptable notion of divine justice can ascribe guilt to infants; only a corrupt judge or tyrant would condemn the little ones. Augustine is a candidate for excommunication because he makes God guilty of a crime.[23]

All agree God is just. For Julian, this means infants cannot be justly damned. For Augustine, justice requires them to be guilty. Augustine welcomes the argument from injustice; children are sometimes born blind, lacking a limb or are just plain stupid. These are punishments, and if God is just, they must be the result of guilt. Their guilt is Adam's guilt, renewed and transmitted by the disobedient member. This recapitulated sin is so great that it justifies any calamity. If a child is deformed, defective or dies of illness, it is a result of an infinite Treasury of Dismerit. Augustine uses their innocence to prove his point; their punishment is derived from their parents' guilt.[24]

Augustine is sure the argument is unanswerable; without original sin, what can be the cause of defects?[25] He repeats the argument many times;

---

18. Aug., *Grace of Christ and Original Sin* 2.6.7.
19. Kelly, *Early Christian Doctrines*, 359.
20. Aug., *Unfinished Work*, 1.53.
21. Aug., *Unfinished Work* 5.9. See also *Unfinished Work*, 1.60.
22. Aug., *Unfinished Work*, 1.54.
23. Aug., *Unfinished Work* 1.48.
24. Aug., *Answer to Julian* 3.6.9.
25. Aug., *Answer to Julian* 3.6.13.

without sin, no one would have been born that way in Eden.[26] All defects are part of the punishment produced and transmitted by generation. While baptism removes the stain of concupiscence, the other punishments such as deformity and stupidity are not, for unexplained reasons.

Julian declares Augustine has a mind as thick as lead; Augustine wittily replies that Julian is the lead-brain. Surely, no one chooses to have a dull mind. Philosophers of great depth are rare, and even they are lead-like compared to the brilliance of Adam before the Fall. Adam is created with an uncorrupted body (Augustine ignores Eve as usual); the concupiscence of our conception corrupts our bodies. Augustine supports the common view that Adam and Eve would have been immortal if they had not sinned. Nevertheless, if they were mortal before the Fall (a position attributed to Caelestius in 411), the soul still would not have been weighed down by the body. Only a person with a thicker brain than most, meaning Julian, would deny this.[27] While the Manichaeans might explain any slowness of mind by the preponderance of evil matter in an individual, Christians cannot use such an explanation since we are formed in God's image. Therefore, Augustine concludes, mental slowness and other failings of infants must be traceable to their parents (and, ultimately, to Adam) because they cannot be the fault of the newborn. The defects of animals are not Adam's fault but are caused by evil spirits, like the demons occupying Gadarene swine. People suffer these defects because of the sin of their parents in conceiving them.[28] Augustine also acquits animals of evil desire because, lacking reason, their desire cannot be disobedient to it. When Julian finds it odd that Augustine exculpates pigs and donkeys, he retorts that if Julian cannot understand why asses can be born free of sin and people can't, then Julian is the ass.[29]

Julian cannot escape the appeal to defects. When he declares that only the Manicheans and the traducianists (Augustine) would ascribe injustice to God, Augustine counters that Julian attributes defects to God. If he thinks God is just, defects must represent God's judgment; he should accept original sin as the only explanation.[30] Nevertheless, Julian denies any sin to infants and Augustine points out that Julian still does not provide any explanation of defects. Julian thinks no one has any doubt about God's justice, but Augustine and the traducianists reverse this—there is no doubt about God's injustice. Augustine ploddingly repeats that because God is just, all

26. Aug., *Unfinished Work* 2.124.
27. Aug., *Unfinished Work* 4.75.
28. Aug., *Unfinished Work* 4.75.
29. Aug., *Unfinished Work* 4.56.
30. Aug., *Unfinished Work* 4.130.

must be worthy of damnation. The presence of defects in children implies God's judgment on them. This is the result of original sin since newborns are stained with filth (Job 14:4–5).[31]

Whatever God's position might be on the status of infants, Augustine maintains we should err on the side of caution; Julian's logic denies infants a salvation they might need. Julian asks how the little ones can be guilty; Augustine replies that since Christ died for them, they must be guilty.[32] Julian is caught in a contradiction, unwilling to abandon infant baptism as a custom, unable to argue it is useful but not essential, and strangely ignoring texts suggesting the innocence of children. For Julian, baptism requires the consent of the believer and his or her commitment to a renewed life—it is an adult decision. For adults, it results in the forgiveness of sins; for children it is a seal; a modern Julian might have called it a vaccination against sin.

In *Marriage and Desire*, Augustine explains the relationship between baptism and original sin. Baptism wipes away the stain acquired by the concupiscence of conception. Afterward, it is not a sin, as long as it remains under the control of the mind.[33] He clarifies the meaning in the *Two Letters*. Julian had compared Augustine's baptism to shaving; it cuts off the hair, but the hair grows back.[34] It is a fair criticism. Even if the child is cleansed from the effects of concupiscence, the first adolescent erection ends the period of grace; the war between spirit and flesh begins. Augustine unambiguously says that sexual desire, the war in the members, is an evil. It certainly is a sin to have sex for pleasure (with some mild dispensation for the married).[35] However, he argues that concupiscence, if it is not acted on, is called sin primarily because it is a result of a sin. This works for virgins and the chaste (after baptism) because they are not at risk for having sex for pleasure. However, even if one confines sex to reproduction, the begetting of the child causes a fresh infection and the transmission of the guilt to the child.[36] Perhaps Augustine means that baptism removes the immediate consequence of original sin while rendering the adult a carrier, a Typhoid Mary, or better, Typhoid Mark, of the contagion.

The infant dying immediately after baptism benefits, but it is harder to see the benefit of baptism for survivors. It does not empower the adult to lead an independent, Pelagian life. It is necessary; God only gives grace

---

31. Aug., *Unfinished Work* 3.7.
32. Aug., *Marriage and Desire* 1.33.56.
33. Aug., *Marriage and Desire* 1.22.24.
34. Aug., *Two Letters* 1.13.26.
35. Aug., *Two Letters* 1.16.33.
36. Aug., *Two Letters* 1.13.27.

to the baptized. However, it is not a guarantee of grace, because if it were, grace would be given as a reward for the merit of baptism. Augustine berates the Pelagians for accepting infant baptism as a custom of the church while denying that the babies have sins that need to be forgiven. However, his own notion of forgiveness is problematic. Original sin is forgiven by baptism but the punishment of that sin, concupiscence, remains. We are all afflicted with the sin that is the punishment of sin. Augustine's reasoning is hard to follow: "For this reason, it is no longer a sin, though it is called a sin, either because it was produced by sin or because it is aroused by the attractiveness of sin, even if one does not consent to it, because the appeal of righteousness prevails."[37] It is unclear how the majority of people can escape the re-establishment of the sin. This may well have been Augustine's intention; only a few will be saved. Taylor mocks Augustine: "Baptism delivers from original sin; Baptism does not deliver from concupiscence; therefore, concupiscence is not original sin."[38]

Having established the dubious privilege of baptism, Augustine returns to the transmission of sin in conception. The Pelagians argue that Rom 5:12 means death, and only death, entered the world through Adam and is inherited with the flesh. Augustine insists on the transmission of both death and sin. If Adam only dies because he sinned, it would be unjust for his descendants to die if they do not sin. However, infants die, so they must have sinned.[39] Augustine overlooks the Caelestian position that Adam would have been mortal without sin; we inherit a natural mortality—Adam's death has nothing to do with his sin. Augustine insists the symmetry between Adam and Christ demands original sin; if Christ saves all, Adam must damn all.[40] He could have said infants start sinless but later sin just as Adam and Eve start sinless and then sin, but this is insufficient for universal damnation.

Julian looks for a rationale for infant baptism without original sin. He quotes Chrysostom, who argues that although infants are not stained with sin, they are baptized to receive them into the fellowship of Christ.[41] Since Augustine doesn't want to accuse Chrysostom of Pelagianism, he claims a correct translation would emphasize that babies had no *personal* sins. Nevertheless, they are still stained because they are conceived in lust, inherited in a direct line from Adam's disobedience by generation. Chryso-

---

37. Aug., *Two Letters* 1.13.27 (Teske, WSA, I/24, 130).
38. Taylor, *Whole Works*, Vol. 7, 564. Second Letter to the Bishop of Rochester.
39. Aug., *Two Letters* 4.4.6.
40. Aug., *Two Letters* 5.5.9.
41. Aug., *Answer to Julian* 1.6.21.

stom omits the crucial word "personal" because, Augustine continues, it is unimaginable Chrysostom could mean anything else.[42] It seems clear that Chrysostom would have supported Julian's interpretation. Chrysostom rejected the idea of any guilt inherited from Adam; "It is not on his account: for neither have you remained without sin: though it be not the same sin, at least there is some other which you have committed."[43] Before Augustine, the story of the Fall is not a description of the destruction of human nature but a warning to Adam's descendants not to abuse the free will in the same way as their progenitor.[44] Julian would agree we inherit the *habit* of disobedience by imitation of our parents. Adam sinned, and we inherit the *capability* to sin; we can freely choose to disobey God's commandments. For Augustine, disobedience is always the disobedience of the male member. Concupiscence is always the enemy against which we struggle and Julian is its secret ally.[45]

Augustine never tires of using the children. He invokes throngs of babies strangling Julian: "The little ones have you by the throat, for we read so many times that they are not killed on account also of their own sins, but only on account of those of their parents."[46] If people find it unjust to punish the children for the sins of the parents, God's judgment is beyond understanding. Julian stubbornly will not listen to the texts showing sins visited on children (Lev 26:39, Num 14:18, and Jer 32:18).[47]

One of the weaker arguments offered by the Pelagians is that the baptism of the parents provides protection for their children. They are only reflecting the pious belief of the times. Chrysostom in his homily on 1 Cor 7 discusses Paul's advice to believing Christians married to unbelievers. Rather than sexual contact with the unbeliever soiling the believer, the unbeliever is made holy. The children are safe as well: "Impurity does not originate in the union of their bodies but in their thoughts and motives."[48] He adds that 1 Cor 7:14 provides the proof, "Otherwise your children would be unclean, but, as it is, they are holy." Pelagius reasons that original sin should not apply to the children of baptized Christians since the sacrament cleanses the sins of the parents. Augustine cannot let any conception be

---

42. Aug., *Answer to Julian* 1.6.22.

43. Chrysostom, *Homily* 17.4. Accessed June 1, 2015, http://www.newadvent.org/fathers/220117.htm.

44. Pagels, "Politics of Paradise," 79.

45. Aug., *Answer to Julian* 2.3.5.

46. Aug., *Unfinished Work* 3.14–3.15 (Teske, WSA, I/25, 290).

47. Aug., *Unfinished Work* 3.21.

48. Chrysostom, *Homily* 19 (Roth and Anderson, 33).

uncontaminated; the righteousness of the parents cannot produce the child without sinful concupiscence even if the sex is only for reproduction.[49] The sinlessness of children might have been plausible with a different sort of sex. However, we are unable to control erections, and that stains the children.[50] Julian could not understand how so much could depend on so small a part of the total human experience. The pleasure of sex is part of God's creation and necessarily good.[51]

Augustine's dedication to the damnation of newborns puzzles many. Jeremy Taylor thinks Augustine's position abominable, calling him the *durus pater infantum* (the cruel father of infants).[52] Jacobs feels the desire to win the argument drives Augustine into extreme positions with unanticipated consequences.[53] He concludes that because Augustine could not shake off the role of controversialist, original sin becomes permanently intertwined with distorted sexuality and tortured children.[54] Heard feels the dispute *provokes* Augustine into an exaggerated position of ascribing not a mere *vitium* (defect) but a *peccatum* (sin) to the entire human race.[55] However, no one tricks Augustine into these views. Nothing forced the old campaigner into an unsound argument, except his old dysfunction. If Augustine had not been ready to explode, he could have ignored the minor pinpricks of Pelagius.

Infant baptism and birth defects are of great tactical value to Augustine. The Pelagian focus on adult responsibility leaves them vulnerable to Augustine's re-purposing of a liturgical tradition, and he uses children as a rhetorical weapon in the debate. Augustine's real concerns are the impotence of the will and the limitation of grace. He sees both of them in the disobedient penis. All men are subject to this tyranny unless God gives them a rare grace. Augustine needs the children as a link between the uncontrollable desire of the father and the uncontrollable desire of the son. Their damnation is incidental but underlines the total despair of the human condition. If the most innocent are damned, even though "it is to such as these that the kingdom of heaven belongs (Mat 19:14)," the situation of sinful adults is truly hopeless. The role of women is again peripheral. They may

---

49. Aug., *Forgiveness of Sins* 2.9.11.
50. Aug., *Forgiveness of Sins* 2.22.36.
51. Aug., *Unfinished Work* 4.29.
52. Taylor, *Whole Works*, Vol. 7, 543–44; letter to the Bishop of Rochester. See also, Coleridge, *Aids to Reflection*, 294.
53. Jacobs, *Original Sin*, 63.
54. Ibid., 66.
55. Heard, *Alexandrian and Carthaginian Theologies*, 161.

be the object of male desire, but the uncontrollable member represents the disobedience in Eden. The chain of original sin runs from father to son, from penis to penis.

## THE POTTER'S CLAY

If infant damnation is a rhetorical strategy, Augustine's pessimism stands on the rock of Rom 9:13–23. Augustine's theory of God's abandonment of the vast majority of humanity depends on acknowledging God's absolute power and incomprehensibility. We must accept our complete impotence. Augustine calls this just on the basis of original sin. The arbitrary predestination of a few illustrates God's mercy.

Paul gives him a good start. God prefers Jacob to Esau, but this is not injustice. God puts us on notice: "I will have mercy on whom I have mercy, and I will have compassion on whom I have compassion (Rom 9:15)." It does not depend on us (there is nothing particularly wrong with Esau or right with Jacob), "but on God who shows mercy (Rom 9:16)." God grants Pharaoh power to demonstrate his superior power (Rom 9:17). Pharaoh is only a puppet in the Exodus drama. "So then he has mercy on whomever he chooses, and he hardens the heart of whomever he chooses (Rom 9:18)." We cannot resist God's decisions (Rom 9:19). We have no right to dispute them: "But who indeed are you, a human being, to argue with God (Rom 9:20)?" We are the clay in the potter's hands; Paul writes in Rom 9:21. "Has the potter no right over the clay, to make out of the same lump one object for special use and another for ordinary use? [KJV: one vessel unto honour and another unto dishonour]." God can use the destruction of a vessel of wrath as a demonstration of his power. This shows his glory to the honorable vessels, "which he has prepared beforehand for glory (Rom 9:23)."

The vessels of wrath exist solely to provide salutary examples for the vessels of mercy. Such examples are not truly helpful because the vessels of honor do not need to learn anything; they are "prepared beforehand for glory." Presumably, the elect can say, more appropriately than usual, "there but for the grace of God, go I," and feel somehow comforted. Perhaps Rebecca West's sense of the childish smugness of the elect is correct.

Augustine explains God's motives in forming two individuals for different fates. They cannot both be honorable vessels lest they believe they deserve it; they cannot both be dishonorable so God can demonstrate his occasional mercy.[56] Julian claims Augustine's God creates life only to destroy it. Augustine replies with an elaborate argument. God makes hu-

---

56. Aug., *Answer to Julian* 4.8.46.

man nature good; people are evil because of a defect God did not make. Nevertheless, no one is made into a dishonorable vessel unless he or she is evil. This argument is vacuous because the evil of being conceived or having sexual desire is sufficient. He verges toward Manichaeism when he reasons that each human is evil because of a defect inserted in his or her nature by the devil, which transforms it into a bad nature.[57] The devil gets a different role in the commentary of Tyconius. All things God creates are good; the devil can change the use of a vessel, but not its nature. They become his *non sua secundum originem, sed sua secundum voluntatem* (not according to their origin, but according to their own will).[58]

The text in Rom 9:20–23 follows Isaiah, "Shall the thing made say of its maker, 'He did not make me'; or the thing formed say of the one who formed it, 'He has no understanding' (Isa 29:16)?" and, "Woe to you who strive with your Maker, earthen vessels with the potter! Does the clay say to the one who fashions it, 'What are you making'? or 'Your work has no handles' (Isa 45:9)?" Neither Julian nor Augustine considers Jer 18:3–11, which expresses divine sovereignty in a more positive way. If the pot goes wrong, the potter reworks and reworks the clay until a new pot is made. If Israel does not repent, God will change his mind about its status as his special nation and repurpose his clay. If Israel, or any nation, repents, God will not inflict his planned punishment. God's power is supreme, but divine actions are contingent upon human ones, particularly upon repentance. Jeremiah and Paul would have understood that the potter does not waste any clay; if the original design does not work, the potter will choose a new one. If we read Romans through the lens of Jeremiah, it leads to unlimited, not limited salvation.[59] Theophilus of Antioch interprets Jeremiah as pointing to our remolding in the resurrection, when we will be broken up and remade "spotless, and righteous, and immortal."[60]

Augustine comes close to saying the clay itself is damned as if it is Manichaean evil matter. The same clay is used for both honorable and dishonorable vessels, and if God does nothing, the vessel is dishonorable by default.[61] We cannot complain about punishment; anyone spared does not deserve it but is only a vessel of mercy, whom "God foreknew, predestined,

---

57. Aug., *Unfinished Work* 1.114.

58. Tyconius. *Book of Rules, Regula 7, on 82*, cited by Clancy "St. Augustine, his predecessors and contemporaries, and the exegesis of 2 Tim 2:20," 248.

59. Heard, *Alexandrian and Carthaginian Theologies*, 327.

60. Theophilus of Antioch, *To Autolycus*, 2.26 (Dods, 104).

61. Aug., *Unfinished Work* 1.126.

called, justified, and glorified."[62] We offer thanks if anyone is saved since all deserve damnation. Any other understanding would be empty words denying Christ and the cross.[63] God does not merely discard the *massa perditionis*, but actively destines the clay to damnation for illustrative purposes.[64] There is no real difference between the damned and saved. If the potter can use the same lump of clay for both honorable and dishonorable purposes, it is all the same clay.[65] God has little regard for the vast majority of humanity:

> But God willed that so many be created and born who he foreknew would not pertain to his grace that they outnumber by an incomparable amount those whom he graciously predestined to be children of the promise for the glory of his kingdom. As a result, even by the very multitude of those rejected he showed that it is of no importance in the sight of the just God how great is the number of those justly condemned.[66]

Taken aback by the God Augustine portrays, Julian retreats to a God he can believe in, "But piety and reason have explained that my God forms no one for a dishonorable purpose."[67] Augustine's reply is "If your God forms no one for a dishonorable purpose, he is not the God of the apostle Paul."[68] Julian says it would be easier to find someone who denies God's existence than to find one who says God is unjust.[69] Augustine replies God is not answerable to human standards.[70] He declares Julian is the selective reader, citing Jesus's words, "apart from me you can do nothing (John 15:5)," as a proof of our impotence without grace.[71]

For Augustine, all people are part of the mass of perdition. Pharaoh's heart begins and ends hard, Jacob and Esau both deserve damnation, and every human pot is dishonorable.[72] The inexplicable thing is that God ever softens a heart, chooses a person for grace, or reshapes a pot for honorable purposes. God's power is absolute and unquestionable: "I will be gracious to whom I will be gracious, and will show mercy on whom I will show mercy

---

62. Aug., *Nature and Grace* 5.5 (Teske, WSA, I/23, 227).
63. Aug., *Nature and Grace* 6.6.
64. Aug., *Simplician* 1.2.18.
65. Aug., *Simplician* 1.2.19.
66. Aug., *Letter* 190.12 (Teske, WSA, II/3, 268).
67. Aug., *Unfinished Work* 1.129 (Teske, WSA, I/25, 137).
68. Ibid.
69. Aug., *Unfinished Work* 3.9.
70. Aug., *Unfinished Work* 3.23.
71. Aug., *Unfinished Work* 3.119.
72. Aug., *Grace and Free Choice* 20.41.

(Exod 33:19)." All would be saved if he truly willed *everyone* to be saved. God must intend most to be damned, contradicting 1 Tim 2:4. Augustine declares, "we should understand all the predestined because every kind of human being is contained in them."[73] "All" means all types of people—Greek, Roman, man, woman, free, slave—not all people.

Origen warns that the hardening of Pharaoh's heart, the choice of Jacob over Esau, and the potter's clay are dangerous topics for the immature exegete. The heretics "practically destroy free will by bringing in lost natures, which cannot receive salvation, and on the other hand, saved natures, which are incapable of being lost."[74] Of course, he was talking about third-century dualists, not Augustine! For Origen, there is no problem of evil. All have turned away from God and fallen into the material world. The different distances each soul has fallen and God's design for bringing each soul back explain any disparities in life. The potter's clay is part of God's individualized redemptive plan. Humanity may be a single lump, but it is a lump meant for redemption and return. Pharaoh's heart is either hardened by his own choice (and the text is a figure of speech) or hardened by God as part of the process for the eventual sake of Pharaoh's soul.[75] God's time is not human time: "For God deals with souls not in view of the fifty years, so to speak, of our life here, but in view of the endless world."[76] The potter reworks the clay patiently and does not abandon the clay until it proves itself unusable. The universalist in Origen hopes no one is unsalvageable, but the free will supporter acknowledges that we can always deny God.

Chrysostom argues people can and do make it impossible for God to save us, otherwise, God would save us all: "Whence then are some vessels of wrath, and some of mercy? Of their own free choice."[77] Chrysostom says Paul's strong statements cannot be interpreted as an attack on free will but are only injunctions to human humility in the presence of God's decisions. He uses the same theme of the choice of the clay in his homily on 2 Tim 2:20–21. This reads, "In a large house there are utensils not only of gold and silver but also of wood and clay, some for special use, some for ordinary [KJV: some to honour and some to dishonor]. All who cleanse themselves of the things I have mentioned will become special utensils [KJV: a vessel unto

---

73. Aug., *Rebuke and Grace* 14.44 (Teske, WSA, I/26, 139). See also *Answer to Julian* 4.8.44.

74. Origen, *On First Principles* 3.1.7–3.1.8 (Butterworth, 168–69).

75. Origen, *On First Principles* 3.1.11. Similar ideas are expressed in Chrysostom's *Homily 16 on Romans*.

76. Origen, *On First Principles* 3.1.13 (Butterworth, 182).

77. Chrysostom, *Homily 16.24 on Romans*, accessed May 1, 2015, http://www.newadvent.org/fathers/210216.htm.

honour], dedicated and useful to the owner of the house, ready for every good work." Chrysostom comments, "Do you see that it is not of nature, nor of the necessity of matter, to be a vessel of gold or of earth, but of our own choice? For otherwise the earthen could not become gold, nor could the golden descend to the vileness of the other."[78] Julian attempts to use Timothy against Augustine, but Augustine undermines any human initiative, pointing to Rom 9:23 to deny that the vessels can clean themselves.[79] He reiterates that the will is prepared by the Lord. Origen has a response to Augustine: "He has prepared these vessels for glory, not from some arbitrary or fortuitous grace, but because they have purged themselves from the aforementioned defilements."[80] The Pelagian debate would have been more interesting if it had included Chrysostom and Origen as active participants.

Augustine can make the resort to God's inscrutability quite moving: "Why this one and this one, why not that one and that one; don't ask me. I'm just a man; I notice the depth of the cross, I can't penetrate it; I shudder with dread, I don't poke and pry."[81] He describes two children, formed from the single lump of perdition. One accidentally suffocates in his mother's bed, but the other lives: "Neither deserved anything good. But 'the potter has power over from the same lump to make one vessel for honorable use, another for disgrace.'"[82] If any of the congregation disputes this, Augustine refers them to God's unfathomable ways.

In *Grace and Free Choice*, Augustine argues that God chooses Pharaoh, already damned by original sin, as a vessel of anger. Pharaoh's heart is hardened as a demonstration of God's power.[83] This power does not persuade people to righteousness. With predestination, there is no ability to repent: no one can be scared straight. Julian cannot accept this notion of God's justice because it is unrecognizable in human terms. Lamberigts describes Julian as believing God still offers a covenant; any special predestined grace was unacceptable.[84] Augustine consistently argues the covenant is only between God and God's predestined elect. The fourteenth-century Dominican, Robert Holcot sides with Julian. The potter's clay metaphor cannot be applied as Augustine wishes to people because the clay had no covenant with the

---

78. Chrysostom, *Homily 6 on Second Timothy*, accessed May 1, 2015, http://www.newadvent.org/fathers/230706.htm.

79. Aug., *Unfinished Work* 1.134.

80. Origen, *Commentary on Romans* 7.18.3 (Scheck, 122).

81. Aug., *Sermon* 165.9, (Hill, WSA, III/5, 206).

82. Aug, *Sermon* 26.13 (Hill, WSA, III/2, 100).

83. Aug., *Grace and Free Choice* 20.41.

84. Lamberigts, "Competing Christologies," 163.

potter, unlike God's creation that has the assurance of God's commitment. God may rework the clay, but he does not discard it.[85]

## DOUBLE, DOUBLE TOIL AND TROUBLE

Augustine's defenders claim he does not advocate double predestination, only the predestination of the elect, but the defense is weak. He never clearly articulates a theory of reprobation in which God damns an individual by name. However, God initially damns us all: "The vessel for dishonor, however, was made first, and then the vessel for honor."[86] The church would not waste its prayers on those predestined to damnation if it could only reliably identify them.[87] God only saves a fixed number of individuals.[88] Limited election requires God to damn the rest. It is not clear why an arbitrary damnation of particular individuals is inappropriate while a blanket condemnation through penile rebellion is acceptable.

Augustine's defense is that the disobedient penis, under the spell of concupiscence, creates the sin; this sin corrupts the good nature of the child. In this way, man (specifically man, not woman: Augustine has no interest in blaming women) is responsible, not God, for the dishonorable character of the vessel. Then, God arbitrarily cleanses a few vessels. The physicians who selected a few to live on the ramp at Auschwitz provide a parallel. They did not operate the gas chambers but, their defenders argue, saved a remnant. This special pleading will not do for God—who not only selects on the ramp but also loads the trains. If each conception is an act of disobedience, Augustine can classify universal damnation as a human act, thereby exculpating God. Julian cannot accept this reasoning.

Given Augustine's willingness for God to abandon the vast majority of nominal believers, it is not surprising he has no tolerance for virtuous pagans. Reflecting Origenist universalism, Pelagians believes God's justice implies a reward for righteous pagans, even if the message of Christ had not reached them. It is possible for the uninstructed to grasp the truth of the creation by God and to live in accordance with his will, as perceived by reason.[89] Origen supports the notion of meriting God's mercy: "[we should never concede that] divine providence does not dispense each one in such a way that each one's merit, which is acquired through freedom of the will,

---

85. Oberman, *Harvest*, 246–47.
86. Aug., *City of God* 15.1 (Babcock, WSA, I/7, 140).
87. Aug., *City of God*, 21.24.
88. See, for example, *City of God* 14.10 and *Revisions* 1.13(12).8.
89. Pelagius, *De Natura*, cited by Augustine in *Nature and Grace* 2.2.

furnishes material to the one who dispenses."[90] Augustine dismisses these efforts to expand God's justice. Merits cannot and should not exist except in the predestined righteous. Virtue can only exist in the righteous, and no one can be righteous without the correct faith.[91] All acts by non-believers are sins because they are not under the mantle of grace. He mocks Julian for considering a special heaven for virtuous pagans[92] as he accuses the Pelagians of proposing for infants.[93] No virtue has value if it is outside of grace; if a pagan clothes the naked, it is a sin because it is not associated with the correct faith.[94]

That faith, which is itself a predestined gift, is central. Even if people lead saintly lives, without the Christian faith Augustine considers correct (it would not be the faith of Julian or Origen), they are damned. When Augustine contrasts the mediocre Christian to the virtuous pagan, the pagans have all the best behavior, incorporating both classical and biblical virtues. The Christians have sex for pleasure, react angrily to offense and seek revenge. No matter how much worse they appear, they are protected by Augustine's faith.[95] The argument is incoherent; if grace is a gift, it cannot depend on faith in Christ if that suggests an action of the believer. God could predestine anyone to grace, regardless of baptism or previous history. Salvation belongs to the predestined; merit, even the merit of faith, is irrelevant. Augustine's rejection of the saintly pagan is a clue to what he means when he says that, without grace, people can only choose between sins. *All* actions, whether they would be judged good or evil by others, are evil if they are not the result of God's predestined grace. Charles Raven declares these views are not only presumptuous restraints on God's justice but also contradict gospel teachings.[96]

The monks in Provence struggle with what leads to salvation. If God places everyone in damnation and arbitrarily saves a few, then belief, prayer, study, and reason have no point. In the *Predestination of the Saints,* Augustine concedes we have reason and are separate from other animals. However, this does not mean human nature has remained good or resembles Pelagian nature. The gift of reason is of no more significance than the fact that some of us are handsome. Human nature cannot lead us to God. Faith

---

90. Origen, *Commentary on Romans* 9.2(16) (Scheck, 204).
91. Aug., *Answer to Julian* 4.3.7.
92. Aug., *Answer to Julian* 4.3.25
93. Aug., *Unfinished Work* 1.50, 2.113.
94. Aug., *Answer to Julian* 4.3.30.
95. Aug., *Two Letters* 3.5.14.
96. Raven, *Natural Religion*, Vol. 2, 164.

is an unmerited gift; we do freely choose to believe or not believe, but the "will is prepared by the Lord," who chooses to prepare only a limited number of wills.[97]

The monks raise the objection that even some who hear the word of the Lord do not believe. Augustine's argument is hard to follow: God gives mercy to the chosen ones but he exercises his judgment to blind the rest. The predestined freely choose to believe and the blinded freely choose not to believe, just as if human actions determined salvation or damnation; the Lord prepares or does not prepare the will. God saves the saved without any cause, but he blinds the blinded as a deserved punishment for original sin.[98] In the *Gift of Perseverance*, Augustine states that the evil deeds of those whose hearts are hardened do not differ from those of the undeserving elect.[99] We cannot merit either salvation or damnation, and we begin damned. Augustine tries to clarify how it works. Predestination prepares us for grace; grace is the giving of the anticipated grace. Predestination implies foreknowledge, but foreknowledge does not imply predestination.[100] In this way, Augustine attempts to separate God's predestination to grace from his foreknowledge of those he will leave in the state of damnation bestowed on them by their conception.

He closes with the little ones; adults might have merits, but for infants "every claim to human merits preceding the grace of God collapses."[101] It does not make sense to say those who die baptized achieve salvation by some foreknowledge of future merits, or those who are damned are damned for future sins never committed. When infants die, their original sin is either removed by God's mercy or remains by his judgment.[102] The only distinction is God's arbitrary choice.

God's foreknowledge is foreknowledge in a trivial sense. Just as an act of the will is necessarily voluntary (we do it, after all), God has foreknowledge of what he predestines. All predestination is before all worlds; the Hellenized God of the fifth century no longer acts in history. Augustine explains we are not called because of our belief but so we will believe.[103] God foreknows himself; predestination is simply God's foreknowledge of the

---

97. Aug., *Predestination of the Saints* 5.10.
98. Aug., *Predestination of the Saints* 6.11.
99. Aug., *Gift of Perseverance* 11.25.
100. Aug., *Predestination of the Saints* 10.19.
101. Aug., *Predestination of the Saints* 12.23 (Teske, WSA, I/26, 168).
102. Aug., *Predestination of the Saints* 13.24.
103. Aug., *Predestination of the Saints* 19.38.

gifts he will give to his elect.[104] The foreknowledge is not God's knowledge of our freely chosen actions, but of his arbitrary choices.

Predestination becomes entangled with the issue of perseverance until death. A vessel may appear to human eyes to be honorable or dishonorable, but no one can be certain. The monks in Provence are puzzled as to why some Christians fall away from the faith. If people lead Christian lives but sin at the end, Augustine says they lack the gift of perseverance. They are among the many called but not the few chosen. They never were part of the predestined elect. Adam is created in the image of God but is not given the grace of perseverance—he does not last past lunchtime. The grace offered now is a better class of grace since perseverance is sometimes given along with faith. On the other hand, if Adam and Eve had not sinned, they would have been immortal. They had both the ability not to sin and not to die. His logic traps Augustine. He wants to defend the standards of the monastery and suggests the gift of perseverance can be merited by prayer and then will be never lost.[105] However, we cannot know whether we have the gift of perseverance until we do or do not persevere. We can only hope; if we are not given the irrevocable gift of perseverance, we may lose our faith.[106] The safe policy is to give God all the credit for any achievement we seem to achieve.[107]

Like all acts of grace, God dispenses perseverance arbitrarily. Augustine explains the role of unelected congregants; God mixes those who will not persevere with the ones who will so the elect do not complacently assume their salvation.[108] Many must be damned to keep a few humble. Augustine doesn't want the elect to be too comfortable. God's opposition to smugness is admirable, but smugness is independent of predestined salvation. Augustine does not know God's reasons but counsels acceptance and trust in God's intentions.[109] Augustine focuses on the mystery; equally unsearchable are God's reasons for granting mercy and his reasons for hardening a person's heart. The latter will have committed sins, but he has done no more evil than the one who is saved.[110]

---

104. Aug., *Gift of Perseverance* 14.35.
105. Aug., *Gift of Perseverance* 6.10.
106. Aug., *Gift of Perseverance* 6.11.
107. Aug., *Gift of Perseverance* 6.12.
108. Aug., *Gift of Perseverance* 8.19.
109. Aug., *Rebuke and Grace* 8.17.
110. Aug., *Gift of Perseverance* 11.25.

There is a hierarchy of gifts, ranging from the beginning of faith to the gift of perseverance, reserved for those who pray.[111] Prayer seems to be a prerequisite for perseverance, but it is not merit. Like baptism, it is mysteriously necessary, but not sufficient. No monk can be sure of the gift of perseverance and, swollen with pride, omit his duty to pray, but praying is no guarantee. Each faltering Christian does so because of his own temptation and fault, but still perseverance is a predestined gift of God. This should not induce despair in the monk but remind him to put his hope in God and not in himself.[112] Underneath the apparent comfort to the praying monks of Provence, there is the echo of Augustine's approach to 1 Tim 2:4. The will is prepared by the Lord, and God predestines the graces and the benefits he will provide. God's predestined plan includes beginning to believe, prayer, and perseverance: "These gifts of God, I insist, are only foreknown by God if there is the predestination which we are defending. But they are foreknown. There is, then, the predestination which we are defending."[113] Augustine's logic is mind-bending. We win God's gifts by faith, but it is a faith God has previously given us. God foreknows he will give those gifts to the ones he predestines and prepares their will appropriately. It then appears that they freely choose to believe. God's foreknown and predestined gifts include everything from the beginning of faith through perseverance to the end. He claims this is so clear that only the very argumentative will not fall silent.[114] The sensation of dividing by zero associated with infant baptism returns in greater strength in Augustine's discussion of gifts.

God's gifts do not arise because of his foreknowledge of an individual's life and deeds—that would imply an unacceptable role for merit. Robertson interprets this passage as saying foreknowledge is interchangeable with predestination for the elect, but they are not equivalent for the reprobate. This does not diminish the mystery; both the predestined elect and the damned are equally likely to have sinned.[115] Mozley finds these distinctions vacuous; abandonment to damnation is equivalent to damning by name.[116]

Although Augustine tries to end the discussion, he admits this is a hard story to explain. Mediocre Christians should be encouraged to run for the prize as directed in 1 Cor 9:24; they will be reassured to be conforming

---

111. Aug., *Gift of Perseverance* 16.39.

112. Aug., *Gift of Perseverance* 17.46.

113. Aug., *Gift of Perseverance* 17.47 (Teske, WSA, I/26, 223).

114. Aug., *Gift of Perseverance* 21.56.

115. Robertson, "Augustinian Ecclesiology and Predestination," 406. See Aug., *Gift of Perseverance* 11.25.

116. Mozley, *The Augustinian Doctrine of Predestination*, Note XX, 412.

with God's foreknowledge. Of course, running is foreknown only for the elect; the others are running pointlessly. "And the foreknowledge of God can perhaps be preached in other ways so one wards off human laziness."[117] The congregation is encouraged in its discipline and morality for the convenience of others and is not told that salvation has nothing to do with righteous behavior.

Augustine explains God brings some to Christ out of mercy but abandons more out of judgment. He rhetorically asks why God does not teach all of humanity to come to his grace. The answer he offers is that God teaches out of mercy and does not teach out of judgment. It is a universal answer. If anyone complains, Augustine turns to Paul and the potter's power over the clay.[118]

Kirwan analyzes the scattered and conflicting references and concludes no other conclusion than double predestination is possible.[119] Bigg declares Augustine is as much a Gnostic as a Manichee; if we are intrinsically damned, it doesn't matter if it is fated as in Gnosticism or the result of a contaminated nature.[120] Rigby attempts to place Augustine's predestination in the context of Wisdom literature; we must go beyond the simple questions of ethics, punishment, and reward to reach the unquestioning love of God.[121] Only a complete narrative of the interaction of justice, grace, and wisdom will explain God's goodness. Rigby asserts that Augustine does not deny our ability to understand God's judgments to defend God; God does not need a defense. Rather we are to abandon our efforts to comprehend him and simply face the *Deus Absconditus,* the hidden God.[122] Julian has no mystical element in his personality. He denies God is hidden; God reveals himself in his creation, his law and scriptures, and the life of Christ. This is sufficient, with the added grace of human reason, to establish a covenant.

Cunningham blames Calvin for distorting Augustine. It is inappropriate to separate God's power, which is unconstrained, from his character, which is to do good.[123] He tries to distinguish Augustine's theory of a man with a weakened will from Calvin's vision of the man with a predestined life. Sadly, Augustine makes it clear the latter is what he means, even if it contradicts scripture and the philosophical speculations about the goodness

---

117. Aug., *Gift of Perseverance* 22.57 (Teske, WSA, I/26, 231).
118. Aug., *Predestination of the Saints* 8.14.
119. Kirwan, *Augustine,* 144–46.
120. Bigg, *Christian Platonists,* 289–90.
121. Rigby, "Augustine's Use of Narrative Universal," 192.
122. Rigby, "The Role of God's 'Inscrutable Judgments,'" 215.
123. Cunningham, *S. Austin,* 96.

of God.[124] Heard dismisses Cunningham's defense; Augustine is responsible for all he says just as Luther and Calvin are responsible for their interpretations.[125] Calvin claims his paternity; he states the earlier church fathers, excepting Augustine, were all confused about the freedom of the will.[126]

Rist believes Augustine makes us puppets, free to sin if unelect, and free from sin if elect.[127] Augustine's free will is only *formally* free; it can be described as free but is actually bound; Augustine has avoided one form of determinism but created another.[128] Freedom that is only freedom when granted as a gift is not freedom. In later work, Rist confesses some of his earlier work should be modified. He does not disavow it; while "puppets" may go too far, suggestions that there might be human choices of love or humility fail because each of them is also a gift.[129]

Augustine is unable to produce a different theory because his center is elsewhere. We cannot earn merit with God, or even take the action of accepting God's covenanted grace, any more than a man can raise his member by a thought. A man cannot reject God's grace if offered, any more than he can command an erection to subside.

Augustine starts with the impotence of the will and the limitation of grace and works backward. We have no *natural* ability to do what we choose unless we choose evil. There is no notion of merit and no mechanism to obey God's commands. Even the apparently righteous pagan sins by his very act of virtue, if he is without the true faith. Only God can give him that faith.[130] All humanity is intrinsically damned. This damnation is not individually earned (otherwise merit might also exist) but is universal. To be universal, it must apply even to an infant a few seconds old—it must be an *original* sin. All the suffering in human life is just because everyone deserves the worst punishment. Augustine derives original sin and infant damnation from his impotence and despair.

The question still arises of why God abandons so many. In Origen's cosmology, there is an explanation of the troubles of this life—the situation of each person reflects the degree of his or her separation from God in the spiritual realm. Nevertheless, after the amazing incarnation of Christ, it is possible for *all* humans to reverse course and return to God. Augustine

---

124. Ibid., 105.
125. Heard, *Alexandrian and Carthaginian Theologies*, 132.
126. Calvin, *Institutes of the Christian Religion*, 1.2.2.4 (Beveridge, 226).
127. Rist, "Augustine on Free Will and Predestination," 241.
128. Ibid., 235.
129. Rist, *Ancient Thought Baptized*, 133.
130. Aug., *Two Letters* 3.5.14.

denies this optimism. While the abandonment of Origen might explain Augustine's rejection of universalism, his limitation of grace is extreme. The motive for his belief in a tiny elect may lie in the utter denial of merit he adopts to make the impotence of the will plausible. If God's grace is arbitrary, there is no reason to hope it is abundant. Augustine makes God in his image. If he feels damned by impotence, then God should also damn, or leave in damnation, the vast majority of humanity. In Augustine's system, God's own justice renders God impotent; God is not allowed to see any difference between the virtuous and vile.

Augustine's concepts of original sin, infant baptism, and the limitation of grace each have logical problems; they are almost impossible to maintain in combination. One can assert the existence of an original sin (Augustine's or some other less penis-centric variety) that results in inevitable damnation. Infant (and adult) baptism is the remedy for that condemnation. The baptized Christian has her sins forgiven and begins a new life. This view of baptism is the view of the early church. There is no room for predestination in this perspective. The life of the Christian in the church consists of prayer, almsgiving, and participation in the sacraments. Alternately, all humanity starts out in a state of damnation. God rescues a few out of his mercy. In this case, there is no real purpose to baptism and holy communion, or any of the other sacraments. Baptism is a sign of initiation into the community and communion is only a memorial. The Catholic Church took the first approach; the Protestants took the second.

# 10

# On the Disobedient Member

THE PREVIOUS CHAPTERS SHOW Augustine defending his deep Fall against the shallow Fall of the Pelagians. The valley floor is stark, depressing, and featureless. Between the cliff of the Fall and the cliff of the Rise, the course of human history is flat without any even brief periods of relative consonance between God and humanity. The whole problem is lust. The disorder in the will distorts our good nature; sexual desire is now necessary to persuade the disobedient penis to become erect and ensure conception. Desire is fundamentally wayward and uncontrollable; our wills are impotent, able only to choose between sins. An arbitrary predestination seals all of this; our conception damns us. We should be grateful a few are arbitrarily lifted from the lust-haunted floor.

The argument Augustine makes can again be read in two ways: either from despair to the penis, or from the penis to despair. If one starts with the observation that humanity is a mess, the next step is to seek an explanation. We appear to be a species that behaves damnably, with a few exceptions. A simple weakness would be insufficient to explain why religious leaders and philosophers have never succeeded in their efforts to educate us into virtue. The ignorance Plato blamed is not enough; we are not just weak, we are helpless and guilty. How can we all be guilty? The only solution, Augustine concludes, is an original sin, dating from prior to birth so not even an infant can escape. In some ways, this approach would be compatible with Origen, who assumes a prenatal sin to provide us all with guilt; for him, the sin was inattention to God. Augustine does not take this route.[1] He seeks a more

---

1. Of course, Origen's original sin story is more of an explanation of our starting point in life and is part of a generally optimistic view of humanity's future rather than

active sin and chooses our conception. Not just any description of concupiscence and conception will do. If Augustine wanted to blame sex and lust for the human condition, it would have been natural in a misogynistic era to blame women. After all, a woman takes the fruit and women continue to be the objects of men's desire. Augustine surprisingly blames the male contribution to desire, the wayward penis. To justify this conclusion, he identifies the disobedience of Adam and Eve with the disobedience of the male member. Augustine believes, or wants us to believe, that his conclusions are the inevitable consequences of an analytic and deductive process, even if some steps (such as why all of this stains the child rather than the parents) are shaky.

On the other hand, the hypothesis of impotence suggests that the process runs in the other direction, from the penis to despair. Cursed with a useless and frustrating penis, Augustine needs to think that the failures of his life are not unique, but are part of the general state of humanity. To him, sex and reproduction are not a natural and pleasurable process but a reminder of his problem, so they must be symbolic of the human dilemma. Impotence would be a virtue if desire were the cause of damnation. The helplessness of the impotent man, especially if still plagued by desire, becomes the emblem of the common human state. A few are spared from this unsatisfiable desire, but they cannot choose to be chaste. It is an arbitrary happenstance, a grace. If this is also to be part of the general condition of humanity, then salvation is random. If the damnation of infants is the darkest part of Augustine's thoughts, the location of all human tragedy in the penis is his strangest.

## FROM FRUIT TO PHALLUS

Everything begins in Eden. There would have been nothing wrong with marriage or reproduction in paradise if Adam had not voluntarily sinned.[2] Augustine sees the cosmic Fall of the Garden in the miniature fall in the bedroom. Although the sin was pride, the punishment was desire. The tempting beauty of the fruit is replaced with the disobedient member.

In any deep Fall, humanity is wounded in some way. Augustine's past prevents him from applying the damage directly to human nature, inherited from Adam and Eve. He eliminates the traducianist possibility because, as Julian repetitiously points out, it would be Manichean. The only option is to inflict the damage on the will, which Augustine separates from human

---

Augustine's pessimistic view of our state.

2. Aug., *Marriage and Desire* 2.26.43.

nature. Augustine makes the injury complete—the will is impotent. No one can make any good choice without direct divine action—the will is only free to sin. This relentless fiat provides the flatness of the valley floor after the Fall. No human effort can improve the state of humanity. God's injunctions to righteousness are lessons in futility. We are to discover the need for unmerited grace by our repeated failures. Since all are born deserving damnation, every human defect or evil in the world is just. God's grace rescues a few selected individuals from this desolate valley, but this salvation is whimsical. Augustine doggedly returns to infants, who are incapable of personal sins, but who die young or are born with defects, to demonstrate the arbitrariness of grace and the logical need for an original taint.

Pride impels Satan's Fall; it is enough to kick Adam out of Eden and be the continuing source of the disobedience of a stiff-necked people. Augustine accepts pride as the Eden sin,[3] but it is not enough to support his theology. He needs sex. The shift from pride to sex would have surprised the early church. While Jerome, Ambrose, and Tertullian emphasize some sexual issues, and Origen and Cyprian wonder about a birth taint, no one goes as far as Augustine. The new element is the identification of the disobedience in the Garden with the disobedience of the penis. Augustine sexualizes the Fall, but without conventional misogyny. He is fully capable of being patronizing toward women; he regards them as inadequate companions to men, suitable only for reproduction and not wholly formed in the image of God. However, there is very little language about temptation; there is no role for seduction in a male-member-disobedience scenario. Misogyny is usually not so generous, but the distinction is often lost on those who take Augustine to be a typical woman-hater. Even experts are inclined to drift into the standard vocabulary of feminine wiles, the weaker vessel, and the seduction of men.[4] Augustine never complains about Eve *seducing* Adam; if the word is taken sexually, there is no seduction before the Fall because sexual desire only comes into existence with the Fall. His theme is unreliability of the male member, not the fallibility of women.

The turning point is Adam's acceptance of the fruit. One disobedience leads to another: "At that moment there came into being that animal arousal of which human beings are rightly ashamed and which caused Adam to be embarrassed by his nakedness."[5] Adam gets an erection, presumably much to his surprise. His erection gives him primacy in embarrassment, if not in

---

3. Aug., *Answer to Julian* 3.6.13.

4. See, for example, Brown, *Augustine of Hippo*, 296.

5. Aug., *Forgiveness of Sins* 1.16.21 (Teske, WSA, I/23, 45). See also Augustine's *Sermon* 151.

disobedience. Embarrassed by this unexpected and unwilled motion, they cover up their newly shameful genitals.[6] In one quick step, the shame of the disobedience moves from the upper body to the lower.

Augustine ascribes to all *men* the punishment of *Adam's* disobedience, making all males slaves to their disobedient members. The obsession with the seductive nature of women running rampant in western culture is a grafting of Augustine on Tertullian. Augustine's rants are not about bishops driven mad with desire by a nun's touch or churches disrupted by uncovered virginal heads. Instead, he focuses on erratic performance. The disobedient member makes sexual desire the symbol of the will run wild. Augustine still has to show it is responsible for the transmission of guilt. The struggle is overtly over the interpretation of Paul in Romans, but one should recall Rist's warning that Augustine reaches a conclusion and then finds an interpretation of scripture that supports it.[7] Some criticism of Augustine's exegesis misses a crucial point: Augustine wants an interpretation that puts the blame on the inconsistency of desire while avoiding the accusation of Manichaeism. The path has to be found; it doesn't have to be smooth or seamlessly logical.

Julian and Augustine spar over the translation of Augustine's proof text, Rom 5:12. Compare the modern New Revised Standard Translation with the Old Latin:

> NRSV: Therefore, just as sin came into the world through one man, and death came through sin, and so death spread to all because all have sinned.

> OL: Sin came into the world, and death through sin, and so death spread to all men, through one man, in whom all men sinned [*in quo omnes peccaverunt*].

In Greek, the last part of the verse is *eph' hoi pantes hermarton*. Modern scholars, Jerome, and Julian claim the *eph' hoi* should be understood as indicating "because of" or "on account of," not the "in whom" (*in quo*) of the Old Latin.[8] Julian says Paul means death is passed to Adam's descendants, not sin.[9]

Rather than sin being the cause of death, some argue death is the cause of sin. Meyendorff suggests the best translation would read, "As sin came

---

6. Aug., *Grace of Christ and Original Sin* 2.34.39. Eve's embarrassment will be discussed in the next section.
7. Rist, *Ancient Thought Baptized*, 20.
8. Aug., *Unfinished Work* 2.174.
9. Aug., *Unfinished Work* 2.64.

into the world through one man and death through sin, so death spread to all men, and because of death, all men have sinned."[10] Theodore of Mopsuestia agreed death was the source of sin, not the other way around.[11] David Weaver suggests this is the common thread in the eastern fathers.[12] Less scholarly than Julian or Jerome and less polemical than Augustine, Pelagius simply interprets 5:12 as implying imitation; one man means, "by example or by pattern. Just as through Adam sin came at a time when it did not yet exist, so in the same way through Christ righteousness was recovered at a time when it survived in almost no one."[13]

Augustine chooses the darkest interpretation of Rom 5:12 to forge a connection to the disobedience of flesh and will. He needs all the negativity of the Manichaean analysis separated, somehow, from Manichaeism. Augustine finds his solution in the *process* of reproduction. Nothing is intrinsically wrong with the flesh; that would be the Manichaean error. However, the disorderly desire that our fallen condition requires for an erection is not a physical disorder, it is a disorder of the will. As a part of this approach, Augustine relentlessly insists on generation rather than imitation as the basis of a correct exegesis. Julian objects to the notion of the inheritance of sin, particularly if it implies an inherited guilt. However, Augustine needs more than just acknowledgement that sin is inherited; it has to be inherited because of concupiscence and conception.

If Rom 5:12 were to imply imitation, Augustine suggests it would mean imitation of the devil (the serpent) since the devil sins first.[14] Julian says we are talking about human sin, not angelic so entering the world means entering the world of humans. Eve is the first sinner, one woman, not one man. Julian explains men are the natural superiors of women and more worthy of imitation. Adam should have been a good example to imitate, but he becomes a bad one. Even if the woman sins first, the responsibility of the imitation of sin falls to Adam.[15] Origen similarly reasons that people attribute posterity to the man through the woman, so Adam is responsible.[16]

Augustine continues; if Paul says "through one man," he must mean Adam and generation.[17] Julian replies that if Paul believes sin is transmit-

---

10. Meyendorff *Byzantine Theology*, 144.
11. Ibid., 145.
12. Weaver." "From Paul to Augustine," 188.
13. Pelagius, *Commentary on Romans* (De Bruyn, 92).
14. Aug., *Unfinished Work* 2.48.
15. Aug, *Unfinished Work* 2.190.
16. Origen, *Commentary on Romans* 5.1.13.
17. Aug., *Unfinished Work* 2.49.

ted by generation, he should have said "by two people" since it is hard to generate with one. Augustine counters that generation starts with the emission of seed, so generation begins with the man.[18] The sophomoric debate goes on and on. The transmission cannot be by semen, *per se*; this is too close to the traducianist material transmission of the soul. Attractive as this idea is for some purposes, it implies a damaged nature, which is ruled out. Nor can it be blamed on intercourse. There would have been some form of intercourse in paradise, to answer the requirement to be fruitful and multiply, up to the predestined number of the elect.[19] Augustine insists that Rom 5:12 means that sin and guilt are transmitted by generation, through the disorderliness of desire. The debate continues throughout Romans, but Augustine has made his point.

Origen turns to Rom 5:18 ("Therefore just as one man's trespass led to condemnation for all, so one man's act of righteousness leads to justification and life for all.") in partial mitigation of the possible harsh interpretations of Rom 5:12. He suggests some of the confusion of Paul's exposition is deliberate concealment: if all have death because of Adam, should not all have life because of Christ? Origen believes in universalism, but it is not that easy. Salvation comes to "those who, by a great deal of effort and sweat, are able to ask for what is not seen, knock on that which is closed, and seek what is hidden."[20] We are all capable of salvation, but we have to choose.

Fitzmyer notes that Rom 5:19 ("For just as by the one man's disobedience the many were made sinners, so by the one man's obedience the many will be made righteous.") does seem to imply that Adam's disobedience leads to humanity's sinfulness.[21] This does not lead directly to Augustine's reading; an inherited propensity to sin suffices. Pelagius maintains his interpretation of imitation: "Just as by the example of Adam's disobedience many sinned, so also many are justified by Christ's obedience."[22] Julian says we do not merit reward unless we imitate Christ, and no one is guilty of sin unless he or she transgresses the law in imitation of Adam. Augustine replies, "This is the hidden and horrid poison of your heresy: you want the grace of Christ to consist in his example, not in his gift."[23] Having identified generation as the transmission channel, he has to be more specific about the source—he has to show how generation recapitulates Adam's sin, adding culpability to

---

18. Aug., *Unfinished Work* 2.56.
19. See, for example, *Revisions* 1.13(12).8.
20. Origen, *Commentary on Romans* 5.1.4 (Sheck, 305).
21. Fitzmyer, *Romans: A New Translation*, 406.
22. Pelagius, *Commentary on Romans* (De Bruyn, 95).
23. Aug., *Unfinished Work* 2.146 (Teske, WSA, I/25, 227).

an inclination. He revisits Rom 7:14–7:25. Paul's description of the human psychological struggle. The Manichees use this text as a proof of their dualistic interpretation of Paul. They argue that the intermingling of good and evil matter within a person is the source of the battle between spirit and flesh (Rom 7:25). The speaker in Romans cannot control himself; it is as if something else makes his choices. Paul says, "I" do not sin, but the sin that dwells within him sins (Rom 7:20). Mani writes, "Concupiscence is the origin of evil, through which wretched souls become enslaved to lust, not of their own accord, since this is what we do only with unwilling mind."[24] The resemblance to Augustine is strong, but Augustine distinguishes his concupiscence, which is a failure of the will, from Manichaean concupiscence, which is the infection of evil matter in the human psyche. Pelagius treats the whole passage as an expression of the development of habit. If we begin to sin, the first occasions are willing, but afterward, "habitual desires, or the persuading of the enemy"[25] begin to control us.

How is the war in the members to be fought in Augustine's new theology? There could be no *struggle* between flesh and spirit with a will only able to choose sin; it is not a struggle if you always lose. He requires a new vision of Paul's psychology; the penis is the principle member waging war against us, and its unruliness is the dominant component of the sin dwelling in us. Since even saints have erections, Augustine concludes that the imprisonment spoken of by Paul, beset with unruly members, persists even after his conversion; he remains carnal. Rom 7:17 reinforces Paul's permanent slavery to this desire, which is created by sin, and tempts us to sin again.[26] The sin that dwells in Paul is not anger or pride, but sexual desire. This particular desire is highly unreliable, reflecting its symbolic role as disobedience. Lust fails to sustain the erection both when it is lawfully employed for procreation and when it is sinfully focused on pleasure. It is inconsistent, dominating the mind with sexual thoughts and deserting the body.[27] The emphasis is on the failure of lust to aid the body. Brown thinks Augustine's awareness of impotence shows the breadth of his psychology. The loss of control in orgasm and the frustration of the impotent are both examples of the body defying the mind and will.[28]

Augustine still has to be careful about how he condemns the flesh. The young Augustine faintly praises the genitals as part of his anti-Manichaean

---

24. Quoted in BeDuhn, *Augustine's Manichaean Dilemma*, Vol. 2, 109.
25. Pelagius *Commentary on Romans* (De Bruyn, 105).
26. Aug., *Answer to Julian* 6.23.73.
27. Aug., *City of God* 14.16.
28. Brown, *Body and Society*, 417. See also Wills, *Augustine's Confessions*, 139.

phase. He points out in *Answer to Faustus* that there is nothing shameful about the members of the saints. They would not be condemned just because they are not as beautiful as the unconcealed parts of the body; the problem is how they are used. Virgins and celibates preserve them unused, and this is best. If the married confine sex to rational procreation and avoid passion, then their use is not shameful.[29] In fact, all parts of the body are good, but because something shameful enters into Adam and Eve's nature, sex becomes the embarrassing action we see today.[30] The *Revisions* retract even this mild praise. Paul calls the genitals dishonorable because the law in these members is at war with the mind on account of sin.[31]

Augustine has backhanded compliments for female genitals as well. He disagrees with those who believe the resurrected bodies of women would be masculine in form; Augustine claims they will be improved: "The female organs will still be present. Now, however, they will be accommodated not to their former use but to a new beauty which will not excite the lustful desire of the beholder, for there will be no lust. Instead, they will evoke praise for the wisdom and compassion of God."[32] Women will be pleased to acquire nobler genitals. Men's genitals don't need improvement, but without the need for even rational control of the genitals, the flaccid penis will be the norm. Augustine's lack of interest in women suggests that he never was the profligate he advertises. He occasionally takes note of gender asymmetries; he recognizes women do not have to be aroused to participate in intercourse, as long as the man is. However, this simply reinforces the notion that the sin in sexual desire is entirely due to the male and not any enticement or seduction by the female.[33]

The battle shifts briefly out of Romans: "For all that is in the world, the lust of the flesh, and the lust of the eyes, and the pride of life, is not of the Father, but is of the world (1 John 2:16)." Being moved by beauty, even of bodies, but also of colors, shapes, and sounds, must be sharply distinguished, Augustine asserts, from sexual desire. Lust battles reason, which is humanity's true nature. Concupiscence always has desires contrary to the spirit, so cannot come from the Father.[34] Julian argues moderation, even in sexual desire, must be distinguished from immoderation. Augustine replies with the example of wine, which is undoubtedly good. There can be both

---

29. Aug., *Answer to Faustus* 29.4.
30. Aug., *Marriage and Desire*, 2.6.16.
31. Aug., *Revisions* 2.7(34).3.
32. Aug., *City of God* 22.17 (Babcock, WSA, I/7, 526).
33. Aug., *Marriage and Desire* 2.15.30.
34. Aug., *Answer to Julian* 4.14.73.

moderate and immoderate uses of wine, and John never mentions wine as a problem. However, Augustine insists, there are no moderate uses of sex.[35] Julian is in error when he identifies sexual desire as a good in the same category as wine. Julian does not think the error is his; Augustine has remained Manichaean, and cannot separate moderation from excess. John, he argues, does not blame concupiscence, in general, but only immoderation.[36] John had not referred uniquely to sexual desire but an excessive use of any of the senses, including a fondness for singing and perfumes.[37] Augustine denies he ever said concupiscence was only sexual. However, concupiscence is sin whenever "the flesh has desires opposed to the spirit (Gal 5:17)," which is always the case for sexual desire.

Pelikan traces Augustine's interpretation of Romans and original sin to Ambrosiaster: "all have sinned in Adam, as it were in the mass, for he himself was corrupted by sin, and all whom he begot were born under sin."[38] Ambrosiaster insists the Latin translations emphasizing the inheritance of sin were superior to the Greek ones, corrupted by heretics, but he confined the consequences to death.[39] Augustine adopts the notion of the mass of humanity, appearing as the *massa perditionis, massa damnata,* or *massa peccati* (mass of perdition, mass of damnation, mass of sin) and many other forms. This terminology conveniently supports his desire to have a general condemnation of humanity rather than individual responsibility for sin and error. Bonner agrees with Julian that Augustine's interpretation is unsupportable; he thinks Augustine is too obsessed with original sin to think critically.[40] Augustine *is* obsessed, and that obsession drives his exegesis. However, the focus of his obsession is not on original sin as we usually think of it. When we disentangle his thoughts, we find the waywardness of sexual desire at his center. The inconsistency of desire embodies every kind of human failure. It is the sin that is the punishment of sin.

## BAD SEX

Augustine uses the inconsistency of the motion of the genitals to demonstrate the disorder inherent in fallen humanity and its shame. The genitals are shameful because reason cannot control lust; erections happen or fail

35. Aug., *Unfinished Work* 4.21.
36. Aug., *Unfinished Work* 4.24.
37. Aug., *Unfinished Work* 4.28.
38. Pelikan, *The Christian Tradition*, 299.
39. Bray, "Ambrosiaster," 21–38.
40. Bonner, *St. Augustine of Hippo*, 372.

to happen without the mind and will. The genitals became subservient to lust as punishment for disobedience: "a certain shameless novelty emerged in the movements of their body. As a consequence, their nakedness was now indecent; it caught their attention and made them embarrassed."[41] Augustine explains their embarrassment: "Was it not that they perceived, he in an external motion, she in a hidden motion, those members acting in disobedience to the choice of their will, though they ought surely to have controlled them like the others by the mere sign of the will?"[42] Augustine expands the vision of Adam's immediate erection to include Eve's hidden motion, whatever that might be. He says, "She, of course, did not cover a visible arousal, but in those same members she experienced in a more hidden way something like the man's experience."[43]

The uncontrolled motion is the source of the shame; the indecent motion would not have been required for procreation if Adam and Eve had not sinned.[44] While Augustine occasionally admits an erection might have been part of reproduction in paradise, it would not have been spontaneous or result from biting fruit, but would be in response to the will. The inability to will an erection, much less an ejaculation, without lust, represents the punishment of the sin of original sin.

Augustine finds an argument in Cicero. Sex is so fantastic it overwhelms the mind. People can have a conversation over dinner while drinking wine, watching the theater, or listening to music. Since we lose control during sex, sexual pleasure is marked off as the only pleasure beyond reason and the will.[45] Even if concupiscence can be used to a good end in marriage, it cannot be a good—it bears the mark of Adam. The overwhelming pleasure obliterates the mind as a reminder of our fallen nature.[46] Augustine has an exalted and unrealistic view of sex. He does not sound like a man who had sex with one woman for fourteen years—some of those moments must have been less than all-encompassing. He imagines the mind-destroying power of sex never fades; it triumphs over the sedately married, inducing them to lose themselves in desire, only to suffer regret when the mind regains control. Married couples with a correctly oriented will would prefer sex without any pleasure, or at least with only limited pleasure. They would also prefer

---

41. Aug., *City of God* 14.17 (Babcock, WSA, I/7, 124–25).
42. Aug., *Two Letters* 1.16.32 (Teske, WSA, I/24, 132).
43. Aug., *Answer to Julian* 4.13.62 (Teske, WSA, I/24, 415).
44. Aug., *Marriage and Desire* 1.5.6.
45. Aug., *Answer to Julian* 4.14.72.
46. Aug., *City of God* 14.16. It is also hard to do algebra in the middle of a sneeze.

to confine sex to procreation.⁴⁷ Augustine has some toleration for marital sex, but the lee-way is small. The married sin if they have sex for pleasure and not children and the unmarried sin if they ever even think about sexual pleasure.⁴⁸

Augustine is obsessed with Julian's sex life. Julian will not admit sex in paradise would never have been for pleasure, but only for the rational conception of children.⁴⁹ Augustine feels Julian's entire philosophy is based on sex. The desire that Julian tolerates obstructs the control of the body by the soul, leading to the shameful movements Augustine fears and condemns. Allowing desire to rule extinguishes the chance for a good life.⁵⁰ Augustine feels Julian is out of control. He imagines Julian even approves of couples having sex at all times of the day, whenever desire appears. If Julian has lived such a disgusting life, he should shut up and let others teach about marriage.⁵¹ For Augustine, Julian is a dangerous cheerleader for concupiscence; praising sex encourages the war between the spirit and the flesh. Augustine says he is not fighting over desire or Julian's obvious affection for it.⁵² He sniffs that he doesn't want to know about Julian's sex life; he is not interested in the private actions of a fan of desire.⁵³

For someone who expresses no interest in what Julian and his wife get up to, Augustine devotes a lot of text to the subject: "Shame! You are that fan of sexual desire. Shame, I say! This sexual desire which pleases you so much, against which it is necessary to fight if one does not want to commit sin by consenting to its enticements."⁵⁴ It is a sin to give in to desire and have sex for pleasure; to speak of it other than pejoratively is incomprehensible. Julian repeats that sexual desire is naturally good like all the senses. Julian says Augustine gives the devil credit for inserting it into our genitals; worse, Augustine uses our normal sense of shame and modesty to support his doctrine. In reply, Augustine insists desire is a foreign element injected by the devil.⁵⁵ Since it is foreign to the good of human nature as God created it, it certainly must be excluded from Jesus.

---

47. Aug., *Answer to Julian* 4.14.71.
48. Aug., *Answer to Julian* 2.10.33.
49. Aug., *Two Letters* 1.17.34.
50. Aug., *Answer to Julian* 3.12.26.
51. Aug., *Answer to Julian* 3.14.28.
52. Aug., *Answer to Julian* 5.7.29.
53. Aug., *Answer to Julian* 5.7.30.
54. Aug., *Unfinished Work* 2.122 (Teske, WSA, I/25, 217).
55. Aug., *Unfinished Work* 3.142.

According to Augustine, sexual desire is the sole desire *always* opposed to the spirit.[56] Christ was conceived by the Holy Spirit and was free of the war between spirit and flesh. Consequently, Christ did not have the desire that is a desire to sin, one of Augustine's many ways of saying he could not have had sexual feelings or reactions. Julian's Jesus has the normal range of desires, including sexual ones— his perfection lies in his resistance to temptations, not the absence of them. Pelagius compares Adam and Jesus in his *Commentary* on Rom 5:14, "As men, they would have been on a par with respect to the temptations of the flesh. Jesus showed his superiority [by resisting these temptations]."[57] Augustine is willing to admit Jesus ate and had hunger, but hunger is not the desire always at war with the spirit. Julian declares Augustine cannot separate sexual desire from hunger so cavalierly. Augustine dehumanizes Jesus; he waves around the word "concupiscence" and takes away Jesus's inner feelings and external senses.[58] If Augustine denies this, he denies Jesus has a human soul, combining the heresies of Apollinaris and Mani.[59] Augustine weakly replies that anyone who believes Christ had desires warring with the spirit should be anathema. He argues, "Christ could have felt this desire, if he had it, and he could have had it, if he had willed to. But heaven forbid that he should have willed to."[60] Julian plows on, claiming Augustine is reducing Jesus's humanity by limiting his senses. In a low blow, Julian remarks that it is not much of an example to imitate an *impotent* Christ.[61] Augustine claims Julian is just being silly.[62]

Augustine constructs Christ in his image. He cannot admit Jesus was capable of sexual activity—although he could thirst, he could not lust. The power of lust is limitless; it even disturbs the chaste in their sleep.[63] He accuses Julian of suggesting Jesus had wet dreams:

> We know that Christ did, of course, sleep, and if your darling was present in him, she at times surely deluded his sleeping senses by such dreams that it seemed to him that he was even having intercourse, and so his flesh aroused by the stimulus of

---

56. Aug., *Answer to Julian* 2.5.12.
57. Pelagius, *Commentary on Romans* (De Bruyn, 93).
58. Aug., *Unfinished Work* 4.46.
59. Aug., *Unfinished Work* 4.47. Augustine's Christology is a subject of considerable dispute. TeSelle, *Augustine the Theologian*, 155, argues Augustine, initially influenced by Origen, is later closer to the Antiochian school, verging on Nestorianism. If one's Christology is both Apollinarian and Nestorian, it is not completely worked out.
60. Aug., *Unfinished Work* 4.48 (Teske, WSA, I/25, 427).
61. Aug., *Unfinished Work* 4.50.1. My emphasis.
62. Aug., *Unfinished Work* 4.50.3.
63. Aug., *Answer to Julian* 3.20.38.

this good of yours would make his genitals uselessly erect and pour forth useless seeds.[64]

Augustine assumes even Julian will recoil from that thought. He will have to admit Christ had no impermissible desires. It would be frustrating for an impotent man to have wet dreams. Augustine admits in the *Confessions* to experiencing pleasure and even nocturnal emissions.[65] He bewails the apparent loss during sleep of the reason that can control desire during the day. He implores God to relieve him of the concupiscence troubling his soul.[66]

Julian's Christ is fully human; Augustine's Christ is arguably less so. Augustine believes some distance is necessary. Sin wounds our good human nature; Christ the physician must heal it.[67] Augustine believes a sick physician cannot heal. Since the sickness is concupiscence, particularly sexual desire, Christ must be free of all sexuality; if Adam and Eve had not sinned, we would all have shared that freedom. Augustine's vision of sex in paradise, before it was corrupted, is modelled on this view of Jesus. Sex would be restricted to reproduction and free of all desire.

## GOOD SEX

Augustine defines marriage outside of Eden as a damaged form of marriage in paradise. In the early *Good of Marriage*, Augustine says three goods moderate the evil of sexual desire, at least within marriage. First, concupiscence has a good end if all intercourse is for reproduction to replace the fallen angels.[68] Second, the sacramental status of marriage shows it is good. Third, *fides,* faithfulness, is a broad concept, extending beyond simple marital fidelity to include the willingness of each partner to have sexual relations with his or her partner, even if one partner prefers chastity. Kevin Guilfoy thinks Augustine supports a positive view overall. Marriage is good because of the friendship between the married partners, based on moderation and respect for each other's sexual needs. The biggest benefit is the mutual support provided to seek the higher good of chastity.[69] Guilfoy goes on to evaluate each of the goods of marriage in the context of the modern availability of Viagra. If Viagra were rationally chosen, it would restore procreation to the control

---

64. Aug., *Unfinished Work* 4.58 (Teske, WSA, I/25, 436).
65. Aug., *Confessions* 10.30.14.
66. Aug., *Confessions* 10.30.15.
67. Aug., *Marriage and Desire* 2.3.9.
68. Aug., *City of God* 14.10.
69 Guilfoy, "Man's Fallen State: St. Augustine on Viagra," 57.

of reason, and Augustine might approve. In contrast, if it were merely an aid to lust, he would not.

Without the first sin, there would have been conception without concupiscence; the genitals would calmly obey the will. Now, even celibates are under the sway of lust; they may resist the temptation to use an erection, but they cannot move the penis with the will.[70] Augustine is obsessed with movement—either the erection or the motions required for ejaculation. He speculates about whether the erection is required; reproduction could have occurred without any shameful motion if the will were in complete control. He marvels, "Do we not also and here is something even more surprising—command the fluid contained within the bladder to flow when we want, even when we are not compelled by abundance, and it obeys."[71] Reproduction in paradise would not require any motion beyond the insertion of the flaccid penis into the vagina stopping short of the maidenhead, or possibly just its placement in the general vicinity. Then, just like urinating, the semen would be released. If this paradisiacal insemination were to return, even a man who is incapable of an erection could participate in the propagation of the species. A man incapable of penetration would find such a theory comforting. Augustine is sure the chaste would prefer to reproduce this way, under the will's command, rather than requiring pleasure. The unchaste enjoy the pleasure that is really a punishment, to the detriment of their minds; they go beyond having sex with mistresses, but even have sex for pleasure with their *wives*.[72]

The first book of *Marriage and Desire* was written in 418 or 419. Augustine's very strange proposal of urinary insemination is offered early in the conflict before Julian writes *To Turbantius* and *To Florus*. Augustine was not provoked into this position; it represents his deepest thought. The urinary model has usually been politely ignored by Augustine's critics and defenders.[73]

Good sex, paradisiacal sex, would have been rational, passion-free, and of limited pleasure. The integrity of a virgin would not be destroyed by intercourse (the hymen would remain intact) because the semen would be deposited at the doorstep and make its way on foot. *City of God* 14.26, explains how sex would have worked in the felicity of Eden:

70. Aug., *Marriage and Desire* 1.7.17.

71. Aug., *Marriage and Desire* 1.31.53 (Teske, WSA, I/24, 88).

72. Aug., *Marriage and Desire* 1.31.53.

73. It has not gone completely unremarked; see, for example, the discussion in McLaren, *Impotence*, 29.

> Rather, the sexual organs would have been moved by the will's command, as the other members are; and, without the enticing goad of sexual heat, the husband would have poured his seed into his wife's womb with tranquility of mind and with no corruption of her bodily integrity.[74]

Maurice Dods leaves this odd passage in Latin, and others translate it euphemistically.[75] Augustine explains that if conception were under the power of the will, the semen could reach the womb without disturbing the hymen, just as the menstrual blood can flow out. Augustine believes the hymen might even have been preserved during a painless childbirth; the infant Jesus passed through the wall of the womb just as the resurrected Jesus could pass through doors.[76]

Rebecca West's discussion of the passage is novel. She believes Augustine both exaggerates sex's importance and has a dread of it more common in hysterical women. She traces this to the "less dignified anatomy of man, a point on which Augustine copiously complained"[77] and to the asymmetrical power of the relationship. Men are exhausted by the act but for women it enhances their power. West is rare among Augustine's biographers in noticing his complaints about male indignity and feelings of powerlessness. Gerard Loughlin speculates even more broadly. He compares Augustine's vision of controlled insemination with the movie *Alien3*, in which a sleeping Ripley is impregnated passively.[78]

Harnack finds Augustine's remarks disgusting and traces them to his Manichaean past. He is surprised Augustine's central concern with the uncontrollability of desire doesn't lead to the conclusion that desire is sinless.[79] Harnack mistakes the complexity of the argument—Augustine cannot allow the defect to lie in nature, but must make the will defective.

---

74. Aug., *City of God* 14:26 (Babcock, WSA, I/7, 134).

75. Bettenson's translation of 14:26 reads in part (Bettenson, 591), "the husband would have relaxed upon his wife's bosom." The translation of Walsh et al. reads in part (Walsh *et al.*, 318), "a man and his wife could play their active and passive roles in the drama of conception without the lecherous promptings of lust." Cavadini, commenting on Andrea Dworkin's *Intercourse*, 190 believes this confused her about Augustine's meaning. *Feeling Right*, 216. Niebuhr echoes the active and passive phrasing in his analysis of self-love in sexual relations. The active male has a tendency to self-deification, and the passive woman has a corresponding tendency to idolatry, although both elements can be present. *The Nature and Destiny of Man*, Vol.2, 237.

76. Aug., *Letter* 137.2.8. By this time, Augustine had adopted the *in partu* virginity of Mary.

77. West, *Saint Augustine*, 37.

78. Loughlin, *Alien Sex*, 114–15.

79. Harnack, *History of Dogma*, Vol. 5, 211.

In Aristotelian terms, a will that is not in the service of the mind is not, technically, the will, but Augustine's will still can corrupt nature and damn all humanity.

Augustine gets some credit for admitting there would have been sex in paradise. Gregory of Nyssa, Ambrose, and Jerome assume the contrary; Eden was the place of chastity and immortality.[80] For them, sex is a result of sin. The mature Augustine believes the human population will increase until the portion of it predestined for salvation can replace the fallen angels.[81] Therefore, anyone arguing against reproduction in Eden would be saying sin was necessary to provide the predestined number of saints. To blunt the horror of giving sex a divine purpose, Augustine decides sex in paradise would have been rational, under the control of reason and the will. There would have been fully worthy marriage and children born without lust, with the penis an obedient servant. Lust is shameful because it usurps the control of the soul over the body. If the will controlled the shameful members, they would not be shameful.[82]

Augustine complains that lust does not completely control the body.[83] The form of his complaint is telling. Any man knows there are many reasons for the lack of an erection: exhaustion, illness, overindulgence, boredom, and even an unconscious *lack* of desire underlying the outward profession of desire. Augustine ignores all other male sexual dysfunctions. For Augustine, the only case of interest is when the mind truly wants to have sex, but the penis will not cooperate.

Augustine argues that this overwhelming but inconsistent concupiscence is not a natural phenomenon. It is the punishment of the Fall. Without the disobedience of Adam and Eve, things in paradise would have been rational and calm. Arousal, if it existed at all, would have been at the command of the will at the direction of the rational soul. The genitals would be moved as we move our hands and feet, the hymen would be preserved in intercourse; there would have been no pain in childbirth.[84] All of this would have occurred without desire or, at least, without any *unreasonable* desire if sin had not entered into Eden. If the unexpected motion had not startled them, no part of the body would have seemed shameful, and no part would have needed to be covered.[85] Reproduction in Eden would

80. Brown, *Body and Society*, 399.
81. Aug., *City of God* 14.10.
82. Aug., *City of God* 14.23.
83. Aug., *City of God* 14.16.
84. Aug., *Grace of Christ and Original Sin* 2.36.40.
85. Aug., *Grace of Christ and Original Sin* 2.36.41.

have been peaceful and not passionate; any motion required would be at the command of the will.[86] Augustine imagines sex by the numbers: (1), up; (2), in (but not very far); (3), squirt; (4), out; and, (5), down. In the flaccid variant, the up and down steps could be omitted. He begs Julian to accept that paradisiacal sex would have been obedient to the will; he asks rhetorically whether Julian's approval of sexual desire extends to the desires troubling the unwilling; are these desires also good?[87] He worries about unnatural forms of sex: would they be too attractive to resist or too shameful to pursue?[88]

He discusses the incredible control some people have over their bodies. He revels in people who can wiggle their ears one at a time, move their scalps up and down, swallow and retrieve items, and combine sweet-smelling farts into a song.[89] Men can do all those remarkable things and still cannot control their erections. Cooper and Leyser think this is a bit of "lowbrow satire of ancient phallocentric pretensions."[90] They suggest that by ridiculing the notion of bodily control, Augustine upsets the Roman concept of self-control as the epitome of masculinity, similarly eliminating the claim of the ascetic to moral authority. The classical comparison between the Roman ideal of the hard man in control of his desires and the soft man who even allows himself to be penetrated, is mistaken. No man has any more control than the soft man does.[91] This is an attractive analysis, and certainly captures Augustine's rejection of any claimed superiority of the Stoic sage or the Pelagian authentic Christian. However, it does not give enough weight to the urgency with which Augustine pursues the erectionalization of theology. Augustine repeatedly contrasts our control over every other action with this particular failure. If reducing the plausibility of self-control through satire is his goal, the emphasis remains on the penis and, at least in this arena, satire does not seem to be his genre.

Adam's erection is the Platonic ideal form of all the erections of his male line, staining them with the same disobedience. This theme has a long life. Montaigne feels the penis is not the only disobedient body part. We sneeze, we blush, and our hair stands on end. Montaigne says his client has been unjustly singled out. If the question is one of sex, the penis has a

---

86. Aug., *Answer to Julian* 3.25.57.
87. Aug., *Answer to Julian* 4.5.34.
88. Aug., *Marriage and Desire* 2.35.59.
89. Aug., *City of God* 14.24.
90. Cooper and Leyser, "The Gender of Grace," 543.
91. Ibid., 544.

partner, the vagina.⁹² According to Angus McLaren, this tongue-in-cheek defense caused Montaigne's work to be placed on the index of forbidden books.⁹³

Loughlin describes Augustine's passionless sex as prostituted sex. Adam is like the porn star earning his salary by performing the sex act without passion or distraction.⁹⁴ While Loughlin's comparison seems outrageous, it raises the question of whether Augustine thinks prostitutes act out of concupiscence or the will. While fourth-century Carthage and Rome may have been more sedate than they were under Tiberius, it would be astonishing if Augustine were unaware of both male and female prostitutes. He might not have known the ancient analog of the fluff girl whose duties include getting the male porn star erect, but Caligula used their services. The erection may not always be at the command of the will, but it can be fluffed. It can also be subject to chemical modification—in ancient times a range of aphrodisiacs but in the modern era, Viagra. The insistence that only lust can move the genitals is oddly naïve. Augustine also shows an obsession with penetration as the only form of sexual interaction. After the sex-soaked life he claims, Augustine should have been aware of more options.

William of Champeaux thinks sex in paradise might be no more pleasurable than "putting your finger in your mouth."⁹⁵ In contrast, Cooper and Leyser conclude Augustine thought it "would have been unimaginably exquisite."⁹⁶ It seems clear Augustine's view is closer to Champeaux's than to Cooper and Leyser's. Sorabji says Aquinas and possibly Augustine think sex in Eden would have been more pleasurable than our common experience, "through not gulping our sex."⁹⁷ This also does not capture Augustine's passionless, rational reproduction.

Augustine is certain the erection would have been at the command of the will in Eden. There would be no sexual desire, or, minimally, desire could be summoned and dismissed by the will.⁹⁸ Any passion would be unthinkable; he cannot believe the spirit and flesh would have been at odds in paradise; sex would have been for reproduction or the body's health.⁹⁹

---

92. Montaigne, *Essays*, 115–16.
93. McLaren, *Impotence*, 28.
94. Loughlin, *Alien Sex*, 192.
95. http://plato.stanford.edu/entries/william-champeaux. Accessed June 1, 2015.
96. Cooper and Leyser "The Gender of Grace," 542.
97. Sorabji, *Emotion and Peace of Mind*, 408–409.
98. Aug., *Answer to Julian* 4.11.57.
99. Aug., *Answer to Julian* 4.14.69.

It is not clear what Augustine meant by reasons of health; perhaps sex was preferable to wet dreams.

Julian believes sex in paradise would have been much like sex out of paradise. There is a natural pleasure associated with sex; Julian associates that pleasure with lustful feelings. He doesn't see where the guilt lies. He cannot understand how Augustine can call the pleasure of intercourse shameful and the arousal of the genitals diabolical, yet the members themselves are innocent.[100] Augustine insists passion would not have had a role in Eden; paradise would have been the ideal place for peace and happiness. While there might have been pleasure, it would not have been the pleasure of passion.[101] Even if there had been some weak form of desire, the penis would be have been used as a tool and desire would follow the will.[102] Everything would have been serene and free of shame without the Fall.

Augustine conjures up the image of a man distributing semen in a broadcast fashion, swinging a hose-like member, watering a garden of recumbent women, arranged in tidy furrows, calmly awaiting fertilization:

> After all, why should we not believe that in paradise God could have granted to man in his blessed state with regard to his seed what we see is granted to farmers with regard to the seeds of grain? Then man's seed would be sown without any shameful lust by the genital organs in obedience to a sign from the will, just as the other seed is sown without any shameful lust by farmers' hands in obedience to a sign from the will.[103]

He repeats this image a decade later: "human beings could in paradise be sown in the fertile fields of women by the male genital organs, just as grain is sown in the earth by the hands of farmers."[104] His model of a urinary, passionless, rational sex in paradise is the fantasy of the impotent man—not a reformed rake.

---

100. Aug., *Unfinished Work* 2.33.
101. Aug., *Unfinished Work* 2.39.
102. Aug., *Unfinished Work* 2.42.
103. Aug., *Marriage and Desire* 2.14.29 (Teske, WSA, I/24, 71).
104. Aug., *Unfinished Work* 5.14 (Teske, WSA, I/25, 528).

# 11

## Augustine's Problem

THIS BOOK HAS ONLY addressed a part of the vast works of Augustine; the portion covered can be simply summarized. Augustinian sin cannot depend on a flawed nature; otherwise, it hints of Manicheanism. The error must lie in the will. It must be inevitable—a choice that is not truly a choice—to ensure the sin is universal. The inevitable sin is the concupiscence of conception, identified as the sin that is the punishment of sin. It is the punishment for Adam and Eve's disobedience but is always renewed in each conception. After this first misstep, the will becomes helpless without God's individual grace, as helpless as a sex-addict or an impotent man. Augustine generalizes his personal incapacity to all humanity. We have the capability of free choice—but only to sin. The ability to be sinless is now lost. God predestines which of us can ever use the will for any good end. We lack even the ability to repent unless God chooses us to repent. The disobedience of the male member recapitulates and symbolizes the primal disobedience. Whether flaccid or firm, it is beyond a man's control. Unconvincingly, he attaches the concupiscence now required for conception to the consequence of the conception—the child—resulting in its just damnation and requiring a compensatory infant baptism. Augustine declares we are all born in a state worthy of damnation; we are all dishonorable vessels, destined for a well-deserved destruction. Anyone who is not damned should be grateful for God's unmerited grace when selected as an honorable vessel. God does not care that the number of people to whom he shows mercy is negligibly small compared to the number abandoned.

Given the oddity of Augustine's positions and the church's efforts to sweep some of them under the carpet, it is surprising most of the Augustinian edifice stands. If it is not the power of his views, the source of his victory has to be sought elsewhere. For all of its influence on the development of the western church, the ins and outs of the controversy are a mystery to most. Brown considers Augustine's rallying of the entire North African church behind him to have been unprecedented—two hundred bishops arrayed against a single layman. Just as startling was the method used to construct a theological edifice on liturgical customs. The challenging issues of grace and free will were dismissed as being fully explained by the custom of infant baptism and the Lord's Prayer.[1] Augustine's success requires an explanation.

Although this struggle is frequently framed as the battle between Augustine and the Pelagians, their perspectives are not the only fifth-century ones available. Jerome has a point of view that, while anti-Pelagian, is not quite Augustinian. John Cassian is anti-Augustinian, without being Pelagian. These alternatives have some influence on the development of the western church but do not challenge the edifice of the great North African saint. The roads not taken highlight Augustine's novelty and provide further evidence for the necessity for a strong psychological motivation underlying his theology.

## WHY DID AUGUSTINE WIN?

Brown emphasizes the importance of the clash of cultures between the North African church and the super-rich refugees fleeing along with Pelagius from Alaric.[2] The refugees were part of the Roman elite, characterized by a robust and firmly held belief in their privileged status, and the correctness of their religion. They listened to the advice of preachers like Pelagius, but they did not take direction. From their pinnacles, they decided how to spend their money. The extreme form of renunciation exemplified by Paulinus of Nola and practiced by some of the newcomers was incompatible with North African sensibilities. Cyprian had established the principle of funneling alms to the bishop of a town rather than throwing money around. Then, sanctified by his control, the bishop could expend the funds as he saw fit. The comfortable and confident Roman elitism was anachronistic. It was the era of Alaric and not the era of martyrs.[3]

Crucially, the refugee Pelagius did not understand the significance of Alaric. Ambrose had, only twenty years earlier, advocated a populist critique

---

1. Brown, *Through the Eye of a Needle*, 369.

2. Brown provides a fascinating account of the transformation of the Church with the shifting patterns of wealth in *Through the Eye of a Needle*, chapters 21–23.

3. Stortz, "Pelagius Revisited," 135.

of the wealthy and their greed. After Alaric, Rome needed the rich to apply their resources to the stabilization of the empire. Constantinople did not want them to please themselves with the whimsical dispersal of funds, either for wasteful games in the circus or poorly capitalized foundations for the poor. Brown argues that Pelagius and Caelestius were not defeated by Augustine but by the reluctance of leading Romans who were rallying around the empire to tolerate another elitist group.[4] Many critics believe the high standards of the Pelagians were inappropriate for the times; only a big-tent church could survive. This certainty may be misplaced; the Donatist church survived its official dismemberment in 411 until the time of the Arab conquest—it found a way to keep a congregation.

The Pelagian approach encouraged dangerous renunciations like those of Melania and Pinianus.[5] An anonymous Pelagian wrote a tract, *On Riches*,[6] excoriating the rich: "take away the rich and you will find no poor (*tolle divitem et pauperem non invenies*)."[7] The author accuses them of building their riches by robbing the poor.[8] Ambrose could well have shared these sentiments, and Jerome would have appreciated skewering the rich, but this sort of anarchistic disruption of the social order was not compatible with the needs of the failing empire.

Augustine responds, "take away pride and riches will do no harm (*tolle superbiam: divitiae non nocebunt*)."[9] Pelagian emphasis on renunciation was misplaced: the rich should provide alms to the church to build up their treasure in heaven. Wealth could be sanctified if arrogant display and abuse of power could be eliminated. Against renunciation, Augustine justified wealth and careful management of capital. Brown believes the Roman world was under too much pressure from civil war and invasion to adopt a social gospel. Even if a generation earlier Ambrose and Chrysostom had excoriated

---

4. Brown, *Religion and Society*, 191.

5. The renunciators seldom completely divested themselves. Melania and Pinianus sold their household slaves on the open market to maximize their value. Dunn, "The Poverty of Melania the Younger and Pinianus," 101.

6. Rees notes that *On Riches* "led John Morris to make his incisive but controversial comment" that "'it is by any text book example socialism.'" *Life and Letters*, Vol. 2, 171.

7. Pelagius, *On Riches* 12.1 (Rees, Vol. 2, 194).

8. Pelagius, *On Riches* 17.1.

9. Aug., *Sermon* 39.4 (Hill, WSA, III/2, 218). The date of the sermon is unknown, possibly ranging from 405 to 420. The phrasing matches the Pelagian work but there is no proof it was composed in response.

the rich and greedy, the writer of *On Riches* had missed his time. Worrying about the poor was less important than the collapse of the empire.[10]

Rather than adopting an Ambrosian condemnation of avarice, Augustine feels wealth is one of God's arbitrary gifts, flowing from God to the rich and from the rich to the church. The Pelagians think wealth is another bad habit, feeding on the poor. Another anonymous Pelagian condemns the diversion of money from the poor to the clergy; "it is better for you not to give alms at all than to cause a great number to be despoiled of money from which you put a roof over the heads of a few, and to strip several of their clothes so as to clothe one."[11]

Appealing to imperial authority against the Pelagians was more likely to have succeeded for economic and political than for theological reasons. Free will was a threat to the institutional church; if people could obey God's commands in isolation, they had no need to come to church. There would be no steady flow of alms for the remission of little sins and no dependence on the authority of the clergy to dispense the sacraments. A weaker church would not be an effective ally of the empire. Pelagian beliefs undermined civil society as well. If on December 8, 1941, Henry Ford had experienced a religious conversion and wanted to rid himself of all his wealth, President Roosevelt would have been horrified—he needed tanks and trucks. The rich had previously displayed their wealth in civic projects. It did the emperor no harm if they took the poor off his hands, but frittering the capital away on shrines or scholarly monks while public needs were unaddressed was not in Constantinople's interest.

No one had any interest in flower-power renunciations. Augustine and Alypius had dissuaded a North African military commander, Count Boniface, from retiring to a spiritual life while the empire needed him.[12] Building a strong local church harnessed wealth for the benefit of the empire. Augustine linked the empire to the church and the church to wealth; his view held into the middle ages.[13] The *noblesse oblige* Ambrose and Pelagius appealed to was dead. The bishop might visit the rich for a contribution to the bell-tower fund, but would not judge them or direct them to deal with the poor. The lines were re-drawn. The North African tradition and the practicalities of the times led to the sacramentalization of wealth; treating it as God's gift is a step closer to identifying money as a positive sign of God's election. The dichotomy between notions of social justice and the use of the rich for the

---

10. Brown, *Through the Eye of a Needle*, 378.
11. Pelagius, *On Christian Life* 12 (Rees, Vol. 2, 120).
12. Aug., *Letter* 189.
13. Brown, *Through the Eye of a Needle*, 377.

organ fund has remained a source of tension in the church. Adam Smith points out the danger of an indulgence of the rich; it causes us to respect their opinions more than those of the poor and corrupts our judgments of ethical issues.[14] Of course, Smith goes on to say such deference serves a useful purpose in maintaining an orderly society—an Augustinian point.

Brown's analysis of the changing implications of wealth and donations in the church provides one key to the surprising effectiveness the Africans demonstrated in the condemnations of the Pelagians. Summoning hundreds of bishops to Carthage was simple; getting them to condemn Pelagian ideas was remarkably easy. Augustine convinced them Pelagianism disrupted the existing African patterns of church governance and were incompatible with the sacramental importance of baptism; the theological niceties and eventual consequences were ignored. The battle with the Donatists was also a struggle for institutional dominance—resulting, not coincidentally, in a transfer of wealth to the victorious Catholics. The fact that Augustinian predestination is equally or more damaging to the relevance of the church may not have been clear to the well-disciplined African bishops. R. D. Hampden stresses the struggle was political as well as theological. The issues were church governance in the failing empire, not the moral earnestness of Pelagius. He was fighting the wrong fight.[15]

The anonymous Pelagian authors of *On Riches* and *On Christian Life* were not just opponents of the rich. As British archeologist and historian J. N. L. Myres points out, the Latin word *gratia* could have the implication of favoritism and corruption. When Augustine asserted an arbitrary grace, the Pelagians heard echoes of arbitrary justice. If God's commandments are impossible, then his decision to save any particular individual is only a personal favor, an act of *gratia*.[16] The harshness of Pelagius's belief in final justice depends on Judgment Day being a fair trial; no *gratia* was needed or wanted. When Augustine called the Pelagians the *inimici gratiae*, the enemies of grace, it may have sounded like "opponents of corruption" to some ears.

The establishment saw such radical critiques of the callousness of the wealthy and the corruption of justice as destabilizing. The number of complaints about judicial corruption, *gratia*, drops abruptly after the suppression of the Pelagians in 418.[17] If this picture of the Pelagian community is

---

14. Smith, *Theory of Moral Sentiments*, Section 1.3.3.

15. Hampden, *Epitome of Hampden*, 11.

16. Myres, "Pelagius and the End of Roman Rule," 27.

17. Ibid., 31. Myres uses the Theodosian Code, a collection of imperial rescripts from the 320s to the 430s.

accurate, it comprised a group of reformed-minded aristocrats who wished to retire from the world, but were also offended by the selfish and corrupt wealthy. They wanted to retain the Roman virtues while adding the Christian virtues to them, as in the *Letter to Demetrias*. It may have been too late.

Myres's thesis that this was *primarily* a dispute about the meaning of *gratia* has met opposition. Cooper and Leyser interpret *gratia* more broadly to include the complex relationship between patron and client in the thinly administered empire. *Gratia* was the grease needed to make it work.[18] Armstrong writes of Myres's analysis that it at least suggests a deep Pelagian conviction that God cannot be a corrupt judge on the Roman model,[19] a view shared by Brown.[20] Pelagius sees God as the ideal judge, dispensing justice that is fair and can be seen as fair. Myres argues Augustine cannot debate Pelagius on social or political issues without compromising his concept of the relationship of God to humanity; if all is predestined, then there is no room for politics or reform.[21] Even if this social critique was important to the Pelagians, there is only limited reference to the rich and poor in the Julian corpus. Augustine's sexualization deflects the argument from the social gospel.

The young Augustine had felt liberated by his conversion. He had achieved some peace by accepting authority (and by avoiding Monnica's marriage plans). By the time of the Pelagian controversy, his world had become stale. Pelagius retained the belief in the ability of the Christian to lead a new, radically different life—often discarding his wealth in the process. Augustine was weighed down by despair; it was not possible for him to shed his impotence. No one could ever change the sorry state of his life. Brown concludes Augustine abandoned the tradition of Christian exceptionalism while Pelagius embraced it.[22] An emphasis on the new person, separated from the old ways and the old society was exactly what the empire didn't need. Even though he spoke to the universality of human responsibility, Pelagius identified with the dedicated faithful, withdrawn from the issues of the world if not fleeing to the desert. As a pillar of the empire, the church had no use for him. Augustine had successfully captured the mood of the time, just as he had earlier correctly gauged the triumph of Ambrose's church. If Pelagius represented the early church, he also, fatally to his cause, embodied

---

18. Cooper and Leyser, "The Gender of Grace," 549.
19. Armstrong, St. Augustine and Christian Platonism," 23.
20. Brown, *Augustine of Hippo*, 343.
21. Myres, "Pelagius and the End of Roman Rule," 29.
22. Brown, *Religion and Society*, 200.

the old ethical concepts of the stoical and Hellenistic past, overwhelmed by the barbarian hordes.

Orlando Patterson provides a related historical analysis. He argues that the character of slavery in each era shapes the concept of freedom. He contrasts the status of freedom in the first centuries after the establishment of the Roman empire with its degraded state in the late fourth and early fifth century. Augustus swept away the old civic freedoms and responsibilities of the Republic. Nevertheless, the early empire supported a notion of personal freedom under the umbrella of the sovereignty of the emperor. Personal freedom was primarily negative: it was the right to equality under the law and freedom from coercion. Patterson compares this to the relationship of master and freedman. The freedman was no longer his master's slave but remained a dependent, owing him loyalty.[23] Paul wrote in the context of this dual freedom, emphasizing the personal freedom of the freedman in Galatians, and the sovereign freedom of God in Romans. In Galatians, Paul says the believer is free from the law; "For freedom Christ has set us free. Stand firm, therefore, and do not submit again to a yoke of slavery (Gal 5:1)." In Romans, freedom is granted as a gift; God frees us from sin in a gratuitous act of emancipation.[24] By Augustine's time, the response to the barbarian assault destroyed this balance of freedoms in the empire. Only the sovereign freedom of the emperor to grant gifts remained. This was responsible for Augustine's misunderstanding, as Patterson sees it, of the careful distinctions in Paul and leads to the dominance of grace as an arbitrary favor.[25] Augustine is not ignorant of the concept of personal freedom, but he despises it. He acts as a disillusioned freedman, who has not achieved happiness.[26] This disappointment is close to that of the impotent man. Pelagians were again living in the past. They believed in personal freedom; reason, human nature, and belief were sufficient resources to define an ethical life. They were not coerced by sin. Instead, they were free individuals living under the eye of a just God. A newly freed slave jealously protected her rights; the Pelagians resented any suggestion they were still slaves. Patterson notes that many of the heretical movements of the middle ages that stressed personal freedom against the sovereign freedom of church and state were essentially Pelagian.[27]

---

23. Patterson, *Freedom*, 258–263.
24. Ibid., 337–343.
25. Ibid., 376–379.
26. Ibid., 380.
27. Ibid., 390.

Beyond these economic and political factors, Augustine was a superb debater and controversialist. The largest advantage was speaking last. Julian responds to *Marriage and Desire*. The later works were all unknown to him. They appear as if they are unanswerable, when they were only unanswered. Augustine trades on his reputation as an enemy of heretics. He debates Manichaeans, writes against the Arians and other heretics, and masterminds the destruction of the Donatists. He had a reputation, while Pelagius, Caelestius, and Julian just had unsteady friends. Displaced from their power center in Rome, they had no place to stand.

Augustine had no equal in finding authorities to bolster his case, even if he reached his conclusions by different routes.[28] His mining of Cyprian built a wall Julian could not breach without being accused of attacking the revered martyr.[29] He does not scruple to re-write Chrysostom[30] and deliberately misreads Tyconius.[31] He inverts the plain meaning of texts such as Zech 1:3, Isa 1:18–19, and Matt 7:7, claiming as support the hijacked texts of Ambrose and Cyprian. He is quite unabashed in using contradictory interpretations. He tells the rich to knock by giving alms[32] while insisting no one knocks without a prior act of grace.[33] He conceals the hardness of his doctrine—the common folk should be encouraged to seek salvation without informing them the outcome is predestined.[34]

Augustine's use of his skills is not evidence of error. Everybody did it; he just did it better. More is going on than this—Augustine correctly judges the drift of the time. The third-century consensus was unraveling in mutually contradictory ways. The fight against dualism, whether of the Marcionite or Manichaean type, concluded with the firm statement of the goodness of the creation *ex nihilo*. The Platonic distinctions between the sensible and intelligible worlds needed to be rebalanced. After the Nicene specification of the equality of Father and Son, the fourth century turns to Christology: what was Christ and what did he mean for humanity? For Origen and the Neoplatonic Christians, the most astonishing thing was the incarnation itself—the eternal Logos manifest in a finite human being. This is the turning point of history. The souls that fell from their original status as pure intellects into the material world have no way of reversing their fall

---

28. Rist, *Ancient Thought Baptized*, 20.
29. Aug., *Two Letters* 4.8.21.
30. Aug., *Answer to Julian* 1.6.22.
31. See Tilly, "Understanding Augustine Misunderstanding Tyconius."
32. Aug, *Sermon* 114B.9.
33. Aug., *Answer to Julian* 4.8.42.
34. Aug., *Gift of Perseverance* 22.57.

by themselves. The incarnation supplies the missing infinite compensating impulse. The souls can now rebound on their bungee cords and begin the process of deification, using their own efforts after this substantial boost. In this view, Christ only has to be the Logos in human form—his existence is sufficient.

As the Christological discussion continues, the Origenist view simply doesn't have enough Jesus in its Christ for the times. The focus shifts from Christ's birth to his life and from his life to his death. The eastern church takes Jesus's life as the paradigm of deification. This is reduced to the more pedestrian Pelagian imitation of Christ as a Roman obligation. The *integri Christiani* replace Vergil's *pius Aeneas* (dutiful Aeneas). It represents a conventional piety lacking the wonder of the eastern view of the incarnation and without much regard for Jesus's death. Augustine feels this focus on daily living and obedience diminishes the role of Christ.[35] Grace is more than teaching and example; human nature needs more than help—it needs to be saved.[36] Augustine is reaching toward some clearer meaning for the cross, an interpretation matching the glory of the incarnation.

Theories of the atonement attempt to reconcile the concepts of God's mercy and God's justice.[37] With this definition, Augustine's theory of grace falls into the general category of an atonement theory, but uncomfortably so. There is no meeting between judgment and mercy, just the separation of those persons who receive mercy for unknowable reasons from the rest, who are left with their default judgment. For the Pelagians, an arbitrary predestination cannot vindicate either God's mercy or his justice. In spite of the failure to establish a coherent doctrine combining Christ's birth, life, and death, Augustine nevertheless identifies the church's future direction. Issues of the nature of God and the nature of Christ seem to be settled and are of no interest to Augustine. The triumphant church has to be able to explain God's judgment and mercy to its congregation. Pelagius, with his dour Puritanism (without the Calvinist predestination), lacks both the grandeur of the eastern concept of the incarnation and the awesome mystery of the cross. There is no pondering of God's relation to humanity; God simply has provided his commandments and the tools to deal with them. Pelagius only stands for hard work; he lacks the depth even of a Jerome and certainly cannot match the understanding of God's love of Cassian.

Finally, Augustine wins because there is a clear sense in which he is right: Pelagius neglects human perversity and overestimates human

---

35. Aug., *Nature and Grace* 40.47.
36. Aug., *Grace of Christ and Original Sin* 1.33.36.
37. Niebuhr, *The Nature and Destiny of Man*, Vol. 2, 64.

capability. Although Augustine's particular form of original sin is inextricably tangled with sexual fantasies, other forms remain viable. The history of humanity demonstrates that we cannot depend on reason, education, and social institutions to overcome the flaws in our nature. There are too few saints to fill a church. The rapidly expanding church of middling Christians needs managing. Augustine builds a system in which ritual and custom can handle any number of congregants and yet is completely consistent with his sense of sin. The growing practice of infant baptism binds the people to the church and supports his theory of original sin. The traditional system of almsgiving is extended from the loving care of a few brothers and sisters in Christ to the mechanical support of the church and the clergy. It changes from a Christian duty to a mechanism for the expiation of sins. Similarly, prayer becomes a constant reminder of our sins and our incapacity. The cycle of birth, baptism, prayer, alms and death can control and comfort the mediocre majority. As Augustine says, there is no need to explain to the congregants that none of these had anything to do with their salvation.

## WHAT ABOUT JEROME?

Augustine's impotence muddles his critics and defenders, making their treatment of the Pelagian challenge clumsy. Jerome's views are not far from those of Pelagius. If they could have changed their natures, and if the anti-Origenist hysteria had not poisoned all discussion, there could have been a different history of the western church. Jerome's *Dialog Against the Pelagians* dates to shortly after the exoneration of Pelagius at Diospolis. Jerome is a biblical scholar, not a theologian. Although familiar with the Greek classics, Jerome does not feel Augustine's need to be reconciled with them, and he confidently rejects the Stoicism that is Julian's foundation. He depends on church tradition and an Origenist exegesis of scripture. Jerome does not care if the texts collide and happily ignores apparent contradictions. He champions asceticism when confronting Jovinian, but his themes in the *Dialog* are humility and mercy, not virginity and grace.[38]

Jerome objects to what he sees as arrogance about the possibility of sinlessness (*impecantia* and *apatheia* are equally despised if not always distinguished). He traces the Pelagian heresy to Plato, for whom evil is ignorance. He believes it is ridiculous to think sinlessness is possible. He cites 1 John 1:8, "If we say that we have no sin, we deceive ourselves and the truth is not in us," a text also used by Augustine. The Apostles sinned, and

---

38. A more polemical version is given in his letter 133 to Ctesiphon, written in 415 before Diospolis.

it is unseemly for us to place ourselves above them.[39] Pelagian citations of righteous men and women fail because they were not perfect. Abraham doubted God's promise of a child to be born to him and Sarah, showing the patriarchs were not free of sin and error.[40] The injunctions to sinlessness are goals rather than commandments. Perfection is never reached, but the goals are not lessons in futility; they are just hard. Like a bowman, we must concentrate to hit the target. We are on a journey: "At every step we take, since we never stand still, but are always on the way, what to us human beings seemed perfect was imperfect."[41] We do our best, striving with all our strength to obtain the prize promised in God's call.[42] He provides advice almost identical to Pelagius's advice to Demetrias.[43] This separates him from Augustine whose predestinationism makes the running pointless because God chooses who will finish the race without regard to effort or achievement. The bowman cannot even aim.

The different levels of holiness and perfection obtained by the saints demonstrate the impossibility of sinlessness.[44] The Pelagian contention that God's commandments would be unjust if they were impossible is answered by inverting the argument. Each commandment is individually within human grasp, but we cannot meet each commandment at every moment. A person may learn music and not master geometry. Each is possible, but not both by the same person at the same time.[45] Jerome admits God can grant sinlessness out of mercy, but he insists only mercy can produce complete sinlessness.[46] No person can be free of sin; this does not lead to universal damnation but to dependence on God. We inevitably fail, but can hope for God's mercy.[47] He finds different texts in Romans to use: "since all have sinned and fall short of the glory of God (Rom 3:23)"; and, "For God has imprisoned all in disobedience so that he may be merciful to all (Rom 11:32)." We are weak, but mercy is available to all.[48] When Jerome says "all," he means "all."

---

39. Jerome, *Dialog* 1.13.

40. Jerome, *Dialog* 1.34. See also *Dialog* 3.12. Jerome say free will can maintain periods of sinlessness; this does not imply one can be perpetually without sin.

41. Jerome, *Dialog* 1.14 (Hritzu, 251).

42. Jerome, *Dialog* 1.18.

43. Pelagius, *Demetrias* 27.3.

44. Jerome, *Dialog* 1.19.

45. Jerome, *Dialog* 1.21.

46. Jerome, *Dialog* 2.16.

47. Jerome, *Dialog* 3.3.

48. Jerome, *Dialog* 2.3.

Jerome rejects Pelagius's view that the will is sufficient *never* to sin, but he does not share Augustine's view that the will can only choose among sins; when we concentrate, a person can limit sin:

> But if he relaxes even for a moment, even as a man rowing his boat upstream immediately slips back if he relaxes his hands and is carried by the current of the river in the opposite direction he does not want to go, so also is the state of man. If it relaxes for even a moment, it gets to know its weaknesses and realizes that it cannot do much of itself.[49]

This is very close to the positions of Pelagius and Origen. It is the human responsibility to climb the stairway or row the boat upstream, but God's assistance is required and will be given to the striver. Jerome retains a belief in repentance, which is largely missing from both Pelagius and Augustine. Pelagius incorporates it into the general ability of the will, and Augustine rejects even the notion of it. Jerome recommends self-examination and an active seeking of God, which Augustine denies is possible and Pelagius over-intellectualizes.[50]

Jerome acknowledges God's foreknowledge and comes close to Augustine's predestination logic, but Jerome's God knows all possible futures. Human actions can affect which future happens; if God foresees that a person will turn to sin, his mercy gives him an opportunity to change his path and repent.[51] Although the future currently unfolding is one of continuing sin and eventual disaster, if the sinner repents, the future can be changed. God offers humanity the gift Dickens gave Scrooge—to change the shadows of the future.

Jerome does support infant baptism, but primarily from a liturgical point of view. He has the same vague understanding of a contagion shared by Origen and Tertullian.[52] There is no theory of concupiscence and sin. He can hold onto a notion of original sin and separate creation of souls at the same time without bothering about the contradiction that puzzles Augustine.[53] If the Pelagians do not wish to maintain a baptism to the kingdom of heaven and are unwilling to accept baptism for the remission of Adam's sin, then he ironically suggests they should return to Origen's solution.[54]

49. Jerome, *Dialog* 3.4 (Hritzu, 352).
50. Jerome, *Dialog* 2.29.
51. Jerome, *Dialog* 3.6.
52. Jerome, *Dialog* 3.18.
53. Clark, *Origenist Controversy*, 221.
54. Jerome, *Dialog* 3.19.

Jerome makes a less successful argument about the Pelagian insistence that all sins must be truly voluntary. He notes the various sins of ignorance listed in the Hebrew Bible, along with their various resolutions and sacrifices. This doesn't adequately address the issue of sins versus accidental transgressions. It may be illegal to trespass, but if you didn't see the sign, it is not sin. Having used the old law to explain sins of ignorance, Jerome then explains away 1 John 5:3 ("His commandments are not burdensome") and Matt 11:30 ("My yoke is easy and my burden is light") by interpreting them as light compared to the law.[55]

Jerome sometimes appears to be an older counselor admonishing the overly enthusiastic Pelagius. Run the race as hard as you can, but recognize stumbles are inevitable. While we should attempt to deserve the heavenly call, we are likely to need God's mercy.[56] He again takes an intermediate position. Our unaided will may be insufficient and require mercy, but we are capable of effort. For Jerome, Pelagius is ungenerous to human failing. He gives too much credit to human capability and not enough to God's mercy. Sounding like Origen, Jerome takes on Pelagius's insistence on the punishment of the unrepentant: "And do you not know that a threat on the part of God at times hints at clemency?"[57] There is not as much distance between Jerome and Pelagius as they each would have claimed. Pelagius says Christians should be spiritual athletes; Jerome corrects this to humble strivers cognizant of failure. Both believe that any one sin can be avoided, and a person should be held responsible for it; Jerome adds we should hope for God's mercy for our frequent missteps.

Jerome constructs a fair criticism of Pelagius. He identifies the Pelagian flaws without a contorted argument on human nature, without the impotence of the will, and without the bizarre erectionalization of the Fall. He has his own sexual obsessions, but they are the more common ones of fear of women and misogyny. Jerome emphasizes effort and the hope of mercy, all of which would be compatible with the pastoral Augustine, but not the theological Augustine. He agrees with Augustine about the improbability if not the impossibility of sinlessness. However, he does not attribute it to a cosmic incapability but our weaknesses and lack of discipline. Although not shy about his scholarly accomplishments, and by no means a stranger to battle, Jerome genuinely believes in the value of repentance and humility. He has far more in common with the earlier traditions of the church than

---

55. Jerome, *Dialog* 2.5.
56. Jerome, *Dialog,* 2.6.
57. Jerome, *Dialog* 1.28 (Hritzu, 272).

## WHAT ABOUT CASSIAN?

John Cassian's principal work, *The Conferences,* is a collection of conversations between Cassian and his friend Germanus and the holy *abbas* (fathers) of the Egyptian desert. The extent to which these represent literary constructions rather than verbatim transcriptions is a subject of active scholarship. Of particular interest are the *Eleventh, Twelfth,* and *Thirteenth Conferences* with Abba Chaeremon. In these, Cassian sketches the outline of a non-Pelagian and non-Augustinian view of perfection, chastity, and grace. He expresses Burnaby's critique; in protecting God's sovereignty, Augustine is unwilling to grant that God truly seeks our love.[58] Cassian wants to reestablish the divine-human cooperation Augustine rejected.

In the *Eleventh Conference,* Chaeremon provides a different parsing of the injunction to faith, hope, and charity. He describes faith as obedience to God's law out of fear, hope as the desire for the rewards of Heaven and charity as the love of virtue for its own sake.[59] We move along a trajectory toward perfection, rising from the status of a slave to a hireling, and then to a son.[60] Cassian echoes Paul: "So you are no longer a slave but a child, and if a child then also an heir, through God (Gal 4:7)." Cassian's ascent is not in a vacuum, but in a plenum filled with God's love and his aid.[61] The adopted son will be generous to his fellows because he knows he is the recipient of God's love.[62] God's grace is more dynamically present than in Pelagius but is also more available than in Augustine. It is an Origenist view; we are surrounded by the river of God's grace in which we can choose to swim—but if we swim, God will provide additional help.

The *Twelfth Conference* focuses on chastity. Chaeremon connects chastity to the ability to give up material wealth; poverty is harder.[63] Chastity is possible and is achievable with God's help. After disciplining himself with ascetic rigors, the monk can be free of the dominion of fleshly desire.[64] The path to chastity has six stages, ranging from immunity from temptation

---

58. Burnaby, *Amor Dei,* 166.
59. Cassian, *Conferences* 11.6.1.
60. Cassian, *Conferences* 11.7.6.
61. Cassian, *Conferences* 11.9.1.
62. Cassian, *Conferences* 11.9.2.
63. Cassian, *Conferences* 12.3.1.
64. Cassian, *Conferences* 12.4.1.

while awake to protection in dreams.[65] Erotic dreams are not sinful because dreams are involuntary, but they do reflect an insufficiently suppressed desire.[66] Even if this high state of chastity is achieved, the man may still be plagued by nocturnal emissions. If they are unaccompanied by erotic dreams, he may blame physical necessity.[67]

Germanus asks about the common phenomenon of an early morning erection induced by pressure from urine in the bladder.[68] Chaeremon responds in two ways; he advises limiting drinking to reduce the provocation, and he invokes a seventh level of chastity—perfect chastity—in which there are no nocturnal emissions and no morning erections. God's love is involved in all human endeavors for good, including the monk's advance through stages one to six. However, the seventh state requires a specific dispensation, an individual rather than general grace.[69]

Cassian is not a defender of marital sex like Julian, but there is none of the extremism of Tertullian, Augustine, or Jerome. When asked how long the first six stages would take, Chaeremon says that if one depends on God's mercy, a monk could achieve it in six months.[70] Although all who devotedly adopt the asceticism and discipline of the desert can do this, they must not pride themselves on it, but attribute all success to God's merciful assistance.

Just as Jerome shows how to be anti-Pelagian without succumbing to sexual oddity, Cassian illustrates in the *Thirteenth Conference* how to oppose Augustinian notions of grace while avoiding Pelagian arrogance. While the two preceding *Conferences* serve as manuals for monastic life, it becomes obvious in the *Thirteenth* that Augustine is a target in all three, even if he remains unnamed. The anti-Augustinian tone prompted Prosper of Aquitaine's attack, *Contra Collatorem* (*Against the Conferences*), and the condemnation of the semi-Pelagians at the Council of Orange in 529.[71]

The *Thirteenth Conference* begins with a subtle discussion of grace and effort. Germanus complains that perfect chastity (the seventh stage, at which the monk is undisturbed by nocturnal emissions) is not achievable except by an act of grace. The farmer tills the soil and harvests the crop—does he not deserve some credit? If the monk achieves chastity, is it not a result of

---

65. Cassian, *Conferences* 12.7.3.

66. Cassian, *Conferences* 12.7.4.

67. Cassian, *Conferences* 12.8.5.

68. Cassian, *Conferences* 12.9.

69. Cassian, *Conferences* 12.10.2.

70. Cassian, *Conferences* 12.15.2.

71. The Canons of the Council of Orange can be found at www.ewtn.com/library/COUNCILS/ORANGE.htm.

his labor? Chaeremon says the farmer's effort, although necessary, cannot succeed if God withholds the rain or sends plagues of locusts. Both effort and mercy are required, but mercy is not denied.[72] In this way, Cassian has no difficulty reconciling apparently contradictory texts about God's judgment and mercy. Cassian consistently emphasizes the dependence on God's grace, but his grace differs from both the grace of Augustine and the grace of Pelagius: it is a continuous flow of mercy. When the desires of the flesh seem strongest, God's mercy and grace will respond in equal strength.[73]

Cassian finds a different lesson in the case of infants than Augustine. God does not want a single child to perish; *a fortiori*, he wants all to be saved (and Cassian means all). It is sacrilegious to believe anything else.[74] Cassian's God continues to cry for our repentance. Cassian quotes Ezekiel, "Say to them, As I live, says the Lord God, I have no pleasure in the death of the wicked, but that the wicked turn from their ways and live; turn back, turn back from your evil ways; for why will you die, O house of Israel (Ezek 33:11)?" Cassian believes in God's desire for universal salvation, denies there is a limited election, implies the persistent sinner can thwart God's will, and supports the call to every human to repent. Christ's grace is always available, "Come to me, all you that are weary and are carrying heavy burdens, and I will give you rest (Mat 11:28)." God wants our salvation; any who are lost are lost against his will, "because God did not make death, and he does not delight in the death of the living (Wis 1:13)."[75]

Chaeremon uses Hosea to illustrate God's infinite patience; if Jerusalem is the adulterer abandoning her husband, God is the man who always seeks her return.[76] His ever-patient love does not decline but increases even more when she sins and fails to come back.[77] It is interesting that Cassian, who holds strictly to desert asceticism, can use such a metaphor. Augustine is often praised for the depth of his psychology, but Cassian understands love. Augustine's fourteen years with his lover left him with less comprehension than Cassian, usually assumed to have been celibate.

God is eager for the smallest sign of our repentance. Cassian cites Isaiah ("Before they call I will answer, while they are yet speaking I will hear (Isa 65:24)." as evidence of God's eagerness to hear our voice.[78] God's de-

72. Cassian, *Conferences* 13.3.2.
73. Cassian, *Conferences* 2.13.6.
74. Cassian, *Conferences* 13.7.2.
75. Cassian, *Conferences* 13.7.3.
76. Cassian, *Conferences* 13.8.2.
77. Cassian, *Conferences* 13.8.3.
78. Cassian, *Conferences* 13.8.4.

sire for us is beyond our understanding, but real. Not only does he respond to those who seek, ask, and knock but also he is "found by those who do not seek, appears openly among these who were not asking for him and stretches out his hands the whole day to a people who do not believe in him."[79] God removes the means for sin and interfers with our attempts to commit evil.

Augustine's God is an arbitrary judge, Julian's God is an impartial judge, and Jerome's God is a forgiving judge. Cassian goes further to depict God as a reluctant judge, seeking an inch of repentance so he may make it a mile of mercy. Chaeremon provides a list of scriptural calls and injunctions and concludes they show a combination of freely made choices with God's subsequent, but necessary, aid. The beginnings of a good will may be a human initiative, but perfection can only be achieved with God's guidance.[80] Nevertheless, make a beginning and God will provide the aid; no one needs to be left behind.

Amy-Jill Levine discusses two Talmudic excerpts in her treatment of the parable of the prodigal son. In the *Deuteronomy Rabbah* 2.24, a father sends word to a son who is too ashamed to return home: "My son, is a son ever ashamed to return to his father? And is it not to your father you will be returning?"[81] The *Pesikta Rabbati* 184–185 describes a son who declares he cannot return home. The father replies "Return as far as you can, and I will come the rest of the way to you." The Talmud continues, "So God says, Return to me and I will return to you."[82] These pictures of God's hope for our repentance align with Cassian and reinforce the covenant theme.

Cassian works his way around the Pauline texts in which Augustine finds predestination. We must accept both the pro-freedom and pro-grace perspectives. It is the same to him whether God's mercy precedes or follows the beginnings of faith and a will dedicated to good.[83] Paul and Matthew are actively summoned, but the thief at Golgotha initiates his salvation by his faith. Grace and free will are only in apparent contradiction; we believe

---

79. Cassian, *Conferences* 13.9.1 (Ramsey, 474). Cassian's source is Isaiah 65:1–2, which he interprets universally. Isaiah's text is the introduction to the description of God's intention to purge Israel of its sinners and idolaters, providing a new heaven and a new earth. When he restores a remnant, God will again open his hand (Isaiah 65:24). Paul refers to the same text in Rom 10:20 and uses it to explain the partial and temporary rejection of Israel in favor of the gentiles.

80. Cassian, *Conferences* 13.11.5.

81. Levine, *Short Stories by Jesus*, 57.

82. Ibid., 58.

83. Cassian, *Conferences* 13.11.1.

in both because both are part of the church's faith.[84] When God sees us turning to him, he meets us halfway, providing strength and counsel. If we do not show repentance, he does not abandon us but continues to work on our will to bring it to the good.[85]

There are implicit criticisms of Augustine. God would never give humanity a will that could only choose sin. That would not be a meaningful free will.[86] Cassian warns against simply attributing good works solely to God, leaving nothing but evil to human nature.[87] The will is truly free and can embrace or reject the grace of God.[88] This is very close to Pelagius's doctrine: "But we say a man is always in a state that he may sin, or may not sin, so as to own ourselves always to be of a free will."[89]

Cassian agrees with Pelagius that effort matters. God offers endless chances, but we have to act on them and act on them vigorously.[90] Still, Cassian is not a Pelagian. It is an error to say the grace of God responds to our faith and merits, but the mistake is not the one Augustine identifies. Cassian says God's grace surpasses anything we can merit.[91] Pelagius's error was to underestimate God's desire to save us all. When Cassian comments on Rom 11:33–34, he does not see mysterious and arbitrary predestination, but the limitless mercy of God. He is always striving for our salvation. If there are interpretations supporting a limitation of grace, they are to be avoided because they act to destroy the faith.[92] Here, he sounds like Origen, warning against immature exegetes of Romans.[93]

While Jerome might be distinguished from Augustine most succinctly by his emphasis on humble human effort, Cassian adds to humility an insistence on God's limitless mercy. We do have free will, but even when our weaknesses overwhelm us in continuing sin, God will be seeking ways to overcome our failings. Neither Jerome nor Cassian accepts a fundamentally corrupted nature. Jerome's advocacy of virginity and asceticism would be incoherent if discipline cannot succeed; Cassian is confident God's creation remains good. Pelagius, Jerome, and Cassian all believe salvation is a process.

---

84. Cassian, *Conferences* 13.11.4.
85. Cassian, *Conferences* 13.11.5.
86. Cassian, *Conferences* 13.12.1.
87. Cassian, *Conferences* 13.12.5.
88. Cassian, *Conferences* 13.12.8.
89. Pelagius, *Libellus fidei* 25.
90. Cassian, *Conferences* 3.19.3.
91. Cassian, *Conferences* 13.16.1.
92. Cassian, *Conferences* 13.18.5.
93. Origen, *On First Principles* 3.1.7–3.1.8.

Pelagius journeys with self-confidence; Jerome walks with a humble awareness of the need for mercy; Cassian is again confident but not in himself, but in the overabundance of God's grace. It is hard to grasp the relationship of humanity to Augustine's capricious God. Julian's God is a stern, but fair, judge. Jerome's God is a coach, encouraging us to strive for virtue. Cassian's God is a forgiving father.

## WHO WAS AUGUSTINE?

If historical analysis explains the immediate outcome of the struggle and Augustine's contemporaries provide alternatives, the portrait of Augustine himself is still incomplete. He is intellectually curious but unsteady in his early philosophical meanderings. He begins with a materialistic Manichaeism, cleanses himself with New Academy skepticism, acquires a dusting of Stoicism, immerses himself in the more spiritual Neoplatonism, and finally ends by accepting the authority of the church. He puts his mind to the service of the institutional church even while transforming it.

This intellectual journey happens within his broader biography. He takes a lover, he fathers a child (or doesn't), becomes a Manichaean and practices superb birth control. He discards his lover brutally, claims a new lover, and becomes engaged to a child. He tries to form an all-male philosophers' commune, dumps the fiancée and is received into the celibate arms of the church. While his intellectual peregrinations have a coherent arc, his personal life is a muddle. It falls into a pattern if it is a continuing effort to deal with his impotence; that is the unspoken confession in his closet. If profligacy is a cover story, then the intellectual, philosophical, and theological content of the post-conversion Augustine takes on a very different character.

Augustine has conditioned theologians and lay Christians alike to see no possibility other than a sexual Fall, but pride and disobedience alone could have sufficed. He writes about pride but realizes he cannot provide a universal original *sin*, with real guilt, based on pride. To turn away from God is an adult choice, and it cannot be used to damn infants, ensure universality, or justify the total impotence of the will. Adam and Eve turned away from God in the best of circumstances—but they might not have made that choice—they were free not to sin.

Augustine needs to destroy the ability not to sin. We cannot choose to keep our gaze on God; something irresistible must distract us. Pride is not a sufficient distraction—it must be sex. Penile disobedience better reflects his feelings of helplessness and utter incapability to act. The re-creation and transmission of guilt have to be sexual since our conception and birth are the only things we all have in common.

His sexual obsessions force a re-evaluation of Augustine's dependence on Manichaeism. Sexual pain informs all of his theology. His diatribes against Julian's presumed hypersexual marital activity show his obsession with sex lasts into old age. Julian's intimate relationship with his wife is deeply disturbing to Augustine. His fantasies about flaccid urinary impregnation go beyond disturbed into the pathological. West concludes Augustine remained Manichaean at his core. Matter and sex stain humanity with guilt; we must accept suffering and renounce pleasure.[94] However, a Manichaean avoidance of sex is quite unlike Augustine's fervent wish for a flaccid, motionless, and rationally commanded intercourse. His critics, including Julian, do not quite understand him. The missing element is Augustine's *need* to avoid a standard marriage. This led to the choice of a child-bride and the desperate, but well-timed, conversion. Manicheism, Neoplatonism, and misogyny are secondary compared to finding a way to conceal his impotence under the cloak of a superficially coherent, but actually deeply incoherent, worldview.

Augustine's sexual obsessions differ radically from the conventional ascetic. He rarely mentions Eve and neglects female sexuality. Milton's Eve is a lot more blameworthy. Raphael warns Adam and Eve that Satan is prowling around Eden. Adam, ever cautious, wants them to stick together while tending the garden, but Eve, as the foolish girl does in every horror movie, suggests they would accomplish more separately. Things go badly, and Milton wonders why God chooses the female to generate humanity.[95] Instead of perseverating on feminine wiles, Augustine sticks to the disobedient member. It failed him, not by leading him into temptation, but by abandoning him in the middle of desire.

Augustine, like most of the clergy of his time, was a proponent of sexual restraint and a fan of virginity. The fifth century is not the sixties; there is no contrast between a rigid conservatism and a sexual liberation movement, even if Julian comes close. We misread Augustine and his contemporaries if we look for anyone with a strongly pro-woman, pro-sex, stance. Nevertheless, he has a distinctive position, corresponding to neither Stoic restraint nor desert extremism.

The Roman approach emphasizes the necessity of controlling disruptive desires, whether for wealth, status, food, or sex. The mind governs all things; the philosopher should cultivate a sense of indifference. There is room for marriage and sufficient sex to guarantee the stable production

---

94. West, *Saint Augustine*, 159.
95. *Paradise Lost*, Book 10, 888–95.

of children. As asceticism grows, fashionable husbands and wives begin to retire from sexuality and live chastely after the children are born. This group includes Julian and the much richer Paulinus of Nola; both disposed of estates to live simpler lives and benefit the poor. Sex, like everything else, has to be regulated, but society requires the family, and the family requires children.

In contrast, the Encratites, the Manichees, and all the other wanderers in the desert adopt a radical rejection of the body. Food is a central concern, but there is also an enormous distance between sex and the holy life. Sex and reproduction are the consequence, if not the causes, of the Fall, and no good can come of them. Although this movement flourishes in female-free monasteries, caves, and retreats, the labeling of women as sources of evil spreads beyond the desert. Virginity is necessary but not sufficient—women would find a way to corrupt men.

Augustine cannot adopt the Stoic path. His struggles with desire make it impossible for him to consider control possible; he does not believe in moderate marital sex. He cannot allow anyone to be in control; if there were successful Stoics (or successful Pelagians), it would show that his sense of helplessness was his and not part of a universal impotence. The lynchpin of his theoretical structure is the impotence of the will; he cannot accept anything that would imply human capability.

On the other hand, he cannot blame women. If he had been a misogynist, he could have relied on commonly held negative views. A woman takes the first prideful step in Eden; it is for her sake that Adam joins her in disobedience. Women are temptresses, enticing noble men into the fearful and messy toils of sex. They are vain, stubborn, and riddled with irrationality, entangling men with all the other sins. These are all things he believed. Positive female images are reserved for virgins, chaste widows, and Mary; even his treatment of Monnica is problematic. If he had blamed women, he could have kept his headship of men. The institutional church and sacraments would retain their meaning—acting as a restraint on women, and providing a place for repentance, cleansing, and absolution. Blaming women is free from the Manichaean taint—it is just a particular continuation of the story in the Garden; the dualism is between male and female, not good and evil forms of matter. The Greek philosophers would not have been disturbed to find that women are the problem. In this theory, virginity can still be prized over marriage, and the rich can be left with their avarice if reliable donations sanctify it. Women can achieve salvation—they are enough of the image of God to do that if they become man-like.

This is not Augustine's path, although, following the Council of Orange, it is arguably the church's path. Augustine cannot use such a theory because women are not his problem. Putting the blame on women does not address the disobedience of the male member. Also, he supports typical Roman values in a modified form; desert celibacy is incapable of meeting the empire's needs for troops.

Augustine cannot choose any of the routes available to others. He feels too out of control to be a Stoic; he is too practical about the character of his congregation to be a renouncer, and too honest about himself to blame women. The softness disturbing him was not theirs, but his. Augustine's brilliance is in finding a new way to reject sexuality. He does not reject women or marriage; he rejects himself. His impotence, generalized to the impotence of the will, is more important to him than the church, the cross, and the headship of men. He needs impotence to explain the impotence causing him so much frustrated desire. Roman homes often had a stone phallus in the courtyard at the center of the house—Augustine's limp phallus is at the center of his heart.

Augustine's inability is displayed everywhere. He believes the male orgasm (he doesn't know much about women's) destroys reason. This is not the statement of a sexually experienced man—it is a possible fantasy for a fourteen-year-old virgin. He is ignorant of aphrodisiacs, male prostitutes, and fluff girls. Augustine could have used them to support our slavery to desire, but they might have contradicted his notion that the erection was always associated with an uncontrollable and all-powerful concupiscence. Perfunctory sex cannot be the source of original sin. He again resembles the celibate professor more than the reformed rake. Finally, his fantasies about sex in paradise resemble the denials of a Freudian child exposed to the primal scene. Although it is a wild surmise, it is more probable Augustine was a virgin than a profligate, Adeodatus being the child of his boyhood friend. Augustine says he lied to establish his image when he was a teenager.[96] It could have *all* been a pretense.

Although his innovation targets the disobedient member and not women, the Augustinian self-loathing eventually re-enforces the Tertullian other-loathing in church history. While Augustine is obsessed with the intermittent emasculation caused by the failure of the penis to respond to lawful desire—a male problem—Tertullian always identifies women as the issue. For all of his influence, Augustine's deepest opinions are often quietly buried. The church dropped extreme predestinationism while retaining original sin and infant baptism. It ignored the idea that the Garden disobedience is recapitulated in the disobedient member, in favor of Eve's and all women's catastrophic seductiveness. The church kept his negative

---

96. Aug., *Confessions* 2.3.7.

assessment of sexuality but transferred the onus to women. The result is a fusion between the Roman reproductive gravity and the revulsion of the desert fathers. Although Augustine is not the sole contributor, Brown still counts this as Augustine's legacy.[97] Augustine's penis is left behind.

Augustine's theory is ultimately fatal to his deepest religious and ecclesiastical concerns. If Pelagian assumptions of human perfectibility endanger the cross, Augustine's predestination burns it to the ground. If unmerited grace not only suffices for salvation but is the only road, then there is no purpose to baptism, no function of the sacraments, no need for the church, no need for the incarnation, crucifixion, and resurrection. Augustine saves his theory of grace at the cost of destroying the basis for Christianity—predestination leaves no room for any other doctrine.

His theory of grace undermines the attitudes toward women. Augustine accepts the theory of female subordination held by his contemporaries. The world is a struggle between male rationality and female irrationality; the male represents contemplation of the eternal and the female, involvement in the temporal. He does not recognize that, if it is all predestination and the penis, the foundation of female inferiority crumbles. If original sin enters the world through "one man," it is hard to maintain the standard misogyny. Nor is predestination compatible with the taming of avarice of the rich. Alms cannot build up treasure in heaven; there is no point of any act of charity, any act of kindness or love, in the face of unmerited grace and near-universal damnation.

Finally, Augustine's theory is unnecessary. O'Donnell correctly observes that the anti-Julian works are the least read of Augustine's work.[98] However, even Aurelius nods. Having expended volumes on how death came into the world through generation, he casually notes that if Adam and Eve had remained in the garden, they would have eaten from the tree of life and been immortal.[99] They became mortal, not because of a corrupted nature or shameful movement, but because they were cut off from the tree of life.[100] While consistent with God's words in Gen 3:21, such an admission undermines his entire argument and is consistent with the Pelagian shallow Fall. The removal from the Tree of Life explains the hardness of our life, not concupiscence. There is no continually renewed sin, but there is a continuing consequence of expulsion. It is a question of location, not generation. Even using a literal interpretation of scripture, there is no need

---

97. Brown, *Body and Society*, 426.
98. O'Donnell, *Augustine: A New Biography*, 283.
99. Aug., *Answer to Julian* 4.14.69.
100. Aug., *Unfinished Work* 6.30.11.

for any connection to male anatomy, obedient or disobedient. There is no need for the will to be impotent. Only Augustine's impotence mandated the impotence of the will and everything that followed. Connecting to the Tree of Life is not a new concept. Wiggers interprets "die in Adam," to mean that Adam and Eve could no longer eat its fruit.[101] The central thesis of James Barr's book, *The Garden of Eden and the Hope of Immortality* is that, while Genesis 1–3 represents a collision of different myths, the final story was centrally concerned with the Tree of Life and the chance that Adam and Eve might have achieved immortality.

In the end, there is only one Augustine. His defenders generally admit his positions become harder during the Pelagian controversy, but they assert his principles on grace are nascent in the middle works. Harrison believes he is consistent from the beginning. She feels he is not a lightly Christianized Neoplatonist, hardened later by his interpretation of Paul and the failure of his philosophical reveries to give him serenity, as Brown supposed. Harrison believes Augustine shows real continuity in his concerns even if he uses a more philosophical vocabulary early and a more scriptural vocabulary later. The form of Augustine's discourses does change—logic-chopping becomes less frequent, and he shows some genuine depth and originality.

Augustine asserts any differences in tone between his earlier and later works are tactical stances adapted to the character of his opponents, Donatists, Manichaeans or Pelagians. Less charitably, he is a political animal like Jerome. In the fourth and fifth centuries, a theologian could plummet into disgrace overnight. As the wind changed, many church leaders learned to pivot on a dime. Augustine's more optimistic early statements about human nature distance him from a Manichaean past and do not necessarily represent a genuinely hopeful state of mind. Augustine shows considerable political acumen in choosing the Nicene side in 386, but he loses his way in the Pelagian controversy, where every step becomes weirder and weirder.

His ideas, desexualized, have merit: we are perversely willful and require every form of aid made available by God and humanity. Pelagian and Stoic optimism are second cousins to arrogance, which impedes the humility necessary for all of us. Understanding that the source of his most controversial positions on the will and sexuality is impotence clarifies things for both his critics and defenders. His peculiar amalgam of fifth-century attitudes, the occasional positive assessments of women, and his sexual revulsion sorts itself out when those elements traceable to his personal impotence can be identified. His moments of brutality and cruelty derive from

---

101. Wiggers, *Augustinism and Pelagianism*, 339.

his pain. Draining those wounds leaves an Augustine whose contributions can be more fairly judged; he is more than "the bitter son of Monica."[102]

If there is one Augustine, it is the impotent Augustine. His impotence creates his guilt, shame, and anger. His pastoral and sacramental concerns are genuine (when he can put aside his contempt for the masses). His psychological insights into the muddle of human volition are groundbreaking, and his influence in completing the fusion of the biblical with Greek ideas has been long lasting. He is willing to throw them all away rather than recognize that his powerlessness is his alone.

Augustine's continuity is not orthodox Catholicism. It could hardly be so—he was ignorant of many basic aspects of Nicene Christianity at the time of his conversion and found Isaiah incomprehensible after his baptism. When he was involuntarily ordained, he still had not plunged into the Scriptures. These are not signs of one passionately embracing his refound Catholic faith, but of an exultant escapee. His surrender to church authority was a great relief—his philosophical angst had been quite real—but the sense of safety was all-important. Augustine was a bright young man who had trouble finding a direction—the church provided him with one. He reformulated his old ideas in his newly adopted context and used his skills to differentiate himself from his former allies. He was a controversialist at his core, but his visions of divine love were not a façade. Within this opinionated, occasionally pastoral, mature individual, there was a cancer gnawing at him—his impotence. It is this, and not his mother's belief, that links all the Augustines.

This in no way implies Augustine was a single-note thinker. Conversion, ordination, consecration, and the Origenist, Manichaean, Donatist, and Pelagian controversies, all created new problems to solve as well as closing off alternate paths. However, the positions of Chrysostom, Cassian, and Jerome show the depth of his darkness was unnecessary. His inner conflict went beyond any intellectual or spiritual evolution. Reading the best of Augustine's defenders makes us long for the Augustine they portray. If Augustine had been free of whatever sexual obsession drove him and had lived in a world in which his Neoplatonic and Origenist impulses were still orthodox, the pastoral Augustine could be seen plain. We are all diminished because the powerful intellect of Augustine never had the time and grace to change his mind.

As for the final disposition of the substantive questions—the roles of grace and faith, divine and human initiative—the twentieth-century cyberneticist and neurophysiologist Warren McCulloch has the last word:

---

102. Wilde, *Intensions*, 96.

Finally, as he has perforce learned from the inadequacies of his best hypotheses, ultimate universal truths are beyond his ken. To demand them is the arrogance of Adam; to come short of them is the impotence of sorry man; but to fancy them known were very hubris.[103]

---

103. McCulloch, *Embodiments of Mind*, 164.

# Bibliography

Abelard, Peter. *Commentary on the Epistle to the Romans*. Translated by Steven R. Cartwright. Washington, DC: Catholic University Press, 2011.

Acton, John Emerich Edward Dalberg-Acton (First Baron Acton). *Selected Writings of Lord Acton, Vol. III: Essays In Religion, Politics and Morality*. Edited by J. Rufus Fears. Indianapolis, IN: Liberty Fund, 1988.

Adams, Marilyn McCord. *William Ockham,* 2 volumes. Notre Dame, IN: University of Notre Dame Press 1989.

Alexander, William M. "Sex and Philosophy in Augustine." *Augustinian Studies* 5 (1974) 197–208.

Allen, Alexander V. G. *The Continuity of Christian Thought*. Boston: Houghton Mifflin. 1884.

Allin. Thomas. *The Augustinian Revolution in Theology*. Boston: Pilgrim Press, 1911.

Altizer. Thomas J. J. "Ethics and Predestination in Augustine and Levinas." In *Levinas and the Ancients,* edited by Brian Schroeder and Silvia Benso, 230–242. Indiana University Press, 2008.

Armstrong, A. H. "St. Augustine and Christian Platonism." In *Augustine: A Collection of Critical Essays,* edited by R. A. Markus, 3–37. Garden City, NJ and New York: Doubleday Anchor, 1972.

Athanasius. *On the Incarnation of the Word*. Translated by Archibald Robertson. From *Nicene and Post-Nicene Fathers, Second Series, Vol. 4,* edited by Philip Schaff and Henry Wace. Buffalo, NY: Christian Literature, 1892. Revised and edited for New Advent by Kevin Knight. http://www. newadvent. org/fathers/2802. htm.

Augustine. *Answer to Adimantus, A Disciple of Mani* (*Contra Adimantum, Manichaei i discipulum*). In *The Works of Saint Augustine: A Translation for the 21st Century, I/19, The Manichaean Debate,* translated by Roland J. Teske, SJ, 165–226. Hyde Park, NY: New City, 2006.

———. *Answer to the Letter of Mani known as the Foundation* (*Contra Epistulam Manichaei quam vocant Fundamenti.*). In *The Works of Saint Augustine: A Translation for the 21st Century, I/19, The Manichaean Debate,* translated by Roland J. Teske, SJ, 227–270. Hyde Park, NY: New City, 2006.

———. *Answer to Faustus, a Manichaean* (*Contra Faustum Manichaeum*). *The Works of Saint Augustine: A Translation for the 21st Century, I/20*. Translated by Roland J. Teske, SJ. Hyde Park, NY: New City, 2007.

———. *Answer to Julian* (*Contra Julianum*). In *The Works of Saint Augustine: A Translation for the 21st Century*, I/24, *Answer to the Pelagians II*, translated by Roland J. Teske, SJ, 221–235. Hyde Park, NY: New City, 1998.

———. *Answer to the Two Letters of the Pelagians* (*Contra dua epistolas Pelagianorum*). In *The Works of Saint Augustine: A Translation for the 21st Century*, I/24, *Answer to the Pelagians II*, translated by Roland J. Teske, SJ, 98–219. Hyde Park, NY: New City, 1998.

———. *On Baptism, Against the Donatists*. Translated by J. R. King and revised by Chester D. Hartranft. From *Nicene and Post-Nicene Fathers, First Series*, Vol. 4. Edited by Philip Schaff. Buffalo, NY: Christian Literature, 1887. Revised and edited for New Advent by Kevin Knight, http://www.newadvent.org/fathers/1408.htm.

———. *The Catholic Way of Life and the Manichean Way of Life* (*De moribus ecclesiae Catholicae et De moribus Manichaeonum*). In *The Works of Saint Augustine: A Translation for the 21st Century*, I/19, *The Manichaean Debate*. translated by Roland J. Teske, SJ, 17–106. Hyde Park, NY: New City, 2006.

———. *The City of God, XI-XXI. The Works of Saint Augustine: A Translation for the 21st Century*, I/7. Translated by William Babcock. Hyde Park, NY: New City, 2013.

———. *The City of God*. Translated by Henry Bettenson. London: Penguin Books, 1972.

———. *The City of God*. Translated by Marcus Dods. In *Nicene and Post-Nicene Fathers, First Series*, Vol. 2. Edited by Philip Schaff. Buffalo, NY: Christian Literature, 1887. Revised and edited for New Advent by Kevin Knight. http://www.newadvent.org/fathers/1201.htm.

———. *The City of God*. Translated by Gerald G. Walsh, Gerald G. Demetrius B. Zema, Grace Monahan, Grace, and Daniel J. Honan, abridged. Garden City. New York: Doubleday Image Books, 1958.

———. *The Confessions* (*Confessiones*). Translated by Maria Boulding, OSB. *The Works of Saint Augustine: A Translation for the 21st Century*, I/1. Hyde Park, NY: New City, 1998.

———. *The Debate with Fortunatus*. In *The Works of Saint Augustine: A Translation for the 21st Century*, I/19, *The Manichaean Debate*, translated by Ronald J. Teske, SJ, 145–162. Hyde Park, NY: New City, 2006.

———. *The Deeds of Pelagius* (*De gestis Pelagii*). In *The Works of Saint Augustine: A Translation for the 21st Century*, I/23, *Answer to the Pelagians*, translated by Roland J. Teske, SJ, 318–383. Hyde Park, NY: New City, 1997.

———. *The Enchiridion on Faith, Hope and Love*. Translated by J. F. Shaw. From *Nicene and Post-Nicene Fathers, First Series*, Vol. 3, edited by Philip Schaff. Buffalo, NY: Christian Literature Publishing Co. 1887. Revised and edited for New Advent by Kevin Knight. http://www.newadvent.org/fathers/1302.htm.

———. *The Gift of Perseverance* (*De dono perseverantiae*). In *The Works of Saint Augustine: A Translation for the 21st Century*, I/26, *Answer to the Pelagians IV*, translated by Roland J. Teske, SJ, 191–236. Hyde Park, NY: New City, 1999.

———. *The Grace of Christ and Original Sin* (*De gratia Christi et de peccato originali*). In *The Works of Saint Augustine: A Translation for the 21st Century*, I/23, *Answer to the Pelagians*, translated by Roland J. Teske, SJ, 284–465. Hyde Park, NY: New City, 1997.

———. *Grace and Free Choice* (*De gratia et libero arbitrio*). In *The Works of Saint Augustine: A Translation for the 21st Century*, I/26, *Answer to the Pelagians IV*, translated by Roland J. Teske, SJ, 70–107. Hyde Park, NY: New City, 1999.

———. *Heresies* (*De Haeresibus*). In *The Works of Saint Augustine: A Translation for the 21st Century*, I/18, *Arianism and Other Heresies*. translated by Roland J. Teske, SJ, 15–80. Hyde Park, NY: New City, 2007.

———. *Letters 1–99*. *The Works of Saint Augustine: A Translation for the 21st Century*, II/1. Translated by Roland J. Teske, SJ. Hyde Park, NY: New City, 2001.

———. *Letters 100–155*. *The Works of Saint Augustine: A Translation for the 21st Century*, II/2. Translated by Roland J. Teske, SJ. Hyde Park, NY: New City, 2003.

———. *Letters 156–210*. *The Works of Saint Augustine: A Translation for the 21st Century*, II/3. Translated by Roland J. Teske, SJ. Hyde Park, NY: New City, 2004.

———. *Letters 211–270, 1\*–29\**. *The Works of Saint Augustine: A Translation for the 21st Century*, II/4. Translated by Roland J. Teske, SJ. Hyde Park, NY: New City, 2005.

———. *Marriage and Desire* (*De nuptiis et concupiscentia*). In *The Works of Saint Augustine: A Translation for the 21st Century*, I/24, *Answer to the Pelagians II*, translated by Roland J. Teske, SJ, 13–96. Hyde Park, NY: New City, 1998.

———. *Miscellany of Questions in Response to Simplician* (*De Diversis Quaestionibus Ad Simplicianum*). In *The Works of Saint Augustine: A Translation for the 21st Century*, I/12, *Responses to Miscellaneous Questions*, translated by Boniface Ramsey, OP, 159–232. Hyde Park, NY: New City, 2008.

———. *The Nature of the Good* (*De natura boni*). In *Augustine: Earlier Writings*, translated by John H. S. Burleigh, 324–348. Philadelphia: Westminster, 1953.

———. *Nature and Grace* (*De natura et gratia*). In *The Works of Saint Augustine: A Translation for the 21st Century*, I/23, *Answer to the Pelagians*, translated by Roland J. Teske, SJ, 204–278. Hyde Park, NY: New City, 1997.

———. *The Nature and Origin of the Soul* (*De anima et eius origine*). In *The Works of Saint Augustine: A Translation for the 21st Century*, I/23, *Answer to the Pelagians*, translated by Roland J. Teske, SJ, 466–562. Hyde Park, NY: New City, 1997.

———. *On Free Will* (*De libero arbitrio*). In *Augustine: Earlier Writings*, translated by John H. S. Burleigh, 102–218. Philadelphia: Westminster, 1953.

———. *The Perfection of Human Righteousness* (*De Perfectione iustitiae humanae*). In *The Works of Saint Augustine: A Translation for the 21st Century*, I/23, *Answer to the Pelagians*, translated by Roland J. Teske, SJ, 279–317. Hyde Park, NY: New City, 1997.

———. *The Predestination of the Saints* (*De praedestinatione sanctorum*). In *The Works of Saint Augustine: A Translation for the 21st Century*, I/26, *Answer to the Pelagians IV*, translated by Roland J. Teske, SJ, 149–90. Hyde Park, NY: New City, 1999.

———. *Propositions from the Epistle to the Romans* (*Expositio quarundam Propositionum ex Epistola ad Romanos*). In *Augustine on Romans*, edited and translated by Paula Fredriksen Landes, 2–51. Chico, CA: Scholars, 1982.

———. *The Punishment and Forgiveness of Sins and the Baptism of Little Ones* (*De peccatorum meritis et remissione et de baptismo parvulorum*). In *The Works of Saint Augustine: A Translation for the 21st Century*, I/23, *Answer to the Pelagians*, translated by Roland J. Teske, SJ, 18–139. Hyde Park, NY: New City, 1997.

———. *Rebuke and Grace* (*De correptione et gratia*). In *The Works of Saint Augustine: A Translation for the 21st Century, I/26, Answer to the Pelagians IV*, translated by Roland J. Teske, SJ, 108–148. Hyde Park, NY: New City, 1999.

———. *Revisions* (*Retractationes*). *The Works of Saint Augustine: A Translation for the 21st Century, I/2*. Translated by Boniface Ramsey, OP. Hyde Park, NY: New City, 2010.

———. *Sermons 20–50*. *The Works of Saint Augustine: A Translation for the 21st Century, III/2*. Translated by Edmond Hill, OP. Hyde Park, NY: New City, 1990.

———. *Sermons 94A–147A*. *The Works of Saint Augustine: A Translation for the 21st Century, III/4*. Translated by Edmond Hill, OP. Hyde Park, NY: New City, 1992.

———. *Sermons 148–183*. *The Works of Saint Augustine: A Translation for the 21st Century, III/5*. Translated by Edmond Hill, OP. Hyde Park, NY: New City, 1992.

———. *Sermons (discovered since 1990)*. *The Works of Saint Augustine: A Translation for the 21st Century, III/11*. Translated by Edmond Hill, OP. Hyde Park, NY: New City, 1997.

———. *On the Sermon on the Mount*. Translated by William Findlay. From *Nicene and Post-Nicene Fathers, First Series, Vol. 6*, edited by Philip Schaff. Buffalo, NY: Christian Literature, 1888. Revised and edited for New Advent by Kevin Knight. http://www.newadvent.org/fathers/1601.htm.

———. *The Soliloquies* (*Soliloquia*). In *Augustine: Earlier Writings*, translated by John H. S. Burleigh, 17–63. Philadelphia: Westminster, 1953.

———. *The Spirit and the Letter* (*De spiritu et littera*). In *The Works of Saint Augustine: A Translation for the 21st Century, I/23, Answer to the Pelagians*, translated by Roland J. Teske, SJ, 140–203. Hyde Park, NY: New City, 1997.

———. *On the Trinity*. Translated by Arthur West Haddan. From *Nicene and Post-Nicene Fathers, First Series, Vol. 3*, edited by Philip Schaff. Buffalo, NY: Christian Literature, 1887. Revised and edited for New Advent by Kevin Knight. http://www.newadvent.org/fathers/1301.htm.

———. *Of True Religion* (*De vera religione*). In *Augustine: Earlier Writings*, translated by John H. S. Burleigh, 218–83. Philadelphia: Westminster, 1953.

———. *The Two Souls* (*De duabus animabus contra Manichaeos*). In *The Works of Saint Augustine: A Translation for the 21st Century, I/19, The Manichaean Debate*, translated by Roland J. Teske, SJ, 107–36. Hyde Park, NY: New City, 2006.

———. *Unfinished Commentary on the Epistle to the Romans* (*Epistolae ad Romanos Inchoata Expositio*). In *Augustine on Romans*, edited and translated by Paula Fredriksen Landes, 52–90. Chico, CA: Scholars, 1982.

———. *Unfinished Work in Answer to Julian* (*Opus imperfectum contra Julianum*). In *The Works of Saint Augustine: A Translation for the 21st Century, I/25, Answer to the Pelagians III*, translated by Roland J. Teske, SJ, 17–721. Hyde Park, NY: New City, 1999.

Bammel, Caroline P. "Augustine, Origen and the Exegesis of St. Paul." *Augustinianum* 32:2 (1992) 341–68.

Babcock, William S. "Augustine's Interpretations of Romans (A. D. 394–396)." *Augustinian Studies* 10 (1979) 55–74.

———. "Sin, Penalty, and the Responsibility of the Soul: a Problem in Augustine's De Libero Arbitrio III." In *Studia Patristica, Vol. XXVII: Papers Presented at the Eleventh International Conference on Patristic Studies held In Oxford 1991*, edited by Elizabeth A. Livingstone, 225–230. Leuven: Peeters, 1993.

Backus, Irena. "Augustine and Leibniz." *Augustinian Studies* 43:1/2 (2012) 179–199.
Bark, William. "The Doctrinal Interests of Marius Mercator." In *Church History: Studies in Christianity and Culture* 12:3 (1943) 210–216.
Barr, James. *Biblical Faith and Natural Theology*. Oxford: Oxford University Press, 1993.
———. *The Garden of Eden and the Hope of Immortality*. Minneapolis, MN: Fortress, 1993.
Barth, Karl. *The Knowledge of God and the Service of God According to the Teaching of the Reformation*. London: Hoddard and Stoughton, 1938.
Bayle, Pierre. *Historical and Critical Dictionary: Selections*. Indianapolis, IN: Hackett, 1991.
———. *A Philosophical Commentary on These Words of the Gospel, Luke 14:23. "Compel Them to Come In. That My House Shall Be Full."* Indianapolis, IN: Liberty Fund, 2005.
Beatrice, Pier Franco. *The Transmission of Sins: Augustine and the Pre-Augustinian Sources*. Translated by Adam Kamesar, Oxford: Oxford University Press (2013). Originally published 1980.
BeDuhn, Jason David. *Augustine's Manichean Dilemma, Vol. 1, Conversion and Apostasy, 373–388*. Philadelphia: University of Pennsylvania Press, 2010.
———. *Augustine's Manichaean Dilemma, Vol. 2: Making a "Catholic" Self, 388–401 C. E.* Philadelphia: University of Pennsylvania Press, 2013.
———. "What Augustine (May Have) Learned from the Manichaeans." *Augustinian Studies* 43:1/2 (2012) 35–48.
Belloc, Hilaire. *Four Men: A Farrago*. Forgotten Books, 2012.
Bigg, Charles. *The Christian Platonists of Alexandria*. Oxford, 1886.
Bonner, Ali. "The Manuscript Transmission of Pelagius' *Ad Demetriadum*: The Evidence of Some Manuscript Witness." In *Studia Patristica, Vol. LXX. Papers presented at the Sixteenth International Conference on Patristic Studies held in Oxford 2011. Vol. 18: St Augustine and his Opponents*, edited by Markus Vinzent, 619–30. Leuven: Peeters, 2013.
Bonner, Gerald. "Augustine's Doctrine of Man: Image of God and Sinner." *Augustinianum* 24:3 (1984) 495–514.
———. "Augustine and Pelagianism." *Augustinian Studies* 24 (1993) 7–47.
———. "Pelagianism and Augustine." *Augustinian Studies* 23 (1992) 33–51.
———. "Pelagianism Reconsidered." In *Studia Patristica, Vol. XXVII: Papers Presented at the Eleventh International Conference on Patristic Studies held in Oxford 1991*, edited by Elizabeth A. Livingstone, 237–41. Leuven: Peeters, 1993.
———. "Rufinus of Syria and African Pelagianism." *Augustinian Studies* 1 (1970) 31–47.
———. *St Augustine of Hippo: Life and Controversies*. Norwich, UK: The Canterbury Press, 2nd edition, 1986.
Børresen, Kari Elisabeth. "Patristic 'Feminism': The Case of Augustine." *Augustinian Studies* 25 (1994) 139–152.
Bray, Gerald. "Ambrosiaster." In *Reading Romans through the Centuries*, edited by Jeffrey P. Greenman and Timothy Larsen, 21–38. Grand Rapids, MI: Brazos, 2005.
———. "Original Sin in Patristic thought." *Churchman* 108, (1994) 37–47.
Bright, William. *Select Anti-Pelagian Treatises of St. Augustine and the Acts of the Second Council of Orange*. Oxford (1880).

Brown, Peter R. L. *Augustine of Hippo*, 2nd edition. Berkeley and Los Angeles: University of California Press, 2000.

———. "Augustine and a Crisis of Wealth in Late Antiquity." *Augustinian Studies* 36:1 (2005) 5–30.

———. *The Body and Society: Men, Women, and Sexual Renunciation in Early Christianity*. New York: Columbia University Press, 1988.

———. *Late Antiquity*. Cambridge, MA: Harvard University Press, 2015.

———. *The Ransom of the Soul*. Cambridge, MA: Harvard University Press, 1987.

———. *Religion and Society in the Age of Saint Augustine*. New York: Harper & Row, 1972.

———. *Through the Eye of a Needle: Wealth, The fall of Rome, and the Making of Christianity in the West, 350–550 AD*. Princeton and Oxford: Princeton University Press, 2012.

———. *The World of Late Antiquity*. London: Folio Society, 2014. Originally published by Thames and Hudson, 1971.

Brunnner, Emil. *Christianity and Civilisation*, 2 vols. New York: Charles Scribner's Sons, 1948.

Burnaby, John. *Amor Dei: A Study of the Religion of St. Augustine*. London: Hodder and Stoughton, 1939.

Burnett, Carole C. "Dysfunction at Diospolis: A Comparative Study of Augustine's *De Gestis Pelagii* and Jerome's *Dialogus Adversus Peleganionos*." *Augustinian Studies* 34:2 (2003) 153–173.

Burrus, Virginia. "*The Sex Lives of the Saints: An Erotics of Ancient Hagiography.*" Philadelphia: University of Pennsylvania Press, 2008.

Burrus, Virginia and Catherine Keller. "Confessing Monica." In *Feminist Interpretations of Augustine*, edited by Judith Chelius Stark, 119–46. University Park, PA: Pennsylvania State University Press, 2007.

Burrus, Virginia, Jordan, Mark D., and MacKendrick, Karmen. *Seducing Augustine: Bodies, Desires, Confessions*. New York: Fordham University Press, 2010.

Calvin, John. *The Institutes of the Christian Religion*. Translated by Henry Beveridge. Grand Rapids, MI: Eerdmans, 1989.

Cassian, John. *The Conferences* (*Collationes*). Translated by Boniface Ramsey, OP. Mahwah, NJ: Newman, 1997.

———. *The Institutes* (*De Institutis coenobiorum*). Translated by Boniface Ramsey, OP. Mahwah, NJ: Newman, 2000.

Catton, Eleanor. *Luminaries*. Boston: Little, Brown, 2013.

Cavadini, John C. "Feeling Right: Augustine on the Passions and Sexual Desire." *Augustinian Studies* 36:1 (2005) 195–217.

Chadwick, Henry. *Augustine*. Oxford and New York: Oxford University Press, 1986.

———. *Early Christian Thought and the Classical Tradition*. Oxford: Oxford University Press, 1966.

———. *The Early Church*. London: Penguin, 1967.

———. *Sentences of Sixtus*. Cambridge: Cambridge University Press, 1959.

Chrysostom, John. *Homily 16 on 1 Corinthians 6:12–6:14*. Translated by Talbot W. Chambers. From *Nicene and Post-Nicene Fathers, First Series, Vol. 12*. Edited by Philip Schaff. Buffalo, NY: Christian Literature, 1889. Revised and edited for New Advent by Kevin Knight. http://www.newadvent.org/fathers/220117.htm.

———. *Homily 19 on 1 Corinthians 7.* In *On Marriage and Family Life*, translated by Catherine P. Roth and David Anderson. 25–42. Crestwood, NY: St. Vladimir's Seminary Press, 1986.

———. *Homilies on Matthew.* Translated by George Prevost and revised by M. B. Riddle. From *Nicene and Post-Nicene Fathers, First Series, Vol. 10*, edited by Philip Schaff. (Buffalo, NY: Christian Literature Publishing Co., 1888.) Revised and edited for New Advent by Kevin Knight. http://www.newadvent.org/fathers/2001.htm.

Clancy, Finnbar G., SJ. "St. Augustine, his predecessors and contemporaries, and the exegesis of 2 Tim 2:20." In *Studia Patristica, Vol. XXVII: Papers Presented at the Eleventh International Conference on Patristic Studies held in Oxford 1991*, edited by Elizabeth A. Livingstone, 242–48. Leuven: Peeters, 1993.

Clark, Elizabeth. *The Origenist Controversy.* Princeton: Princeton University Press, 1992.

———. *St. Augustine on Marriage and Sexuality.* Washington, DC: Catholic University Press, 1996.

Clement of Alexandria. *Stromata.* Translated by William Wilson. In *Ante-Nicene Fathers, Vol. 2*, 299–341. Edited by Alexander Roberts *et al.* Buffalo, NY: Christian Literature, 1885. Reprint, Peabody, MA: Hendrickson, 1999.

———. *Stromateis, Book 3.* Translated by John Ferguson. Washington, DC: Catholic University of America Press, 1991, www.ccg.org/s/B3.html.

Coleridge, Samuel Taylor. *Aids to Reflection.* New York: Swords, Stanford & Co. 1839.

———. *Notes on English Divines*, in two volumes. London: Moxton, 1853.

Cooper, Kate. "Augustine and Monnica." In *Motherhood, Religion, and Society in Medieval Europe, 400–1400: Essays Presented to Henrietta Leyser*, edited by Conrad Leyser and Lesley Smith, 7–20. Farnham, England: Ashgate, 2011.

Cooper, Kate, and Conrad Leyser. "The Gender of Grace: Impotence, Servitude, and Manliness in the Fifth-Century West." *Gender & History* 12:3 (2000) 536–51.

Copleston, Frederick. *A History of Philosophy, Vol. 1, Part II.* Garden City, NY: Image, 1962.

Couenhoven, Jesse. "St. Augustine's Doctrine of Original Sin." *Augustinian Studies* 36:2 (2005) 359–396.

Cunningham, William. *S. Austin and his place in the History of Christian Thought.* London: C. J. Clay and Sons, 1886.

Davenport, Guy. *7 Greeks.* New York: New Directions, 1995.

Davies, Oliver and Thomas O'Loughlin. eds. *Celtic Spirituality (Classics of Western Spirituality).* Mahwah, NJ: Paulist Press, 2000.

De Simone, Russell J. "Modern Research on the Sources of Saint Augustine's Doctrine of Original Sin." *Augustinian Studies* 11 (1980) 205–227.

Djuth, Marianne. "The Hermeneutics of *De Libero Arbitrio, III*: Are there two Augustines?" in *Studia Patristica, Vol. XXVII: Papers Presented at the Eleventh International Conference on Patristic Studies held in Oxford 1991*, edited by Elizabeth A. Livingstone, 281–291. Leuven: Peeters, 1993.

Dodaro, Robert, OSA. "«Ego miser homo»: Augustine. The Pelagian Controversy, and the Paul of Romans 7:7–25." *Augustinianum* 44:1 (2004) 135–144.

———. "Note on the Carthaginian Debate over Sinlessness, A. D. 411–414 (Augustine, Pecc. Mer. 2. 7. 8–16. 25)." *Augustinianum* 40:1 (2000) 87–202.

Dunn, Geoffrey D. "Augustine, Cyril of Alexandria, and the Pelagian Controversy." *Augustinian Studies* 37:1 (2006) 63–88.

———. "The Call to Perfection, Financial Asceticism, and Jerome." *Augustinianum* 52:1, (2012) 197–218.

———. "The Poverty of Melania the Younger and Pinianus." *Augustinianum* 54:1 (2014) 93–115.

Dunphy, Walter. "Marius Mercator on Rufinus the Syrian: Was Schwartz mistaken?" *Augustinianum* 32:2 (1992) 279–288.

———. "A Lost Year: Pelagianism in Carthage, 411 A. D." *Augustinianum* 45:2 (2005) 389–466.

———. "Ps-Rufinus (the 'Syrian') and the Vulgate: Evidence Wanting!" *Augustinianum* 52:1 (2012) 219–256.

———. "Rufinus the Syrian: Myth and Reality." *Augustiniana* 59 (2009) 79–157.

Dworkin, Andrea. *Intercourse*. New York: Basic Book, 2006.

van Egmond, Peter J. "*Haec fides est*: Observations on the Textual Tradition of Pelagius's '*Libellus fidei*.'" *Augustiniana* 57 (2007) 345–385.

———. "Pelagius and the Origenist Controversy in Palestine." In *Studia Patristica, Vol. LXX. Papers presented at the Sixteenth International Conference on Patristic Studies held in Oxford 2011. Vol. 18: St Augustine and his Opponents*, edited by Markus Vinzent 631–47. Leuven: Peeters, 2013.

Erasmus, Desiderius. *The Free Will*, excerpted in *The Battle over Free Will*, edited and translated by Peter Macardle, 1–31. Indianapolis, IN: Hackett, 2012.

Evans, Robert F. *Pelagius: Inquiries and Reappraisals*. Eugene, OR: Wipf and Stock, 1968.

Featley, Daniel. *Pelagius Redivivus: Or Pelagius Raked Out of the Ashes by Arminius and His Schollers (1626)*. Early English Books Online reprint, 2012.

Ferguson, John. *Pelagius*. Cambridge: W. Heffer & Sons, 1956.

Fitzmyer, Joseph A. *Romans: A New Translation*. Anchor Bible, Doubleday, 1992.

Foucault, Michel. *The History of Sexuality, Vol. 2: The Use of Pleasure*. Translated by Robert Hurley, Vintage Books, 1990.

Fredriksen, Paula. *Augustine and the Jews: A Christian Defense of Jews and Judaism*. New York: Doubleday, 2008.

———. *Original Sin: The Early History of an Idea*. Princeton and Oxford: Princeton University Press, 2012.

Freeman, Charles. *A. D. 381*. New York: Overlook Press.

Gaarder, Jostein. *Vita Brevis, A letter to St. Augustine*. Translated by Anne Born, London: Phoenix, 1998.

Gaumer, Matthew Alan. "The Development of the Concept of Grace in Late Antique North Africa." *Augustinianum* 50:1 (2010) 163–187.

Gaustad, Edwin S. *Faith of the Founders: Religion and the New Nation*. Baylor University Press, 2011.

Gibbon. Edward. *The Decline and Fall of the Roman Empire*, in seven volumes. London: Methuen, 1909 Reprint, New York: AMS, 1974.

Gregory of Nazianzus. *Letters*. Translated by Charles Gordon Browne and James Edward Swallow. From *Nicene and Post-Nicene Fathers, Second Series, Vol. 7*, edited by Philip Schaff and Henry Wace. Buffalo, NY: Christian Literature, 1894. Revised and edited for New Advent by Kevin Knight. http://www.newadvent.org/fathers/3103.htm.

Gregory of Nyssa. *Catechetical Oration.* Translated by the Venerable J. H. Strawley, DD. London: Society for Promoting Christian Knowledge, 1917. University of Michigan reprint, 1971.

Guilfoy, Kevin. "Man's Fallen State: St. Augustine on Viagra." In *The Philosophy of Viagra: Bioethical Responses to the Viagrification of the Modern World*, edited by Thorsten Botz-Bornstein, 57–70. Amsterdam. New York: Rodopi, 2011.

Hadot, Pierre. *Philosophy as a way of life.* Translated by Michael Chase. Edited by Arnold Davidson. Malden, MA: Blackwell, 1995.

Hall, Christopher A. "John Chrysostom." In *Reading Romans through the Centuries*, edited by Jeffrey P. Greenman and Timothy Larsen, 39–57. Grand Rapids, MI: Brazos, 2005.

Hampden, Renn Dickson. *An Epitome of the Bampton Lectures of the Rev. Dr. Hampden.* London: Joseph Masters, 1848.

Harmless, William, SJ. "Christ the Pediatrician: Infant Baptism and Christological Imagery in the Pelagian Controversy." *Augustinian Studies* 28:2 (1997), 7–34.

———. "A Love Supreme: Augustine's "Jazz" of Theology." *Augustinian Studies* 43:1/2 (2012) 149–177.

Harnack, Adolph. *History of Dogma*, Vols. IV-V. Translated by Neil Buchanan. London: Constable, 1900. Reprint New York: Dover, 1961.

Harper, Kyle. "*From Shame to Sin: The Christian Transformation of Sexual Morality in Late Antiquity.*" Cambridge, MA and London: Harvard University Press, 2013.

Hauerwas, Stanley. *With the Grain of the Universe.* Grand Rapids, MI: Brazos Press, 2001.

Harrison, Carol. *Augustine: Christian Truth and Fractured Humanity.* Oxford: Oxford University Press, 2000.

———. "Delectatio Victrix: Grace and Freedom In Saint Augustine." In *Studia Patristica, Vol. XXVII: Papers Presented at the Eleventh International Conference on Patristic Studies held in Oxford 1991.* Edited by Elizabeth A. Livingstone, 298–302. Leuven: Peeters, 1993.

———. *Rethinking Augustine's Early Theology*, Oxford: Oxford University Press, 2006

Heard, J. B. *Alexandrian and Carthaginian Theology Contrasted. The Hulsean Lectures 1892–1893.* Edinburgh: T. & T. Clark, 1893. .

Hodgson, Leonard. *For Faith and Freedom (the Gifford Lectures 1955–57).* London: SCM Press, 1968.

Hopkins, Jasper. *Philosophical Criticism: Essays and Reviews.* Minneapolis, MN: Arthur Banning Press, (1994).

Hunter, David G. "Augustinian Pessimism? A New Look at Augustine's Teaching on Sex, Marriage and Celibacy." *Augustinian Studies* 25 (1994) 153–177.

Irenaeus. *Adversus Haereses (Against Heresies).* Translated by Alexander Roberts and William Rambaut. From *Ante-Nicene Fathers, Vol. 1*, edited by Alexander Roberts, James Donaldson, and A. Cleveland Coxe. Buffalo, NY: Christian Literature, 1885. Reprint Ex Fontibus Press, 2010.

Jacobs, Alan. *Original Sin: A Cultural History.* New York: Harper One, 2008.

James, William. *Variety of Religious Experiences.* In *Writings, 1902–1910*, 1–478. New York: Library of America. 1987.

Jaspers, Karl. *The Great Philosophers: The Foundations.* New York: Harcourt Brace World, 1962.

Jerome. *Against Jovinian.* Translated by W. H. Fremantle, G. Lewis and W. G. Martle. In *Nicene and Post-Nicene Fathers, Second Series,* Vol. 6, edited by Philip Schaff and Henry Wace. Buffalo, NY: Christian Literature, 1893. Revised and edited for New Advent by Kevin Knight, http://www. newadvent. org/fathers/30091. htm.

———. "*The Apology against the books of Rufinus.*" In *St. Jerome: Dogmatic and Polemical Works,* translated by John W. Hritzu, 47–222. Washington, DC: Catholic University Press, 1965.

———. *The Dialog against the Pelagians.* In *St. Jerome: Dogmatic and Polemical Works,* translated by John W. Hritzu, 223–380. Washington, DC: Catholic University Press, 1965.

———. *On Illustrious Men.* Translated by Thomas P. Halton. Washington, DC: Catholic University Press, 1999.

———. *Letters.* Translated by W. H. Fremantle, G. Lewis and W. G. Martley. From *Nicene and Post-Nicene Fathers, Second Series,* Vol. 6, edited by Philip Schaff and Henry Wace. Buffalo, NY: Christian Literature, 1893. Revised and edited for New Advent by Kevin Knight, http://www. newadvent. org/fathers/3001. htm.

Johnson, Paul. *A History of Christianity.* New York: Atheneum, 1977.

Justin Martyr. *Dialogue with Trypho.* Translated by Marcus Dods and George Reith. From *Ante-Nicene Fathers,* Vol. 1, edited by Alexander Roberts, James Donaldson, and A. Cleveland Coxe. Buffalo, NY: Christian Literature Publishing Co. 1885. Revised and edited for New Advent by Kevin Knight. http://www. newadvent. org/fathers/0128. htm.

Kane, Robert. Editor. *The Oxford Handbook of Free Will,* 1st ed. Oxford: Oxford, 2005.

———. *The Oxford Handbook of Free Will,* 2nd ed. Oxford: Oxford, 2010.

Kaufmann, Walter. *Without Guilt and Justice.* Wyden, 1973.

Keech, Dominic. *The Anti-Pelagian Christology of Augustine of Hippo.* Oxford: Oxford University Press, 2012.

Kelly, J. N. D. Early Christian Doctrines. San Francisco, CA: HarperSanFrancisco, 1960.

———. *Jerome: His life, writings, and controversies.* Peabody, MA: Hendrickson, 1975.

Kenny, Anthony. *A New History of Philosophy, Volume II, Medieval Philosophy.* Oxford: Clarendon Press, 2005.

Kirwan, Christopher. *Augustine.* London and New York: Routledge, 1989.

Komline, Han-luen Kantzer. "Grace, Free Will, and the Lord's Prayer: Cyprian's Importance for the "Augustinian" Doctrine of Grace." *Augustinian Studies* 45:2 (2014) 247–279.

Lancel, Serge. *St. Augustine.* Trans. Antonia Nevill. London: SCM Press (2002).

Lamberigts, Mathijs. "Competing Christologies: Julian and Augustine on Jesus Christ." *Augustinian Studies* 36:1 (2005) 159–194.

———. "A Critical Evaluation of Critiques of Augustine's View of Sexuality." In *Augustine and his Critics: Essays in Honour of Gerald Bonner,* edited by Robert Dodaro, OSA, and George Lawless, 176–97. London and New York: Routledge, 2000.

———. "Julian Aeclanum on Grace: Some Considerations." In *Studia Patristica, Vol. XXVII: Papers Presented at the Eleventh International Conference on Patristic Studies held In Oxford 1991,* edited by Elizabeth A. Livingstone, 342–349. Leuven: Peeters, 1993.

Lecky, W. E. H. *History of the Rise and Influence of the Spirit of Rationalism in Europe.* London: Longmans, Green, 1913.

Leibniz, Gottfried Wilhelm. *Theodicy: Essays on the Goodness of God, The Freedom of Man, and the Origin of Evil*. Trans. E. M. Huggard, 1710. Republished by Cosimo, 2009.
Levine, Amy-Jill. *Short Stories by Jesus*. HarperOne, 2014.
Lewis, C. S. *A Grief Observed*. San Francisco: Harper and Row, 1989.
———. *Mere Christianity*. San Francisco: HarperSanFrancisco, 2001.
Loughlin, Gerard. *Alien Sex: The Body and Desire in Cinema and Theology*. Oxford: Blackwell, 2004.
Lössl, Josef. "A Shift In Patristic Exegesis: Hebrew Clarity and Historical Verity in Augustine, Jerome, Julian of Aeclanum and Theodore of Mopsuestia." *Augustinian Studies* 32:2 (2001) 157—175.
———. "Who attacked the Monasteries of Jerome and Paula in 416 A. D.?" *Augustinianum* 44:1 (2004) 91–112.
Luther, Martin. *The Enslaved Will (De servo arbitrio)*. Excerpted in *The Battle Over Free Will*. Edited and translated by Clarence H. Miller, 32–126. Indianapolis, IN: Hackett, 2012.
MacIntyre, Alasdair. *Whos Justice? Whose Rationality?* Notre Dame, IN: University of Notre Dame Press, 1988.
Mantel, Hilary. *Bring up the bodies*. New York: Henry Holt, 2012.
Markus, R. A. *The End of Ancient Christianity*. Cambridge: Cambridge University Press, 1991.
Mathewes, Charles T. "The Career of the Pelagian Controversy: Introductory Essay." *Augustinian Studies* 33:2 (2002) 201–212.
Matter, Ann E. "Christ, God, and Woman In the thought of St. Augustine," in *Augustine and his Critics: Essays in Honour of Gerald Bonner*, edited by Robert Dodaro and George Lawless, 164–75. London and New York: Routledge, 2000.
———. "*De cura feminarum*: Augustine the Bishop, North African Women, and the Development of a Theology of Female Nature." *Augustinian Studies* 36:1 (2005) 87–98.
McCulloch, Warren S. "Mysterium Iniquitatis: of Sinful Man Aspiring to the Place of God." In Embodiments of Mind, 157–165. Cambridge, MA: MIT Press, 1965.
McDuffie, Felecia. "Augustine's Rhetoric of the Feminine in the Confessions: Woman as Mother, Woman as Other," in *Feminist Interpretations of Augustine*, edited by Judith Chelius Stark, 97–118. University Park, PA: Pennsylvania State University Press, 2007.
McLaren, Angus. Impotence: A cultural history. Chicago and London: University of Chicago Press, 2007.
Meyendorff, John. Byzantine Theology: Historical trends and doctrinal themes. New York: Fordham University Press, 1979.
Miller, Julie B. "To Remember Self. To Remember God: Augustine on Sexuality, Relationality, and the Trinity," in *Feminist Interpretations of Augustine*, edited by Judith Chelius Stark, 243–80. University Park, PA: Pennsylvania State University Press, 2007.
de Montaigne, Michel. Essays. Translated by M. A. Screech. London: Penguin (2003).
Moorhead, John. "What names did the Anti-Nicenes use for Catholics and Arians?" *Augustinianum* 50:2 (2010) 423–441.
Mosshammer, Alden A. "Historical Time and Apokatastasis in Gregory of Nyssa." In *Studia Patristica, Vol. XXVII: Papers Presented at the Eleventh International*

Conference on Patristic Studies held in Oxford 1991, edited by Elizabeth A. Livingstone, 70–93. Leuven: Peeters, 1993.

Mozley, James Bowling. The Augustinian Doctrine of Predestination. London: John Murray, 1855.

Myres, J. N. L. "Pelagius and the End of Roman Rule in Britain." Journal of Roman Studies 50 parts 1 and 2 (1960) 21–36.

Newman, John Henry. Apologia pro vita sua. London: Penguin Classics, 1994.

Niebuhr, Reinhold. The Nature and Destiny of Man, 2 volumes. Louisville, Kentucky: Westminster John Knox, 1996.

Nolan, John Gavin. Jerome and Jovinian: Abstract of a dissertation. Washington, DC: Catholic University Press, 1954.

Oberman, Heiko Augustinus. The Harvest of Medieval Theology: Gabriel Biel and Late Medieval Nominalism. Cambridge, MA: Harvard University Press, 1963.

O'Donnell, James J. Augustine, a new biography. London and New York: Harper, 2005.

O'Donovan, Oliver. The Problem of Self-love in St. Augustine. Eugene, OR: Wipf and Stock, 2006.

———. Resurrection and Moral Order: An Outline for Evangelical Ethics, 2nd edition. Leister, England: Eerdmans, 1994.

Orosius, Paul. "Book In Defense against the Pelagians (liber apologeticus). In Iberian Fathers, Vol. 3. Translated by Craig L. Hanson, 115–67. Washington DC: Catholic University Press, 1999.

Origen. Commentary on the Epistle to the Romans, Books 1–5. Translated by Thomas Scheck. Washington DC: Catholic University of America Press, 2001.

———. Commentary on the Epistle to the Romans, Books 6–10. Translated by Thomas Scheck. Washington DC: Catholic University of America Press, 2002.

———. On First Principles. Translated by G. W. Butterworth. New York: Harper Torchbooks, 1966.

Orwell, George. All Art is Propaganda. Orlando, FL: Harcourt, 2008.

Ottley, R. L. Studies in the Confessions of St. Augustine. London: Robert Scott, 1919.

Pagels, Elaine. Adam, Eve, and the Serpent. New York: Random House, 1988.

———. "The Politics of Paradise: Augustine's Exegesis of Genesis 1–3 versus that of John Chrysostom." Harvard Theological Review 78:1–2 (1985) 67–99.

Pamphilus. Apology for Origen, in St. Pamphilus: Apology for Origen with the Letter of Rufinus: On the Falsification of the Books of Origen, translated by Thomas Scheck, 35–120. Washington DC: Catholic University of America Press, 2010.

Pater, Walter. The Renaissance: Studies In Art and Poetry. London: Folio Society, 2013.

Pelagius. On Bad Teachers, in Pelagius: Life and Letters, translated by B. R. Rees, Vol. 2, 212–252. Woodbridge, UK: Boydell, 1998.

———. On Christian Life (De vita christiana), in Pelagius: Life and Letters, translated by B. R. Rees, Vol. 2, 105–126. Woodbridge, UK: Boydell, 1998.

———. Declaration of Faith (Libellus fidei). Translated by W. Wall, 1819. http://earlychurchtexts.com/printable/latin/pelagius/letter_and_confession_to_innocent_printable_01.html.

———. Letter to Demetrias, in Pelagius: Life and Letters, translated by B. R. Rees, Vol. 2, 29–70. Woodbridge, UK: Boydell, 1998.

———. On the Rich (de divitiis), in Pelagius: Life and Letters, translated by B. R. Rees, Vol. 2, 171–211. Woodbridge, UK: Boydell, 1998.

———. *Pelagius's Commentary on St. Paul's Epistle to the Romans*. Translated by Theodore De Bruyn, Oxford: Clarendon Press, 1993.

Pelikan, Jaroslav. "An Augustinian Dilemma: Augustine's Doctrine of grace *versus* Augustine's Doctrine of the Church." *Augustinian Studies* 18 (1987) 1–29.

———. *The Christian Tradition: Vol. 1. The Emergence of the Catholic Tradition (100–600)*. Chicago and London: Chicago University Press, 1971.

———. *What has Athens to do with Jerusalem?* Ann Arbor, MI: University of Michigan Press, 1997.

Pope, Marvin H. Translator. *Job: A new translation*. Anchor Bible, Doubleday (1965, 1973)

Possidius. *Sancti Augustini Vita (Life of Saint Augustine)*. Translated by Herbert T. Weisskotten. Merchantville, NJ: Evolution Publishing, 2008.

Power, Kim E. *Veiled Desire: Augustine on Women*. New York: Continuum, 1996.

Priestley, Joseph. *A History of the Corruptions of Christianity*. Kessinger Publishing, reprint of the 1871 edition.

Rackett, Michael R. "Anti-Pelagian Polemic in Augustine's *De Continentia*. *Augustinian Studies* 26:2 (1995) 25–50.

———. "What's Wrong with Pelagianism? Augustine and Jerome on the Dangers of Pelagius and his Followers." *Augustinian Studies* 33:2 (2002) 223–237.

Radice, Betty. Trans. *The Letters of Abelard and Heloise*. London: Penguin Books, 1974.

Ramirez, J. Roland E. "Demythologizing Augustine as Great Sinner." *Augustinian Studies* 12 (1981) 61–88.

Ranke-Heinemann, Uta. *Eunuchs for the Kingdom of Heaven*. New York: Doubleday (1990).

Raven, Charles E. *Natural Religion and Christian Theology*, two volumes. Cambridge: Cambridge University Press, 1953.

Rawls, John. *A Brief Inquiry Into the Meaning of Sin and Faith*, with *On my religion*. Thomas Nagel. ed. Cambridge, MA: Harvard University Press, 2009.

———. *Lectures on the History of Political Philosophy*. Edited by Samuel Freeman. Cambridge, MA: The Belknap Press of the Harvard University Press, 2007.

Rebillard, Eric. "*Dogma Populare*: Popular Belief in the Controversy between Augustine and Julian of Eclanum." *Augustinian Studies* 38:1 (2007) 175–187.

Rees, B. R. *Pelagius: Life and Letters*. Woodbridge, UK: Boydell, 1998. Originally published in two volumes: *Pelagius: A Reluctant Heretic* (Boydell, 1988); and *The Letters of Pelagius and his Followers* (Boydell, 1991).

Rigby, Paul. "Augustine's Use of Narrative Universals in the Debate Over Predestination." *Augustinian Studies* 31:2 (2000) 181–194.

———. "The Role of God's 'Inscrutable Judgments' in Augustine's Doctrine of Predestination." *Augustinian Studies* 33:2 (2002) 213–222.

Rist, John M. *Augustine: Ancient Thought Baptized*. Cambridge. Cambridge University Press, 1994.

———. "Augustine on Free Will and Predestination," in *Augustine: A Collection of Critical Essays*, edited by R. A. Markus, 218–52. Garden City, NJ and New York: Doubleday Anchor, 1972. Originally published In *Journal of Theological Studies* 20 (1969): 420–47.

Robertson, Charles D. "Augustinian Ecclesiology and Predestination: An Intractable Problem?" in *Studia Patristica, Vol. LXX. Papers presented at the Sixteenth International Conference on Patristic Studies held in Oxford 2011. Vol. 18: St*

*Augustine and his Opponents*, edited by Markus Vinzent 401–409. Leuven: Peeters, 2013.

Rowe, William L. "Augustine on Foreknowledge and Free Will," in *Augustine: A Collection of Critical Essays*, edited by R. A. Markus, 209–18. Garden City, NJ and New York: Doubleday Anchor, 1972. Originally published in *The Review of Metaphysics* 18 (1964) 356–63.

Ruether, Rosemary Radford. "Augustine: Sexuality, Gender, and Women," in *Feminist Interpretations of Augustine*, edited by Judith Chelius Stark, 47–68. University Park, PA: Pennsylvania State University Press, 2007.

Scruton, Roger. *Sexual Desire: a philosophical Investigation*. London: Phoenix Press, (2001).

Sébastien, Louis. *Life of Augustine*. Trans. Frederick Van Fleteren. New York: Peter Lang, 2010.

Seneca. *Letters from a Stoic*. Edited and translated by Richard Mott Gummere. New York: Digireads.com, 2013.

———. *The Stoic Philosophy of Seneca*. Edited and translated by Moses Hadas. New York: Norton (1958).

Smith, Adam. *Theory of Moral Sentiments*. London: Penguin Classics, 2009.

Sorabji, Richard. *Emotion and Peace of Mind: From Stoic Agitation to Christian Temptation*. Oxford: Oxford University Press, 2000.

Southey, Robert. *The Book of the Church*, in two volumes. Boston: Wells and Lilly, 1825.

Stark, Judith Chelius. "Augustine on Women: In God's Image but Less So," in *Feminist Interpretations of Augustine*, edited by Judith Chelius Stark, 215–42. University Park, PA: Pennsylvania State University Press, 2007.

Stortz, Mary Ellen. "Pelagius Revisited." *Word and World*, 8:2 (1988) 133–140.

Taylor, Jeremy. *The Whole Works*, in ten volumes. London: Longman, Brown, Green and Longmans, 1850. Reprinted by Google Books.

Tennant, F. R. *The Origin and Propagation of Original Sin: Being the Hulsean Lectures Delivered before the University of Cambridge, 1901-2*, 2nd ed. Cambridge: Cambridge University Press, 1908.

Tertullian. *Against Marcion*. Translated by Peter Holmes. From *Ante-Nicene Fathers, Vol. 3*. Edited by Alexander Roberts, James Donaldson, and A. Cleveland Coxe. Buffalo, NY: Christian Literature, 1885. Revised and edited for New Advent by Kevin Knight, http://www.newadvent.org/fathers/0312.htm.

———. *On the Apparel of Women*. Translated by S. Thelwall. In *Ante-Nicene Fathers, Vol. 4*, edited by Alexander Roberts *et al*. Buffalo, NY: Christian Literature, 1885. Revised and edited for New Advent by Kevin Knight, http://www.newadvent.org/fathers/0402.htm.

———. *On Baptism*. Translated by S. Thelwall. From *Ante-Nicene Fathers, Vol. 3*, edited by Alexander Roberts *et al*. Buffalo, NY: Christian Literature, 1885. Revised and edited for New Advent by Kevin Knight. http://www.newadvent.org/fathers/0321.htm.

———. *On Exhortation to Chastity*. Translated by S. Thelwall. In *Ante-Nicene Fathers, Vol. 4*, edited by Alexander Roberts *et al*. Buffalo, NY: Christian Literature, 1885. Revised and edited for New Advent by Kevin Knight. http://www.newadvent.org/fathers/0405.htm.

TeSelle, Eugene. *Augustine the Theologian*. London: Burns & Oates, 1970.

———. "Rufinus the Syrian, Caelestius, Pelagius: Explorations in the Prehistory of the Pelagian Controversy." *Augustinian Studies* 3 (1972) 61–95.

Teske, Roland J., SJ. "Saint Augustine as Philosopher: The Birth of Christian Metaphysics." *Augustinian Studies* 23 (1992) 7–32.

Theophilus of Antioch. *To Autolycus*. Translated by Marcus Dods. In *Ante-Nicene Fathers, Vol. 2*, edited by Alexander Roberts et al., 85–121. Buffalo, NY: Christian Literature, 1885. Reprint, Peabody, MA: Hedrickson, 1999.

Ticciati, Susannah. "Augustine and Grace Ex Nihilo: The Logic of Augustine's Response to the Monks of Hadrumetum and Marseilles." *Augustinian Studies* 42:2 (2010) 410–422.

Tilly, Maureen A. "Understanding Augustine Misunderstanding Tyconius," in *Studia Patristica, Vol. XXVII: Papers Presented at the Eleventh International Conference on Patristic Studies held in Oxford 1991*, edited by Elizabeth A. Livingstone, 405–408. Leuven: Peeters, 1993.

Toczko, Rafał. "Heretic as Bad Rhetorician: How Augustine Discredited Pelagius." *Augustinian Studies* 42:2 (2011) 211–231.

———. "Rome as the Basis of Argument in the So-Called Pelagian Controversy (415–418)," in *Studia Patristica, Vol. LXX. Papers presented at the Sixteenth International Conference on Patristic Studies held In Oxford 2011. Vol. 18: St Augustine and his Opponents*, edited by Markus Vinzent, 649–59. Leuven: Peeters, 2013.

Toews, John E. *The Story of Original Sin*. Eugene OR: Pickwick, 2013.

Toynbee, Arnold. *An Historian's Approach to Religion*. London: Oxford University Press (1956).

Trout, Dennis E. *Paulinus of Nola: Life, Letters, and Poems*. Berkeley and Los Angeles: University of California Press, 1999.

Weaver, David. "From Paul to Augustine: Romans 5:12 In Early Christian Exegesis." *St. Vladimir's Theological Quarterly* 27:3 (1983) 187–206.

Webb, Melanie. "'On Lucretia who slew herself': Rape and Consolation in Augustine's *De ciuitate dei*." *Augustinian Studies* 44:1 (2013) 37–58.

West, Rebecca. *Saint Augustine*. Chicago: Thomas More Press, 1982.

Wetzel, James. "Snares of Truth: Augustine on free will and predestination," in *Augustine and his Critics: Essays in Honour of Gerald Bonner*, edited by Robert Dodaro and George Lawless, 124–41. London and New York: Routledge, 2000.

Wiggers, G. F. *An Historical Presentation of Augustinism and Pelagianism from the Original Sources*. Translated by Ralph Emerson. New York: Gould. Newman and Saxton, 1840. Reprint, Bibliolife, 2009.

Wilde, Oscar. *Intentions*. New York: Brentano's, 1907.

Wiley. Tatha. *Original Sin: Origins, Developments, Contemporary Meaning*. New York, Mahwah, NJ: Paulist Press, 2002.

Williams, Norman Powell. *The Ideas of the Fall and of Original Sin: A Historical and Critical Study being Eight Lectures Delivered before the University of Oxford in the year 1924 on the Foundation of the Rev. John Bampton, Canon of Salisbury*. London: Longmans, Green, 1927.

Williams, Patricia. *Doing without Adam and Eve: Sociobiology and Original Sin*. Minneapolis, MN: Fortress, 2001.

Wills, Garry. *Augustine's Confessions: A biography*. Princeton: Princeton University Press, 2011.

Yamada, Nozomu. "The Influence of Chromatius and Rufinus of Aquileia on Pelagius—as seen In his Key Ascetic Concepts: *exemplum Christi, Sapientia, and imperturbabilitas*," in *Studia Patristica, Vol. LXX. Papers presented at the Sixteenth International Conference on Patristic Studies held In Oxford 2011. Vol. 18: St Augustine and his Opponents*, edited by Markus Vinzent 661–70. Leuven: Peeters, 2013.

Zevit, Ziony. *What Really Happened In the Garden of Eden*. New Haven: Yale University Press, 2013.

www.ingramcontent.com/pod-product-compliance
Lightning Source LLC
Chambersburg PA
CBHW050341230426
43663CB00010B/1950